"Lazy, Improvident People"

DATE DUE

OCT 0 1			
GAYLORD			PRINTED IN U.S.A.

"Lazy, Improvident People"

Myth and Reality in the Writing of Spanish History

RUTH MACKAY

CORNELL UNIVERSITY PRESS

Ithaca & London

This book is published with the aid of a grant from the Program for Cultural Cooperation between Spain's Ministry of Education, Culture and Sports and United States Universities.

First published 2006 by Cornell University Press
First printing, Cornell Paperbacks, 2006

Printed in the United States of America

Library of Congress Cataloging-in-Publication Data

MacKay, Ruth.
    "Lazy, improvident people" : myth and reality in the writing of Spanish history / Ruth MacKay.
        p. cm.
    Includes bibliographical references and index.
    ISBN-13: 978-0-8014-4462-3 (cloth : alk. paper)
    ISBN-10: 0-8014-4462-4 (cloth : alk. paper)
    ISBN-13: 978-0-8014-7314-2 (pbk. : alk. paper)
    ISBN-10: 0-8014-7314-4 (pbk. : alk. paper)
    1. Spain—Historiography.   2. National characteristics, Spanish—History.
3. Work ethic—Spain—History.   4. Labor—Spain—History.   I. Title.
    DP63.M295 2006
    946.0072—dc22

                                                    2005037251

To the memory of my father, Donald MacKay:
journeyman carpenter, Stornoway man

Contents

Acknowledgments

More than once, this tale of apparent sloth threatened to self-destruct. It survived because I was blessed with good advice and financial generosity. Also, I confess, I worked very hard.

Grants from the Fulbright Commission and the American Council of Learned Societies gave me a year off early on for writing and research. The San Francisco Public Library's interlibrary loan service worked to perfection, a miracle in a time of budget cuts. Without it, this book simply would not exist. Sections of the project were delivered to seminars at the Universidad Autónoma de Madrid, Tulane University, and the University of Minnesota. I am grateful to Jim Amelang, Jim Boyden, and Carla and William Phillips, respectively, for these invitations and for the suggestions made by workshop participants.

For their time and ideas, I wish to thank Jim Amelang (above all), Carolyn Eastman, Tamar Herzog, Angela Muñoz (though she didn't know it), Helen Nader, José Nieto, Beth Remak, Peter Sahlins, Marie Salgües, Jeff Sklansky, Suzanne Walker, Elizabeth Wingrove, David Wood, and Bartolomé Yun Casalilla. My thanks, too, to John Ackerman, of Cornell University Press, for his enthusiasm and expert advice.

Finally, most of this book was written during a nine-month stay at the Newberry Library, in Chicago, where I was a Mellon/National Endowment for the Humanities fellow. The intellectual companionship I found there convinced me not to turn my back on scholarship, a possibility I was seriously considering at the time. My gratitude to the Newberry Library and my fellow fellows is boundless.

Abbreviations

AAS	Archivo del Arzobispado de Sevilla
ACC	Actas de las Cortes de Castilla
AGI	Archivo General de Indias
AGS	Archivo General de Simancas
	CG Contadurías Generales
	CJH Consejos y Juntas de Hacienda
	GA Guerra Antigua
AHN	Archivo Histórico Nacional
	Inq. Inquisición
	CS Consejos Suprimidos
AMB	Archivo Municipal de Burgos
AMSeg	Archivo Municipal de Segovia
AMSev	Archivo Municipal de Sevilla
AMT	Archivo Municipal de Toledo
AMV	Archivo Municipal de Valladolid
ARCV	Archivo de la Real Chancillería de Valladolid
AV	Archivo de Villa (Madrid)
BN	Biblioteca Nacional
	VE Varios Especiales
CODOIN	Colección de documentos inéditos para la historia de España
CSIC	Consejo Superior de Investigaciones Científicas

ABBREVIATIONS

caja	box
chap.	chapter
escr.	escribanía (notary)
exp.	expediente (file)
leg.	legajo (bundle of documents)
sec.	sección (section)
tit.	título (title)
tomo	volume

"Lazy, Improvident People"

Introduction

Sometime in 1704, when British troops were fighting the French on the Iberian peninsula to ensure that an Austrian archduke would be named king of Spain, an unnamed officer in the Royal Navy sent a letter home "to a Person of Quality." In it, he described his unwilling host country.

> Spain, in the general, is a large Garden of Butter-Flies, or rather a Hive of Idle Drones, where neither Wit nor Industry is encourag'd: A Spaniard is a sort of Amphibious Animal, that is neither Fish nor Flesh, nor Good Red-Herring, that is, neither Fool nor Knave, but both; that has more Pride than Merit, that has more Impudence than a Dozen of Watermen, more conceit than Six Country Squires, and as much Courage as a Goose.[1]

The officer, though original in his metaphors, was reiterating assessments that had survived for several centuries and would survive for several more. This book is an exploration of the notion that Spaniards would do practically anything rather than besmirch their honor by working. It is a widespread notion; indeed, this project began as an exploration of a category of workers referred to as vile and mechanical, whose existence I had no reason to doubt, though if I had thought more clearly I would have noticed from the start that there was something wrong with the story.

The story is that certain manual laborers or artisans in early modern

---

[1] *A Trip to Spain, or a True Description of the Comical Humours, Ridiculous Customs, and Foolish Laws of that Lazy Improvident People the Spaniards. A Letter to a Person of Quality from an Officer in the Royal Navy* (London 1705), 3, available on the database Eighteenth-Century Collections Online. The War of Spanish Succession resulted in a victory for the French Bourbons.

Spain were considered vile and mechanical because of the work they did. Their crafts also were considered vile and mechanical, which meant no one wanted to perform them. All people who worked with their hands were shunned, most work being off-limits to low-level nobles and those above them precisely because it was dishonorable, and those who performed vile and mechanical tasks were especially shunned, the story goes. This ostracism was emblematic of a society of rigid social classifications and race-based barriers, and it went a long way toward explaining why Spain did not progress like other nations.

One of the principal themes of Spain's historiography is the effort to explain the existence of these barriers and the damage they caused. Depending on the variant of the story, they had positive or negative derivations. They could be positive, in that one must refrain from working in order to pursue more lofty objectives: "Very early, it seems, foreign travelers and attentive Spaniards noted [Spaniards'] lack of interest in manual labor and, more generally, their poor opinion of labor. . . . The Spanish ideal, then, was in fact absence of work, the contemplative life."[2] Or they could be negative, in that those who had no choice but to work suffered shame and disdain: "In Castile there was widespread prejudice against the 'mechanical work of laborers,' which the enlightened rulers of the eighteenth century strongly opposed."[3] Negative also in that Spain got off the track of developed nations: "Spaniards' aversion to manual trades was generally recognized in the seventeenth century. . . . Spain was still steeped in medieval spirit; the mechanical trades were still dishonorable."[4]

My previous book was a study of the obstacles in the path of the monarchy as it tried to raise an army in the 1630s. I read many petitions to Philip IV and his advisers from men asking to be excused from military service, and as I read them I was struck by a paradox: most of the petitioners were extremely humble, miserable men. They worked with their hands; they were poor; they lived in isolated small towns. Yet they wrote to the king as if they expected to be listened to, and their confidence was often rewarded. These men were not behaving like vile and mechanical refuse. So I set out to discover who was vile and mechanical and why. Immediately I ran into problems. Nowhere in sixteenth- or seventeenth-century documents did I

[2] Bartolomé Bennassar, *The Spanish Character: Attitudes and Mentalities from the Sixteenth to the Nineteenth Century* (Berkeley: University of California Press, 1979), 117–118. Bennassar, a pioneering Hispanist, brought the *Annales* school of history to Spain with his 1967 study of Valladolid.

[3] Pere Molas Ribalta, *Los gremios barceloneses del siglo XVIII* (Madrid: Confederación Española de Cajas de Ahorros, 1970), 40. The author, for years the preeminent Spanish historian of labor in the early modern period, gives no explanation for the internal quotation marks.

[4] Miguel Herrero García, *Ideas de los españoles del siglo XVII* (1927; repr., Madrid: Editorial Gredos, 1966).

encounter workers being shunned specifically because of the labor they performed. Instead, I found them arguing their cases before judges and city councils, as articulate and tenacious as workers whose status allegedly was higher. So something was wrong with what historians had learned and repeated for generations. Lists of vile and mechanical trades may have existed (though I found none except in treatises), but the terms were so infrequent and unreliable that they were useless for describing the actual social structures of early modern Spain.

So the project changed shape. Now, it is about how work and workers were regarded in sixteenth- and seventeenth-century Spain, how we think they were regarded, and how the discursive differences between these two sets of values explains much about how the history of Spain was written. It is about the alleged disdain for labor in the early modern period and the alleged restoration of the dignity of labor in the Enlightenment. It studies concepts such as exclusion, indolence, pride, honor, and failure; it draws those concepts from archival documents, normative treatises, dramatic literature, executive edicts, and scholarly accounts. It links very different forms of thought and speech across very different time periods. It presents fragments and juxtaposes them, and sometimes the lines between them are tenuous. There is the speech of philosophers, of policemen, of artisans, of priests, historians, and governors. The book draws at various threads; sometimes it is chronological and narrative, other times it is thematic. It jumps back and forth in time and from side to side in concept. Readers may think I am counterposing apples and oranges, but apples and oranges, after all, do have something in common. The language of artisans, the rhetoric of treatises, the prohibitions of laws, the laments of patriots, and the findings and inventions of historians are all part of one long story that was continually rewritten as words were redefined and descendants grew weary or impatient or ashamed of their ancestors. The semiotics of labor changed as political and economic structures changed. Each generation of thinkers and workers had a new arsenal of words, a new past to imitate or abjure, a new future to which they aspired. For all of them, throughout modern Spanish history, work was a fundamental part of their explanation for why their society functioned—or didn't—as it should.

One of my objectives is to refute historiography apparently determined to deny political consciousness to people beyond a certain point in history or beyond a certain social class. I argue that by working, producing, and selling, common Castilians of the sixteenth and seventeenth centuries knew they were essential to their community and to the common good. They said so, and they acted as if that were true. The organic, republican language they used did not reflect timelessness or a lack of opportunity to rise above their station that would be available to them only after the fall of the Old Regime. On the contrary, it assigned them a place from which they could contribute and negotiate. They did not speak a special, marginal language of their own; they spoke a shared language, which both God and the king understood. Artisans had access to much of the same news and religion as their betters; they heard the same town criers, attended the same church, marched in the same processions, frequented the same courtrooms. They were poorer, to be sure, but not marginal. They may or may not have been *vecinos,* or citizens, but their formal legal status mattered little. What counted was how one behaved. If subsequent observers have failed to see this, then we must ask why. The answer, I propose, has a great deal to do with the Enlightenment.

The words and actions of the eighteenth-century writers and reformers known as the *ilustrados* stand between us and the early modern period. Their descriptions of the era that preceded theirs and the remedies they proposed for taking their country into the succeeding era (which included assigning honor to all manual occupations) established a scene whose properties have remained virtually unchanged in the modern mind. It is a spectacle of an obstinately irrational world awaiting correction in which actors either are condemned to live in scorn because of the work they do or pass their days aspiring to do nothing. The fanciful images come as much from Golden Age literature as from enlightened political treatises, but they were sealed as fact by being so fiercely condemned by the eighteenth-century reformers. They must have been true if their elimination was a necessary step toward progress. This argument regarding the Enlightenment's role in essentially writing our historiography of the early modern period points to the existence of a series of interpretive and discursive barriers between us and the object of our analysis. I do not mean to suggest that the closer to the "facts," the more "true" the analysis; contemporaries in the sixteenth and seventeenth centuries, we will see, had their own problems in describing the world around them. But each successive barrier complicates the story a bit more. As we clear each one, we must account for networks of relationships in the actual past, the texts that people in those relationships produced, and how both those things have been described by successive historians, all of whom left a sort of script, and thus new barriers, for their successors.[5]

If one of my purposes is to show that early modern Castilian artisans as a class were not vile, marginal, or shunned, another is to argue that Castile was not all that different from the rest of Europe and that the burden of exceptionalism should be cast off. The construction of Spain (and especially Castile) as a foreign planet is largely the work of Spain's erstwhile European enemies, though Spaniards themselves participated in it. It be-

---

[5] Robert Berkhofer Jr., *Beyond the Great Story: History as Text and Discourse* (Cambridge, Mass.: Harvard University Press, 1997), 20 and chap. 6.

hooves European and American historians to take account of the inaccuracies, stereotypes, and excesses of Spanish historiography because Spain has worked for them as their opposite: Catholic, resistant to industrial capitalism, a failed empire. If Spanish noblemen were not eager to work (and many were not), nor were their counterparts elsewhere. Noblemen in England had no legal obstacle in their way, as the French did, and in fact sometimes apprenticed their sons as merchants, but many would have regarded occupation in a trade as a humiliation: "Tradesmen in All Ages and Nations have been reputed ignoble," Edward Chamberlayne pronounced in 1619.[6] While they praised hard work, Puritans on both sides of the Atlantic also extolled moderation, charity, and the common good, words that would not have sounded at all unusual to Catholic churchgoers in Salamanca or Palencia. In seventeenth-century England, wage earners were regarded as unfree, "journeyman" was a pejorative term, and Utopia was a place where one did not have to work.[7]

My sources, as I said, are a varied lot. From the sixteenth and seventeenth centuries I relied on guild documents simply because that is where I could find people who worked with their hands; I must caution that this is not a book about guilds per se. I examined lawsuits, petitions, and complaints between or by craft guilds and individual artisans. I also read dramatic and fictional literature from that period. From the entire early modern period from the late fifteenth century to the eighteenth century I read political and economic treatises. From the nineteenth and twentieth centuries I read histories of Spain and labor. And from the past few decades I read theoretical works that helped me better understand this vast array of paper and offered me logical and meaningful ways of arranging events and concepts.

I am admittedly casual in my use of certain terms. Nearly all the artisans described or quoted in this book are urban. They are producers and vendors, and probably both. I refer to them variously as workers, laborers, mechanics, artisans, journeymen, and craftsmen, and I do not think the differences much matter. The general term for artisans at the time was *oficiales*, which can mean journeymen in the strict sense of middle-rung members of guilds or, more broadly, all skilled artisans. Generally, craftsmen were referred to by their specific occupation: a tailor was Juan Pedro Pérez, *sastre*. Larger class groupings probably would have made little sense, and we rarely encounter *trabajadores* or *artesanos;* instead they referred to themselves as *vecinos, el común, hermanos*.

---

[6] Lawrence Stone, *The Crisis of the Aristocracy, 1558–1641* (Oxford: Clarendon Press, 1965), 40.

[7] Christopher Hill, "Pottage for Freeborn Englishmen: Attitudes to Wage Labour in the Sixteenth and Seventeenth Centuries," in *Socialism, Capitalism and Economic Growth: Essays Presented to Maurice Dobb,* ed. C. H. Feinstein (Cambridge University Press, 1967), 338–350.

Parts 1 and 2 are similarly organized: each has two chapters, the first devoted to ideological contexts, the second to describing how those contexts helped structure the lives of working people in, respectively, the seventeenth and eighteenth centuries. Chapter 1 briefly examines the legacy of biblical and classical attitudes toward labor and then offers a more detailed exploration of artisans' passage through city halls and courts of law, where they articulated their quarrels and demands as citizens and members of a republic, using statute and custom as the basis for their arguments. Chapter 2 addresses more subjective identities and characterizations of labor and laborers, largely concerning sloth, honor, and exclusion. It explores the hierarchies of labor minutely described in treatises yet conspicuously absent in daily life, absent even in court transcripts that by definition are a record of the past, its grievances, and its meaning. Legal precedent was (and is) a way of writing the past, yet artisans who went to court chose not to mention shame and exclusion. There was a reason for their silence.

Part 2 moves to the eighteenth century, though it looks back from time to time in order to assess how words and concepts changed significance as they changed hands. Law, science, and the marketplace were among the criteria used by Bourbon reformers to justify and explain the measures they thought necessary for increasing production and happiness, and in chapter 3 I examine each one by setting their normative words aside the documentary words of artisans. Chapter 4 returns to what I originally thought was going to be this book's starting point: exclusion on the basis of occupation. I find indications of a rise in an array of exclusionary practices in the eighteenth century. Together with the facts that such practices as regards labor cannot be found in the previous era, that the enlightened reformers were anxious to mold a docile workforce whose rationalization would be that much easier if it comprised elements previously said to have been regarded as vile, and that Spanish historians often base their assessments of the early modern era on eighteenth-century data and treatises, this sheds light on how the role of early modern Castilian artisans has been so simplified and misunderstood. Readers will see that I am less than enthusiastic about the attitude of the eighteenth-century reformers toward manual laborers and about the later adulatory historiography of their era. I do not mean to be dismissive. They were remarkable, brave, intelligent, curious, idealistic, and sometimes even modest men whose confidence in learning is sometimes breathtaking. "My desire for the good of this country devours me," Gaspar Melchor de Jovellanos once wrote.[8] But their legacy to historiography has been mixed, though the fault is not entirely theirs.

[8] Letter to Father Posada, in Gaspar Melchor de Jovellanos, *Obras*, vol. 2, ed. Cándido Nocedal, Biblioteca de Autores Españoles, vol. 50 (Madrid, 1859), 180.

Part 3 moves ahead to the nineteenth century, again with detours. The subject in chapter 5 is national character and empire. I examine the long tradition of national stereotyping, of which the anonymous officer quoted above was a fine example, with particular focus on laziness. I argue that Spaniards' alleged antipathy for labor was a crucial component of the relationships between Spain and its American colonies and between the rest of Europe and Spain. Attitudes toward labor bore an imperial imprint and were integral to Spain's vision of itself as an imperialist nation, which would become especially evident at the end of the nineteenth century with the final collapse of the empire. Finally, chapter 6 serves as a conclusion, presenting an analysis of Spanish exceptionalism and some final considerations on Spanish historiography in general.

This book entails a lot of time travel. Perhaps I am making a virtue of necessity, but I think in some ways that emphasizes one of my points. I wish to suggest the possibility of simultaneity in many forms: freedom and regulation, economics and politics, markets and ethics, justice and hierarchy, rights and obligations, stratification and mobility, public and private, capitalism and corporativism. At the same time I argue against such dualities, against a teleological imperative that one mode necessarily succeeds the next. Discourses and practices can coexist with their alleged opposites. People can adopt different roles; in the words of Giovanni Levi, there are "intersticial forms of action between parallel and contradictory normative systems."[9] Sin and virtue cohabited along the Calle de los Cuchilleros, in the Plaza Mayor, or anywhere else in Castile that was a site of production, of republican living, and of civic virtue. So, too, did "old" and "new" values coexist. Rather than the former refusing to step aside for the latter, which is what often is said to have happened in Spain until the welcome arrival of the eighteenth century, I suggest that old ideas and practices were incorporated and redrawn. Discourses survived by acquiring new meanings. Spaniards did not cling to archaic ways any more or less than anyone else; if later economic accounting proved unfavorable, it cannot be blamed on persistent "traditional" thought.

Righting an erroneous historiographic path entails more than pointing at those who got us lost. However true it is that many historians over many years have simply believed what Quevedo and Pedro Rodríguez de Campomanes, to name two of the best-known culprits, said about Spaniards' unhealthy dislike for work, repeating their words as if they were unambiguously transparent, it also is true that the problems go beyond misreading sources or reading the wrong ones. There is also the matter of placing our subject—in this case work, not-work, and antiwork

---

[9] Giovanni Levi, *Inheriting Power: The Story of an Exorcist* (University of Chicago Press, 1988), 126.

in early modern Castile—in a mesh of simultaneous considerations, of locating it, in William Bouwsma's words, "in the largest possible context of significance."[10] In the following pages I have tried to do that, to right the path and remove manual laborers from their undeserved exile on the margins.

[10] William J. Bouwsma, *A Usable Past: Essays in European Cultural History* (Berkeley: University of California Press, 1990), 6.

PART ONE

SEVENTEENTH-CENTURY CASTILE

Prologue

CASTILE AND CRAFTSMEN IN THE EARLY MODERN PERIOD

In 1520–1521, townspeople throughout Castile rose up against the crown and its representatives in what is known as the Revolt of the Comuneros. The rebels, many of them artisans, though many more were merchants, churchmen, and low-level nobles (*hidalgos*), declared that true sovereignty did not rest with the newly arrived (and quickly departed) Charles V, who was regarded as a foreigner, but with the Reino, the kingdom, the people. In the absence of a legitimate ruler (though they proclaimed Charles's mother, Juana, the rightful monarch and acted in her name), they established what they called the Santa Junta, which guided the course of the ultimately doomed uprising for almost a year. It was an event that shaped both the early part of the Hapsburg monarchy in Spain and subsequent historiography. For centuries, champions of popular representation and freedom (regardless of the terms they used to describe those things) would look back to the remarkable and valiant fight and then at the imposition of a dynasty said to be foreign as a turning point for Spanish political and economic development. The defeat of Europe's "first modern revolution," in the words of José Antonio Maravall, was one of the principal explanations for Spain's everlasting exceptionalism. But though vanquished on the battlefield, Castilian urban elites never let the crown forget that sovereignty was not a settled question. The notions that just government was a prince's duty and that his vassals participated in ensuring that that was the case were among the legacies of the revolt that shaped the world of the artisans who populate the following pages.[1]

---

[1] José Antonio Maravall, *Las Comunidades de Castilla: Una primera revolución moderna* (Madrid: Alianza Universidad, 1963).

Charles V's maternal grandparents, Isabel and Ferdinand (usually called the Catholic Monarchs), through their marriage enabled their respective kingdoms of Castile and Aragón to themselves enter into a sort of political marriage, though each retained its own jurisdictions, powers of taxation, and representative assembly. (The peninsula's third major kingdom, Portugal, was joined to the others after Philip II declared himself the rightful heir to its empty throne in 1580. The union lasted until the 1640 rebellion by Portugal.) The history of Hapsburg Spain, which lasted nearly two hundred years and covered the reigns of Charles and four of his descendants, is the history of, in J. H. Elliott's oft-repeated expression, a composite monarchy.[2] Kings had to balance the rightful demands of cities, regions, estates, towns, and other jurisdictions, not to mention provinces and colonies throughout Europe, Asia, and America, with the increasingly pressing economic needs of the throne, which could be satisfied only through repeated requests and demands for money and men.

Such urgency arose in large part from the fact that Spain was at war for most of the sixteenth and seventeenth centuries. In Europe, the intermittent Hapsburg-Valois wars with France (many of which took place in Italy) ended with the treaty of Cateau-Cambrésis in 1559. War with the Ottoman Empire also was a constant, coming more or less to an end with the Battle of Lepanto in 1571. The Dutch Revolt and, of course, war with England also occupied the reigns of Charles and his son, Philip II. After the 1609 Twelve-Year Truce with the Netherlands gave both sides a chance to rearm, war commenced again in 1621, by which time Spain also had over twenty thousand troops engaged in what would become the Thirty Years' War. War again was declared between Spain and France in 1635, and that was followed by the twin revolts of Catalonia and Portugal in 1640. The various conflicts came to their respective ends with the Treaty of Westphalia in 1648, Barcelona's surrender in 1652, the Peace of the Pyrenees in 1659, and Portuguese independence in 1668. In the rest of the world, Spain had to contend not only with the expense of maintaining a vast empire but also with increasingly effective attacks on its fleets by its European enemies.

To all intents and purposes, Hapsburg Castile comprised eighteen districts, each of which was represented by its leading city in the Cortes, the representative assembly (also, significantly, referred to as the Reino). The power, or lack thereof, of the assembly has been the subject of substantial revisionist literature, largely concerned with its role in raising and assessing taxes, which obviously were crucial to the crown.[3] Cities and towns were

---

[2] J. H. Elliott. "A Europe of Composite Monarchies," *Past and Present*, no. 137 (November 1992): 48–71.

[3] Pablo Fernández Albaladejo, *Fragmentos de Monarquía* (Madrid: Alianza Universidad, 1992); José Ignacio Fortea Pérez, *Monarquía y Cortes en la corona de Castilla* (Valladolid: Cortes de Castilla y León, 1990), 271–298; Charles Jago, "Habsburg Absolutism and the Cortes of

central to Castilian politics; indeed, they defined it, the comuneros' defeat notwithstanding. Each had a multitude of particular rights and jurisdictions, granted as a result of actions taken on behalf of the monarchy during the Reconquest era or of royal favors since then. Each province was governed by a royal governor, or *corregidor,* and each municipality had a town council. Residents of towns could become legal citizens, or *vecinos,* though their prerequisites, obligations, and rights varied from place to place, from time to time, and from person to person.[4]

The Castilian economy triumphantly and famously rose in the sixteenth century, fueled by the gold and silver of America, and contracted in the seventeenth century.[5] Population, agriculture, trade, and manufacturing followed a similar arc, whose downward course had repercussions throughout Europe and the rest of the world. Sectorial, demographic, chronological, and regional peculiarities of the long depression have been brought to light during recent decades, thanks to Spanish historians' work in local archives and innovative interpretations of what was once considered merely a classic case of economic misjudgment and illness. But even accounting for those variations, by the turn of the seventeenth century many villages throughout Castile reported with alarm on their declining population, masterless men were said to be clogging country roads as they fled hunger and traveled to larger towns and cities, and the peninsula's urban network collapsed as great textile towns such as Segovia, Córdoba, and Toledo and the great commercial towns of Medina del Campo and Burgos became shells of their former selves. As the century turned, a deadly plague swept much of the country. Taxes were both inequitably assessed and inadequately collected; the mass of the population paid while the hidalgos and the aristocracy contributed nothing, though great noblemen themselves complained to the king that their entailed estates were a burden from which they could extract less and less for the royal service. The crown several times declared bankruptcy. Shipping tonnage declined steadily. Monetary policy was simply chaotic. Merchants put their money into the export of raw materials (especially wool) rather than into manufacturing, resulting in widespread insecurity, unemployment, and poverty.

In the early seventeenth century, especially during the reign of Philip

---

Castile," *American Historical Review* 86 (April 1981): 307–326; I. A. A. Thompson, "Crown and Cortes in Castile 1590–1665," *Parliaments, States and Representation* 2 (June 1982): 29–45.

[4] Tamar Herzog, *Defining Nations: Immigrants and Citizens in Early Modern Spain and Spanish America* (New Haven: Yale University Press, 2003).

[5] For works in English, see especially I. A. A. Thompson and Bartolomé Yun Casalilla, eds., *The Castilian Crisis of the Seventeenth Century: New Perspectives on the Economic and Social History of Seventeenth-Century Spain* (Cambridge University Press, 1994); and Carla Rahn Philips, "Time and Duration: A Model for the Economy of Early Modern Spain," *American Historical Review* 92 (June 1987): 531–562.

III, a group of writers called the *arbitristas* put a name to the monarchy's predicament: *declinación,* or decline. Their proposals—covering such matters as agriculture, taxation, foreign policy, sumptuary laws, class relations, and manufacturing—called for the *restauración,* or restoration, of a kingdom that clearly had lost its way. The monarchy itself established a string of committees (*juntas*) to examine a host of problems and implement reforms, a policy that continued through the mid-seventeenth-century reign of Philip IV and his favorite, the Count-Duke of Olivares.

With fewer raw materials available, disposable income scarce, and an infrastructure that hindered rather than encouraged enterprise, the subjects of this study, manual laborers and craftsmen, were often living on the edge of poverty or in the midst of forced idleness. Although neither the seventeenth-century Hapsburg monarchs nor the arbitristas attempted specifically to reform, abolish, or strengthen the craft guilds, the plight of their members obviously was of interest to them. More important to my argument, craftsmen's activities, complaints, claims to rights, and contributions mattered to the crown because through them the righteousness and purpose of the monarchy was tested.

Traditionally, historians of Spain assumed that guilds were ineffective albeit colorful organizations. They were, by the seventeenth century, "useless machinery, dead weight, which, far from fulfilling their purpose, were a serious obstacle to progress and the development of labor."[6] They were powerless, they were history, which is why their formal elimination was greeted by some with such a sigh of relief. This attitude became particularly noticeable during the 1960s and 1970s, when social historians looking forward to the Industrial Revolution dismissed traditional corporations as archaic and anti-modern. Although this is not the place to explore this issue at length, I would like to make two points. First, guilds were far from irrelevant in seventeenth-century Spain, as we shall see. The political relationship between them and the cities or the crown was more complicated than has been described, and each of the three benefited in different ways. Corporations were part of a mesh of reciprocity. Guilds were both useful and a nuisance to rulers; their ordinances on the one hand could exercise claims, but on the other they were susceptible to co-optation. The Catholic Monarchs in 1500, for example, issued ordinances governing cloth manufacturing that may have undercut guilds in such places as Segovia, an important textile center, leaving effective power in the hands of merchants.[7] Those ordinances were rewritten and reissued several times

---

[6] Juan Uña Sarthou, *Las asociaciones obreras en España* (Madrid: Estab. tip. De G. Juste, 1900), 240.

[7] María Asenjo González, "El obraje de paños en Segovia tras las ordenanzas de los Reyes Católicos," in *La manufactura urbana i els menestrals (ss. XIII–XVI)* (Palma: Govern Balear: 1991). The ordinances are widely reproduced, for example in Paulino Iradiel Murugarren.

during the following half-century, and in 1552 Charles V, in what has been seen as a further attempt to reinforce royal power, ordered all guilds to again rewrite (or perhaps just resubmit) their ordinances. The order does not appear to have been obeyed in any significant fashion. That same year he also banned guilds' religious confraternities, though in fact they continued to exist throughout the early modern period.

At the same time, and perhaps paradoxically, guilds did not incarnate all the economic ills ascribed to them, neither in Spain nor in the rest of Europe. The forces opposing them were not always those one might expect. Guilds were not necessarily antithetical to economic freedom and growth, nor were they necessarily synonymous with regulation. Regulation, under certain circumstances, can be seen as a progressive manner of marshaling science. Corporativism, in short, was not necessarily a fetter on growth or on citizenship, not even the new citizenship later envisioned by the Enlightenment figures known as the *ilustrados*: "Citizens could represent various corporate bodies to the state, and they could represent the power of the state in these corporate bodies," according to a Latin American historian, and the same was true for Spain.[8] In large part, as should become evident in part 2, the notion that guilds were guilty of fatal sins including restrictions on labor, barriers to technological innovation, monopolies, and price-fixing (none of which apparently contradicted their other sin, that of being irrelevant), is a legacy of the Enlightenment.

Guilds have been defined as "free associations of laymen who acknowledged a common identity as townsmen, as practitioners of the same trade, as spiritual brothers."[9] The primary purposes of guilds in Castile, as elsewhere in Europe, were to discourage competition, ensure quality, establish a monopoly over supplies, control the labor supply, and take care of their members.[10] Cities with an important Muslim artisanal legacy were the first to have incipient guilds: Valencia and Seville in the late thirteenth century, Murcia in the late fourteenth century. Tailors in Seville had a confraternity

---

Evolucion de la industria textil castellana en los siglos XIII–XVI: Factores de desarrollo, organización y costes de la producción manufactura en Cuenca. (Universidad de Salamanca, 1974), 355–389.

[8] Claudio Lomnitz, "Nationalism as a Practical System: Benedict Anderson's Theory of Nationalism from the Vantage Point of Spanish America," in *The Other Mirror: Grand Theory through the Lens of Latin America,* ed. Miguel Angel Centeno and Fernando López-Alves (Princeton University Press, 2001), 333.

[9] Richard Mackenney, *Tradesman and Traders: The World of the Guilds in Venice and Europe, c. 1250–c. 1650* (London: Croom Helm, 1987), xii.

[10] James R. Farr, *Artisans in Europe, 1300–1914* (Cambridge University Press, 2000), 22–32. This survey includes excellent brief bibliographies with each chapter. Also useful on European guilds are Antony Black, *Guilds and Civil Society in European Political Thought from the Twelfth Century to the Present* (Ithaca, N.Y.: Cornell University Press, 1984); Geoffrey Crossick, ed., *The Artisan and the European Town 1500–1900* (Aldershot, U.K.: Ashgate, 1997); and James R. Farr, *Hands of Honor: Artisans and Their World in Dijon, 1550–1650* (Ithaca, N.Y.: Cornell University Press, 1988).

organized by 1250, just two years after the city was taken from the Muslims, and by 1500 there were almost fifty hospitals there run by guilds.[11] Throughout Castile, guilds appeared generally in the fifteenth century, later than in the rest of Europe. In the New World, artisans also established guilds soon after their arrival. In Mexico there were guild ordinances for blacksmiths already in 1524 (apparently motivated by their habit of over-charging), for printers in 1539, for embroiderers in 1546, and for painters in 1557.[12]

It is impossible to know what percentage of the working population was affiliated with guilds, and anyway the numbers would vary dramatically with each town. It is possible, however, to know roughly how many guilds there were in certain cities. In Madrid there were probably over one hundred in 1640, and a tally in the minutes of the Cortes shows there were still around that many in 1657.[13] A map of Valladolid identifies fifty-two separate crafts, though not all were organized as guilds.[14] Málaga in the eighteenth century had around seventy-five.[15] Toledo's municipal archive has ordinances from around forty different occupations, though there may be some repetition among them and some may be missing. In Murcia in the mid-seventeenth century there probably were around thirty.[16] Seville in 1527 compiled and published all the city's craft ordinances and came up with fifty-seven, though there were seventy-five different crafts at the time, some of which shared ordinances. Authors of a modern, comprehensive study of Seville's guilds found mention of a total of eighty occupations during the early modern era.[17] Guilds' structure was generally the same from place to place. Crafts were organized in three tiers: apprentices, journey-

[11] J. N. Hillgarth, *The Spanish Kingdoms, 1250–1516*, 2 vols. (Oxford: Clarendon Press, 1976), vol. 1, 74.
[12] *Copia paleográfica de los antiguos Libros de Cabildo del Exmo. Ayuntamiento de Esta Capital*, 6 vols. (Mexico, 1849), Newberry Library, Ayer ms. 1143, vol. 1, 5; Manuel Carrera Stampa, *Los gremios mexicanos: La organización gremial en Nueva España, 1521–1861* (Mexico City: EDIAPSA, 1954). The word *ordenanzas* in early sixteenth-century Mexico often referred to prices as much as it did to rules for craftsmen.
[13] AV 3–420–1; *Actas*, 23 June 1657 (Madrid: Real Academia de la Historia, 1987).
[14] Máximo García Fernández, *Los viejos oficios vallisoletanos* (Valladolid: Michelin, 1996), 35. The map has no date.
[15] Siro Villas Tinoco, *Los gremios malagueños (1700–1746)*, 2 vols. (Universidad de Málaga, 1982).
[16] José Javier Ruíz Ibañez, "Vecinos y forasteros: La división de la fuerza de trabajo en la ciudad de Murcia en la primera mitad del siglo XVII," in *El trabajo a través de la historia*, Actas del II Congreso de la Asociación de Historia Social, ed. Santiago Castillo (Madrid: Centro de Estudios Históricas, 1995), 191.
[17] Vicente Romero Muñoz, "La recopilación de ordenanzas gremiales de Sevilla en 1527," in *Revista de Trabajo*, no. 3 (February 1950): 225–231; Antonio Miguel Bernal et al., "Sevilla: De los gremios a la industrialización," in *Estudios de historia social*, no. 5–6 (1978). The 1527 edition was republished in 1632 by Andrés Grande: Víctor Pérez Escolano and Fernando Villanueva Sandino, eds., *Ordenanzas de Sevilla* (1632) (Seville: Oficina Técnica de Arquitectura e Ingeniería, 1975).

men, and masters, though the divisions between the groups were not always hard and fast. Masters might act as nascent capitalists employing quasi-proletariats, but journeymen sometimes operated their own shops, at least judging from the number of complaints about the practice. The number of apprentices was limited by law to two per shop, but it can be assumed that more than one master managed to employ a few extra free apprentices rather than pay a journeyman, and this was certainly the case by the late seventeenth century.

For the most part, the artisans and guilds discussed in the first part of this book come from Madrid, Seville, Valladolid, Toledo, and Segovia. I cannot estimate what percentage of the total population artisans accounted for, though it is very clear that few male artisans did nothing but tend to their shops. Most worked in the fields as well, except in the largest cities, and both activities probably were seasonal. Artisans who made things probably also sold them. Scholars who have studied Philip II's famous surveys, the *Relaciones topográficas,* whose subjects generally lived in much smaller places than those I studied, all have observed that there was no distinction between artisans and peasants.[18] During the off-season, peasants took care of other business: they wove cloth, made shoes, built homes, or made soap. Some did this work in their own villages, while others were itinerant during part of the year. Their manufacturing activities were secondary to the agricultural activities, David Vassberg says, but exactly how secondary is hard to know: "It is impossible to be precise about the proportion of villagers involved in crafts or artisanal activities. Early modern Castilian censuses do not consistently list professions, and even when they do we cannot be sure that they include the full range of people's economic activities."[19] Readers will see later that eighteenth-century reformers were convinced that guilds in large cities stifled crafts in villages and small towns and actually prohibited peasants from engaging in manufacturing. Judging from the *Relaciones topográficas,* this was not so, though it is true that small-town craftsmen often were prohibited from bringing their manufactured wares into the city for sale.[20]

[18] The Madrid and Toledo surveys are in Carmelo Viñas y Mey and Ramon Paz, eds., *Relaciones de los pueblos de España ordenadas por Felipe II,* 3 vols. (Madrid: Instituto Balmes de Sociología, 1949). The Guadalajara survey can be found in *Memorial Histórico Español,* vols. 41–43 and 45–47 (Madrid: Real Academia de la Historia, 1903). The Cuenca survey is in Eusebio Julián Zarco-Bacas y Cuevas, ed., *Relaciones de pueblos del Obispado de Cuenca hechas por orden de Felipe II* (Cuenca: Biblioteca Diocesana Conquense, 1927). The survey of Murcia is in Aurelio Cebrián Abellán and José Cano Valero, eds., *Relaciones topográficas del Reino de Murcia* (Universidad de Murcia, 1992). See also David Vassberg, *The Village and the Outside World in Golden Age Castile: Mobility and Migration in Everyday Rural Life* (Cambridge University Press, 1996), especially chap. 3; and Noël Salomon, *La vida rural castellana en tiempos de Felipe II* (Barcelona: Planeta, 1973).

[19] Vassberg, *Village and the Outside World,* 58.

[20] For example, Gaspar Melchor de Jovellanos's "Informe dado a la Junta general de Co-

Glovers might easily buy a little extra leather and sell it to shoemakers, or a tanner might pick up some extra cash by selling the meat from the animals whose skins he worked. A man's named craft might not indicate what he actually did, how he survived, or how he put food on the table. This makes it difficult to figure out who did what and what they considered themselves to be. The subjects of Philip II's surveys themselves were imprecise.[21] Most towns did not mention what we would consider artisanal occupations. Of the ninety (including the capital) questioned in Madrid, for example, only nine mentioned crafts. Of the 181 towns surveyed in Toledo, 23, or 13 percent, mentioned them. Of the 150 surveyed in Guadalajara, 19, or 12 percent, mentioned them. In Cuenca, the figure was just 6 out of 132, or 4 percent. It is possible, though unlikely, that only 10 percent or less of these towns had tailors or shoemakers or bricklayers and that the rest of the towns and villages were serviced by travelers or that their inhabitants had to visit cities to buy clothes. But even the hometowns of the itinerants do not appear to count them. The answers are at times contradictory. In Alcabón (Toledo), "there are no businesses or commerce or cultivation, nor anything, for there is no one in the town who has money to cultivate as they are all so poor, and there is nothing to work, much less journeymen, except a blacksmith, a tailor, a velvet weaver and other ordinary occupations." Others go out of their way to mention their artisans. In Carranque (Toledo) "most people work in the fields, and other people bake bread and work in other occupations, hatters, carders, shoemakers, and other occupations"; "The [740 *vecinos*] of [Dos Barrios de Ocaña, Toledo] are mostly peasants, some of them are tailors and shoemakers and blacksmiths and carpenters and laborers and there are four shopkeepers, and in all there are some twenty craftsmen [*oficiales*]"; "Some of the *vecinos* in Puebla Nueva [Toledo] have enough to eat, and others not so much, and others are poor and live off their work making bread and working the land and livestock and their occupations as tailors, shoemakers, laborers, carpenters, and day laborers."

---

mercio y Moneda sobre el libre ejercicio de las artes," 9 November 1785, in Jovellanos, *Obras*, vol. 2, ed. Cándido Nocedal, Biblioteca de Autores Españoles, vol. 50 (Madrid, 1859), 39.

[21] I looked at three questions on the surveys that alluded to people's occupation. These were Question 35 from the 1578 survey: What way of life and what cultivation (*granjerías*) do the people of the said town have and what things are made or worked there better than anywhere else; Question 40 from the 1575 survey: If the citizens are all *labradores* or if some of them are hidalgos, and the number of hidalgos there are, and which privileges and exemptions they enjoy; and Question 42 from 1575: If the people of the said town are rich or poor, the cultivation, businesses and occupations by which they live and the things that are made there or worked there that are better than in other places. My model in using the *Relaciones* is William Christian, whose pathbreaking study of local religion was based on the replies to two questions. See William A. Christian Jr., *Local Religion in Sixteenth-Century Spain* (Princeton University Press, 1981).

So most towns did not find it necessary to mention artisans, even though they were there. One's occupation, it appears, did not necessarily define one, and occupations could be multiple and transient. Vassberg offers one example of a peasant who decided he would rather be a carpenter.[22] A twenty-five-year-old man in Illescas (Toledo), Pedro Sánchez, a defendant in a minor Inquisition case, repeatedly was identified as a cutler in the proceedings, but the only work he actually was described doing was in the fields.[23] Castilians primarily devoted to agriculture might spend several months a year doing something quite different. People changed, according to the time of year, their gifts, their need, their desires. Occupational distinctions were imprecise, as were their reputations. The social structure, then, though certainly not entirely fluid, was neither unyielding nor impervious to the possible virtues and talents of manual laborers, whose fate was not sealed by their occupation, vile and mechanical though it was said to have been.

[22] Vassberg, *Village and the Outside World,* 62.
[23] AHN Inq. leg. 75.4.

CHAPTER ONE

The Republic of Labor

Castilian workers often are said to have lived in a world apart, beaten
down by a rigid, dominant ideology of honor and caste that condemned
them for who they were and what they did. Yet the political, rhetorical, and
ideological structures that emerged from previous centuries and conditioned their lives, labor, and language were the same ones that shaped the
worlds to which they allegedly were strangers. The words of Jesus and Aristotle reached them, directly or indirectly, and were transformed into social
practice. Identifying links between prevailing moral and political notions
of human society and the way in which work and workers were understood
and understood themselves is a difficult task. The links were indirect. But
there clearly were points of contact. Common people discussed theology,
as we know from Inquisition trial transcripts. They speculated about sin.
They laced their petitions with the language of treatises, though most likely
they had never read them. As litigants, producers, taxpayers, and citizens,
they invoked the common good. They were capable of theorizing their
lives, and they did so in a language that meant something to them.

The Philosophical Legacy

The Book of Genesis provided Christians with two stories relevant to our
exploration of the meaning of work: God as the craftsman of the universe,
and man's expulsion from Eden. Theologians struggled to reconcile the
two: on the one hand craftsmanship and labor appeared to be extolled; on
the other they were a punishment. Generally, they argued that work had

20

been pleasurable before the Fall and painful afterward, but in both cases it was a duty. Using different terms, they agreed that Adam had had a calling in Paradise. As one historian of Puritanism wrote, "The Fall introduced sweat and weariness into the world; work had already been here."[1] For St. Augustine (345–430), work in Paradise had been pleasurable and born of freedom, not necessity: "When all is said and done," he asked, "is there any more marvelous sight, any occasion when human reason is nearer to some sort of converse with the nature of things, than the sowing of seeds, the planting of cuttings, the transplanting of shrubs, the grafting of slips?"[2] God Himself had labored at creating the universe, though early hexaemeral commentarists tended to use God's artisanship more as a metaphor of his power and aesthetic perfection than as an indication of his workmanlike skill. Augustine's Creator "is not to be imagined as measuring out the heavens with a compass or, worse yet, molding the human form from the mud of Eden."[3]

Yet "thy hands fashioned and made me," Job had said to his maker (Job 10:8). One Spanish theologian who cited the verse, the Jesuit Pedro de Guzmán (1557–1616), went on to explain: "When He made man He said, 'Let us *make* man,' which among us is a term not of one who orders others but of one who works with his hands. . . . Without doubt, our God in speaking thus wanted to approve, for man, working with one's hands." Guzmán asked if the form of the human body did not prove that God always meant for us to work, and he used Galen and Aristotle to praise the strength, delicacy, and adaptability of man's hands. No wonder Aristotle had called them "instruments of instruments," he marveled. Indeed, he opened his treatise by announcing, "There is nothing that man's perverse inclination flees and hates as much as that for which he was born: labor and sweat."[4]

Another writer who saw God rolling up his sleeves during the creation was a late-seventeenth-century *letrado*, Melchor de Cabrera Nuñez de Guzmán, who wrote an impassioned defense of the printing trade depicting God as the First Printer and each of the days of the first week as a different book. The immense, starry firmament was a "shining parchment, in which the innumerable, brilliant stars are letters that order and teach us the omnipotence of God." The third book was man, "and we should not be surprised if God put his own Image and Stamp in the press. . . . He wanted to please himself with so many copies of his myste-

---

[1] Timothy Hall Breen, "The Non-Existent Controversy: Puritan and Anglican Attitudes on Work and Wealth, 1600–1640," *Church History* 35 (1966): 279.

[2] *De genesi ad litteram*, cited in Peter Brown, *Augustine of Hippo: A Biography* (Berkeley: University of California Press, 1967), 143.

[3] George Ovitt Jr., *The Restoration of Perfection: Labor and Technology in Medieval Culture* (New Brunswick, N.J.: Rutgers University Press, 1987), 64.

[4] Pedro de Guzmán, *Los bienes del honesto trabajo y daños de la ociosidad, en ocho discursos* (Madrid, 1614), 1–8.

rious Original."[5] God's assistants also got their hands dirty: a funeral sermon by Luis de Rebolledo (1549–1613) referred to Purgatory as a stonemason's yard where souls were hewn into shape.[6]

If Adam had not been expelled, the physician Huarte de San Juan (c. 1530–1592) speculated, then we would have no mechanical arts or sciences. There would be no tailors, shoemakers, carders, or carpenters, nor would there be philosophers, laws, or medicine: "Adam's sin thus gave practical commencement to all the arts and sciences we have mentioned, because all were necessary for remedying his misery and need."[7] Once expelled, Adam surely was grateful, looking up at heaven and thanking God for providing him with the means for shunning sloth, Guzmán surmised: "You did not give me the house built, the table laden, the clothing sewn, or satisfy the rest of my needs. You gave me just the materials, so that I would give them form. . . . Well then, as long as life should last, I shall work with my hands (*manos a labor*)."[8]

If one were to feel tempted by idleness, cautioned one of the most famous of sixteenth-century preachers, Luis de Granada (1504–1588), a Dominican, one should look at the example of Jesus, who had labored just as his father had in Genesis:

> Think of the labors Christ performed for you from the beginning to the end of his life, how he spent sleepless nights in the mountains praying for you, how he walked from one province to the next teaching and curing the sick, how he was always occupied with our salvation and how in the Passion he bore on his weary, holy shoulders that large and heavy wooden cross.

Think, too, he said, repeating a common topos, that God had created nothing idle. The sun, the stars, the trees, the ants, and the bees all move and grow and work. "Will you not be ashamed, then, you, a man capable of reason, of your idleness, a state abhorred, by natural instinct, by all irrational creatures?"[9] The Franciscan Diego de Estella (1524–1578) also depicted a universe in a state of perpetual motion:

[5] Melchor de Cabrera Nuñez de Guzmán, *Discurso legal, histórico, y político . . . del arte de la imprenta* (Madrid, 1675), 3–4. The author's aim was not so much to equate creation with printing as to elevate printing to the level of divine providence.

[6] Hilary Dansey Smith, *Preaching in the Spanish Golden Age: A Study of Some Preachers of the Reign of Philip III* (Oxford University Press, 1978), 148.

[7] Huarte de San Juan, *Examen de Ingenios* (1575), ed. Guillermo Serés (Madrid: Cátedra, 1989), 180–181. *Examen de Ingenios* was published in Venice in 1586 and 1600; in Paris in 1661; and in London in 1596, 1616, and 1698. The author is also known as Juan Huarte Navarro and Juan Huarte de San Juan.

[8] Guzmán, *Los bienes del honesto trabajo*, 11.

[9] "Remedio contra la pereza," in "Compendio y explicación de la doctrina cristiana," *Obras de Fray Luis de Granada*, vol. 3, Biblioteca de Autores Españoles (Madrid: M. Rivadeneyra, 1945), 130. Granada's *Libro de la Oración*, first published in 1554, went through twenty-three editions in five years and in 1559 was put on the Index.

Not for one moment are the elements idle. The heavens are always moving, and the planets produce their fruits. There is but one monster in the world, and that is the idle man. . . . Running water breeds delicious fish, but stagnant and idle water breeds only toads and snakes, and its fish are tasteless and harmful. What, then, can you breed if you are idle but vain, dishonest and lazy thoughts?[10]

There are those who live by their hands, the poet Jorge Manrique wrote, and then there are the rich.[11] Madrid residents Ana de Leyba and her daughter were too poor to pay a 1640 tax because "they support themselves by the work they do with their hands" and "they have nothing but what they earn with their hands."[12] Another petitioner protested that he provided for his wife and four children "with just the work of his hands, with no other way of supporting them."[13] Work literally was synonymous with hardship, and it was a frequent recourse in petitions from the poor: I work, therefore I cannot pay. A velvet weaver, Alonso Tofiño, wanted to move from Toledo to America because he and his family could not "support themselves with the honor of their ancestors, and they suffer hardship" (*padecen trabajos*).[14] Farther to the south, another hopeful emigrant, Alonso Ruiz de Vera, explained he was "a poor man, and needy, as I have no property or savings with which to support myself except with my work, and therefore I would like to go to the said New Spain, because in [Seville] I am enduring much hardship" (*paso muchos trabajos*). His neighbor, Alonso López, said a relative had invited him to America "because he knows I am poor and in this city I am undergoing many hardships."[15] The burdens were unfortunate but not a curse. They could be remedied.

Along with the Bible, classical writers were an inspiration for Spaniards as they thought about labor. Aristotle (384–322 B.C.) had compared manual workers to "certain inanimate things which act but do so without understanding that action, as in the case of fire which burns."[16] The term "mechanical," he said in the *Politics,* "should properly be applied to any occupation, arts, or instruction, which is calculated to make the body, or soul, or mind, of a freeman unfit for the pursuit and practice of goodness."[17]

---

[10] Diego de Estella, *Libro de la vanidad del mundo,* 3 vols. (Barcelona, 1582), vol. 3, 143v–144.

[11] Jorge Manrique, "Coplas por la muerte de su padre." Manrique lived from 1440 to 1479.

[12] AGS CJH leg. 1749, 30 March, 3 April.

[13] AGS CJH leg. 1756, memorial Francisco de Mesa.

[14] AGI Indiferente General, leg. 2055, exp. 88.

[15] AGI Indiferente General, leg. 2071.

[16] *Aristotle's Metaphysics,* trans. Hippocrates G. Apostle. (Bloomington: Indiana University Press, 1966), 981b, 13.

[17] *The Politics of Aristotle,* ed. Ernest Barker (Oxford University Press, 1962), book VIII, chap. II.5, 334. He added: "Much the same may also be said of the liberal branches of knowledge. Some of these branches can be studied, up to a point, without any illiberality; but too much concentration upon them, with a view to attaining perfection, is liable to cause the same evil effects that have just been mentioned."

Elsewhere he said, "none of the occupations followed by a populace which consists of mechanics, shopkeepers, and day laborers leaves any room for excellence," and "a state with an ideal constitution . . . cannot have its citizens living the life of mechanics or shopkeepers, which is ignoble and inimical to goodness."[18]

"Must mechanics be also included in the ranks of citizens?" he famously asked.[19] The answer depended on the constitution. If excellence was a requirement for citizenship, then a laborer could not be a citizen. But, Aristotle added, the good man and the good citizen are not always identical, and it may be possible in some states for a not-good man to be a citizen. One could extend his argument by positing that it then might also be possible, in some states, for a not-citizen to be a good man. In other words, perhaps an artisan can have virtue. Virtue and excellence were not absolute; they depended on the constitution under which one lived. If that was so, then the force of Aristotle's condemnation loses some of its edge. That admittedly optimistic reading is buttressed by Aristotle's own concession that the Many, the "people at large," may in certain situations rise above themselves. "Each of them by himself may not be of a good quality; but when they all come together it is possible that they may surpass—collectively and as a body, although not individually—the quality of the few best."[20]

One of the most fundamental influences on later Spanish thinking about manual labor was Cicero's *De officiis,* largely based on the writing of the Stoics, who constituted an exception to the generally negative assessment of labor in classical literature.[21] In the work, Cicero (106–43 B.C.) instructed his son about the moral and public duties of men, both in warfare and in peace, the nature of justice and virtue, the commendability of moderation and prudence, and the utility and grace of conversation and rhetoric. The passage on work and commerce quoted in virtually every Spanish treatise on the subject is the following:

> First, those means of livelihood that incur the dislike of other men are not approved, for example collecting harbor dues, or usury. Again, all those workers who are paid for their labor and not for their skill have servile and demeaning employment; for in their case the very wage is a contract to servitude. Those who buy from merchants and sell again immediately should also be thought of as demeaning themselves. For they would make no profit un-

---

[18] Ibid., book VI, chap. IV.12, 265, and book VII, chap. IX.3, 301.

[19] Ibid., book VII, chap. IX.3, 301.

[20] Ibid., book III, chap. XI.2, 123.

[21] See Birgit van den Hoven, *Work in Ancient and Medieval Thought: Ancient Philosophers, Medieval Monks and Theologians and Their Concept of Work, Occupations and Technology* (Amsterdam: J. C. Gieven, 1996), 21–71; Marcia L. Colish, *The Stoic Tradition from Antiquity to the Early Middle Ages,* 2 vols. (Leiden: E. J. Brill, 1985), especially vol. 1, 143–152, on *De officiis.*

less they told sufficient lies, and nothing is more dishonorable than falsehood. All handcraftsmen are engaged in a demeaning trade; for there can be nothing well bred about the workshop. The crafts that are least worthy of approval are those that minister to the pleasures: fishmongers, butchers, cooks, poulterers, fishermen . . . ; add to this, if you like, perfumers, dancers, and the whole variety show.

Other arts either require greater good sense or else procure substantial benefit, for example medicine, architecture or teaching things that are honorable. They are honorable for those who belong to the class that they befit.

On the other hand, there was no better life than that of the farmer: "If a merchant, satiated, or rather satisfied with his profits . . . shall from the harbor step into an estate and lands, such a man seems most justly deserving of praise. For of all gainful professions, nothing is better, nothing more pleasing, nothing more delightful, nothing better becomes a well-bred man than agriculture."[22]

St. Thomas of Aquinas (1224–1274), in writing about the intellectual virtues, followed Cicero's hierarchy in declaring that "the liberal arts are more excellent than the mechanical arts," but he left it at that:

> The speculative habits . . . are called arts by a kind of similitude, but liberal, to distinguish them from those arts which are ordered to their work by the exercise of body. The latter are in some way servile, insofar as the body is a servant to the soul and a man is free thanks to his soul. . . . The fact that liberal arts are more noble does not mean that they are more properly called arts.

Aquinas also differed with Aristotle in saying that art itself is not a virtue, because a bad product can make an artisan's good intentions irrelevant. The virtue lies in the piece, though it is also true

> that in order for a man to use well the art he has, a good will is needed, which is perfected by moral virtue. Therefore, the Philosopher says that there is a virtue of art, namely moral virtue, insofar as some moral virtue is needed for its good use. It is obvious that the artisan is inclined by justice, which causes rectitude of will, to make a faithful work.[23]

---

[22] Cicero, *On Duties,* ed. M. T. Griffin and E. M. Atkins (Cambridge University Press, 1991), book I, 150–151, 58–59. Colish remarks that Cicero is "falling back on social prejudices of a sort that no Stoic would tolerate" (*The Stoic Tradition from Antiquity to the Early Middle Ages,* 2 vols. [Leiden: E. J. Brill, 1985], vol. 1, 147). Aristotle, it is worth pointing out, was less enthusiastic about rural life than Cicero and excluded both farmers and mechanics from the priesthood: *The Politics of Aristotle,* book VII, chap. IX.9, 302–303.

[23] Question 57, "Distinguishing the intellectual virtues," *Summa theologiae,* I-2, 18, in Thomas Aquinas, *Selected Writings,* trans. Ralph McInerny (London: Penguin Books, 1998), 670–681.

"Faithful work," translated into Spanish as *obra leal,* would become part of craft guilds' vocabulary, their term for a work that had passed an inspector's muster. When they fought for the dignity of their craft and the objects they created, they were defending their *obra leal.*

Classifications of human knowledge and activities became a common pastime in the late Middle Ages. When the moralist Enrique de Villena (1384–1434) wrote about the labors of Hercules, he naturally started off by defining all the social orders and suborders and all their members.[24] A few years later, Rodrigo Sánchez de Arévalo (1404–1479) in a mirror book also classified all eight arts (wool, metal, navigation, hunting, farming, theater, medicine, and commerce), reiterating that just because something was necessary did not make it virtuous and advising that "the mechanical arts should be exercised only by those who cannot do something better."[25] St. Bonaventure (1221–1274) classified seven sorts of servile work—agriculture, cloth, metal-stone-wood, food, pigments and potions, merchants, and theater—and three general types of labor: purely servile, continuously necessary, and completely pleasureful.[26] Hugh of St. Victor's *Didascalicon* (c. 1120) sorted the practical, theoretical, and mechanical arts, the latter of which were a precondition for the higher forms. Cicero's hierarchy remained intact, but the lower forms were considered necessary and even admirable in that they were part of a process leading to a higher end.[27] In thinking thus, Hugh perhaps was drawing from Aristotle, who in the *Ethics* had separated actions from their ends, the latter of which were superior to the former:

> All skills of that kind which come under a single 'faculty'—a skill in making bridles or any other part of a horse's gear comes under the faculty or art of horsemanship, while horsemanship itself and every branch of military practice comes under the art of war, and in like manner other arts and techniques are subordinate to yet others—in all these the ends of the master arts are to

[24] Enrique de Villena, *Los doze trabajos de Hércules* (1483), ed. Margherita Morreale (Madrid: Real Academia Española, 1958). The author was Enrique de Aragón, marquis of Villena. See also G. Karl Galinsky, *The Herakles Theme: The Adaptations of the Hero in Literature from Homer to the Twentieth Century* (Oxford: Basil Blackwell, 1972); and Marianne Breidenthal, "The Legend of Hercules in Castilian Literature Up To the Seventeenth Century" (Ph.D. diss., University of California, Berkeley, 1985). I am grateful to Emilie Bergman for sharing this dissertation with me.

[25] Rodrigo Sánchez de Arévalo, *Spejo de la vida humana* (Zaragoza, 1491).

[26] Steven Epstein, *Wage Labor and Guilds in Medieval Europe* (Chapel Hill: University of North Carolina Press, 1991), 173.

[27] *The 'Didascalicon' of Hugh of St. Victor: A Medieval Guide to the Arts,* trans. and ed. Jerome Taylor (New York: Columbia University Press, 1961). Some historians have interpreted Hugh's classification as marking a substantial change in the way learned men looked at the mechanical arts, a position disputed in William Eamon, *Science and the Secrets of Nature: Books of Secrets in Medieval and Early Modern Culture* (Princeton University Press, 1994), 83.

be preferred to those of the subordinate skills, for it is the former that provide the motive for pursuing the latter.[28]

Struggling with this problem centuries later, Gaspar Gutiérrez de los Ríos seemed to despair as he drew up his own classification of mechanical arts and occupations and liberal arts, with Aristotle and Cicero crowding the margins. The writer, a professor of law and letters at Salamanca, went beyond the static lists of his predecessors; instead, he described arts and occupations (both liberal and mechanical) as processes of learning, innovation, and inspiration. Liberal arts were those in which understanding played the leading role; mechanical arts were those performed primarily by the body; mechanical occupations required hardly any learning at all. But Gutiérrez de los Ríos decided that as all higher classes of labor depended upon the lower ones, and mechanical arts generally all used liberal arts (e.g., a tailor must use geometry), then mechanical arts could become liberal ones. He noted that some occupations, such as cooking, had been regarded as vile in one era but later praised as an art; others were considered servile only because slaves were allowed to learn them; even swimming had once been thought liberal, he said.[29] This recognition of the mutability of regard, the "instability of opinions and alterations in times, uses, and customs," represented an important step in centuries of classifications of labor.[30] Labor was timeless neither in its virtue nor in its contemptibility.

The list making gradually died out in the early modern era, though there survived a notion of crafts more noble than others—or, at least, advocates of one or another craft pretended that such a universally accepted notion existed. Such was the belief of Seville's arquebusiers, who argued in 1635 that they should have new ordinances like other "occupations of less consideration and importance."[31] And such was the opinion of the Buscón's father: "Son, this thieving business is a liberal, not a mechanical art."[32]

Misreadings of early modern Castilian attitudes toward labor in large part stem from excessive reliance on normative treatises, whose obsession with categories of labor, particularly with identifying those crafts held to be vile and mechanical, reflected as much the authors' need or desire to continue an interpretive tradition as it did what they saw around them.

---

[28] *The Ethics of Aristotle*, ed. J. A. K. Thomson (Baltimore: Penguin, 1953), 25–26.
[29] Gaspar Gutiérrez de los Ríos, *Noticia general para la estimación de las artes* (Madrid, 1600), 28, 46, 95.
[30] Ibid., 86.
[31] AMSev Sec. X, Actas, 2a escr., 24 January 1635.
[32] Francisco de Quevedo, *El Buscón* (1626) (Madrid: Clásicos Castalia, 1990), 78.

Tract writers were responding to their predecessors, not describing their world. They certainly were not describing the world of the tailors, farriers, and shoemakers whose litigation and petitions form the bulk of the documentary evidence for this book. For those artisans, categories of labor might prove useful from time to time, but they did not regard themselves as inanimate objects or refuse, no matter which job they performed. To be sure, their society was a stratified one, and there were stigmas to be lived with or overcome, just as there are today. But these workers' classical legacy was one of inclusion, not exclusion.

The Common Good and the Law

The commonweal, the common good, *el bien público, el bien común*—this was the essence of what the republic meant. Though there were various strains of republicanism in early modern Europe and Spain, with debts to humanism, natural law, Aristotle, constitutionalism, and Roman law, there was virtually no contemporary document regarding work that did not appeal to the common good. Few normative descriptions of good government did not mention work.

The republic, a term that embraced relations of both authority and cohabitation, often was depicted in late medieval and early modern times with the metaphor of the body. One diseased organ could spell doom for the rest, and therefore a prince had the obligation to ensure that the body remained healthy. Human society, wrote Gutiérrez de los Ríos in his 1600 appeal for social harmony and mutual respect, should imitate the human body, "in which the head does not bite the hands, nor do the hands tear apart the other members."[33] In a less graceful use of the metaphor, Francisco Martínez de la Mata in 1650 warned that "if the feet and the hands of the body of this republic are the consumers, and the mouth is the arts, which grant existence to us all, then it is clear that the needs of the head, which is Your Majesty, and the weakness of the entire body, and all the ills that Spain suffers, are the result of this mouth not eating."[34] Like other writers, the Augustinian prior Marco Antonio de Camós (1543–1606) identified the feet as the member corresponding to working people, which held up the rest of society: "And because they are so near to the ground, stepping on stones and pebbles and other impediments that might make them stumble, it is necessary to take even greater care of them, considering the service they provide and how they are missed when they are weak

[33] Gutiérrez de los Ríos, *Noticia general*, 332–333.

[34] *Memoriales y discursos de Francisco Martínez de Mata* [*sic*], ed. Gonzalo Anes (Madrid: Moneda y Crédito, 1971), 300. The author's name sometimes includes the definite article and sometimes not.

or sick."[35] More powerfully, in his criticism of Aristotle for having shunned artisans, the Italian Tommaso Campanella (1568–1639) asked, "just because [the foot] is not the eye, is the foot for that reason not part of the body? Here stands the most valid argument of [St. Paul] based on nature. Let Aristotle blush."[36]

Aristotle and Cicero were not the only classical writers Spaniards read, of course; Horace, Virgil, and Ovid were on their bookshelves as well, and much of the political theory of the late medieval and early modern period is filled with visions of bygone rural perfection. Writers such as Antonio de Guevara (1480–1545) counterposed the vice-ridden court (not yet settled in Madrid) to the bucolic, innocent village where friendship was sincere and men worked honestly to reap the fruits they harvested. The village was not a place for contemplation; it was a place for tilling and spinning and sweating. Cicero, it will be remembered, believed that "nothing better becomes a well-bred man than agriculture." At a time when Castile's representational system and political culture was predicated on the municipality, its idealized past was rooted in the countryside, where everyone grew what they needed, unafraid and unashamed to get blisters on their fingers.[37]

The pastoral utopia was joined by utopias set somewhere completely different—America, for example, or the moon. The humanist priest Juan Maldonado (1485?–1545?) composed a dream voyage on which he was accompanied by María de Rojas, the deceased widow of Pedro de Cartagena, who Maldonado believed had betrayed the interests of the 1520 comuneros revolt. On the moon, he was astounded to encounter lush meadows and orchards, but María reminded him that his world, too, had once known such beauty: "In those days, when people were not yet poisoned by avarice and lust, the vast majority, including rulers, lived in the countryside and in the villages, and they fed their families with the fruits their property yielded with no taxes." How could such a world have been lost? he asked her. Ah, Maldonado, she sighed, "What disappeared was sense and honesty. . . . The ancient heroes were satisfied in their frugality, they saw mortal life as a voyage or as an inn along the road. The riches of this world were regarded as quirks of fate, as tokens that would soon be re-

---

[35] Marco Antonio de Camós, *Microcosmia y govierno universal del hombre* (Barcelona, 1592), 220. Camós was a military and diplomatic official under Philip II who entered the Augustinian order after his wife and children died. He was appointed archbishop just before his death.

[36] Cited in John M. Headley, "On Reconstructing the Citizenry: Campanella's Criticism of Aristotle's 'Politics,'" *Il Pensiero Politico*, no. 24 (1) (1991): 35.

[37] In this sense Castile was unlike sixteenth-century Germany, with its mythic guildsmen's past, what Lyndal Roper has called an "independent household-workshop Utopia" (*The Holy Household*. [Oxford: Clarendon Press, 1989], 31). On Guevara, see F. Márquez Villanueva, *"Menosprecio de corte y alabanza de aldea" (Valladolid, 1539) y el tema áulico en la obra de Fray Antonio de Guevara* (Santander: Universidad de Cantabria, 1999).

claimed."[38] From the moon the unlikely pair traveled to America, where they found that there, too, everyone had what they needed. Nobody was poor, property was shared, the shops were full, and there were no guards. As astonished as he had been on the moon, Maldonado asked an old man how such harmony could reign with no Spanish doctors of the church there to instruct them, the latter having left America after fighting among themselves. "It is true we have none," the old man conceded, "but those who practice the priesthood among us, after the death of the Spaniards, use just their reason to instruct us," and that seemed to be plenty.[39]

To ensure the common good, the republic should be ruled wisely and moderately. It should be inhabited by citizens who helped one another and who were mostly alike. It should emulate the simple values of the rural world of the *labradores,* those hardworking, honest country folk who had not yet become contaminated with urban vice. This utopia was not a land where people lolled around. They worked, and that was good.

Just how good it was can be seen from one of the finest allegorical treatises of the sixteenth century, Luis de Mejía y Ponce de León's *Apólogo de la ociosidad y el trabajo.* It is the story of Labricio Portundo, a Spanish descendant of Jupiter, Saturn, and Hercules; and Doña Ocio (Lady Indolence), who reigns with her two chief servants, Fraud and Hypocrisy, over Sybaris, the mythical Greek city, where the Olympic Games have stalled and philosophy has ceased. Ocio is looking for a husband, Labricio is single, and her people get in touch with his people. Labricio seems willing, and as a first step he sends his future bride some presents: He sends a rooster (symbolizing a clock) and a monkey (for ingenuity). Instead of perfume, he sends two barrels of his own sweat, "so you know that just as men work outside the home until they sweat to earn money with which to sustain their honor . . . so, too, women inside the home should govern their finances and their family in the same manner." He also sent her an ass, which his messenger explained thus:

> This, madam, though it may appear to be a vile animal, unworthy of admiration, is nonetheless very useful for the home, the family, and the republic. Furthermore, I tell you that no matter how lofty a person's lineage, status, or condition, he should not look down upon the low or disdain those who appear to be abject, because oftentimes they are the bases upon which their betters support themselves.[40]

---

[38] Juan Maldonado, *El sueño* (1532), in *Sueños ficticios y lucha ideológica en el Siglo de Oro,* ed. Miguel Avilés (Madrid: Editora Nacional, 1981), 159. In Maldonado's account of the comunero uprising, Cartagena, who represented Burgos on the insurgent junta, did everything the city's wealthy merchants wanted him to do: Juan Maldonado, *El movimiento de España, o sea Historia de la revolución conocida con el nombre de las Comunidades de Castilla* (Madrid, 1840).

[39] Maldonado, *El sueño* (1532), 173.

[40] Luis de Mejía y Ponce de León, *Apólogo de la ociosidad i el trabajo* (1546), in *Obras que*

Ocio, not surprisingly, did not like her presents, so she expelled the messenger and turned down Labricio's offer of marriage. This turned out to be a good thing for all concerned. While Ocio went off to Jerusalem, persuading everyone along the way to stop working and follow her, Labricio married Diligence, one of Minerva's servants. Everyone in history and mythology apparently was on the guest list for their wedding party, at which Mercury (the god of trade) took Labricio aside and gave him four servants: Prudence, Justice, Temperance, and Fortitude. He also offered him much advice about marriage and governance and the following words about work and moderation:

> You should also procure very perfect masters in all the arts so that people in your republic wisely use the time they spend learning. Journeymen should neither be so rich that they scorn a job well done, nor so poor that they cannot buy the instruments necessary for using their art perfectly. The former, because of insolence, and the latter, because of poverty, will be unable to properly teach what they should of the customs and art by which they live and which benefit the republic.[41]

One of Labricio's ancestors, I noted, was Hercules, whose labors made frequent appearances in the literature of the late medieval and early modern period. In general, he was a moral hero, often taking on the aspect of a knight errant, a living illustration that good deeds could ensure salvation. Don Quixote included him when he enumerated the great and virtuous men in history who had been maliciously slandered.[42] Enrique de Villena called his hero a "great guardian of the common good."[43] Gutiérrez de los Ríos followed a common Renaissance trope when he introduced Hercules into his treatise on labor: The young Hercules went walking one day in the countryside and sat down to meditate on which of two paths to choose in life, *ocio* or labor. Just then two women appeared. One was "honest, of noble appearance, her body naturally clean, her eyes shy, her figure chaste and draped in a white dress." The other was a disturbing contrast: "Fleshy

---

Francisco Cervantes de Salazar ha hecho glosado i traducido, ed. Francisco Cervantes de Salazar (Madrid, 1772), 15–17. Mejía (b. 1524) and Cervantes de Salazar both were followers of Erasmus; Cervantes de Salazar dedicated his edition of Mejía's work to Juan Martínez Siliceo, archbishop of Toledo, tutor to the future Philip II, and instigator of Toledo's controversial 1547 *limpieza de sangre* statute. For more on Mejía's allegory, with a particularly interesting analysis of the importance of marriage, see Alain Milhou and Anne Milhou-Roudié, "Le concept de travail dans les courants utopiques en Espagne et en Amérique (1516–1558)" in *Les utopies dans le monde hispanique,* ed. Jean-Pierre Etienvre (Madrid: Casa de Velázquez, 1990), 171–190.

[41] Mejía y Ponce de León, *Apólogo de la ociosidad i el trabajo,* 114.

[42] The others were Julius Caesar, Alexander the Great, Amadís de Gaula, and Amadís's brother, Galaor (Miguel de Cervantes, *El ingenioso hidalgo Don Quijote de la Mancha,* II.2).

[43] Breidenthal, "The Legend of Hercules in Castilian Literature," 166.

and flabby . . . her figure appeared more artificial than real, her eyes rest-less and open, dressed so beautifully that she gazed at herself and won-dered who was looking at her." They each pitched their way of life to the future hero, who made the correct choice, demonstrating, Gutiérrez de los Ríos wrote, that "everybody, without exception, has the obligation to work."[44]

Mercury's advice to Labricio was published in the same decade as a dia-logue by Alfonso de Valdés, a leading Erasmist, whose ideal king recalled in a long speech how he had governed his republic:

> I expelled from my court con men, tricksters, and vagabonds, leaving only those who were in need; and to avoid idleness, from which infinite ills are born, I ordered all my gentlemen to teach their children mechanical arts along with the liberal arts. And knowing how important it is that he who makes the law abide by it, I put my sons and daughters to learning occupations, and everyone followed me.[45]

Work was still linked to sin—it was good because it removed the possiblity of sinful idleness—but it had acquired civic importance as well. In spite of Aristotle, workers were becoming citizens.

How did workers themselves use the language of the common good and the republic? Silk twisters in Toledo met in 1627 to discuss "matters con-cerning the good government of the shops of this art and compliance with and execution of its ordinances and to find a way to address the malice of those who, embracing the baseness of words, act against the intent and the principal aim of some of the ordinances that are most important for the public good and utility."[46] When Madrid's turners met in 1654 to draw up new ordinances they said they were meeting "to discuss matters con-cerning the common good."[47] Makers of capes asked Seville's city council to allow their ordinances to be publicized because "it is in their right and it serves the common good that the ordinances be made public so as to impede many contradictory things that greatly harm the common good."[48] Even Philip III, when stepping between Madrid's tailors and braid makers, began by telling the corregidor that "concerning the common good, the tailors have told us . . ."[49] In disputes over manufacture or sale, "malice," "fraud," and "false" often were the terms used to describe objec-

[44] Gutiérrez de los Ríos, *Noticia general,* 290–298.

[45] Alfonso de Valdés, *Diálogo de Mercurio y Carón,* ed. Rosa Navarro (Madrid: Cátedra, 1999), 216–217. Valdés (1490–1532) perhaps is best known for his ringing defense of Charles V in 1528 after the sack of Rome.

[46] AMT Gremios leg. 1231, 20 June 1627.

[47] AV 2.309.31.

[48] AMSev, Sec. X, Actas, 2a escr., tomo 119, 30 April 1635.

[49] AV 2.245.12, 1 August 1609.

tionable products or behavior. The words imply the breaking of a contract, the creation of discord among peaceful citizens, the transgression of justice, the violation of order. They are words that go beyond corporate bickering. They are political terms whose meaning resonated within a commonwealth.

One instance of an occupation judged in republican terms was that of the master builders or architects (*alarifes*) of Seville, who had responsibility over an array of overlapping construction crafts.[50] The title originated in Muslim Spain and encompassed both moral and technical authority over subservient guilds. The alarifes' ordinances, whose original date is unknown, state that theirs is a noble art requiring technical knowledge justly rewarded by monarchs when performed well. Most important for our purposes, "they serve God to enter Holy Paradise because they make peace among men, judging their rights and relieving them of great conflicts."[51] By the sixteenth and seventeenth centuries, alarifes were elected by carpenters and laborers guilds and then approved by the city council. But in May 1634, the Seville city council announced it would put the post up for sale, a decision that met with protests from the interested parties. The protests seem to have prospered, because the city announced the identical intention two years later. Bartolomé Vázquez pleaded before the council on his comrades' behalf, predicting great harm for the republic if the sale were to go ahead. Master builders, he said, had studied "all the mechanical and liberal arts" such as architecture, geometry, and arithmetic: "Alarifes must be men of good life and customs, fearful of God and their conscience, skilled in all arts, old Christians . . . skillful in measuring and assessing and giving everything its proper due, giving everyone what is his, making peace among men, relieving disputes and sorrows [and ensuring] calm in the Republic."[52] Without them, he said, lawsuits and discord would ensue. Once again, the city took note, and the sale was stopped.[53]

[50] Architects and master builders were sometimes, but not always, the same person, and at times laborers and carpenters shared alarifes. On alarifes, see María Angeles Toajas Roger, *Diego López de Arenas: Carpintero, alarife y tratadista en la Sevilla del siglo XVII* (Seville: Diputación Provincial de Sevilla, 1989), chaps. 1–2; On architects, see Alicia Cámara Múñoz, *Arquitectura y sociedad en el Siglo de Oro* (Madrid: Ediciones el Arquero, 1990), chap. 3.

[51] Víctor Pérez Escolano and Fernando Villanueva Sandino, eds., *Ordenanzas de Sevilla* (1632) (Seville: Oficina Técnica de Arquitectura e Ingeniería, 1975), 141v–142. The ordinances in this collection were written in the sixteenth century but were compiled only in 1632.

[52] AMSev Sec. X, Actas, 2a. escr., vol. 120, 13 March 1636. The office is also the subject of discussion in vols. 118, 119, 122, 123, 128, and 129. See part 2 for a discussion of the requirement that members be Old Christians, or not descended from Jews.

[53] Though the division of labor among alarife, master builder, and architect was never clear, everyone agreed they had to be well-read; Seville's plans to put the office up for sale may have thinned the job pool, judging from the laborers' alarife's complaint that he was being called upon to fix jobs botched by illiterate colleagues and his request that the city guarantee that alarifes at least know how to read and write. AMSev Sec. X, Actas, 2a. escr., tomo 129, 27 January 1645.

The instruments with which Castilian communities ensured the common good were codified law and custom, along with price ceilings, mutual aid, and production regulations overseen by guilds. Law was the manifestation of government and of history, of a people's past and its relationship to its ruler. It was a mark of justice, not distant in consideration from what they heard in church. If a forestaller was said to have "shown no fear of God or justice" by concealing eggs beneath her market stall, it was because God and justice were close neighbors.[54] Carders in a Segovia town who allegedly had carried out improper inspections were said to have shown "little fear of God, their consciences, or the justice that Your Mercy administers."[55] Responding to wage complaints by Segovia's cloth shearers, the assistant corregidor referred the matter to city councilmen, telling them to "address what is most fitting for the service of God, our Lord, and the good of this republic."[56] Proposals for charity projects in Seville noted they served God and the common good, together referred to as the "two majesties."[57] The charges against Cantabrian shoemakers who were moonlighting as tanners said they had acted "with little fear of God, in detriment to the common good, and in disregard of the right justice that Your Mercy administers."[58] Guild ordinances, which, as we will see, took on the quality of law in litigation, were written in the name of God. The masters of harp and guitar strings, who had never had ordinances before, wrote their first ones "in the name of the all-powerful God and the eternally virgin Mary."[59] The turners whom we saw earlier meeting for the common good also were gathered "for the glory of God our Lord and the Holiest Virgin and the glorious Saint Joseph," their patron.[60]

Law was what made the republic good. In the late fifteenth century, Sánchez de Arévalo wrote: "The law should be applied only insofar as it aids the common good of the city or kingdom for which it exists, and not for any particular gains. The law also should be common to all, applicable and constraining to rich and poor, powerful and weak, unlike the spider's web, which catches weak animals but does not extend itself to the strong."[61] And Alonso Morgado, a sixteenth-century chronicler of Seville, introduced the various judicial institutions of his city by affirming that jus-

[54] AHN CS leg. 42.482, exp. 188.

[55] AMSeg 908–31.

[56] AMSeg Libro de Actas 1030, 12 October 1626.

[57] Cited in Valentina K. Tikoff, "Assisted Transitions: Children and Adolescents in the Orphanages of Seville at the End of the Old Regime, 1681–1831" (Ph.D. diss., Indiana University, 2000), 14.

[58] ARCV Pleitos Civiles Pérez Alonso (O) 43.2 (1696–1698).

[59] AV 2.309.41, 11 November 1679.

[60] AV 2.309.31.

[61] Rodrigo Sánchez de Arévalo, *Suma de la Política* (1454–1455), ed. Juan Beneyto Pérez (Madrid: CSIC, 1944), 115.

tice was "the true Peace of the People, the Stability of the Fatherland, the Liberty of the People, the Temperance of the Air, the Serenity of the Sea, and what fertilizes the land, without which (as St. Augustine divinely says) no Republic can remain nor preserve itself nor call itself a Republic."[62] The laws Sánchez de Arévalo and Morgado were familiar with were those of the Catholic Monarchs' predecessors, starting with Alfonso X, who compiled Roman and canon law into the famous *Partidas* in the mid-thirteenth century. Ferdinand and Isabel ordered the compilation (the *Recopilación*) of all previous laws, a late edition of which included a prologue stating the conditions of good law: "The first, to remove and uproot vice. Second, to put in order subjects' customs and actions. Third, to bring happiness to men. Fourth, to plainly and clearly order the truth. And the final object of law is the tranquil and peaceful condition of the people."[63] During the reign of Philip II, the various laws of what by then was a united kingdom were again compiled and edited into the *Nueva Recopilación,* which would go through a subsequent re-edition in the seventeenth century. The new law code, in the words of James Casey, reflected "the all-embracing nature of law, in which administration, morality, and adjudication seem to be gathered together in a way which leaves little room for that separation between public and private space characteristic of a modern society."[64] Put another way by a seventeenth-century magistrate, the law was "a virtue and manner of life."[65]

Disputes and claims over work in seventeenth-century Castile often bumped up against the proximity of law and custom. Gutiérrez de los Ríos, as was noted earlier, recounted how certain mechanical arts could, over time, come to be considered liberal arts. That was the result of custom overtaking prescription. Cabrera Núñez de Guzmán, in making his point that printers deserved their privileges, commented on Gutiérrez de los Ríos's treatise by saying that "custom, no matter how barbarous, has the power to make a servile Art liberal, and vice versa."[66] Aristotle had drawn attention to the problem when he wrote, "It is from habit, and only from habit, that law derives the validity which secures obedience."[67] Law, then, could be respected only if it conformed with habit and if it promoted the common good.

The school of sixteenth-century Spanish philosophers known as the neo-scholastics also addressed the relationship between law and custom.

---

[62] Alonso Morgado, *Historia de Sevilla* (Seville, 1587), 59v.

[63] Diego Pérez de Salamanca, ed., *Ordenanzas reales de Castilla* (Salamanca, 1560).

[64] James Casey, *Early Modern Spain: A Social History* (London: Routledge, 1999), 166.

[65] Mateo López Bravo, *Del rey y de la razon de gobernar* (1627), in *Mateo López Bravo: Un socialista español del siglo XVII,* ed. Henry Mechoulan (Madrid: Editora Nacional, 1977), 172.

[66] Melchor de Cabrera Núñez de Guzmán, *Discurso legal, histórico, y político . . . del arte de la imprenta* (Madrid, 1675), 26.

[67] *Politics of Aristotle,* 73.

35

Domingo de Soto, for example, concluded that custom could overtake law and that, indeed, a custom might indicate the existence of a long-forgotten law.[68] A custom could become a precept, he wrote, as in the case of the Dominican order's rule and practice of saying certain prayers at certain times, which surely was the result of informal custom over hundreds of years. But a bad custom could not replace a good law and, he cautioned, if the prince does not agree with the acceptance of the custom as law, acceptance will not take place. One of the most important of the neo-scholastic legal scholars, Francisco Suárez, a Thomist Jesuit who studied at Salamanca and spent most of his career in Coimbra, was especially concerned with popular consent and the legitimacy of rule, and he devoted considerable attention to the conditions under which custom could be transformed into unwritten law. In general, he said, custom must be shared and voluntary and must meet the criteria for law. Under certain conditions, custom could abrogate written law but, he wrote, differing with Soto, a monarch must consent to such abrogation.[69] For Jean Bodin, a judge could not rule based on conscience in the presence of either a contrary custom or a law, which for him had equal standing.[70] Jurist Jerónimo Castillo de Bobadilla (1547?–1605) also told corregidores they had as much obligation to observe custom as to observe law, though he admitted that the question of exactly when a custom acquired the force of law, which depended on how long it had been practiced and by how many people, was open to debate. "There is no civil law or common opinion that cannot be altered through custom," he wrote in his manual for governors. Kings must confirm all reasonable customs, "and thus he who judges custom over law must be excused, particularly when the law is abrogated by contrary use."[71] Later on in his manual, when discussing judicial appeals, he enter-

---

[68] Domingo de Soto, *De la justicia y del derecho* (1556), book I, qu. 7, art. II (Madrid: Instituto de Estudios Políticos, 1967), vol. 1, 76–78. On Soto and in general on the School of Salamanca see José Barrientos García, *Un siglo de moral económica en Salamanca (1526–1629)*, vol. 1: *Francisco de Vitoria y Domingo de Soto* (Universidad de Salamanca, 1985); José Barrientos García, "El pensamiento económico en la perspectiva filosófico-teológica," in *El pensamiento económico en la Escuela de Salamanca*, ed. Francisco Gómez Camacho and Ricardo Robledo (Universidad de Salamanca, 1998); J. A. Fernández-Santamaría, *The State, War and Peace: Spanish Political Thought in the Renaissance 1516–1559* (Cambridge University Press, 1977); Marjorie Grice-Hutchinson, *Early Economic Thought in Spain 1177–1740* (London: Allen and Unwin, 1978); and Bernice Hamilton, *Political Thought in Sixteenth-Century Spain* (Oxford University Press, 1963).

[69] Francisco Suárez, *De legibus* 7.14.8, cited in Arthur P. Monahan, *From Personal Duties towards Personal Rights: Late Medieval and Early Modern Political Thought, 1300–1600* (Montreal; McGill-Queen's University Press, 1994), 173.

[70] Jean Bodin, *Six Books of a Commonweale*, book I, chap. 10.

[71] Jerónimo Castillo de Bobadilla, *Política para corregidores*, 2 vols. (Madrid, 1597), vol. 1, 568. On Castillo de Bobadilla, see Benjamín González Alonso, *Sobre el estado y la administración de la corona de Castilla en el antiguo régimen* (Madrid: Siglo Veintiuno, 1981), 85–140; and Benjamín González Alonso, *El corregidor castellano* (Madrid: Instituto de Estudios Administrativos, 1970).

tained the case of a municipal custom that allowed sentencing after the expiration of a deadline. Is such a sentence valid? Yes, for several reasons, he said, among which: "municipal custom and customs of the patria [are] considered law and they silence law (*hace callar las leyes*). . . . Fourth, because immemorial custom is based on reason, though it may be contrary to law, it is considered approved by the king, and must be observed with no further notice required."[72]

In fighting before city councils and in courts, seventeenth-century Castilian workers made use of the relative merits and weight of custom and law. The distinction between the two was often murky. Decisions by the king or the Council of Castile were more obvious examples of law than were previous court rulings or guild ordinances, but all bore the king's signature, directly or indirectly. They were written and enforceable. But it is also true that they could be modified or appealed on the basis of long-standing custom. The fact that something was written did not make it immutable; the fact that something was considered a custom did not mean it was not written. Indeed, the fact that so many historians in recent years have noted the proclivity with which early modern Spaniards creatively used the law to their own advantage is an indication that "law," as we define it today, is perhaps the wrong word for sixteenth- and seventeenth-century codes. More apt, perhaps, would be to think of them as norms, or broad social rules.

Guild ordinances sometimes were seen not as law ordered by the king but as tacit admissions of custom sanctioned by practice, sort of a starting point for negotiations. In 1606, for example, the city of Valladolid declared that a shoemakers confraternity's privilege to appoint inspectors, which was written, had become null and void because it was not being used.[73] Nor was longevity decisive. Mack Walker has pointed out that in Germany "the assumption that a Custom was ancient was a legal fiction or at best expressed the faulty memory of a generation. . . . There is just as much reason to believe in the relative novelty of a Custom as in its antiquity."[74] In often insisting on the primacy of custom over positive law, Castilian workers to some degree were affirming the primacy of the common good over the individual good. But when custom had ceased serving their interests, they just as easily could point to the greater justice of innovation, and the authorities could do the opposite. When certain basket weavers in Seville, for example, wanted new ordinances in 1641 so as to end confusion with

---

[72] Castillo de Bobadilla, *Política para corregidores*, vol. 2, 301–302.

[73] AHN CS leg. 29.581.

[74] Mack Walker, *German Home Towns: Community, State, and General Estate, 1648–1817* (Ithaca, N.Y.: Cornell University Press, 1971), 36. See also Harald Deceulaer, "Guilds and Litigation: Conflict Settlement in Antwerp (1585–1796)," in *Statuts individuels, statuts corporatifs et statuts judiciaires dans les villes européenes (Moyen âge et temps modernes). Actes du colloque tenu à Gand les 12–14 Oct. 1995*, ed. Marc Boone and Maarten Prak (Leuven: Garant, 1996).

another sort of basket weavers, the city dictated "Let custom prevail."[75] When Madrid shoemakers came up against the leather sellers, as they so frequently did, each bearing rulings and orders that proved their case, they said the Alcaldes de Casa y Corte (royal judges with jurisdiction over the capital) had the obligation to find with them "because any novelty is hateful, and the rule is to order that custom be followed even in those cases in which a case has not been decided (*ejecutoriada*), as in this one."[76]

Guilds, then, generally took a two-pronged approach to their lawsuits. In their "incursions into the past," to quote an Italian historian, they appealed to law and precedent, which could either compel a certain legal action or simply guide legal actors. They inserted ordinances from decades or even centuries earlier and reminded the court that the king had previously found with them, as he invariably had at some point. But, at the same time, they appealed to custom, which they said had prevailed since time immemorial.[77]

A suit between Segovia's tailors and hosiers that arose after the city's corregidor had decided tailors could cut and make *greguescos* (a type of breeches) illustrates how litigants used both custom and law.[78] Segovia in the sixteenth century had been a city of artisans who worked mostly in textiles and wool and with related finished products. Before the 1604 trial, the hosiers marshaled seven witnesses who were each asked five questions; the tailors had eleven witnesses who each were asked twelve questions. Most people agreed that breeches had been in use for over thirty years and that during that time the hosiers had overseen production and had administered examinations to the tailors. The hosiers enjoyed, as several of their witnesses said, peaceful ownership (they were *en quieta y pacífica posesión*) of the craft and were the ones who did it best. Things were changing, though, and tailors were taking over. The tailors explained the change by appealing to the common good, which stood to gain because there were so few hosiers left in Segovia, a city they called "very large and populated" (one witness echoed "it has always been and is very big"). With twelve thou-

---

[75] AMSev, Sec. X, Actas, 2a. escr., tomo 125, 27 September 1641.

[76] AHN CS leg. 36.276 (1658).

[77] Angela Groppi, "Jews, Women, Soldiers, and Neophytes: The Practice of Trades under Exclusions and Privileges (Rome from the Seventeenth to the Early Nineteenth Centuries)," in *Guilds, Markets and Work Regulations in Italy,* ed. Alberto Guenzi et al. (Aldershot, U.K.: Ashgate, 1998), 392; Austin Sarat and Thomas R. Kearns, "Writing History and Registering Memory in Legal Decisions and Legal Practices: An Introduction," in *History, Memory, and the Law,* ed. Austin Sarat and Thomas R. Kearns (Ann Arbor: University of Michigan Press, 2002), 4–6. "Time immemorial" and variations are ubiquitous forms of appeal. In France one finds "de tous temps et hors de mémoire d'homme"; in England it was "long usage," defined in 1610 as "such time whereof the memory of man is not to the contrary, time out of mind, such time as will beget a custom." See David Underdown, *A Freeborn People: Politics and the Nation in Seventeenth-Century England* (Oxford: Clarendon Press, 1996), 56.

[78] ARCV Pleitos Civiles Pérez Alonso (F) 1539.3.

sand vecinos and only six hosiers, prices would tend to stay high, the tailors said.[79] While to the hosiers the common good was a matter of quality,
to the tailors it was a question of the best price.

The hosiers had tradition and custom on their side, at least since the
breeches had come into fashion; the tailors had the corregidor's ruling
and a high court verdict in a similar case in Madrid. Nonetheless, the
tailors spent as much time pointing to practice as to law. Tailors made
greguescos in a long list of cities, they said. They summoned witnesses who
had lived in those places and who agreed it was a "universal custom," which
they said was precisely why they had won in Madrid. One after another, in
numbing repetition, witnesses for both sides recalled that for years and
years things in Segovia had been a certain way. According to the tailors,
everybody knew their craft was far older than the hosiers': "The occupation of tailors, both in the said city of Segovia and in other cities and towns,
is and always has been very old and it began many years before the hosiers',
because in olden times men and women, as is known, dressed in long garb
down to their feet, without *greguescos*," said the witness Francisco Bueno, a
fifty-year-old tailor.

At nearly the same time as the makers of breeches in Segovia were arguing points of law and custom, wax makers in Seville were doing the same.
There the issue was a common one: how guild inspectors should be chosen. The city council had decided to ignore the wax makers' own candidates and appoint its own. The guild appealed to the king. According to
the ruling, the city said it was

> in possession, use, and custom, since time immemorial, with no opposition
> and with the wax makers and chandlers and other crafts seeing, consenting,
> accepting, and not contradicting, of the appointment of city council mem-
> bers to name the said inspectors, both of the said crafts of wax makers and
> chandlers as well as of other crafts, and the said city confirmed and approved
> the said appointments and at no time did the said craftsmen among them-
> selves ever, as the wax makers now say, choose their own inspectors.[80]

The Council of Castile decided on 20 August 1602 to let custom stand,
which meant that the city could continue appointing inspectors. The wax
makers appealed, saying the law was on their side "and in no way could they

---

[79] Twelve thousand vecinos would mean approximately 54,000 inhabitants (using 4.5 as
the multiplier), a fantastic figure. The economic historian Angel García Sanz estimates that
Segovia's population in 1580 was 25,000 and had fallen to about half that by the mid-seven-
teenth century. Angel García Sanz, "Castile 1580–1650: Economic Crisis and the Policy of
'Reform,'" in *The Castilian Crisis of the Seventeenth Century: New Perspectives on the Economic and
Social History of Seventeenth-Century Spain*, ed. I. A. A. Thompson and Bartolomé Yun Casalilla
(Cambridge University Press, 1994), 27.

[80] AMSev Sec. I Privilegios, caja 26, exp. 308.

be denied what they asked because it was in conformance with the said law and the ordinance" and better served the common good. Once again, the council sided with the city "because everything [the wax makers] alleged is excluded by the immemorial custom with which the city had been governed with none of the drawbacks the [wax makers] presented." On the contrary, the council said, letting guilds choose their own inspectors was sure to lead to fraud.

In this case, the crown chose custom over its own laws. I do not know to which law the wax makers referred in their appeal, but surely it existed, in the form of a precedent. The ordinances certainly existed, and they were by definition approved by the king. Many guilds had ordinances giving them the right to choose their own inspectors. Cities, apparently Seville in particular, disliked such rules, and so would argue on the basis of tradition rather than code. The Seville silk weavers in 1614 had the same fight as the wax makers, and they pointed to a privilege from Alfonso XI giving them the right to choose their inspectors. This time, the king told the city to desist.[81] Continuing with silk weavers but returning to the province of Segovia, in a battle over allegedly improper inspections by carders of weavers' shops, the weavers said the carders had violated anti-usurpation laws. The carders, whose inspectors were being held in jail, did not even bother replying; instead they said they had been conducting such inspections "for so long that no man can remember when it was not the case. . . . And [this is the case] not only in [Piedrahita] but in other places where silk is produced, principally in the city of Segovia, and this right has always been protected, not only in custom but by law."[82]

Shoemakers in Madrid got involved in a different sort of dispute after the *alguaciles,* the ever vigilant and often overruled law enforcement officers, accused them of fraudulently passing off one-layer soles as two-layer, two-layer as three-layer, and so on. The jailed shoemakers protested that the shoe insert (*palmilla*) counted as a sole. It always had counted as one, it did in Madrid and Valladolid and the rest of Spain, that was how one defendant's father had done it, and no one had ever heard of doing things otherwise. "This is an inviolable custom," they concluded, with the lawyer adding, "my clients are honorable and upright people of much truth and legality." Nine months after filing the appeal, the shoemakers won their case.[83]

Gilders, too, found themselves debating customs and codes. In 1634, Antonio González passed his master's examination in Guadalajara and immediately began working in Madrid. Just one day after he opened his

---

[81] AMSev Sec. I Privilegios, caja 26, exp. 335.

[82] AMSeg 908–31.

[83] ARCV Pleitos Civiles Pérez Alonso (F) 2480.5. The lawyer's statement was: "Mis partes [son] personas honradas y principales de mucha verdad y legalidad."

shop, the guild (which then comprised both gilders and swordmakers) denounced him, and he and a colleague were arrested.[84] Examinations in Guadalajara were a shoddy affair, the guild said, and were causing serious problems in Madrid. Apprentices routinely received master's diplomas they had not earned; and examinations for both occupations were combined into one day, though each should properly take six days. Moreover, they did not include requisite tests in the making of specific masterpieces: "It is public knowledge that by bribing [the examiners] and inviting them to cake and wine, examinations will consist of no tests at all; and when those who come from Guadalajara are asked in Madrid which tests they took, they reply 'cake and wine.'" Gilders unwilling or unable to make the trip to Guadalajara could simply mail in their money and receive a master's diploma in return, the guild said.

But according to González and his co-defendant, the Madrid ordinances, which of course had been approved by the Council of Castile, had never been obeyed and were being invoked now just to make the guild look good. Several sixteenth-century precedents concerning overlooked ordinances were included in the proceedings. Everyone took their examinations in Guadalajara or other cities, González said, "because they don't have the money to pay the Madrid examiners and it is much cheaper to take the examination elsewhere." So corruption does not seem to have been confined to Guadalajara. But the Alcaldes de Casa y Corte, the royal judges who heard the case, chose to listen to the guild: "The ordinances of the swordmakers and gilders of this court, confirmed by the council and presented in this suit, should be obeyed and executed." The two men were prohibited from opening their shops until they were examined in Madrid. Nearly 150 years later, the reformist royal minister Pedro Rodríguez de Campomanes in his famous pamphlet on the education of artisans specifically mentioned refreshments at examinations as one of the corrupt practices that had to be eliminated.[85]

Custom, then, was not something archaic that benefited craftsmen alone, nor was it something they clung to in an effort to halt some inexorable march of progress. It was a useful, collective possession that had a history and embodied implicit rights and enjoyments. Custom often was virtually synonymous with law and was linked to the common good. If things had always been done a certain way, it was probably because a community had seen and learned that it was thus better served. In cases in which time immemorial was not an ally, one could always appeal to codes or to changing times. The convenience of having two lines of argument

---

[84] AHN CS leg. 50.965, caja 2. I am grateful to José Nieto for showing me this case.

[85] Pedro Rodríguez de Campomanes, *Discurso sobre la educación popular,* ed. F. Aguilar Piñal (Madrid: Editora Nacional, 1978), 138.

was not lost on the parties in dispute. When the Alcaldes de Casa y Corte in 1652 told shoemakers to abide by a 1593 edict and work on Mondays, for example, they specified it was not a holiday, "even if they say it is the custom."[86] Custom used in this way helped artisans establish defensive and offensive lines. At stake was ownership and control of the craft by the guild and its practitioners and, implicitly, affirmation of their citizenship. In this regard, the frequent assertion that a guild or craft was "in possession" of a task is particularly meaningful: custom (or tradition) was invoked to essentially establish law. To quote Michael Sonenscher, who was writing about eighteenth-century France, "customs conferred a quasi-institutional stability upon trades whose composition and boundaries were anything but permanent or precise."[87] They also permitted a certain reciprocity. In the words of Francisco Sánchez-Blanco, custom "establishes a far more subtle servitude than law in that it both invokes and establishes the collective will without resort to a constitutional act."[88] In the possible absence of law, custom ensured that rights would be upheld. But this is not a teleology. Custom and law coexisted and were intertwined.

Guild ordinances were among the laws that artisans took with them to court in their efforts to seek punishment for transgressors or approval for innovations. The procedure to enact or change them consisted of several steps, and there were always variations. Masters generally would meet in a church, convent, or hospital and agree that new ordinances were needed.[89] (Alternatively, the crown might order a city to tell its guilds to draw up new ordinances, as Charles V did in 1552, though compliance took years.) The guild would notify the city council, which would then appoint a member or a committee to oversee the matter. Once the ordinances were drawn up (by the guild and/or municipal authorities, depending upon the place, time, and craft), they would be approved by the city council and then were sent on to the king or the Council of Castile. After the crown gave the green light, they were sent back down to the city, where they were entered into the city council minutes and a town crier read them out in the most central locations of the city, an event sometimes repeated one week later. On 30 January 1574, for example, "in the Puerta

[86] AHN CS leg. 7162, doc. 9. Punishment included public shaming and four years of exile from the capital. The order was one of several in 1652 attempting to enforce previous disciplinary edicts that set off a protest by guild members and a reprimand by the Council of Castile of the alcaldes for their *novedades*.

[87] Michael Sonenscher, *Work and Wages: Natural Law, Politics and the Eighteenth-Century French Trades* (Cambridge University Press, 1989), 205.

[88] Francisco Sanchez-Blanco, *El Absolutismo y las Luces en el reinado de Carlos III* (Madrid: Marcial Pons, 2002), 218.

[89] A study of the eighteenth century reports that meetings were held in convents, churches, workshops, and private homes; the author found 146 in shops and 118 in religious and public buildings. See Antonio Manuel Moral Roncal, *Gremios e Ilustración en Madrid (1775–1836)* (Madrid: Actas Editorial, 1998), 62–63.

de Guadalajara at nine or ten in the morning, in front of many people," a notary accompanied by an alguacil read aloud the hatters' new ordinances, and from there the pair went on to the Plaza Mayor to do the same.[90] In Zamora, the cap makers' ordinances were read by town crier Juan Benito on 24 May 1569, market day, "in a loud and intelligible voice . . . *de verbo ad verbum.*"[91] In Mexico City, viceregal officials sometimes accompanied the crier as he made his rounds, reading ordinances aloud so no artisan could later plead ignorance.[92]

Guilds petitioned authorities for new ordinances for a variety of reasons. Madrid's locksmiths in April 1587 told the corregidor they were extremely worried about the familiar problem of journeymen taking their master's examinations elsewhere, and they proposed the addition of new provisions to remedy it. After that, they had to formally question a series of journeymen about the problem, with a notary recording their replies, which were then forwarded to the corregidor, who authorized the locksmiths to vote on the changes. The unanimous vote took place in the church of San Miguel on 28 June, witnessed by the alguacil mayor.[93] Sometimes we find new crafts, dependent on older guilds, petitioning to have their own rules. Such was the case of Córdoba's silk workers, who argued that theirs was a noble occupation because it created beautiful objects for the best people and it was not right that they did not have their own rules and examinations "when many occupations of less quality have them."[94] When silk twisters in Seville went to the city council in 1639 to say that their ordinances needed to be updated, the council appointed a member who spent seven months consulting a long list of experts, including "merchants who know a lot about this matter" and finally recommended the changes suggested by the craftsmen.[95] Also in Seville, master silk dyer Juan de Manzanares went before the council in 1688 to point out that the city had no examination for dyers, unlike the city of Córdoba, a lacuna which predictably threatened the common good with an influx of badly (or "falsely") dyed foreign cloth. The city council agreed to his proposal to name a coun-

[90] AHN CS leg. 705. The requirement to read the ordinances aloud at major intersections appears to have disappeared by the early eighteenth century.

[91] María del Carmen Pescador del Hoyo, "Los gremios de artesanos de Zamora," *Revista de Archivos, Bibliotecas y Museos* 78 (July–December 1975): 681–682.

[92] Manuel Carrera Stampa, *Los gremios mexicanos: La organización gremial en Nueva España, 1521–1861* (Mexico City: EDIAPSA, 1954), 151.

[93] AV 2.245.8. This case appears unusual in that it bypassed the city council, although it is possible that the corregidor was asserting his royal prerogative over the Madrid city council, which was less powerful than its counterparts elsewhere because Madrid was the capital.

[94] José Ignacio Fortea Pérez, *Córdoba en el siglo XVI: Las bases demográficas y económicas de una expansión urbana* (Córdoba: Monte Piedad y Caja de Ahorros de Córdoba, 1981), 378. Fortea notes that Córdoba lagged behind other Castilian cities with regard to the development of guilds.

[95] AMSev, Sec. X, Actas, 2a escr., tomo 123.

cilman to look into the matter. Two months later the appointee died, but another took his place, and the following month the enterprising Manzanares had collected copies of ordinances from Toledo and Córdoba to use as models. (The authors of the Toledo ordinances commented in theirs that they, in turn, had looked at Granada's, which they deemed "worthless"; the 1550 Toledo ordinances also were consulted by Seville in 1688.)[96]

In 1587, master hatters in Madrid gathered to alter their ordinances "for the service of God and the common good so that their craft be performed with more perfection and rectitude and that all fraud cease."[97] They wanted inspectors' elections to be switched from the first Sunday of March to the first Sunday after the Day of Santiago (25 July) because they had recently established a confraternity in honor of Santiago. They wanted new dying techniques incorporated into their examinations and resolved that the examination fee should be raised from 16 reales to 30 *reales,* a hefty increase; 8 *reales* were to go to the examiners and the other 22 went to the new confraternity. Widows would now be allowed to keep their husband's store forever instead of for just two years. Hatters would oversee the retail business of the rope makers. Over a hundred years later the guild requested new changes, this time concerning outsiders opening shops in Madrid. It is likely that there had been no other changes in the interim.

These were all fairly typical items. Ordinances generally were prefaced with dedications to God, Jesus, Mary, or the saints and with declarations of the guild's devotion and commitment to the common good. From there, they presented general information about the guild and then discussed rules of access, the structure of labor relations, raw materials, production, barriers to competition, internal authority, assistance to members, and religious and ceremonial matters.[98] Apprenticeships, inspections, fines, the occasional enormous technical detail, and foreign materials and craftsmen were all generally included. Some ordinances were more technical than others, but they were all designed to regulate and discipline their occupation. Historians sometimes describe them as being emblematic of the guilds' hermetic nature, their unresponsiveness to changing economic conditions, and their impulse to stifle innovation. But such a view of ordinances places them exclusively in the realm of production. The process by which they were written, publicized, and enforced, and the conditions that led to their amendment suggest their meaning went far beyond stipulations about the quality of felt or the sheen of silk. For the *xervilleros* of Seville, for example, ordinances were nothing less than part of the proper

[96] AMSev. Sec. IV, Escr. de Cabildo 25/144.
[97] AHN CS leg. 705.
[98] Antonio Miguel Bernal et al., "Sevilla: De los gremios a la industrialización," *Estudios de historia social,* no. 5–6 (1978). These are the categories developed by the authors in their detailed study of some 140 ordinances from the fifteenth to the nineteenth centuries.

ordering of the world: "The governance of human nature does not consist only of supplies and food, but they are necessary and speak to human weakness and sustain us through this long life, and because it is necessary for the Republic that supplies be orderly, it is right that remedies be found in the matter of footwear."[99]

Regardless of whether they were normative, descriptive, assertive, or defensive—and historians of early modern Spanish labor have spent far too much time parsing them—ordinances embodied political, civic, economic, and discursive relationships. They were part of a grid, not one step along a flow chart on which guilds necessarily were subservient to cities or crown. The fact that the ordinances' oral presentation in the Plaza Mayor by the town crier was what made them real "was sufficient to demonstrate the municipality's authority over the guilds," Juan Uña Sarthou wrote a century ago, an assessment echoed countless times since.[100] But there are plenty of examples of guilds or individual workers going directly to the king or to the courts with their grievances and disobeying or ignoring municipal orders. In 1641, the Madrid city council admitted it had no idea what the content of most guilds' ordinances even was.[101] Although councilmen were supposed to supervise the redaction, guilds clearly took the initiative in many cases. The origin of these documents is, in short, a muddled affair, and one cannot be distracted by the city's seal of approval or its alleged authorship. Though they were laws, ordinances were not edicts one could easily keep track of among the rungs of Castilian bureaucracy, not even physically. For one thing, they not infrequently got lost, and often they ended up being the center of litigation when they were being recopied. In Seville, for example, packsaddle makers reported that

> these ordinances were entrusted to an *albardero* who lived in the Santa Catalina district and who, at the time of the debates and questions between the duke and the marquis, was robbed and he fled the city, so the said ordinances were lost, and certain journeymen . . . knowing that the said ordinances were lost, are daring to go against the good uses and customs of their forebears.[102]

Contested literal ownership of the ordinances, their provenance, and their physical location meant they were laws difficult to categorize but no less

---

[99] Vicente Romero Muñoz, "La recopilación de ordenanzas gremiales de Sevilla en 1527," *Revista de Trabajo* (February 1950): 225–231. The original of "orderly" is *que se ponga regla cierta*. I have been unable to ascertain exactly what the *xervilleros* did.

[100] Juan Uña Sarthou, *Las asociaciones obreras en España* (Madrid: Estab. tip. de G. Juste, 1900), 253.

[101] AV 2.309.16. The city told the guilds to submit copies, an order the guilds seemingly ignored.

[102] Romero Muñoz, "La recopilación de ordenanzas gremiales," 228.

(or perhaps even more) useful. They did not describe a static set of hierarchical relations. As laws, they lived on the streets and in the workshops and in marketplaces, and the neighbors lived with them. They were inserted into lawsuits, copied, recopied, read aloud, and then read aloud again decades later to remind the disobedient of the price of their infractions and to show everyone that the business of the republic was a joint venture. Guilds and individual artisans were the members of the republic encharged with making this possible.

The discourse of the republic was shared by magistrates and shoemakers, but it is worth asking if they had the same republic in mind and to what end they used this language. Was the workers' use of republican discourse merely imitative? Was it subversive? Was it parallel? Or was it an appropriation? Did the workers understand in literal terms what more educated citizens understood in theoretical terms? As with a lawyer today who in mentioning a point while questioning a witness opens up that line of questioning to the opposing attorney, Castilian authorities, by employing republican discourse, made it available for wider use. The nature of the republican discourse was broad and all-inclusive. That was its danger and its utility. It applied to all equally, and in many ways it defined the community. More important than individuals' epistemological understanding of republican terminology, however, are the ways in which the discourse, as a vehicle, allowed different parties to assert themselves and achieve their aims and how it helped reproduce political and productive practices. By using the language of the law, artisans could transform their localized conflicts into public causes. If notions of community or the common good were shaped by production relations, as is logical, then it also is possible that guilds' positions on production issues may implicitly have reflected their attitudes about community and their place in it. That is why I have chosen to look at production and consumption disputes to determine the place workers occupied in the early modern Castilian republic. Municipalities, the most visible manifestation of the republic and the site and jurisdiction for production and consumption, will be where we turn next.

Citizenship

If workers could be citizens of the republic they could also, of course, be citizens, or *vecinos,* of a city, that best and most natural of all forms of social organization. The city was the embodiment of the republic, and there was virtually no classical writer who did not sing its praises. The organization of a city—its laws, its coordination, and its spirit—personified a society's values. If a republic could be likened to a body, all of whose members had to exist in harmony, then the metaphor was even more obviously apt with a city. Moderation would allow Christian harmony to flower, unlike in overcrowded and ungovernable London, "a port and overmuch populous, which Aristotle doth disallow."[103]

The requisites for a good and bountiful city in the eyes of Francisco Eiximenis, a fourteenth-century Catalan who lived and preached in Valencia, were material sustenance, money, liberty, nobility, peace, wisdom, science, knowledge, wealth, generosity, good laws, mechanical workers, weapons, and servants.[104] This vision of the city as the site of virtue and efficacy was not incompatible with the pastoral utopia. In the imaginary, pre-urban state, people did not live alone on mountain tops; they inhabited villages, tiny republics. For Sánchez de Arévalo, the principal reason for establishing cities and civic communities was to ensure that citizens lived virtuously. According to the author—a lawyer, theologian, diplomat, papal defender, and onetime archbishop of Zamora—a city should be self-sufficient, homogeneous, well supplied, and well fed, which meant there must be agriculture, production, and commerce, though the last should be limited to satisfying inhabitants' needs. A ruler should make sure his vassals had abundant resources so they would be able to "fulfill the needs and utility of human and political life." There was no room in the republic for those who did not work, he wrote: "Everyone in the city must contribute through industry or occupation to the honor and benefit of the city."[105]

So public or civic virtue and the common good were linked to abundance and self-sufficiency, which clearly was possible only if a city was populated by industrious workers. Petitions to city councils in the sixteenth and seventeenth centuries show that workers understood what their place was in this republic. They were a key component of the common good. They supplied the city with bread, made it possible for poor people to have cheap shoes and for priests to wear proper vestments, built the king's ships, and cleaned city streets. All these tasks and hundreds more, even the simplest ones and those that paid the least, were necessary and useful for the health of the municipal republic.

Many of the workers who petitioned city councils or appeared in lawsuits, either as witnesses or defendants, were vecinos of their cities or towns. *Vecindad*, among other things, entailed a series of municipal, fiscal, and judicial privileges and obligations, depending on the place.[106] A 1487 letter

---

[103] Edmund Grindal to William Cecil, cited in Susan Brigden, "Religion and Social Obligation in Early Sixteenth-Century London," *Past and Present*, no. 103 (May 1984): 69.

[104] Soledad Vila, *La ciudad de Eiximenis: Un proyecto teórico de urbanismo en el siglo XIV* (Valencia: Diputación Provincial de Valencia, 1984), 127. The citation is from Eiximenis's *Dotzè del Crestià* (1484), chap. 131, f. 60. Eiximenis lived from 1327 to 1409.

[105] Sánchez de Arévalo, *Suma de la política*, 52, 94, 110.

[106] Tamar Herzog has shown that *vecindad*, whose definition was never fixed, had far more to do with recognizing rights already being practiced than with legal enactments (*Defining Nations: Immigrants and Citizens in Early Modern Spain and Spanish America* [New Haven: Yale

from the Catholic Monarchs, for example, gave vecinos of Seville the privilege of having their lawsuits heard in local courts even if they were sued by an outsider and said they did not have to pay customs excises when bringing merchandise into the city. Such privileges motivated people to apply under false pretenses, leading Seville to specify that no vecino of an outlying town or village could become a vecino of the city and that "all should be taxed and pay in the place where they live and are accustomed to live."[107] Often in Castile, applicants just wanted access to communal grazing lands and had no intention of actually establishing themselves in a new town. Such dishonesty was apparently widespread, judging from a 1581 manual of Christian conduct among whose moral dilemmas was the sinfulness of lying about one's true residence to gain vecindad elsewhere.[108]

Requests to become a vecino were made to the city council, which generally referred the matter to one of its members, who then investigated the applicant. Witnesses were summoned to confirm that the applicant was a permanent resident of the city and planned to stay there. Indeed, many applicants had lived in their city for as long as thirty years.[109] In seventeenth-century Madrid, applicants whose cases reached the city council included shopkeepers, vegetable vendors, glovers, tavern keepers, laborers, clothiers, trim makers, carpenters, doublet makers, shoemakers, and bakers. There is virtually no craft not represented, and the procedure for investigating applications was the same as that used for nobles. In a typical exchange, the carpenter Juan de Ocaña said that he had lived in Madrid for more than thirty years in his own home with his family and had always wanted to be a vecino. His neighbor, a carpenter who already was a vecino, confirmed that he had heard Ocaña say many times he wanted to be a vecino. So did all the other witnesses. Witnesses also generally confirmed that the applicant would be sure to pay his taxes and whatever supplementary assessments the city might levy.[110]

The litigants and petitioners described in this book were vecinos not just

---

University Press, 2003]). See also David Vassberg, *The Village and the Outside World in Golden Age Castile: Mobility and Migration in Everyday Rural Life* (Cambridge University Press, 1996), 14–18.

[107] Pérez Escolano and Villanueva Sandino, eds., *Ordenanzas de Sevilla* (1632), 64–67v.

[108] Antonio de Córdoba, *Tratado de casos de consciencia* (Zaragoza, 1581), 405. Córdoba, a Franciscan, said it was indeed wrong and that the sinners must repay the taxes they improperly had denied their true hometowns.

[109] According to Herzog, this shows that the status of a town's residents could be consensual for years and then suddenly come into doubt (*Defining Nations*, chap. 2).

[110] AV 2.347.29. The case is from 1624. Unlike in Germany or England, guild membership and marriage were not requirements for citizenship. On guilds and citizenship in England, see Steve Rappaport, *Worlds within Worlds: Structures of Life in Sixteenth-Century London* (Cambridge University Press, 1989), chap. 2; on Germany, see Walker, *German Home Towns*, chap. 4.

in the sense of citizenship; they also were neighbors, which is the present-day definition of the word. Thus dyers in Córdoba in 1485 specified in their ordinances that inspectors "must be our neighbor [*nuestro vecino*] and . . . able and skilled and of good conscience and reputation and experience."[111] Eiximenis had recommended that cities be divided up into quarters, each to be populated by a mendicant order (the author was a Franciscan) and a mix of craftsmen "so that all necessary occupations can be found in each of the four parts of the city, and the peasants should be near the entrance closest to the orchard or the land or the fields, and in each of the four parts there should be a butcher, a fish seller, a grain market, and everything that its inhabitants require.[112] The idea was that by scattering artisans among the neighborhoods they would not become isolated, they could better satisfy the needs of people throughout the city, and social harmony would ensue. In Burgos, for example, a 1502 lawsuit between the city and various of its neighborhoods ended with the Catholic Monarchs ordering members of certain trades to live in certain areas. Silversmiths, coal vendors, and makers of cork-sole shoes had their shops in the upper part of the city; they could live below, but not work there. Secondhand clothing dealers could live in a newer part of the city but were not allowed to go into the old Jewish district. Ragpickers, turners, and saddlers had to live on Calle Tenebrosa and were not allowed to live anywhere in the lower city. The Council of Castile confirmed this arrangement in 1536 and again the following year.[113] Around that same time, a visitor to Burgos was favorably impressed:

> There are no idle or useless people. . . . All work, women as well as men, with young and old seeking their living with their hands and the sweat of their brow. Some exercise mechanical arts, others the liberal arts. . . . Those who rule and govern the republic seek the common good, unlike many others who seek their own interests and destroy their peoples. Thus each person does as he should, and every day the city grows and becomes more noble.[114]

The demographic distribution of seventeenth-century Madrid might have pleased Eiximenis, though surely the crowds would have startled him and he would have found the noise and filth distressing. As with all European cities, Madrid's street names are an occupational map. But though

---

[111] Cited in Fortea Pérez, *Córdoba en el siglo XVI,* 272.

[112] Vila, *La ciudad de Eiximenis,* 108. The citation is from Eiximenis's *Dotzé del Crestiá* (1484), chap. 110.

[113] AMB Hi-3138. I do not know if the order was a victory or a defeat for the workers, nor is it clear how the *vecindades* were legally constituted as litigants.

[114] The visitor was the Italian humanist Lucio Marineo Siculo (1460–1533), a member of the courts of Ferdinand the Catholic and Charles V. Cited in Antonio María Fabié, ed., *Viajes por España* (Madrid: Librería de los Bibliófilos, 1879), 565–566.

members of a given occupation tended to concentrate on a particular block, the neighborhoods were mixed, with different crafts and social classes within earshot of one another. This may have furthered social harmony or social bickering, or both, but it certainly made production and producers a visible part of every city dweller's life. As David Garrioch has observed about eighteenth-century Paris, occupational ties overlapped with neighborhood ties. Some workers were stationary, others itinerant. Some just manufactured, others sold. Some were outdoors and visible, others indoors, in the back rooms of shops. Some worked on their own, others worked as a team in larger workshops. All these factors influenced the degree to which occupation or neighborhood would dominate a craftsman's sense of home and loyalty. In any case, the crisscrossing communities of church, marketplace, workshop, family, neighborhood, and sales, supply, or repair routes collectively contradict a vision of seventeenth-century Castile as a society of rigid social orders in which workers were pushed aside, excluded, and scorned.[115]

Madrid's neighborhoods in particular belie such a notion. Noblemen had their large houses smack in the center of crowded parishes, surrounded by the dwellings of their dependants. Studies of Madrid's city council and the Council of Castile show that members lived throughout the capital's parishes, not in ghettos of the well-to-do.[116] Residents of a parish probably all attended the same church even if they moved in different social circles; they may not have sat in the same pew, but they shared a loyalty to their church's relics and a familiarity with the landmarks and events of their neighborhood. Confounded foreigners often remarked on such unhealthy mixing, usually while commenting on the puzzling pride of poor Spaniards. In 1550s England, for example, when pamphleteers vehemently protested the imminent marriage of Queen Mary to Philip II, John Bradforth wrote—accurately or not—that if she were to go to Spain the English queen could expect "to see sitting among her grace's yeomen curriers, car-men and cobblers, woodmongers, vintners and waggoners, [lace-makers], pinners and pedlars, shoemakers, surgeons and saddlers, bookbinders, bakers, brewers, and all kind of lousy loiterers."[117]

[115] José Antonio Maravall, for example, in "Trabajo y exclusión: El trabajador manual en el sistema social español de la primera modernidad," in *Les problèmes de l'exclusion en Espagne (xvi–xvii siècles)*, ed. Augustin Redondo (Paris: Publications de la Sorbonne, 1983), repeatedly describes what he called workers' "tremendous marginalization." See David Garrioch, *Neighborhood and Community in Paris, 1740–1790* (Cambridge University Press, 1986), especially chap. 3. There is an excellent map of Madrid's occupational neighborhoods in Moral Roncal, *Gremios e Ilustración en Madrid*, 92–93.

[116] Janine Fayard, *Les membres du Conseil de Castille à l'époque moderne 1621–1746* (Geneva: Droz, 1979); Ana Guerrero Mayllo, *Familia y vida cotidiana de una élite de poder: Los regidores madrileños en tiempos de Felipe II* (Madrid: Siglo Veintiuno, 1993), 290–298.

[117] J. N. Hillgarth, *The Mirror of Spain, 1500–1700: The Formation of a Myth. History, Lan-*

So much for the marginal lives of manual laborers. This alarming egalitarianism continued in 1701, when an anonymous traveler, equally polemical, wrote that if it were not for the red and green crosses painted on their capes, "it would be impossible to distinguish a Spanish gentleman from a shoemaker."[118]

Inquisition cases in the parishes around Madrid's Plaza Mayor offer an idea of one neighborhood's diversity and also of how closely people watched each other. In a broad investigation into a nest of religious seers there in the 1630s, the witnesses against Mateo Rodríguez, all of whom lived in the neighborhood, included hidalgos, priests, hatters, tailors, shoemakers, painters, farriers, gilders, makers of grass mats (Rodríguez's trade), and servants of noblemen. They knew about each other (making them useful witnesses), they knew about each other's jobs, and they knew if the rest had visited Rodríguez and seen one of his alleged raptures. A servant of the Constable of Castile, Spain's second-highest grandee, for example, "knows that nearly every night many men of these and other mechanical occupations go to Brother Mateo's house to hear the good doctrine he teaches . . . and he has heard that some of those who go there have raptures . . . and they especially go on Saturday night after finishing their work, and also on Sunday afternoons." Rodríguez and his friends organized theatrical performances at his house which appear to have been religious (sacrilegious, in the minds of the inquisitors, being that Rodríguez sometimes dressed in women's clothing). The audience members, who were neighbors, shared their devotion despite their class differences. They did so bunched up on benches or on the floor of what must have been a very small room.[119]

Other cases also attest to the neighborly (albeit not friendly) proximity of artisans and their betters. In a case not heard by the Inquisition but by secular judges, shopkeepers along the Calle de Toledo in 1666 asked authorities to enjoin mattress makers (or sellers) from blocking the street in front of the home of the count of Humanes, which apparently had been going on for some time.[120] Francisco Enríquez de Villacorta, a member of the Madrid city council and a knight of Santiago, complained in 1645 about his neighbors on the Calle Imperial, also near the Plaza Mayor, whose activities had led his servants and renters to threaten to leave: "[The

guages, and Cultures of the Spanish and Portuguese Worlds (Ann Arbor: University of Michigan Press, 2000), 355–356.

[118] Patricia Shaw Fairman, *España vista por los ingleses del siglo XVII* (Madrid: Sociedad General Española de Librería, 1981), 217.

[119] AHN Inq. leg. 106.2, caja 1. See also María José del Río, "Representaciones dramáticas en casa de un artesano del Madrid de principios del siglo XVII," in *Teatros y vida teatral en el siglo de oro a través de las fuentes documentales,* ed. Luciano García Lorenzo and J. E. Varey (London: Tamesis Books, 1991), 245–258.

[120] AV 2.244.24.

renters] suffer great damage and injury from the women who sell mutton and cow parts there. [The women] block the doorways and low windows of the said neighbors, especially one where the women leave refuse such as rotten livers, tripe, bones, hooves, heads, and filthy water, inflicting bad smells, damage, and injury to the said house." Don Francisco had begun his campaign to evict the women more than seven years earlier, he said, but neither his daily complaints to the women nor the authorities' orders had had any effect. The women again were ordered to clear the sidewalk in front of his house, but there is no reason to think the cohabitation ended then.[121] In mid-seventeenth-century Seville, meanwhile, the convent of San Antonio de Padua got into a long-running fight with the tanners next door, who routinely dumped the foulest of waste matter right before the eyes (and noses) of churchgoers and neighbors, who were described as very respectable people (*gente tan principal*). The city council wrestled with the problem but apparently could do nothing as long as a lawsuit brought by the tanners, in which they claimed dumping rights, was pending before the Council of Castile.[122]

One of the best ways of finding residents of a neighborhood, of course, is to follow the crown's steps as it tries to tax them. During the reign of Philip IV, the crown levied repeated *donativos*, "donations" by the kingdom's vassals to aid their monarch in his time of need. In 1625, after the English attacked Cádiz, the king or his chief minister, the Count-Duke of Olivares, established the Junta del Donativo, one of the myriad ad hoc committees for which Philip's monarchy was noted, whose purpose it was to establish how much each locality could pay and then collect the money.[123] The 1625 donativo was followed by around ten more by the end of his reign, though it is impossible to say exactly how many there were because they dragged on for years and overlapped. Some were collected directly by the crown; others were under the administration of the corregidor. Some were levied on guilds, others on towns or their parishes, still others on individuals. No method was especially effective, and so one thing after another was tried.

A well-documented collection drive (or drives) began after France and Spain declared war on each other in March 1635. The donativo had been approved by the Cortes to pay for its most recent *millones* subsidy to the crown, another of the serial contributions that characterized seventeenth-

---

[121] AHN CS libro 1230, 13 January 1645.

[122] AMSev Actas, 2 escr., 22 March 1642.

[123] On finance during the reign of Philip IV, see Antonio Domínguez Ortiz, *Política y hacienda de Felipe IV* (Madrid: Ediciones Pegaso, 1983); and J. H. Elliott, *The Count-Duke of Olivares: The Statesman in an Age of Decline* (New Haven: Yale University Press, 1986). On the juntas, see Ruth MacKay, *The Limits of Royal Authority: Resistance and Obedience in Seventeenth-Century Castile* (Cambridge University Press, 1999), 25–32.

century Castilian finance.[124] In Madrid, fiscal targets included the city's thirteen parishes and the many guilds whose members populated the central district's crowded streets. The king had decreed that local judges would divide up the guilds among themselves and, simultaneously, that members of the Council of Castile would be assigned to particular parishes. The jurisdictions were confused from the very start.[125]

In the summer of 1636, representatives of each guild met with their designated judge in the presence of a notary to tell him how many members it had and how much each one could pay.[126] These representatives were called *repartidores,* because their job was to *repartir,* or divvy up, the payments among members. Speaking for the tailors guild, for example, five masters offered Alcalde Juan de Quiñones 1,500 silver reales. (In fact, it appears 104 members of the guild paid a total of around 980, probably in copper. It is also worth noting that for a donativo drive in 1659, authorities believed there were 504 tailors).[127] Another of the alcaldes, Lope de Cuevas, met with tanners, shoemakers, secondhand clothing dealers, barbers, mat makers, carders, laborers, gilders, and eight more guilds. The corregidor, Juan de Castro y Castilla, the count of Montalvo, met with a total of thirty-one guilds, including hatters, slipper makers, carpenters, dyers, locksmiths, clothing merchants, and vinegar vendors.

The promised amounts either were unsatisfactory or not forthcoming, however, because a few months later the archbishop of Granada, who also was president of the Council of Castile, sent off new instructions to the judges to remind them how best to fill the king's coffers. "You must meet with the repartidores of each guild and explain to them what dire straits the royal treasury is in," he wrote. If the guilds could, they should pay up front; if not, in installments. Silver was preferred, and the judges

---

[124] There is an immense literature on the *millones* which, unlike indirect sales taxes, affected both the clergy and the nobility. See Antonio Domínguez Ortiz, "Concesiones de votos en Cortes a ciudades castellanas en el siglo XVII," in his *Crisis y decadencia de la España de los Austrias* (Barcelona: Ariel, 1979); José Ignacio Fortea Pérez, *Monarquía y Cortes en la corona de Castilla* (Valladolid: Cortes de Castilla y León, 1990), 271–98; Charles Jago, "Habsburg Absolutism and the Cortes of Castile," *American Historical Review* 86 (April 1981): 307–326; Felipe Ruiz Martín, "Credit Procedures for the Collection of Taxes in the Cities of Castile during the Sixteenth and Seventeenth Centuries: The Case of Valladolid," in *The Castilian Crisis of the Seventeenth Century,* ed. Thompson and Yun Casalilla (Cambridge University Press, 1994), 169–181; José Ignacio Ruiz Rodríguez, "Estructura y recaudación del servicio de millones 1590–1691," *Hispania* 52, no. 3 (1992): 1073–1088; and I. A. A. Thompson, "Crown and Cortes in Castile 1590–1665," *Parliaments, States, and Representation* 2 (June 1982): 29–45.

[125] AGS CJH leg. 1759, Archbishop of Granada to Luis de Paredes, 7 September 1635.

[126] AGS CG leg. 3251, libro 61. A list compiled by the Alcaldes de Casa y Corte in April 1636 showed there were fifty-eight guilds in Madrid (AHN CS libro 1221). In 1640, a list drawn up by the corregidor for a military levy contained 108 guilds (AV 3–420–1). Five years later, sixty-seven guilds were listed for an accounting of how much each had contributed to a conscription levy (AV 2.433.3). None of the lists is reliable.

[127] AV 2.315.32.

were to tolerate no bargaining concerning outstanding crown debts to workmen.

> If, after having summoned the repartidores of each guild and calling upon them with the said arguments and others to be be left up to the prudence and Christianity of the collectors, there was anyone who, minimizing the present situation, was so stubborn as to refuse to give or offer a just amount, the collector may do with him as he sees fit, except for prison or violent force, using equally effective but less cumbersome methods, including the use of *votos secretos,*

secret votes being a detailed investigation into someone's financial affairs followed by the summoning of witnesses to confirm that the subject could, and should, donate more graciously.[128]

Quiñones, who knew his city well, had his doubts. Repartidores were notoriously dishonest and would surely assign greater amounts to their less popular guild brothers, he said in reply to the instructions. Some smaller guilds did not even have repartidores and would object to another guild collecting on their behalf. Moreover, he pointed out, guilds as corporations had no wealth, implying that it made more sense to tax individuals, not guilds. (Unlike guilds in Catalonia, Castilian guilds owned no real property; their revenues consisted of fines and fees.) Antonio de Valdés, of the Council of Castile, replied rather weakly that it was worth a try, particularly as it had worked with military conscription levies.

That was exactly the problem, I would guess. Guilds already were working overtime taxing and impressing their own, and neither the repartidores had energy for more nor did the journeymen have much patience left. Sometime between December 1636, when the instructions were written, and the summer of 1637, the donativo was taken away from the guilds and assigned to the parishes. The same thing happened in Seville, where the king's envoy, the loyal, effective, and ubiquitous Diego de Riaño, warned that collecting from guilds was *"dificultosísimo."*[129] There also are indications that in Valladolid the donativo was first assigned to guilds and then removed to the parishes.[130] Guilds were at the outset the natural vehicle for tax collection, but lack of coordination on the part of too many officials, insufficient donations, and what appears to have been consistent footdragging combined to make them more trouble than they were worth. They were occasionally used in subsequent tax drives in Madrid, but rarely, as far as I can tell. In other cities, guilds were not tapped at all.

They had been the first objective in Toledo in 1625, when the donativos

---

[128] AGS CG leg. 3251, libro 61.
[129] AGS CJH leg. 1738, Riaño to king, 9 September 1636.
[130] AMV Libros de Actas, libro 51, 5 April 1636.

were initiated. As in Madrid a decade later, the city's top officials met with guild representatives to work out how much each could pay. Corregidor Diego Hurtado de Mendoza met with some sixty-five guilds over a two-month period. On 4 January, it was the shoemakers' turn. Hurtado de Mendoza described "His Majesty's needs and the kingdom's hard times and asked them to come to the service of His Majesty with as much generosity as possible, and having vividly explained how just and necessary it is that everyone serve His Majesty and that nobody fail to do so, the said guild and its officials, one at a time, offered the following:" The city council minutes then go on to list fifty-four men, each one of whom obviously was in the room with Hurtado de Mendoza, and the amount pledged.[131]

A few months later the same thing occurred in Madrid, where shoemakers met with Castro y Castilla (not yet a count) in the presence of a prior, a city council member, and a notary. One by one, the artisans declared their intentions: "I, Juan de Cabañas, a maker of new shoes, who live on Calle Aluche at the corner of Calle de las Rosas in my own house, offer to serve His Majesty with 24 copper reales. . . . I, Melchor de Herrera y Reyes, who live on the Calle de las Descalzas in a house owned by the San Martín convent, offer to serve His Majesty with 20 reales. . . . I, Pedro Ortega, a hosier in the Plazuela de los Herradores, who live in the house of Francisco de Soto, a shoemaker, offer to serve with 8 reales. . . . I, María de Mella, daughter of María Lucas, widow of Alonso de Mella, a tanner, in the name of my mother, who live in the tannery below the Rastro in my own house, offer to serve His Majesty with 30 copper reales. . . . I, Catalina de Alva, a locksmith, wife of Juan de las Casas, who live at the entrance of the Cava de San Francisco in a house owned by Don Juan de la Guia, offer to serve with 4 reales . . . ," and on and on and on. There were ninety-five clothiers and hosiers, fifty-seven hatters, hundreds of tailors. Each apparently stepped forward and said his or her lines. Many of them signed their names to their statements.[132]

It was one thing to offer; it was quite another to pay. It is impossible in the case of the 1625 donativo to track how much each person promised and how much he or she ended up paying, but it is certain that the latter was less than the former.[133] By the late 1630s, when the guild donativo in Madrid had been handed over to the parishes, residents were negotiating reductions in their assessment based on their alleged poverty, and the lan-

[131] AGS CG leg. 3251, libro 16.
[132] AGS CG leg. 3251, libros 59 and 86.
[133] According to calculations by José Nieto based on AGS CG libros 59 and 86, seventy-seven people (just 2.3 percent of the population) affected by the 1625 donativo in Madrid put up 70 percent of the tax. He estimates that 65 percent of the capital's population were artisans. See José A. Nieto Sánchez, "La organización social del trabajo en una ciudad preindustrial europa. Las corporaciones de oficio madrileñas durante el feudalismo tardío" (Lic. diss., Universidad Autónoma de Madrid, 1993).

guage of their appeals equated poverty and work. The Council of Castile itself cautioned crown officiales in 1644 not to request too much from "journeymen who earn bread for their wives and children by working." One assumes there was no other kind.[134]

The man in charge of collecting the 1637 donativo in Madrid's San Ginés parish, clustered along the Calle Mayor, was Juan Adam (or sometimes Adán) de la Parra, a disagreeable inquisitor recently transferred from Murcia. Valdés told him to spare no one: "Many people have tried to be excused, saying they are poor . . . but you must solicit from everyone, excluding no one, except for this: From the poor, not counting the notoriously poor (*pobres de solemnidad*), you should take what is offered, but everyone must give something." Though some people might try to show they were poor by saying they lived in a rented house, Valdés cautioned, they might well own their own home elsewhere.[135] Likewise, De la Parra's counterpart in Cuenca, Pedro Pacheco, was instructed to ferret out duplicitous artisans by checking dubious claims of poverty against local tax records and then interrogating two witnesses apiece about their neighbors' financial state. But he was also allowed to skip over the *pobres de solemnidad,* "who support themselves on the limited wage of their sweat and are the majority of the population in Sr. D. Pedro's district."[136] Juan de Chacón Ponce de León, collecting in Toledo in 1632, had been instructed to solicit from "servants, even if they have very low occupations, and even from the servants of the servants, if they should exist."[137]

De la Parra and his assistants set out to squeeze all they could from San Ginés.[138] Lists of hundreds of residents—name after name, amount after amount, craft after craft—attest to their diligence. If at first they failed, they tried again: "[De la Parra] arrived in his carriage at the home of the

---

[134] AHN CS leg. 7.145, cited in Domínguez Ortiz, *Política y Hacienda de Felipe IV,* 369. Though after 1637 the guilds no longer were the object of the Madrid fund raising, there were exceptions: cooks, pastry chefs, blind people who sold song lyrics, blacks, water carriers, and porters (*ganapanes*) were still targeted by occupation (or race). I do not know why.

[135] AGS CJH leg. 1764, Valdés, 10 August 1637. See the following section for a discussion of *pobres de solemnidad.*

[136] AGS CJH leg. 1756, instructions 21 February 1636; report May 1636 (?). Pacheco, the marquis de Castrofuerte, was a member of several royal councils.

[137] AGS CJH leg. 1744. Chacón, a judge at the Valladolid Chancillería, also was a member of several royal councils.

[138] The total population of the capital in 1597 was between 83,000 and 90,000, around one-fifth of whom lived in San Ginés. Twenty years later, the city's population was between 118,000 and 135,000, of whom a similar proportion lived in San Ginés (by then combined with the parish of San Luis). The other most populous parishes were San Sebastián, to the southeast, on both sides of Calle Atocha and into Lavapiés; and San Martín, extending north across Calle Arenal. See María F. Carbajo Isla, *La población de la Villa de Madrid desde finales del siglo XVI hasta mediados del siglo XIX* (Madrid: Siglo Veintiuno, 1987), chap. 6; and Claude Larquié, "Barrios y parroquias urbanas: El ejemplo de Madrid en el siglo XVII," *Anales del Instituto de Estudios Madrileños* 12 (1976).

draper Mateo Porta, on Calle de las Postas, and asked him how much he had offered to the Alcaldes for the donativo, and when [Porta] replied that he had promised 30 or 40 reales, though he could not remember well, [De la Parra] responded that that was nothing, and that it was up to him to establish the amount . . . and after negotiating, the two agreed on 80 *reales de quartos.*"[139] Domingo de Paz, a vecino and a tailor, said De la Parra had assigned him 34 ducats, which he could not pay "because I am poor and have no other way of supporting myself except with my personal labor." Diego de Zamora, whose craft is unknown, complained that De la Parra had based his assessments on the San Ginés census. If he investigated further, Zamora said (surely the neighborhood's worst nightmare), De la Parra would see that Zamora was so poor he should be given alms, not assessed taxes. The embroiderer Jacinto de Villan, who lived in the Plaza Mayor, said De la Parra had assessed him 100 silver *reales* even though he was "a poor journeyman who has nothing but his labor, with a wife and family to support."[140] Two braid makers testified that Miguel Esteban, a vecino and fellow braid maker, "is an unmarried assistant (*mancebo*) and has no more than what he earns with his work and he has no other occupation than that of braid maker." Another witness said he swore he knew Antonio La Puerta, a vecino

who lives in the Calle de la Sal, near the Calle de las Postas and the Plaza Mayor, where he has a shop of secondhand clothing of little worth, and he is married and has children, and he works for Doña Angela del Balverde, the wife of Marcos Martín, a merchant on the Calle de las Postas, whom he accompanies as a servant, and he has no other occupation . . . and if he had any considerable wealth I would know, because I have known him a long time.[141]

By the 1640s, those alleging poverty generally were allowed to reduce the total amount and pay in installments. The number of residents affected by the crown's clemency was 312 in March 1640, 167 the following month, 88 the month after that, and it declined continually from there, probably reflecting the fact that everyone by then had been accounted for.[142]

In 1639 and 1640, all Madrid's guilds had to sign a statement saying they had not actually ever paid the amounts they had been assessed back in 1636 and 1637, being that the donativo was now being managed through parishes. In fact, it appears not one maravedi ever had been collected from the guilds. At least fifty guilds signed these declarations. Representatives of the shoemakers, for example, swore before a notary that on 11 May 1637

---

[139] AGS CJH leg. 1764.
[140] AGS CJH leg. 817.
[141] AGS CJH leg. 1749.
[142] AGS CJH leg. 1756.

"they had promised Francisco Camarena, His Majesty's notary, to pay 3,300 reales for the donativo of their guild . . . and they swore that they had neither assessed nor collected any of that amount." Slipper makers, who had promised the count of Montalvo that they would give 800 silver reales, also swore they had collected nothing. Four clothiers, all of them vecinos and repartidores of one tax or another, swore they had met with Quiñones some two and a half years earlier after having conferred with the masters and promised before a notary to pay 3,000 *reales de plata doble* in various installments. But now, they said, "His Majesty and the gentlemen of the Junta del Donativo General have annulled, as is known, the offerings made by guilds . . . and various judges have been put in charge of soliciting from all the vecinos of this city, from everyone individually in their parish, because the donativo is greater this way."[143]

Why this detour into tax collection? Because guild members were taxpayers, tax evaders, writers of petitions, neighbors, and good vassals, both poor and relatively wealthy. They were citizens, even if they were not always legal vecinos. Because, at least at first, when the crown had to seek money (or soldiers), it looked to the guilds.[144] It negotiated with them, bullied them, and respected them. Though historians may try to demonstrate that Castilian guilds as institutions were powerless by the sixteenth and certainly by the seventeenth centuries, the crown does not seem to have shared that opinion. One could argue, perhaps, that the crown was so desperate for money it would have negotiated with anyone and that there was no honor in being asked. But that does not fully explain why the corregidor of Madrid, a nobleman with a very long résumé, would spend hours listening to the fiscal promises of hundreds of shoemakers. They were not merely being squeezed, although that was certainly part of what was going on. They were being summoned, consulted, included. Implicit in this relationship, in which the crown used guild officials, judges, and ministers as intermediaries, was a recognition of guilds as corporate institutions that embodied workers' political identity. Guilds were the guardians of the eco-

---

[143] AGS CJH leg. 1764. De la Parra did not fare well in the end. A onetime protegé of the Count-Duke of Olivares, he made enemies everywhere. Pacheco, his former fellow tax collector and later inquisitor general, probably ordered De la Parra arrested in 1642 for writing an inflamatory pamphlet. See J. H. Elliott, "Nueva luz sobre la prisión de Quevedo y Adam de la Parra," *Boletín de la Real Academia de la Historia* 169 (January–April 1972). According to Antonio Valladares de Sotomayor, writing in 1787, the Count-Duke ordered De la Parra murdered, and he died of his stabbing wounds on the Calle Mayor, in the same neighborhood where he once collected the donativo. Valladares called him a great poet ("Noticia de quién fue Adan de la Parra," in *Semanario Erudito*, vol. 1, 111–112).

[144] For a study of how Venice used its guilds for military levies, see Richard Mackenney, *Tradesmen and Traders: The World of the Guilds in Venice and Europe, c. 1250–c. 1650* (London: Croom Helm, 1987). On Rome, see Laurie Nussdorfer, *Civic Politics in the Rome of Urban VIII* (Princeton University Press, 1992), chap. 8. On Castile, see my *Limits of Royal Authority*, especially chap. 4.

nomic morality that formed the backbone of the republican discourse so familiar to all petitioners. Guild membership, or even just craftsmanship, though it may not have been a requirement for vecindad, was closely linked to a sense of citizenship. When a shoemaker and a judge spoke face-to-face about gracious donations, these two worlds met.

The apparent contradiction of holding guilds to be, on the one hand, irrelevant, co-opted, or subservient to crown and city, and, at the same time, annoying obstacles to progress that finally were swept aside by the rational, forward-looking forces of the Enlightenment, can to some degree be elucidated by looking at how their production rules were enforced. It was a function hotly disputed by city and guild that illuminates a complex world in which guilds were more than stubborn, self-justifying anachronisms and agents of the crown and the city did not necessarily serve modern masters. Guild inspectors, or *veedores*, championed craftsmen when it suited their and their guilds' interests, but they also attacked them in courts, raided their workshops, and, if plaintiffs are to be believed, carried out personal vendettas. Like their brothers in seventeenth-century London, whose duty the authorities said was to seize "false and deceitful wares," veedores were the guardians of the craft and the monopoly and the enforcers of production relations they said were designed to ensure the common good.[145] It was a task they jealously guarded, and at times they seemed to be competing with their municipal counterparts as often as they were disciplining artisans. Veedores spoke before judges, supervised examinations, notified the city council when someone had become a master, authorized punishments, and were present at inspections. They were paid for their troubles and, of course, enjoyed considerable privilege as a result of their responsibilities.

When King Ferdinand in the early sixteenth century established (or confirmed) the post for the clothing guilds, he ordered that city councils appoint "the [two] most able and skilled and wealthy" among the members. He protected them from insult and abuse by guild members and ordered that appeals of their rulings go straight to the corregidor.[146] Generally (though not always), they were masters elected by other masters at meetings that may have been the only such gatherings held all year. The men solemnly swore to the city council to serve their craft and the good of the republic, after which their appointments were entered into the city council minutes. In theory, they served for one year, but clearly there were

[145] James R. Farr, *Artisans in Europe, 1300–1914* (Cambridge University Press, 2000), 82. Inspectors had different titles in different parts of Spain; *veedor* was the most common term in Castile. For a discussion of their French counterparts, the *jurés*, see James R. Farr, *Hands of Honor: Artisans and Their World in Dijon, 1550–1650* (Ithaca, N.Y.: Cornell University Press, 1988), 29–35.
[146] *Nueva Recopilación*, libro 7, tit. 13, leyes 108–110.

guilds who routinely re-elected the same men; witness the sad case of the wineskin makers Andrés Gil and Pedro de Talamea, who had held the job for twenty years and pleaded with the Seville city council to release them from their bondage, saying they were old and suffered from gout, but the city would have none of it.[147] There was also the unfortunate case of Pedro Hernández, a Toledo pastry cook expelled by the other masters because, they said, he was poor and owed them money and therefore could not be relied on to levy fines as he should. Hernández naturally protested, alleging he was the victim of personal grudges. He had held the job for twenty-four years, he pointed out, and not once had there been a complaint.[148]

The appointment or election of veedores gave rise to frequent conflicts between guilds and city councils regarding their respective right to decide who would hold the post. Charles V's 1552 *pragmática* on guilds and confraternities explicitly stated that city councils should be the ones to pick them, and his will was upheld in the case of the wax workers we saw earlier who failed to change the Seville city council's mind.[149] Yet silk weavers in Seville managed to convince Philip III in 1614 that they should retain their appointing privilege (which they said dated from the fourteenth-century reign of Alfonso XI), which the city was trying to undermine.[150] In a better-documented case in Valladolid, the confraternity (not the guild) of shoemakers and makers of half boots (*borceguineros*) and of cork clogs (*chapineros*) found itself during the reign of Philip III being stripped of its long-standing power to name its veedores.[151] According to the confraternity's ordinances, first approved by Queen Juana in 1509 and then by her son, Charles V, journeymen shoemakers were to be examined by men appointed by the confraternity. (The ordinances also provided that journeymen, not masters, conduct inspections.) A hundred years later, the city struck back. Winding up a dispute over the distribution of fines collected by inspectors, the city agreed to a compromise solution but pointed out that it, not the confraternity, had the right to appoint the inspectors who were collecting those fines, and it offered a 1596 verdict as evidence. The confraternity responded by presenting its own ordinances, repeatedly confirmed by the monarchs, which stated just the contrary. The city's list of arguments was illustrative of all craft litigation: inspectors were "so-called inspectors" and the ordinances were "so-called ordinances." The city said it had not been consulted when the ordinances were first written a century earlier and that they anyway violated the public good. Confraternities were

---

[147] AMSev. Sec. X, Actas, 2a. escr., tomo 128, September 1644.
[148] AMT Exámenes de oficios, caja 1. The case ran from 1597 to 1602.
[149] AMSev Sec. I Privilegios, caja 26, exp. 308.
[150] AMSev Sec. I Privilegios, caja 26, exp. 335.
[151] AHN CS leg. 29.581.

not even supposed to exist, it (correctly) pointed out, referring to another 1552 edict by Charles V. Royal law provided that cities appoint inspectors, it said, adding that it had been doing so since time immemorial. Finally, the city stated that the confraternity's privilege (which it could not deny) "is null and void by royal law and by lack of use and by contrary use" (*por el no uso y contrario uso*). Though the resolution of the case is unknown, in 1644 the crown sold the confraternity of San Crispín y San Crispiniano the right to name inspectors and examiners, indicating that the shoemakers may have lost in 1606.[152] City council minutes in 1651 confirm that such appointments were taking place.[153] But in 1683 the city again sued, and two years later it won a decision wresting the appointments away from the confraternity. Even there, however, the matter did not end, as there is evidence the confraternity continued appointing whom it pleased.[154]

Appointments notwithstanding, records of elections, direct and indirect, demonstrate that guilds were not mere appendices of cities, or at least that they were unwilling ones. The Toledo municipal archive has tally sheets recording how each member voted in guild elections. In Madrid on 1 January 1725, fifteen master canvas weavers swore in the presence of a crown notary that they constituted a majority of their guild and had unanimously chosen two of their members as veedores and examiners.[155] In Seville, seventy-one master laborers met one day in April 1691 in the chapel (*ermita*) of San Andrés in the presence of a city council member and a crown notary to choose two veedores and two examiners from a list of eight nominees. The laborers each had four little balls. One by one they went before the notary, who before him had nine tin money boxes, eight with the names of the candidates and one blank. "Each one of the said masters swore an oath and named four different people, two for alcaldes alarifes and the other two for examiners . . . and the notary read them the names on each of the money boxes and with their own hand they put the balls in those they wished." The four winners received sixty-one, forty-one, thirty-nine, and thirty-seven votes, with the losers getting between eleven and and thirty votes. "And the said election was conducted quietly and peacefully without contradiction by anyone, and the four [winners] swore to use their offices well and faithfully and to defend the mystery

---

[152] Máximo García Fernández, *Los viejos oficios vallisoletanos*. (Valladolid: Michelin, 1996), 149. The author gives no archival citation. Crispín and Crispiniano were themselves shoemakers, and brothers, who preached by day and cobbled by night. The Battle of Agincourt, in Shakespeare's *Henry V*, takes place on their saint's day: "And Crispin Crispian shall ne'er go by, / From this day to the ending of the world, / But we in it shall be remembered—We few, we happy few, we band of brothers. "

[153] For example, AMV Libro de Actas 55, 2 January 1651.

[154] García Fernández, *Los viejos oficios vallisoletanos*, 149. Again, the author gives no archival citation.

[155] AV 2-244-27.

of the pure and immaculate conception of Our Lady and the Holiest Virgin."[156]

So city councils certainly were involved in the selection of inspectors. Sometimes their wishes were decisive. But minutes show that often they had to be reminded, and not just once, that it was time for the guild to choose new veedores. This apparently casual attitude could reflect the city's distance from guild discipline, which it left up to the artisans. It also, of course, could indicate that veedores did not really matter because the *sobreveedores,* council members sometimes appointed to oversee each craft, were really in charge. The city council appointed *sobreveedores* at the start of each calendar year. It never forgot to do that.

Like lightning rods, inspectors often found themselves attacked by cities or journeymen for not having properly defended the craft and/or its practitioners. Córdoba in 1582 accused silk veedores of cozying up to merchants in exchange for easy access to silk, and two years later the journeymen filed the same complaint. In this case, the city would prove to be a far better ally for the silk workers, with whom it shared an antipathy toward the merchants, than would guild authorities.[157] City officials in Seville sued the esparto workers' veedores in 1682, saying, "they do not conduct nor have they conducted the required inspections, and all that is being made is false and violates the ordinances, and the said veedores are to blame."[158] City councils often got in the middle of disputes in which guild members alleged elections had been fraudulent, usually because not enough members were present, a sign that direct versus indirect democracy was a sensitive issue. A remarkable indication that democracy (and the crown treasury) was in trouble can be found in Valladolid, where in 1636 and 1637 the king awarded (or sold) certain hatters, dyers, locksmiths, and other artisans lifetime appointments as veedores or the lifetime right to appoint the veedores they wished. The city vehemently protested but was forced to hear the new inspectors' oaths.[159]

Regardless of how veedores were chosen, they were not necessarily champions of their constituents. Though authorities in Seville, Madrid, and Toledo (and probably elsewhere) routinely granted licenses good for four months to a year allowing poor journeymen to operate businesses prior to taking their exams, and they ordered veedores to leave the petitioners in peace in the meantime, beneficiaries of such licenses often com-

---

[156] AMSev Sec. XIII, Siglo XVII, tomo 3, no. 10, Papeles Importantes. I found this document thanks to the very useful Toajas Roger, *Diego López de Arenas.*

[157] Fortea Pérez, *Córdoba en el siglo XVI,* 385.

[158] AMSev. Sec. IV, Escr. de Cabildo 16/9.

[159] AMV Libros de Actas, libro 51 (July–December 1636) and libro 52, August–September 1637. The privileges were contained in *autos* signed by Bernardo de Ipeñarreta, a magistrate who also was a member of the Council of Castile.

plained they were being harassed. There were also plenty of cases of vee-dores refusing to examine journeymen, essentially condemning them to maintain illegal shops. In one such case in Seville, veedores in 1677 re-lentlessly went after Gregorio Martín, a master cooper with official papers from Gibraltar, who assured the city council that the inspectors hated him because he was a better craftsmen than they. The city ordered the veedores to leave Martín alone, but the cooper insisted they were cutting off his wood supply. The inspectors, in their own defense, said Martín's ineptitude was common knowledge in Seville. They were ordered to prison.[160] In a similar case, silk dyers in Toledo consented to examine Alonso de Morales, who passed, but for twelve months they refused to give him his *carta de exá-men,* without which he could not open a shop. The city in 1602 ordered them to give Morales what was rightfully his.[161] With protection like this, it should come as no surprise that litigious artisans often dispensed with inspectors' services in courts of law. Instead, they directly petitioned the king or their city council, or they hired a lawyer themselves.

Inspections, or *visitas,* generally were governed by ordinances, but the ones we read about today, those that were challenged by their targets, sound more like raids than visits. It is possible that many went off without a hitch; indeed, they might be welcomed by artisans anxious to gain their guild's seal of approval. James Farr describes pre-announced visits by Lon-don livery companies in which the inspectors, "clad in costumes and proudly carrying the guild's insignia on its banner, marched in a pro-cession from the guild hall through the city, stopping at and inspecting shops along the way."[162] Locksmiths in Madrid surely would have scoffed at such ceremony; after the Alcaldes de Casa y Corte prohibited them from making inspections without prior permission, the veedores protested that if they announced their intentions ahead of time everyone would hide their false wares.[163] Veedores of guilds throughout Castile, probably with good reason, shared the locksmiths' assumption that inspections would in-variably uncover wrongdoing.

Inspections were supposed to be a collective affair; neither veedores nor alguaciles could conduct them on their own. Each had to be accompanied by the other, as well as by a notary. In the perfect world described in the 1567 ordinances of Burgos's locksmiths, "in order that the said veedores may best carry out .[the above duties] we order that all journeymen of the said occupation be obliged to show them their stores and their homes and all the work contained therein and that they be received politely and that not a rude word be uttered during the inspections, nor can there be any

---

[160] AMSev. Sec. I Privilegios, caja 161 exp. 394.
[161] AMT Exámenes de Oficios, caja 1.
[162] Farr, *Artisans in Europe, 1300–1914,* 89.
[163] AHN CS libro 1198, f. 92.

other discourtesy."[164] But good manners often were conspicuously absent. Madrid's cobblers (*zapateros de viejo*) complained that inspectors for the shoemakers (*zapateros de nuevo*), "because of the hatred they harbor toward the cobblers because we are our own guild with our own ordinances," as well as to cut the market out from under the cobblers, who sold mainly to the poor, staged unannounced and unaccompanied inspections during which they took away cobbled shoes they claimed were new.[165] Also in Madrid, veedores persecuted an old widow, prohibiting her from teaching braidmaking to her daughter and an orphaned nephew, and they harassed another widow who was trying to keep her son's locksmith shop open while he was at the front.[166] In all three cases, the Alcaldes ordered the veedores to desist. But what goes around comes around, at least in Segovia, where master tailors alleged that journeymen appointed to inspect shops to see that masters were not employing more than two apprentices "maliciously go in and out of the masters' homes at all hours, adding insult to injury by saying they must keep their doors open."[167]

When not fending off attacks from their own, artisans in Madrid were doing battle with the alguaciles, those guardians of the law who were supposed to accompany veedores on their rounds. City councils and the Alcaldes de Casa y Corte routinely slapped the alguaciles' hands, instructing them again and again to leave inspections to the guilds, and the Cortes and the king regularly heard complaints about their excesses and their attempts to interfere. Why they would want this responsibility, especially when magistrates were telling them it was not theirs, is hard to figure out. But their determination to raid shops whenever possible, never mind their motivation, cannot be taken as an indication that cities "really" regulated and disciplined the crafts to the detriment of the irrelevant guilds. There are too many contradictory instances.

That said, the alguaciles were a royal pain in the neck. ("That's not a man, that's an alguacil," Quevedo wrote.)[168] Encharged with policing the streets and marketplaces, making arrests, and watching over prices, weights, and measures, the alguaciles were an arm of the Alcaldes de Casa y Corte, who in turn depended on the Council of Castile. Each alcalde had a group of alguaciles under his command; and the number grew at an alarming rate in the early seventeenth century, alarming both for their victims and for the Cortes, which repeatedly tried to rein them in. During

---

[164] *Boletín de la Institución Fernán González,* no. 207 (1993).

[165] AHN CS libro 1229, 30 May 1644. In Dijon, shoemakers had the right to inspect cobblers. See Farr, *Hands of Honor,* 19–20.

[166] AHN CS libro 1200, October 1609; AHN CS libro 1226, April 1641.

[167] AMSeg 1165–11 (1702).

[168] Francisco de Quevedo, "El alguacil endemoniado," *Los Sueños,* ed. Ignacio Arellano (Madrid: Cátedra, 1991), 144.

most of the seventeenth century there were ninety-six alguaciles, sixteen for each of Madrid's six *cuarteles,* or districts. In 1650 the Alcaldes ordered that the number be reduced to sixty, which does not seem to have occurred, since in 1657 the Cortes heard a petition by a Madrid city councilman making exactly the same request, which had been made by the Cortes itself in 1632 as a condition of the millones.[169] They were routinely accused of accepting bribes, exceeding their mandate, and using gratuitous violence. The Council of Castile in 1638 had to instruct the Alcaldes to make sure that the alguaciles did not leave Madrid on their own, independent missions.[170] Again in 1645, having been informed of "the excesses and disorders" by alguaciles and notaries and "the aggravation of some alguaciles who inspect homes and shops on the pretext of alleged violations or that the merchandise sold there is illegal," the Council of Castile prohibited any inspections or hindrance of commerce without prior written reports from the Alcaldes.[171] All to no avail. They had a terrible track record in court, with their putative employers (who were judges) nearly always ruling against them—at one point the Alcaldes admitted that alguaciles' cases were getting thrown out of court because of their failure even to properly identify themselves when they made arrests— yet they persisted.[172] The veedores' treatment of poor artisans and their widowed mothers paled in comparison. The alguaciles hunted down shoe-makers, hosiers, pastry makers, locksmiths, fruit vendors, hatters, and vendors of snacks, detecting endless imaginary violations that cost magistrates untold hours to sort out and finally dismiss. They even harassed two boys who were collecting old shoes for their uncle, a disabled cobbler unable to get out of bed.[173]

One nicely documented case concerned shoemakers, ten of whom denounced the alguacil Fulano Montero (meaning they did not know his first name) for leading a series of raids in and around the San Ginés parish in 1629 aimed at seizing inner sheepskin soles (*palmillas*) from shops.[174] There were no veedores present, the shoemakers said, in violation of the Alcaldes' orders. Although it was true that the occasional *palmilla* could be found in their shops, that was because of the hard times and shortages everyone was undergoing and the "impossibility of our doing anything else until God makes things better." For four days, notaries heard testimony from around a dozen shoemakers who reported on the raids: At 11 a.m. on 18 March, Montero and his henchmen marched into the home of the

[169] Actas de las Cortes de Castilla, 30 May 1657.
[170] AHN CS libro 1223, 21 August 1638.
[171] BN VE 142–43, auto, 6 February 1645, reissued on 10 June 1645.
[172] AHN CS libro 1230, 24 April 1645.
[173] AHN Consejos Libro 1206, ff. 183–185. The Alcaldes sided with the boys.
[174] AHN CS libro 1214, ff. 311–322.

master Pedro Arias on Calle del Carmen and took thirty pairs of shoes. One of Arias's journeymen reported that, "not content with examining the shop, [Montero] wanted to enter [into Arias's home], until the master swore there were no more." Cristobal González, who had a shop on Callejuela de San Ginés, said another alguacil named Torres took nine [sic] shoes. A child who lived on Calle del Pez described Montero's raid across the street from his house. One after another, the shoemakers or their neighbors testified that alguaciles had entered their shops, loaded up on shoes, and marched out again, ignoring all protests and pleas. Francisco del Muro, who lived on Calle Ancha de San Ginés, said he had asked the alguacil how he, who was not a veedor, could possibly do this with no order, and furthermore, how he could identify a shoe as false when he knew nothing about shoes. Six days later, Muro happily testified, the alguacil returned the shoes, which turned out not to be false after all. The shoemakers won the suit in July, and other craftsmen took note; ten years later, the *coleteros,* who made leather jerkins and by then belonged to the shoemakers guild, asked the Alcaldes to declare that they were covered by the same ruling, which the Alcaldes did.[175]

This little story of inner soles and law enforcement tells us a few things about guilds as institutions that inhabited a municipal republic. To what degree did guilds really police themselves? The alguaciles' actions might make us think, not at all; they trampled over guild ordinances and the pertinent laws, and in this last case it was individual shoemakers, not the guild, who successfully fought them off. Yet the shoemakers did so in part by appealing to the authority of the absent veedores and to the guild itself, its tradition and its place in the order of things. The men scoffed at the alguaciles' ignorance and expressed genuine horror at the invasions to which they had been subject. As craftsmen and as vecinos, they had been violated. From our point of view, these raids made little sense, judicially or economically. Were pigheaded constables just being overzealous? Or hoping to be paid off? Possibly. But whatever the reasons for the raids, the shoemakers' response was organized, legal, articulate, political, and successful. They were speaking to a crown as worried about excesses and disorder as they. Guilds in many ways were modeled after municipal governments, and the division of labor within the guilds to some extent mirrored that of the commonwealth at large; participation, mutual aid, and economic regulation all were aimed at assuring the common good and civic peace. Cities could be allies of artisans or their enemy. They could allow guilds to run themselves or they could co-opt them. The point is that they spoke the same language, obeyed the same laws and customs, and, at least in theory, aspired to the same ends. Guilds were creations of the municipalities but

[175] AHN CS libro 1224, October 1639.

not necessarily their creatures. They were both subject to and part of the city.

Community allegiance and loyalty verging on the xenophobic is a much commented-on characteristic of Castilian life. Outsiders (*forasteros*) upset civic harmony, according to the treatises, and they certainly manufactured inferior goods, according to the locals. David Vassberg has shown that there was far more coming and going in villages than the older literature had led us to believe and that villages were not the stagnant, hermetic places they had been depicted as being.[176] Nonetheless, prejudice against products from elsewhere and, inversely, praise for what was locally made, clearly were part of working people's understanding of community. A town or a city parish had civic, religious, spatial, and social meaning for its inhabitants, but it was also a center of economic activity, and if that was a point of pride, then knife makers or potters or weavers could share in the glory. Indeed, they thought, they were largely responsible for it.

Local histories commissioned by towns and cities became especially popular in the sixteenth century, in Spain as well as in the rest of Europe. These chronicles, often aimed at specific political ends, were an opportunity to celebrate whatever it was a town did best. Most were proclaimed to be heaven on earth. Though few authors spent much time describing the local artisanal class, preferring royal, mythological, and Biblical inhabitants, many enumerated the alleged cornucopia of products that spilled from their hands. The self-described "unworthy priest" Alonso Morgado, for example, a most worthy booster, praised Seville's bread, oil, grains, meat, fish, markets, and the infinite number of products sold on its many streets; and he took particular pride in the city's monopoly over the sea trade with America.[177] A Madrid chronicler immodestly noted that the capital "cedes not to the most celebrated [cities] of the planet."[178]

The degree to which chronicles, sermons, and festivals promoted pride in the *patria chica* is impossible to calibrate, but there is little doubt that such a notion of community and citizenship existed and that it was tied to production. Pedro de Rabanero, a master shearer from Segovia, showed up in Seville in 1637 confident that he could overcome local suspicion because "he is examined in the city of Segovia, where he says the best cloth in Spain is made and where great care is taken in examining journey-

---

[176] Vassberg, *Village and the Outside World*.

[177] Morgado, *Historia de Sevilla*, especially book 2.

[178] Alonso Nuñez de Castro, *Libro histórico político* (Madrid, 1658), chap. 2. It is unlikely many artisans read these chronicles, but Richard Kagan has found that common citizens were treated to oral summaries of their glorious and productive past in sermons and festivals: "Clio and the Crown: Writing History in Habsburg Spain," in *Spain, Europe, and the Atlantic World: Essays in Honour of John H. Elliott*, ed. Richard L. Kagan and Geoffrey Parker (Cambridge University Press, 1995), 98.

men."[179] The city council of Toledo "has been informed, as is well-known, that the steel needles made in this city are the best in all the kingdom of Castile."[180] Toledo's tailors noted in their ordinances that "there is no place in Spain where clothes are made as well as in Toledo."[181] Residents of Palencia were sure in 1460 that their town "made better white and beige cloth than any other city, town, or village in all of the kingdom of Castile," and they accused others of falsely using their good name.[182] The *Relaciones topográficas*, which in many ways formed part of the tradition of local history, specifically asked about each town's relative advantage: Which "things made or grown there are better than those of other places?"[183] Although the economic downturn by then was such that for many localities artistic pride was a thing of the past, even their complaints were revealing. Alcorcón, today a suburb of Madrid, reported that "what is made here better than anywhere else are jugs, pots, and pitchers, and they are made so well and the clay is so ideal for the craft that they are sold in faraway places and esteemed in all the kingdom." These pots were made by women, the town notary added. In nearby Getafe, "what is made in this town better than anywhere else in the region are drills [*barrenas*] for cartwrights and other occupations, and people come forty and fifty leagues for them, and our hoes are nearly as famous." Talavera de la Reina, whose ceramic pottery is still prized, had seen better days: "What this town makes better than others is glazed clay and tiles and other similar crafts, which are sold throughout the kingdom and Portugal and the Indies, and the journeymen in this occupation used to be rich and now they are poor, and some have left their trade because they cannot afford to maintain it."

The inevitable corollary of one's own town making the best products was that everyone else's town made worse ones. Outsiders were given little benefit of the doubt. Either they were fraudulently taking advantage of their competitor's good reputation (as in the case of Palencian cloth) or they were dumping inferior goods.[184] A variation on the theme was the problem of artisans examined elsewhere coming to town to practice, the assumption being that standards were necessarily inferior wherever the interlopers had received their papers. Generally, craftsmen with out-of-

[179] AMSev Actas Sec. X 2a. escrib., tomo 121, 13 November 1637.

[180] Título 31 of the needle makers' sixteenth-century ordinances, in *Ordenanzas para el buen régimen y gobierno de la muy noble, muy leal e imperial Ciudad de Toledo* (Toledo: José de Cea, 1858), 42.

[181] Cited in Uña Sarthou, *Las asociaciones obreras en España*, 247.

[182] César González Mínguez, "Los tejedores de Palencia durante la Edad Media," *Publicaciones de la Institución "Tello Tellez de Meneses,"* no. 3 (1992): 112.

[183] Question 42 in the 1575 survey and Question 35 in the 1578 survey.

[184] A Dutch historian writes that Dutch guilds also always portrayed outsiders as acting out of self-interest while they themselves sought to benefit the community. See Maarten Prak, "Individuals, Corporation, and Society: The Rhetoric of Dutch Guilds," in *Statuts individuels, statuts corporatifs*, ed. Boone and Prak, 272–276.

town papers had to present their credentials to the guild inspectors and/
or to city authorities. Sometimes these were accepted without problem, but
at other times, depending on the place, the craft, and the economic climate, they were not. In Seville, shoemakers complained in 1634 that *sevil-
lanos* were going to Carmona and Ecija, where the examinations allegedly
were easier.[185] The silk twisters in that city had the same problem, with
Juan Cortés, inspector of his guild, saying that craftsmen went elsewhere
"because they are not capable or skilled (*capaces ni suficientes*), and they do
so to avoid this city's examination."[186] Glovers sued to stop Bernabé de
Góngora, who had "maliciously" taken his examination in Ecija, from
opening a shop in Seville. They asked the city to take their side, reminding it that it had agreed in 1626 to prohibit any vecino from taking his examinations elsewhere (though Góngora seems to have located a city edict
admitting examinations from Cortes member-cities, which was useful to
him, as he claimed he had papers from Córdoba.)[187] The Madrid locksmiths who in 1587 asked the corregidor for permission to add to their ordinances stipulations prohibiting nonexamined locksmiths from spreading
their false wares throughout the capital also asked to add the following to
the list of questions put to prospective masters: Did they know that locksmiths who do not properly know their craft often leave Madrid and go to
Mora, Cuenca, Soria, and other towns

> where the examiners are not experts in the art or the occupation, rather they
> are sometimes farriers and leather-strap makers and blacksmiths chosen by
> lot by the priors of their confraternity, and they are examined orally and do
> not have to forge or produce a single work, and then they come to open shop
> in this court, and they do all this in two weeks' time, resulting in harm to the
> community [*al común*] and dishonor to good journeymen.[188]

In Toledo, silk twisters met in 1627 to put an end to this plague of deceit.
Fifty years earlier, their ordinances had allowed outsiders with legitimate
credentials to do business in Toledo. But now, they said, incompetent
craftsmen were taking advantage of the situation, obtaining fraudulent papers, and relying on the trust of the Toledo guild. The motive was malice,
the republic suffered, and the silk was false and shoddy and dishonest. This
was no minor matter in Toledo, famed for its textiles. Silk that was easily
ripped, and thus "useless," was a fraud; "and the art and manufacture of
this city, famed and known to everyone, is discredited." As a result, from

---

[185] AMSev Actas Sec. X 2a. escr., tomo 118, 29 May 1634.

[186] AMSev Actas Sec. X 2a. escr., tomo 120, 6 October 1636.

[187] AMSev Actas Sec. X 2a. escr., tomo 124, 13 March 1640; tomo 125, 20 November 1641
and ff. Toledo in the 1690s had a similar rule (AMT Gremios leg. 1226).

[188] AV 2.245.8, 6 and 26 April 1587.

now on, craftsmen who wanted to open shops in Toledo with outside papers were to be assumed guilty before proven innocent.[189]

There were many motivations for so strongly guarding a town's control over its craft and its craftsmen. I have suggested that pride of place and pride of craft were closely related. There was also, of course, the not unimportant question of economic survival, and it is not surprising that Toledo's largesse in the sixteenth century had disappeared by the seventeenth century. Protectionism had noble and less noble motivations. Sometimes, too, it was the last refuge of losers. Cloth craftsmen in late seventeenth-century Castile who were threatened with cheaper, lighter foreign textiles were sure the foreign products were a fraud. They looked good but clearly would not last, they said. Rather than trying to make their own cloth competitive, they insulted the imports. Such attacks, José Ignacio Fortea Pérez has written of Córdoba, "revealed an absolute incomprehension of the inherent possibilities of the new draperies. They also concealed the obvious technical inferiority of the Córdoba workshops."[190] Fortea is right, of course, but it would be a mistake to overlook the political underpinnings of protectionism, regardless of its economic consequences. As we have seen, the very word "fraud," used time and again to describe competitive products both Castilian and foreign, implied a broken pact, an act of betrayal.

The guilds existed to protect the quality of their products and to impede competition, which they generally understood to be the same thing. Excluding outsiders was a way of ensuring that the quality of the goods remained high, however that was defined. Implicit in that stance is, I believe, a statement about the value of Castilian labor and of the value of labor in general. A sense of community, preoccupation with production standards, and economic protectionism were not separate issues. In protecting their members, in insisting that things be done a certain way, in their assurance that their handiwork was better than anyone else's, guilds and their members gave form, color, shape, and utility to citizenship. They defended both the common good and the particular good. The limits underlined the importance of community as much as they did the danger of invasion.

In refuting a historiography that has taken for granted the topos of the shunned, vile, and mechanical laborer, for which there is little or no documentary evidence except treatises whose condemnations and celebrations may not have corresponded to fact, my aim has been to remove Spanish workers from life on the margins, an existence allegedly ruled

[189] AMT Gremios leg. 1231 (formerly caja 7).

[190] José Ignacio Fortea Pérez, "The Textile Industry in the Economy of Córdoba at the End of the Seventeenth and the Start of the Eighteenth Centuries: A Frustrated Recovery," in *The Castilian Crisis of the Seventeenth Century,* ed. Thompson and Yun Casalilla, 142.

more by colorful processions and others' denigration than by law or politics. I am trying to determine how it is that we came to think that that was the world workers inhabited. The archival documents used in this section have focused on ways in which workers' lives or their words embraced, disputed, or just made their peace with what they and everyone around them called *la república,* the commonwealth of king and kingdom in which they were vassals and actors. Artisans shared responsibility for ensuring the common good. Their complaints, their lawsuits, and their labor were all aimed, or so they said, at making this possible; and they explicitly framed their protests and justifications in political terms. They were at an economic and social disadvantage, of course. It was true that workers and vendors generally were worse off than nobles and hidalgos, and they probably often disliked one another. But nonetheless they lived side-by-side, and each knew how the other contributed. In the most literal sense of the word, there were few petitions by guilds or individual workers that did not point out (and complain) that craftsmen contributed as taxpayers by paying the *alcabala* and other assessments. In the broader sense, just as the aristocracy justified its privileges with a social ethic based on public virtue exercised in the name of the common good, so, too, workers had a similar ethic, which they argued gave them the right to manufacture or sell or behave themselves in a certain way. Their productive lives lay within a mesh of moral considerations. Their contributions, both material and political, were obligations and entitlements.

Law, custom, and a shared belief in God were what bound citizens of a republic together, and republican rhetoric was familiar to and used by working people. Work, Gutiérrez de los Ríos wrote, "is good for man as an animal, as a man, as a political man constituted in a republic, and as a Christian."[191] But how did republican theory work out in practice for those who worked? Was their discourse of social harmony spoken in a world of exclusion? How common was the common good?

[191] Gutiérrez de los Ríos, *Noticia general,* 270–271.

CHAPTER TWO

The Life of Labor

Members of the republican body closest to the feet were not always in good standing. Classificatory lists of occupations had not disappeared by the seventeenth century, though they became less common. Castillo de Bobadilla, for example, in his 1597 guide for corregidores displayed the old categorical concerns when he wrote that gambling was prohibited to journeymen on work days, "and by journeymen I mean not just mechanics, but soldiers and clerics and farmers and notaries."[1] The *vulgo*, a late seventeenth-century lexicon told readers, "does not apply to the entire mass of citizens, nor to the masters of the more noble arts, but to tailors, shoemakers, coachmen, puppeteers, *and others of similar classification*."[2] But for every writer who insisted on the innate inferiority of blacksmiths or notaries, there were others who disagreed with de facto segregation or the theory that supposedly allowed it. Already in 1537, Alejo Venegas, a Toledo theologian, had listed among Spain's four vices the fact that "only in Spain is it dishonorable to have a mechanical occupation," a statement that could refer more to theory than to practice, but which certainly shows he dissented.[3] Juan Luis Vives in 1531 encouraged scholars not to be "ashamed to enter into shops and factories and to ask questions from craftsmen and

---

[1] Jerónimo Castillo de Bobadilla, *Política para corregidores* (Madrid, 1597), vol. 1, 673–674.
[2] Otis H. Green, "On the Attitude toward the Vulgo in the Spanish Siglo de Oro," *Studies in the Renaissance* 4 (1957): 194, citing an unpublished work by José Alcázar. My emphasis, aimed at pointing to the indeterminate nature of such classifications, more on which below.
[3] Alejo Venegas, *Agonía del tránsito de la muerte* (1537), Nueva Biblioteca de Autores Españoles, vol. 16 (Madrid: Bailly-Baillière, 1911), 174.

to get to know about the details of their work."[4] Gutiérrez de los Ríos sounded positively Brechtian in 1600 when he asked, "Who shoes us, who clothes us, who builds our homes, who serves us, who accompanies us, who sustains us in peace, who in war, but those who work?"[5] Of course, one might well remark that he doth protest too much; rather than responding to a particular state of affairs, it is likely, again, that these men were speaking to one another, continuing a tradition of scholarly debate over the proper place of labor in society.

Work was denigrated and celebrated, workers were rabble and citizens. They were the basest members of the republic and the base on which everyone depended. Everyone had his or her own notion of which trades were vile and mechanical, and no one seemed averse to loosening or restricting the various and unreliable criteria for inclusion, among which were the nature of the raw materials used in a particular craft, whom the guilds served or sold to, how long they had existed, and how much time or skill was involved in the manufacture of goods. There was always going to be someone ill-considered, but it was not always going to be the same person. Even with obvious candidates for vileness, there was room for maneuver. Butchers sometimes were shunned, though not always, as in the case of a lucky one in Avila whose city council regarded him as too important to give up for a conscription levy.[6] Tanners today are considered to have been beyond the pale, but they also were tireless litigators and often wealthy. Vileness and wealth are not mutually exclusive, but the ease and frequency with which tanners moved through royal courtrooms suggests they did not worry about their station. A widely read Italian treatise on labor referred to tanners and skinners as vile while going on to praise them; the Spanish edition, going further, said they had been regarded as noble since ancient times.[7] When Jacques Le Goff tried to come up with a list of reviled professions in medieval Europe, he concluded that if region, document, and era were accounted for, all professions would have to be included.[8] Much the same can be said for early modern Spain.

[4] *De tradendis disciplinis* (1531), book 4, chap. 6, cited in Pamela H. Smith, *The Business of Alchemy: Science and Culture in the Holy Roman Empire* (Princeton University Press, 1994), 37.

[5] Gaspar Gutiérrez de los Ríos, *Noticia general para la estimación de las artes* (Madrid, 1600), 257.

[6] AGS GA leg. 1290, 23 February 1639.

[7] Tommaso Garzoni, *Plaza universal de todas ciencias y artes,* trans. and ed. Christóbal Suárez de Figueroa (Madrid, 1615), 363–364. In Italian: Tommaso Garzoni, *La piazza universale di tutte le professioni del mondo* (1585), ed. Giovanni Battista Bronzini (Florence: Leo S. Olschki Editore, 1996), vol. 2, 792. Garzoni (1549–1598) was an Augustinian monk. His work describes over 150 (the Spanish edition contains 187) occupations; in addition to the usual suspects we find princes, exorcists, heretics, and historians.

[8] Jacques Le Goff, "Licit and Illicit Trades in the Medieval West," in Le Goff, *Time, Work, and Culture in the Middle Ages.* (University of Chicago Press, 1980), 59. He reached a similar conclusion in *Your Money or Your Life: Economy and Religion in the Middle Ages* (New York: Zone

"Servile labor" and "vile occupation" existed as categories in some form or another under Justinian, Carolingian, and church law, but they were never firmly established. By the early modern era in Spain, the relationship between the rhetoric of the vile and mechanical trades, on the one hand, and practice and attitudes, on the other, was not always parallel. To paraphrase Paul Freedman, there was a certain elite ambivalence about work and workers.[9] In his study of attitudes toward the peasantry in medieval Europe, Freedman found that a vocabulary of contempt coexisted with the uncomfortable recognition that peasants fed everyone and that their very lowliness placed them in a privileged position vis-a-vis God. Similarly, we have seen that manual labor was regarded as worthy in part because it entailed austerity and suffering, but also because it was useful and advantageous to the republic. With that in mind, the following pages present glimpses into the lives of sixteenth- and seventeenth-century Castilian craftsmen, attempting to catch them at those moments when their worth was questioned or asserted. The discourse used by them and about them provides us with evidence of their often secure, always potentially ambivalent, but rarely marginal status.

Honor

Good artisans knew they had a gift. One such man, a forty-eight-year old master farrier named Juan García Sierra, got into trouble with the Inquisition in 1631 precisely because he was so sure of himself. He worked in the queen's stables, so it is likely he was very skilled. In a case that lasted nearly a year, he was accused of having replied to praise for his work (*que tenía mucha gracia en la que hacía*) by saying that his gift (*la gracia*) lay within himself rather than having come from God. Responding to the charges (from his wife, his mother-in-law, and other farriers who, he said, disliked him because he had criticized their work), García Sierra denied the blasphemy but affirmed his superiority: "He had always said that it was God who gave him his gift, and with that and his skill (*habilidad*), he earns his living." He gave God his due but insisted on his own talent.[10]

Juan Díaz, a master locksmith who also worked for the royal family, in his case in the Alcázar of Toledo, a castle, was equally sure of himself. He told the royal public works commission (Junta de Obras y Bosques) that at his own expense he had constructed a special drill to perform the wrought-

---

Books, 1988), 47, in which he ends a long list of shunned trades, with no particular rhyme or reason, with the words "and so forth."

[9] Paul Freedman, *Images of the Medieval Peasant* (Stanford University Press, 1999). See his introduction.

[10] AHN Inq. leg. 35.34.

iron work on some balconies he was making for the castle but that a Portuguese craftsmen was claiming that he, not Díaz, had invented the drill and that he had a *privilegio* of sole use. Díaz was imprisoned over the matter, and the dispute went before the corregidor of Toledo, who agreed that Díaz's drill was different from Francisco de Silva's. After Silva appealed, Díaz asked the crown to stop the appeal from going forward because he could not pay his legal bills. The junta agreed, Díaz was released, and he continued using his novel drill.[11]

Even St. Augustine had a tolerant view of pride when it came to craftsmanship; it was praiseworthy for journeymen to want to be better than the rest, he wrote, and "speaking of diverse arts he said that they all had confidence in their hands, by which they lived."[12] They had confidence in their hands, which is to say they had confidence in themselves. But in their daily activities—their holidays, their petitions, their scrapes with the law, and their attempts to emigrate or collect back wages—did they speak as if their words would be listened to? Or were they ashamed of what they did?

Unfortunately for us, they rarely talked about their work except when they were litigating. In his study of artisan autobiography throughout Europe, James Amelang found that workers tended to write about the same sorts of things that better-educated writers did: family, health, war, and public rituals. In general, he found, these were people who, at least as long as they had a pen in their hand, saw themselves as writers and observers, not as laborers. It was less a statement about their view of labor than it was about their aspirations as citizens, for chronicle writing was a form of involvement in urban affairs. Amelang says, "The act of authorship expressed the desire, and provided the means, to help shape the content of civic discourse."[13] It also may indicate that in our determination to see artisans as such and only as such we force a collective identity on them that is not warranted.

But though they did not write about their work, artisans nonetheless frequently identified themselves (or were identified) as craftsmen. Sometimes they wore a label, other times they did not. It is not possible to say if authorities were more likely to identify artisans by occupation than were the artisans themselves. Rather, it seems to have depended on the occasion. Most property leases identified the lessee as, for example, Juan Pérez, *sastre*. The well-to-do author of a chronicle of the Morisco uprising in the Alpujarras mountains almost always signed documents (and books) as

---

[11] AGS Casas y Sitios Reales, leg. 307, doc. 474, 9 March 1629.

[12] Paraphrased in Marco Antonio de Camós, *Microcosmia y govierno universal del hombre christiano* (Barcelona, 1592), 228.

[13] James Amelang, *The Flight of Icarus: Artisan Autobiography in Early Modern Europe* (Stanford University Press, 1999), 221. An appendix lists over 200 autobiographies from men and women throughout Europe and America, 25 of which are from present-day Spain.

Ginés Pérez de Hita, *zapatero,* though he apparently had not worked as a shoemaker since he was young.[14] Legal papers generally identified witnesses, plaintiffs, and defendants in the same manner, even when a person's occupation was of no apparent relevance: "Manuel de la Plaza, a blacksmith, tried to kill his wife." Inquisition trial transcripts repeatedly identified the defendant by his craft every time a new witness began his or her testimony. Something similar occurred with what passed as news items: on 3 July 1621, for example, "Eugenio Hernández, a hatter, threw himself down the San Miguel well. People say he was out of his mind."[15] Unless the hatter's livelihood was the explanation for his mad behavior, one wonders what it was doing there. But people's occupations were markers of something. In these cases, of all the information that notaries or chroniclers could give us about their subjects, that is what they chose.[16]

In some instances that seem to beg for occupational identification, the records are silent. When Toledo distributed poor relief to its parishes, it rarely mentioned how recipients had made their living in better times; in 1573, only 16 of 518 recipients in the San Isidro parish were identified by job; William Callahan reports a similar omission in Madrid.[17] Petitions for vecindad did not necessarily mention how petitioners made their living. Military conscription often was channeled through guilds, in which case men always were identified by their craft, but when conscripts found substitutes to replace them, the substitutes were sometimes identified by trade, but usually not: "Juan de Cáceres, braidmaker, who was picked in his guild's lottery, offers Juan de Torres in his place"; "Juan Pérez, twenty, strong body, dark skin, smallpox scars, enlisted in my company September 7 for Domingo Morán, master pastry cook."[18] Once conscripts became soldiers, the label was dropped, with only a physical description of the man remaining. For reasons I do not think we can guess at, corporate identity was invoked or ignored depending on the respective needs and desires of the subject and officialdom, and more than one such identity was possible.

Most male emigrants to America presumably were tradesmen, yet the passengers' catalogue rarely mentions their professions.[19] This may sug-

[14] Manuel Muñoz Barberán and Juan Guirao García, *De la vida murciana de Ginés Pérez de Hita* (Murcia, 1987). Pérez de Hita, who was born in 1537 and died without a trace, also sometimes signed or was referred to as *poeta y cronista* and *vecino.*

[15] Antonio León Soto, "Noticias de Madrid," BN ms 2395.

[16] For a study of women and labor labels in Portugal, see Darlene Abreu-Ferreira, "Work and Identity in Early Modern Portugal: What Did Gender Have to Do with It?" *Journal of Social History* 35, no. 4 (2002): 859–887.

[17] Linda Martz, *Poverty and Welfare in Habsburg Spain* (Cambridge University Press, 1983), 205; William J. Callahan, "A Note on the Real y General Junta de Comercio, 1679–1814," *The Economic History Review* 21 (December 1968): 109. The Madrid Hermandad needed to know only if supplicants had a permanent home, in which case they qualified for assistance.

[18] AV 3–419–2.

[19] Archivo General de Indias, *Catálogo de pasajeros a Indias durante los siglos XVI, XVII y XVIII,*

gest that on crossing the ocean, one left one's profession (or unemployment) behind, or it may simply suggest that data on emigrants was collected irregularly or later omitted from the catalogues in favor of one's parents or hometown. In their letters home, some emigrants urged relatives to join them, saying they would not have to work at their present occupation; others, on the contrary, praised the New World as a place where work was not looked down on, as it was at home, and where the possibilities were endless. Alonso Ortiz, a tanner, wrote his wife from Mexico: "God led me to be a tanner, and in this land there is no better occupation. With the desire I brought with me, and which I still have, to take advantage of my God-given health and not waste time, I have worked diligently, I try to spend my money carefully, and I earn more than enough to eat." Juan Sedeño wrote to the "most magnificent Señor Diego López, locksmith," that "your occupation is very good for this land and you would earn plenty to live on if you should come." Juan de Córdoba, who told his wife in Madrid that there was not enough paper in all America to describe how much he missed her, suggested that an acquaintance who was a leather worker should emigrate too, because "good men are valued here and are not so wretched as they are in Spain."[20]

If workers often omitted their occupation, how did they describe themselves? Above all, as vassals and as poor. "For the good of the poor and the entire Republic," was the heading on a petition from Madrid's lard vendors.[21] Virtually all prospective emigrants said they were poor (*pobres*) and that their relatives in America were rich (*ricos*), the former predicament usually being confirmed by witnesses. (*Rico* and *pobre* also were the two options towns had for describing themselves in the *Relaciones topográficas*.)[22] "I am dying of hunger because I have nothing other than what I earn from my work," wrote Juan Díaz, a shoemaker, in a typical equation of work with poverty. Others described their poverty not only as something to be pitied but worthy of indignation: the shoemaker Fernando Romero wrote that "he cannot sustain himself in Spain in conformity with the quality of his person."[23]

When presenting themselves or asking for something, artisans used the language of charity, obedience, and poverty. Economic relations were embedded in that language. One was poor *because* one had to work. If one

---

7 vols. (Seville: Archivo General de Indias, 1940–1986). In vol. 1, for example, covering 1509–1534, there are six shoemakers, four tailors, and three hosiers; in 1586–1599 there was one shoemaker, one tailor, and no hosiers.

[20] Enrique Otte, ed., *Cartas privadas de emigrantes a Indias, 1540–1616* (Seville: Junta de Andalucía, 1988), letters 52, 334, 337.

[21] AHN CS libro 1213, f. 31.

[22] Question 42 in the 1575 survey asked *si la gente del dicho pueblo es rica o pobre*.

[23] AGI Indiferente General, leg. 2029 exp. 58; leg. 2071.

had to work, one surely was poor. This was in part a linguistic question (*trabajo* as travails), but it also opened up possibilities for a rhetorical strategy. Dozens of palace employees, for example, some of whom had been owed back wages for nearly thirty years, finally got paid in the 1630s when the king dipped into the donativo pot; they achieved this by arguing not that they were owed the money but that they were poor. The passementerie Gabriel Montero and the tailor Juan Varela told the Count-Duke in 1634 that their debts went back to 1618, as a result of which "they find themselves in need and cannot attend the royal service of His Majesty as they wish." In another case, the king worried that his stable workers, who also had petitioned for back wages, were "in such need that they cannot keep going."[24] Here we do not see a fair exchange of labor for wages. Rather, the two parties, king and vassal, graciously provided services to each other. In another instance, proving that the palace was not the best place to be employed, Philip III's tailor, Lorenzo Varela, wrote that he was owed 10,000 ducats (a fortune) for work performed over the preceding four years, and his creditors were threatening to send him to prison. The king, it appears, had awarded Varela two certificates of noble status (*hidalguías*), but nobody would pay Varela enough for them to compensate for his wages. Varela said he was starving and pleaded that the king "for God's sake take pity on his need and have the mercy" to intervene in the matter. Philip finally ordered that his tailor be paid "without delay, because God cannot permit such need and hardship."[25] The queen's carpenter, meanwhile, had not been paid for three years: "I ask and plead that Your Majesty, mindful that I am very poor and needy, order that I be paid" what he was owed, Gabriel Garcés wrote in 1610. The order went out, but the money did not come in, and two years later Garcés again petitioned, with the bill naturally having gone up in the interim. "I ask and plead Your Majesty, given that there is a special decree for Your Majesty's servants, that I be paid from the properties of moriscos and from the millones."[26]

Privileged artisans in these cases were arguing they were poor when surely they were not (at least insofar as we define poverty in economic terms), but the language was useful to them. On rare occasions, the pretense was dropped and petitioners spoke plainly (or, to use an illustrative idiom, *hablaron en plata*). Two carpenters who had constructed platforms for a Madrid bullfight in 1636 still had not gotten paid the following year, and they wrote the Alcaldes de Casa y Corte to ask that "we be paid the usual amount and that we be issued an order of payment, because it is jus-

[24] AGS CJH leg. 1755.
[25] AGS CJH leg. 554.16.
[26] AGS CJH leg. 494.16.17; leg. 500.21.31. The moriscos, former or practicing Muslims, had been expelled from Spain in 1609 and their property confiscated.

tice we ask for."[27] Philip III's locksmith in Aranjuez pointed out that for the past seven years he had worked diligently fixing locks and clocks at very moderate prices, but it was time for a raise. The locksmith, Antonio Francés, earned 10,000 *maravedíes* a year plus a fixed amount per job, but as there were no jobs at present, according to the Junta de Obras y Bosques, he could not make ends meet. The junta, taking into account what a good locksmith could earn in Madrid, recommended to the king that the petitioner be given 20,000 or 25,000 a year on condition that he remain in Aranjuez and be permanently on call, as it would be costly and inefficient to have to hire from Madrid. The duke of Lerma answered for the king: Francés would get just a one-time bonus of 15,000 maravedíes.[28]

Some artisans could bargain even with the king: a goldsmith conditioned his payment of a 1629 donativo on withdrawal of an ordinance prohibiting goldsmiths from working with silver and silversmiths from working with gold.[29] Also in 1625, artisans placed conditions on donativo payments. Some wanted back wages, such as the blacksmith Antonio Hernández, who offered to pay 100 of the 725 reales he was owed for a balcony he had made for the royal palace; records for the 1632 donativo indicate Hernández's deal was accepted.[30] Alarife Pedro de Pedrosa insisted that if the city of Madrid paid him 600 reales ("although my claim is for a greater sum"), he would "donate" that amount to the king; if the city paid less, he would pay 300 in copper coinage in two months' time.[31] Other craftsmen tried to pay the donativo using IOUs from third parties. By the time of the 1636 donativo drive that directly targeted guilds, collectors were instructed that debts not be accepted as offerings.[32]

Poverty, then, real or not, was not necessarily a stigma. (A fleeting remark in an Inquisition trial even suggests unexpected benefits: when the bad Catalina de Sepúlveda proposed that the good and unmarried María de Castilla have sex with a man, María resisted, to which Catalina replied, "Come on, in your case, being poor, it's not a sin."[33] Students applying for scholarships had to argue they were *pobres,* but in this case "the poverty requirement became a minimum threshold of wealth."[34] Parents claimed they were poor to gain admittance for their children to orphanages.[35] No-

[27] AHN CS libro 1222.
[28] AGS Casas y Sitios Reales leg. 304, doc. 203.
[29] AV 2.315.46.
[30] AGS CG leg. 3251, libro 86, 12 February 1625; AGS CG leg. 3251, libro 85.
[31] AGS CG leg. 3251, libro 86, 1 January 1625.
[32] AGS CG leg. 3251, libro 61.
[33] AGS Inq. 73.34.
[34] Dámaso de Lario, "El requisito de pobreza en los colegios mayores españoles," *Pedralbes,* no. 15 (1995): 169.
[35] Valentina Tikoff, "Assisted Transitions: Children and Adolescents in the Orphanages of Seville at the End of the Old Regime, 1681–1831" (Ph.D. diss, Indiana University, 2000).

bles were *pobres* when they refused to provide the king with money during wartime; city councilmen were *pobres* when they tried to get out of assignments they did not want. If one had less money than one thought one should, one could call oneself poor, and one generally did. The language of poverty offered both sides a way in which to discuss something else. It was not a strategy that either side necessarily adopted, but it was at their disposal when they perceived it would help them. Likewise, the language of poverty was not unrelated to the more obviously political language of the republic, in that it implied mutual service and the desirability of justice. Many artisans who petitioned the king to reduce taxes or to allow them to emigrate were, indeed, very poor. Not everyone who used the language was, however. Poverty was a question of social rank and unmet expectations.

But if in using the language of poverty, workers were not demeaning themselves, they certainly could point to their low status if it promised rewards. Inquisition testimony offers some especially self-effacing speeches by artisans. (Being on the stand is always a good moment to show humility.) Lucas de Santa María, a carder in Torrijos (Toledo) who was accused in 1616 of the bizarre crimes of having declared he would like to be a Moor and that the Son of God had told him to go back to being one, as well as chatting with Muslim slaves, denied it all by saying that because "he was a man of work and drinks wine" the occasional offensive words might have escaped his lips.[36] (Drunkenness often was accepted as a mitigating circumstance.) The silk weaver Gonzalo de Cepeda, who in 1608 had huffed and puffed about being an hidalgo and therefore much loftier than Inquisitor Gaspar de Quiroga, in whose garden he was caught trespassing, later explained that it was all a big mistake: "For the love of God he asked the Inquisitor and other gentlemen to pardon him because he is a poor man and a journeyman . . . and confessed he knows little."[37]

Workers, like everyone else, were expected to wear a certain type of clothing. Already in Renaissance Florence, similar laws had used social categories to regulate clothing, decoration, and even meals. Sumptuary legislation from the Middle Ages onward prohibited Spanish artisans from dressing up but, as one eighteenth-century writer noted, the laws nearly all began with "exclamations of inobservance."[38] In one, which was typical, tailors, shoemakers, carpenters, blacksmiths, weavers, and a long list of other craftsmen, along with day workers and field workers, and their women were prohibited from wearing silk except for caps in the case of the men and petticoats and a little trim on their capes in the case of the

---

[36] AHN Inq. 40.8. The denouncers included most of his in-laws.

[37] AHN Inq. 122.18. He got off with a warning.

[38] Francisco Roma y Rosell, *Las señales de la felicidad de España y medios de hacerlas eficaces* (Madrid, 1768), 149. Roma y Rosell was the *abogado de pobres* for Catalonia.

women.[39] The crown did not want members of one social class to look like another, a practice in Spain commented on regularly by foreign visitors. Luis Ortiz, in his 1558 *memorial* to Philip II, though he argued in favor of overturning laws [*sic*] that discriminated against mechanical craftsmen, also suggested limiting their attire. Admiring the ancient Romans and contemporary Genoans and Flemings for their restraint, Ortiz recalled a recent *pragmática* stating that workers wearing silk would inflict "great damage on the republic." Rich and honorable journeymen had obeyed the law, Ortiz said, but certain "vile people" had not, which was "such a bitter thing it could not last."[40] Melchor Macanaz, a bureaucrat in the Bourbon court of Philip V, told his king, "Today it is truly impossible to distinguish a noble from a plebian, the rich from the poor, the honorable from the vile. . . . If the peasant's son sees himself dressed in an outfit meant for the powerful, he imagines himself, he judges himself, and he sees himself as too delicate for hard work. He becomes torpidly inactive, making him a rotten [*podrido*] member of his estate."[41]

Laws aimed at craftsmen who wore or made luxurious clothes existed elsewhere, of course. A 1363 English law went into great detail to avoid class confusion, starting off with a complaint of the "contagious and excessive apparel of divers people against their estate and degree."[42] In France, according to James Farr, the crown's declaration of who could wear silk and who could not, and who could wear velvet and how much and where, corresponded less to any established hierarchy than to an elite perception of what the hierarchy should be.[43]

Spanish authorities certainly got it wrong in late 1691 when the latest sumptuary law, which banned certain craftsmen from wearing silk and silk blends except in the case of sleeves and stockings, included farriers but exempted *maestros de obras*, silversmiths, painters, book merchants, and surgeons who did not work as barbers. A petition by members of the farriers guild who worked in the royal stables (descendants of the cocky Juan Gar-

---

[39] *Nueva Recopilación,* libro 7, tit. 12; also the *Novísima Recopilación,* libro 6, tit. 13. This particular law survived until at least 1723, when it was confirmed by Philip V.

[40] Luis Ortiz, *Memorial del Contador Luis Ortiz a Felipe II* (1558) (Madrid: Instituto de España, 1970), 32–35. Laws prohibiting commoners from wearing clothes unbecoming to their status often bore a paternalist stamp: foolishly aping their betters, lawmakers said, the poor spent all their money on clothes and thus would never improve their lot. The disorder in apparel was so great, the Cortes told the king in 1559, that the "kingdoms are being destroyed" (Real Academia de la Historia, *Cortes de los antiguos Reinos de León y de Castilla,* 5 vols. [Madrid, 1903] vol. 5, 826).

[41] Cited in Juan Sempere y Guarinos, *Historia del luxo y de las leyes suntuarias de España* (Madrid, 1788), vol. 2, 159–160. Sempere was opposed to sumptuary laws and said Macanaz was mistaken.

[42] Christopher J. Berry, *The Idea of Luxury: A Conceptual and Historical Investigation* (Cambridge University Press, 1994), 79.

[43] James R. Farr, *Hands of Honor: Artisans and Their World in Dijon, 1550–1650* (Ithaca, N.Y.: Cornell University Press, 1988), 123–125.

cía Sierra) complained that the original law had not specifically mentioned farriers and that their mistaken inclusion now was causing them enormous sorrow. Forever and ever, they said, their profession had been considered an Art, even a Science, one of the most necessary to the Republic and one that had been repeatedly honored by kings, emperors, and princes. Indeed, farriers not only made horseshoes, they acted as veterinarians, and in their opinion they differed from physicians "only in the object of the cure." What did it matter if their patients were irrational, they asked, being that rational beings depended on them? Forsaking rhetoric in favor of law, the farriers also pointed out that silversmiths some 130 years earlier had appealed a similar sumptuary law by Charles V and won.[44]

For the farriers, this was a question of honor, that behavior or attitude as much a part of Spanish historiography as the disdain for labor, and obviously the two questions are related. Honor has been regarded as the leading social discourse of early modern Spain, the chief way society had of defining itself and policing its boundaries. There was no honor in work, we have been told, or at least one did not acquire it because of work. On the contrary, common people's desire to mimic the behavior of their betters was simultaneously a form of disparagement toward their own class and an internalization of the scorn from above, which together impeded the development of any viable middle or working class. The anthropologist Julian Pitt-Rivers long ago distinguished two sorts of honor: that deriving from virtuous conduct and that emanating from an intrinsic right to precedence.[45] The honor usually attributed to craft guilds, which trickled down to its members, was a variation of the latter. Membership in the hatters guild, for instance, with its traditions and privileges and history, all given a public face during civic rituals, bestowed honor on the individual hatter. But I am arguing that craftsmen also could obtain honor through virtuous conduct, that is, through good citizenship. The loss of honor, a subject that has preoccupied generations of anthropologists and historians with an avid interest in Spaniards' sexual behavior, could, I believe, extend to a failure to fulfill one's obligation to the commonwealth. It was not enough to be a hatter; one had to be a good one, or at least a responsible one, or at least one had to try. I put little credence in a "code of honor"; anyone who has spent time working in Spanish archives knows rules were meant to be broken and that codes are far more useful to academics who devise them than to common people who were oblivious to them. So the links among work, citizenship, and honor that I am proposing do not con-

[44] BN VE 210–128. The 30 September 1552 edict in favor of the silversmiths, the result of an appeal by a man named Cristóbal Alvarez, appears in Gutiérrez de los Ríos, *Noticia general*, 205–210.

[45] Julian Pitt-Rivers, "Honour and Social Status," in *Honour and Shame: The Values of Mediterranean Society*, ed. J. G. Peristiany (University of Chicago Press, 1966), 19–77.

stitute a rule. But they do allow us to see that private honor and public duty could be closely related, as was noted in the eighteenth century by one of the guilds' most fervent defenders: "We have not been able to establish a happy medium between the high honor of the nobility . . . and honor fitting for an artisan (*menestral*), which is based more on public opinion than on a particular legal distinction."[46]

From the Greeks on, everyone understood the family to be a miniature republic, and male petitioners' claims of poverty almost inevitably mentioned parents, wives, and children who depended on them as their breadwinner. In putting food on the table, a man's good name was at stake. As James Casey has noted, "a man's reputation in the marketplace could be undermined by failure to control and run his household."[47] A family was a training ground for masculine and feminine civic virtues, and the division of labor therein was reminiscent of the organic harmony of the republic at large. It was a private enclave within the public realm, not separate from it, and honor and law resided in both. For many early modern Spanish moralists, the antidote to excess of any type, be it violence in the New World or indolence at home, was hard work and a nuclear family, especially a rural one. If idle hands made the devil's work, bachelorhood did too, many thought, and praise for work often went hand-in-hand with praise for marriage.[48] In the section of his Hercules chronicle devoted to the labors' moral lessons, for example, Enrique de Villena used matrimony as a metaphor for the virtuous life; if an artisan worked hard and well, he said, "he will wed the good and legitimate life."[49] Women, too, were instructed to keep busy. The symbol of a good wife was the spinning distaff; the model for all wives, wrote Fray Luis de León (1527–1591), should be the *labradora,* and those not lucky enough to be one should emulate their more humble sisters:

[46] Antonio de Capmany [Ramón Miguel Palacio, pseud.], *Discurso político económico* (Madrid, 1778; repr., Madrid: Almarabu, 1986), 12. In a recent study of sex-crime litigation in Vizcaya, Renato Barahona makes the important point that, contrary to what most historians have thought, loss of honor did not extend to the kin of the person whose honor was lost (Renato Barahona, *Sex Crimes, Honour, and the Law in Early Modern Spain: Vizcaya, 1528–1735* [University of Toronto Press, 2003], 32 and chap. 5, *passim*). For another important discussion of honor in the context of sexual relations, see Abigail Dyer, "Seduction by Promise of Marriage: Law, Sex, and Culture in Seventeenth-Century Spain," *Sixteenth Century Journal* 34, no. 2 (2003): 439–455. Scott Taylor, "Women, Honor, and Violence in a Castilian Town, 1600–1650," *Sixteenth Century Journal* 35, no. 4 (2004): 1079–1097, examines village disputes to argue that the rhetoric of honor is far broader than had been thought.

[47] James Casey, "Household Disputes and the Law in Early Modern Andalusia," in *Disputes and Settlements: Law and Human Relations in the West,* ed. John Bossy (Cambridge University Press, 1983), 196.

[48] The same was true for Germany: see Lyndal Roper, *The Holy Household: Women and Morals in Reformation Augsburg* (Oxford: Clarendon Press, 1989), especially chap. 2.

[49] Enrique de Villena, *Los doze trabajos de Hércules* (1483), ed. Margherita Morreale (Madrid: Real Academia Española, 1958), 79.

And if those who call themselves duchesses and queens are not convinced, they can experience this for a short time, pick up the distaff, arm their fingers with thimble and needle and, surrounded by their maids, perform sweet labors with them. . . . And if such labors were not necessary for themselves or their homes (although there is no house so grand or royal that such works will not bring honor and benefit) . . . still they can perform them for the remedy and comfort of one hundred poverties and one thousand needs of others.[50]

I propose that men's creditworthiness and ability to feed their families could be as important for honor and standing in a community as their ability to avenge sexual transgression; indeed, it is logical to think that it would be more important simply because sexual transgression of the sort that required avenging did not happen in most towns most days. Francisco Gómez Angel, for example, born and raised in Orgaz (Toledo), was interrogated by an Inquisitorial tribunal in 1611. He was fifty-two. A neighbor, the chief witness against him, reported that Gómez, a *labrador*, and his wife, Catalina, had been fighting because he allegedly was not providing for her. The quarrel broke out when she had served him three sardines (although Gómez later specified there were only two, and the wife testified there were three plus an egg) and he complained. Well, Catalina said, your two daughters and I ate just bread and oil, and three sardines is more than enough for someone who doesn't work. St. Paul, she went on, said that he who does not work should not eat. She had read this, she added, to which the husband yelled that Paul was a liar because nobody could go without food.[51] The inquisitors were more interested in this last remark than in the wife's logic, but Catalina's complaint, which surely was not unusual, illustrates the connection I am trying to establish. On the one hand, it is simply common sense and practice that working men should support their families; on the other, this assumption implicitly links labor and the common good.

The authorities themselves made the connection at times when dealing with poor working men who were trying to avoid military service. The Council of War told the king of the case of Francisco Jiménez, who was lame (and therefore would not be of much use anyway) and was needed by his mother and his wife and their two children, "whom he supports with his work and they are in extreme need."[52] Manuela Ortiz wrote to the authorities that "my husband was a journeyman tailor and we got by with his work, with no other occupation, property, or money," and she desperately needed his pay.[53] Juan Alonso de Náxera, the only hatter in Palenzuela (Valladolid) pleaded to be excused because "I am married and I have a

[50] Fray Luís de León, *La Perfecta Casada* (1583) (Madrid: Taurus, 1987), 105.
[51] AHN Inq. leg. 203.17. Gómez got off with a warning.
[52] AGS GA leg. 1346, January 1641. Jiménez was excused.
[53] AV 3–420–1.

small daughter to raise and my wife is pregnant and my mother is old and disabled and my unmarried sister is old enough to marry and I support them all with no other means but my occupation because I am *pobre de toda solemnidad.*" The presiding judge was sympathetic, noting that "the occupation of hatter is very necessary in this town because he is the only one and if he left, the alcabalas and other taxes would greatly decrease."[54] Taxes aside, the point was that these men contributed to the well-being of their families and their towns by working and by being good vecinos.

If one could suffer shame by not working, as Francisco Gómez Angel had, it stands to reason that to some extent work bestowed honor, or at least it enhanced one's reputation. Spanish writers in the sixteenth century praised the patron saint of fathers, St. Joseph, precisely because he had worked with his hands, like God before him when he created the universe. (Some said Joseph was not a carpenter at all, but rather a blacksmith or a farrier, a matter resolved in 1597, but the point was that his hands got dirty.)[55] Honor was not solely a matter of individual qualities; it was a question of one's relationship to one's community and one's responsibility toward family, neighbors, and colleagues. Nor were lost and restored honor as easily defined as some have thought; I disagree with Pitt-Rivers's assertion in his discussion of the relationship between honor and legality that "to go to law for redress is to confess publicly that you have been wronged, and the demonstration of your vulnerability places your honor in question."[56] On the contrary, going to court may well have been an assertion of strength, not a confession of weakness. Letting one's children go hungry or passing off shoddy merchandise as quality goods was as much an affront to a moral code as was sexual innuendo, as long as we understand morals to extend beyond the intimate sphere. In this regard, when James Farr notes that French artisans were especially likely to go to court over honor disputes— suits were filed when plaintiffs were called usurers, thieves, or cuckolds, when craftsmen's marks were defaced, when hats were knocked off, and when garbage was tossed—he implicitly and, I believe, mistakenly suggests honor concerned only private affairs, that it was somehow separate from craft and community, that "culture" had liberated itself from politics, and that honor was a matter for the rash, not the reasonable.[57]

---

[54] AGS GA leg. 1450, May 1642. Náxera was excused after the intervention of Francisco Valcárcel, a high-ranking royal jurist.

[55] Charlene Black, "Trabajo y redención en la España del Siglo de Oro: Imágenes de San José en el taller de carpintero," *Estudios josefinos* (Valladolid), no. 101 (January–June 1997): 13–14.

[56] Pitt-Rivers, "Honour and Social Status," 30.

[57] Farr, *Hands of Honor,* 177–195. I. A. A. Thompson has noted that the honor system as concerned the nobility was similarly predicated on community participation: "Hidalgo and Pechero: The Language of 'Estates' and 'Classes' in Early-Modern Castile," in *Language, History, and Class,* ed. Penelope J. Corfield (Oxford: Blackwell, 1991), 69.

Honor was not the ideal standard it is often made out to be. While the proverbial craftsman was swaggering around imitating a nobleman, preachers were instructing their flocks to shun ostentation. Juan de Avila (1499–1569) wrote, for example, of how "we must scorn vain and worldly honor and of the great strength Christ has given us with which to overcome it." It was no wonder that Christ chose the most dishonorable way to die, "because he knew how powerful a tyrant is the love of honor in the hearts of so many." If we realize the irony of the fact that Christ was proclaimed to be evil while we are praised for virtue, he said, "not only will you lose the desire for worldly honor, but you will desire scorn, to be more like the Lord."[58] It is hard to imagine parishioners embracing public scorn, but one must keep in mind that the dominant culture so often posited by historians had to contend with dissenting voices, in this case none other than that of Jesus, and that allegedly honor-crazed artisans also were devout Catholics. When the Franciscan Diego Murillo (1555–1616) scoffed at those who he said carried their honor about with them in a glass flask, terrified of all bumps and slights, his listeners surely agreed that honor dwelled elsewhere.[59] "No bait draws a hawk to one's hand and no spurs drive a horse as he begins a race as effectively as honor makes a man run, even if it be uphill," remarked Tomás de Mercado, commenting on the "horrible confusion" of bestowing honor on those who did not deserve it.[60]

Both for contemporary writers and for historians, the notion that manual labor was dishonorable was linked to rules prohibiting nobles from working, a subject treated extensively in most histories of Spain. Though Alfonso X in the thirteenth century declared that a nobleman should not engage in commerce or "any low manual occupation," his *Partidas* explained that in years past, knights had been selected for their strength, and thus hunters, carpenters, blacksmiths, masons, and even butchers (because they were not shocked by blood) were good choices.[61] Nonetheless, a 1417 law in the reign of Juan II declared it was "public and notorious" that a gentleman (*caballero*) would not work as a "tailor or skinner or carpenter or stone mason or blacksmith or shearer or barber or grocer or reseller or shoemaker, nor would [he] have other low and vile occupations."[62] Of course, it was unlikely that a gentleman would work as a skin-

---

[58] Juan de Avila, *Obras del Padre Maestro Juan de Avila, Predicador en el Andaluzia* (Madrid, 1588). Libro Espiritual, cap. 3, f. 287.

[59] Hilary Dansey Smith, *Preaching in the Spanish Golden Age: A Study of Some Preachers of the Reign of Philip III* (Oxford University Press, 1978), 128. Both in literature and in proverbs, a woman's honor also was frequently compared to glass, easily broken and impossible to repair.

[60] Tomás de Mercado, *Suma de tratos y contratos* (1569), ed. Nicolás Sánchez-Albornoz (Madrid: Instituto de Estudios Fiscales, 1977), vol. 2, 675.

[61] *Partidas* II, tit. XXI, ley II.

[62] *Ordenanzas Reales de Castilla*, libro 4, tit. 1, ley 9; *Nueva Recopilación*, libro 6, tit. 1, ley 3.

ner (and one would expect the skinners guild to have objected if he had), but in the two centuries after Juan's reign it was not at all unlikely that at least some of his revenues should come from business of one sort or another. Recent studies have confirmed that nobles throughout Spain were engaged in estate management, farming, commerce, transportation, manufacturing, and banking, much of it far more profitable and productive than they had been given credit for.[63] The Cortes of Aragón in 1626 passed a law allowing the nobility to benefit from the manufacture and sale of cloth as long as it did not take place in their dwellings. On 13 December 1682, the crown declared that nobility was not incompatible with owning textile factories, though actually working with one's hands remained off-limits. The new edict has been described as having "removed legal obstacles" to noble participation in economic activity, but the alleged obstacle had been no more precise than the list of supposedly proscribed crafts. Discrimination against manual labor was less a matter of law than it was of pressure from the nobility, anxious to preserve its privileges.[64]

Early modern Spanish writers who sang the praises of labor either took pains to reinterpret and take issue with Juan II's law or they simply ignored it. They used a double-pronged attack: they asserted that the Spanish nobility in fact could and did work; and they criticized those who did not, sometimes with a vehemence that suggested that the lazy objects of their attacks were more imaginary than real. Luis Ortiz suggested to Philip II that all boys ten years or younger and all those born in the future forevermore be taught letters, arts, or mechanical occupations "even if they are the sons of grandees and gentlemen."[65] The arbitrista Martín González de

---

According to Gutiérrez de los Ríos, the original wording caused an outcry (*grandes pleitos*) and had to be rewritten. See Gutiérrez de los Ríos, *Noticia general,* 203.

[63] This question is part of the larger debate concerning the aristocracy's role in Spain's economic development in the sixteenth and seventeenth centuries. See Charles Jago, "The 'Crisis of the Aristocracy' in Seventeenth-Century Castile," *Past and Present,* no. 84 (1979): 60–90; I. A. A. Thompson and Bartolomé Yun Casalilla, eds., *The Castilian Crisis of the Seventeenth Century: New Perspectives on the Economic and Social History of Seventeenth-Century Spain* (Cambridge University Press, 1994); I. A. A. Thompson, "The Purchase of Nobility in Castile, 1552–1700," *The Journal of European Economic History* 8 (Fall 1979): 313–360; I. A. A. Thompson, "The Nobility in Spain, 1600–1800," in *The European Nobilities in the Seventeenth and Eighteenth Centuries,* ed. H. M. Scott (London: Longman, 1995), 174–236; and the articles collected in Bartolomé Yun Casalilla, *La gestión del poder: Corona y economías aristocráticas en Castilla (siglos XVI–XVIII)* (Madrid: Akal Ediciones, 2002). For an instructive local empirical study, see Mario García-Oliva Pérez, "'Oficios mecánicos' en la nobleza montañesa," *Hidalguía,* no. 46 (May–June 1961): 299–304. The Basque Country was a special case because of nearly universal hidalguía, which led to frequent litigation.

[64] *Nueva Recopilación,* libro 7, tit. 13, ley 100; John Lynch, *The Hispanic World in Crisis and Change, 1598–1700* (Oxford: Blackwell, 1992), 191. According to Thompson, the 1682 decree was ignored ("The Nobility in Spain, 1600–1800," 228). See also William J. Callahan, *Honor, Commerce and Industry in Eighteenth-Century Spain* (Boston: Baker Library, Harvard University, 1972).

[65] Luis Ortiz, *Memorial del Contador Luis Ortiz a Felipe II,* 32.

Cellorigo stated flatly that "there is no law that says he who works is no longer noble and very honorable and worthy of all the honorable posts of the republic."[66] Bernabé Moreno de Vargas (1576–1648), a perpetual city councilman (*regidor*) in Murcia and author of a study of the nobility, said that while it was true that in France and other kingdoms a nobleman could lose his privileges by working (Frenchmen were excluded from commercial and industrial activities on pain of *dérogeance,* or the permanent loss of rank, although they found ways of getting around the rule, especially in major cities and ports),[67] that was not the case in Spain: "It is a very ancient custom [in Spain] that one does not lose nobility or hidalguía by practicing [vile and mechanical] occupations, as many authors have pointed out, and as for which occupations are vile and mechanical, that is left to the common opinion and custom." (That last comment should serve as yet another warning for those who take for granted a fixed hierarchy of labor.) Moreno went on to say that the non-stigma applied to the children and descendants of hidalgos,

> because even if [hidalgos] have mechanical occupations and do not live nobly, their children should not have to give up their hidalguía. . . . Thus we can see the harm some contemporaries have done in saying that hidalguía granted by the Prince is lost by using low and vile occupations . . . basing themselves on laws from the *Partida* and others from the *Nueva Recopilación* that appear to prove them right. But the truth is that in Spain, ancient or newly granted nobility and hidalguía is not lost by using vile and mechanical occupations.[68]

Admittedly, Moreno proved nothing; he merely made an assertion (several times). We have to assume, however, that he spoke for other men of his rank, either hidalgos and nobles anxious to work or well-to-do working men anxious to improve their status by acquiring a title. Other writers who looked abroad saw not lazy Frenchmen, as Moreno de Vargas did, but aristocratic, industrious Venetians and Flemings who, in the words of Marco

[66] Martín González de Cellorigo, *Memorial de la política necesaria y útil restauración de la república* (1600), ed. José L. Pérez de Ayala (Madrid: Instituto de Estudios Fiscales, 1991), 85. González de Cellorigo was a Valladolid jurist, "one of the most acute of the *arbitristas*," in the words of J. H. Elliott.

[67] Gaston Zeller, "Une notion de caractère historico-social: la dérogeance," in his *Aspects de la politique française sous l'Ancien Régime* (Paris: Presses Universitaires de France, 1964), 336–374; Roger Mettam, "Definitions of Nobility in Seventeenth-Century France," in *Language, History, and Class,* ed. Corfield, 79–100. H. M. Scott and Christopher Storrs, in their introduction to *The European Nobilities in the Seventeenth and Eighteenth Centuries,* vol. 1, 18, note that Breton aristocrats who wanted (or needed) to engage in commerce could put their noble status on hold and then reclaim it once their commercial activities were completed.

[68] Bernabé Moreno de Vargas, *Discursos de la nobleza de España* (1636) (Madrid, 1659), 50v.

Antonio de Camós, had "ennobled their country" by working.[69] Such attitudes were not premature harbingers of capitalism by those "ahead of their time" or anomalies marking a break with the "dominant ideology." They were perfectly coherent with a moral political culture that discussed honor and the common good in the same breath. Not all well-born men desired to work, and their bad habits surely did prove a pernicious example to some. Mid-seventeenth-century nobles and hidalgos in Seville, for example, frequently refused to take on municipal responsibilities, pointing to their social status as an impediment.[70] But though there is little doubt that rich people in general worked less than poor people, and they certainly worked less with their hands, Spain was not the only country in which work was to some degree off-limits to the nobility, and, just as in the rest of Europe, such limits were anyway of questionable efficacy and implemented irregularly.

Not-working

The surest way of losing the sort of honor I have linked both to labor and to family was to be *ocioso,* which can be translated as lazy, shiftless, idle, indolent, or just unemployed. (The word *ocio* today means leisure.) What people thought about not-working can illuminate what they thought about working. Not-working such as religious contemplation or writing poetry, to name just two activities worthy of clerics and scholars, was in a different category and I do not discuss it here. Instead, I am concerned with the indolence of those who breached their obligation to contribute to the common good or were doing it harm.[71]

The quintessential ocioso was the *pícaro,* that protagonist of Golden Age literature whose adventures, desires, and failings are too often read as a faithful record of seventeenth-century social tensions. Some modern

---

[69] Marco Antonio de Camós, *Microcosmia y govierno universal del hombre christiano* (Barcelona, 1592), 197.

[70] In one such example, efforts by the roving royal minister Diego de Riaño to persuade Seville to participate in a donativo campaign in 1635–1637 were stonewalled by the nobles' refusal to take on the job. See AMSev, Sec. X, Actas, 2a. escr., tomo 120; and AGS CJH legs. 1738 and 1779.

[71] Contemporaries at times treated bad activities as if they were not activities at all, implicitly making them ociosos: "That which does not bring about glory to God, an example to one's neighbors, or good to the republic, cannot properly be called an occupation," the letrado Laureano counseled his childhood friend Florino, a reformed gambler, in one of many contemporary allegorical dialogues on the question (Francisco de Luque Faxardo, *Fiel desengaño contra la ociosidad y los juegos* (1603), ed. Martín de Riquer [Madrid: Real Academia Española, 1955], 123). This is a five-hundred-page dialogue between repentance and erudition; for the modern reader, it is hard to say which is worse.

scholars have taken pains to separate characters from their originals, as they must also separate the novels' narrators from their authors.[72] But José Antonio Maravall's influential work on the picaresque often floats from literature to society and back again with little warning and with only the words of fictional characters and treatise writers as guides. The fact that picaresque literature arose when and where it did is significant and tells us a great deal about the anxieties and limitations of seventeenth-century Spain, but to aver, as Maravall does, that "every" worker was on the verge of poverty, that there was an "insurpassable dichotomy" between rich and poor, that mechanical laborers were "socially disqualified," and that manual labor was held in the "lowest regard," this last remark flowing seamlessly out of a discussion of Mateo Alemán's *Guzmán de Alfarache,* confuses portrait with testimony and understands social status and hierarchy in anachronistic terms.[73] Similarly, a standard study of Madrid's eighteenth-century merchants informs us that "even the pícaros, the lowest social stratum, had a profound aversion to manual labor or any business occupation. . . . [There was] a haughty disdain for the manual arts." The source for this observation was *Lazarillo de Tormes.*[74] The pícaro was an essential character into which dramatists and novelists converted their anxiety and the material reality of the economic and political crisis around them. He distilled the economic disaster, the fatal flaws, the colorful, the wily, the lost opportunities, the turning away from God. At the same time, work, or notwork, was fundamental to the characterization of Spain's shortcomings, an explanatory vehicle, and it obviously has lain heavy on descriptions of Spain's past ever since. But conflating the stage character with the stage is a grave error. Lope de Vega himself distanced himself from his plots. In the words of one writer, his plays were "believable but not true."[75]

Not all idlers were pícaros; many were just plain poor, and writers of the early modern period, both in Spain and elsewhere, labored to distinguish the deserving poor (or the true poor) from the undeserving, or false poor. First in Protestant countries and later in Spain, the virtue of poverty came to be perceived as too much of a good thing. Laws, the church, confraternities, and the great charitable hospitals established in previous decades were unable to clear city squares and country roads of the poor and the unemployed, or so writers claimed. Work and activity therefore began ap-

[72] For one such study, see Anne J. Cruz, *Discourses of Poverty: Social Reform and the Picaresque Novel in Early Modern Spain* (University of Toronto Press, 1999).

[73] José Antonio Maravall, *La literatura picaresca desde la historia social* (Madrid: Taurus, 1986), 71, 148, 169, 173.

[74] Miguel Capella and Antonio Matilla Tascón, *Los Cinco Gremios Mayores de Madrid* (Madrid, 1957), 10–11.

[75] Richard Boyer, "Honor among Plebeians: 'Mala Sangre' and Social Reputation," in *The Faces of Honor: Sex, Shame, and Violence in Colonial Latin America,* ed. Lyman L. Johnson and Sonya Lipsett-Rivera (Albuquerque: University of New Mexico Press, 1998), 154.

pearing more praiseworthy than poverty and contemplation. Treatises, both philosophical and economic, reflected the contradiction between Christian charity and the idealization of poverty, on the one hand, and the recognition of its social price. They proposed workhouses, poorhouses, and job training, along with handouts, to alleviate the pressure of emigration from rural villages unable to support their inhabitants.[76]

Throughout the sixteenth century, as the economic situation in Spain became more onerous, the crown issued a multitude of orders punishing vagrancy and setting up licensing procedures for beggars. A thirteen-point edict from 16 January 1597, for example, ordered beggars to prove their state of need by providing a long list of biographical data in return for which they received a license and a little rosary that functioned as a sort of dog tag. They could sleep in shelters equipped with a large patio and straw mattresses and rough blankets. Those who already had a place to stay were required to check in on Sundays to hear Mass. Those who authorities determined were not truly in a state of need were first given a warning and then were punished if they continued to beg.[77]

The false poor offended the republic by not working and offended the genuinely poor by effectively stealing their alms. Soon after the 1597 edict was issued, the chronicler Francisco de Ariño described the rounding-up of beggars in Seville: Two thousand men and an unspecified number of women were examined by doctors over three or four days. Licenses were issued to "the lame, the one-armed, the palsied and the aged" to continue begging, while the rest were ordered to find a job within three days on pain of a hundred lashes.[78] Picaresque literature, of course, is full of frauds who pretended to have dread diseases and useless limbs that reduced them to begging; Sancho Panza, as governor of the island of Barataria, took the trouble to appoint a special sheriff to inspect beggars' alleged disabilities, "for behind feigned missing limbs and counterfeit sores lurk sturdy thieves and hale drunkards."[79] Quevedo complained that rather than seek to rem-

[76] The outstanding sixteenth-century treatises on poverty are Miguel de Giginta, *Tratado de remedio de pobres* (1579); Cristóbal Pérez de Herrera, *Discursos del amparo de los legítimos pobres* (1598); Domingo de Soto, *Deliberación de la causa de los pobres* (1545), and the reply that same year by Juan de Robles (also known as Juan de Medina); and the humanist Juan Luis Vives's *Tratado del socorro de los pobres* (1526).

[77] "Lo que parece que es conveniente para el amparo de los pobres mendigantes" (Hispanic Society of America ms. 1682). For poor relief in general, see William J. Callahan, *La Santa y Real Hermandad del Refugio y Piedad de Madrid, 1618–1832* (Madrid: CSIC, 1980); Michel Cavillac, introduction to Crístobal Pérez de Herrera, *Amparo de Pobres* (Madrid: Espasa-Calpe, 1975), lxxiv–cciii; Cruz, *Discourses of Poverty*, chap. 2; Martz, *Poverty and Welfare in Habsburg Spain*; and Augustin Redondo, "Pauperismo y mendicidad en Toledo en la época del 'Lazarillo,'" in *Hommage des Hispanistes Français à Noël Salomon* (Barcelona: Editorial Laia, 1979), 703–717.

[78] Cited in James Casey, *Early Modern Spain: A Social History* (London: Routledge, 1999), 125.

[79] Miguel de Cervantes, *El ingenioso hidalgo Don Quijote de la Mancha*, book II, 51 (Madrid: Clásicos Castalia, 1978), 433.

edy their misfortune, the disabled made an occupation of their defects: "He that lacks an arm could be a weaver, he that is missing a leg could be a tailor. Instead, they buy crutches, learn to wail and complain . . . and go from church to church and house to house."[80]

As with their constructions of hierarchies of labor, treatise writers and canonists were tireless in producing categories and subcategories of poverty, though the terms were relative and the delimitations hazy. *Pobres de solemnidad* often were excused from taxes and other financial obligations, and supplicants for any relief usually presented themselves as such. How poor did one have to be to be considered a *pobre de solemnidad*? Impossible to say, though by the eighteenth century one could obtain a notarized certificate (which was not cheap) proving one's solemn status.[81] Cynthia Milton has documented how the royal courts of Quito were flooded with petitions for such declarations of solemn poverty, a category principally reserved for whites which reflected colonial social relations as much as it did economics.[82] Petitions, which could take months to process and involved testimony from a wide range of sources, generally stressed merit as much as want. *Pobres vergonzantes* (shamefaced poor), in contrast, in the words of Cristóbal Pérez de Herrera (1556–1620), were those who, "because they are honorable, do not want to reveal their need by begging door to door"; the 1597 edict mentioned above made special mention of these people who were not living in the manner to which they had once been accustomed. As for the ordinary deserving poor, Pérez de Herrera described what people accepted into a shelter should look like: they should be men or women who were crippled, blind, old, or who had limbs missing, and children seven years or younger, "such that they are practically of no service or use to the republic."[83]

Once the deserving poor were dealt with, either in treatises or with policies, that left the deliberately indolent, who became a veritable obsession. Mejía y Ponce de León wrote his tale of Doña Ocio's failed courtship in around 1525. Nearly a century later, the humanist Pedro de Valencia could still write that there was no vice worse than ocio. Adultery, homicide, and robbery were bad, he conceded, but they could not be universal and were difficult to commit, unlike indolence, which really does not have to be

[80] Francisco de Quevedo, "Capitulaciones de la vida de la Corte," xlix, cited in Eusebio Julián Zarco-Bacas y Cuevas, ed., *Relaciones de pueblos del Obispado de Cuenca hechas por orden de Felipe II*, 2 vols. (Cuenca: Biblioteca diocesana conquense, 1927), vol. 1, xlix.

[81] Elena Maza Zorrilla, *Pobreza y asistencia social en España* (Universidad de Valladolid 1987), 22.

[82] Cynthia Milton, "The Many Meanings of Poverty: Colonial Compacts and Social Assistance in Eighteenth-Century Quito" (Ph.D. diss., University of Wisconsin, 2002), chap. 3. Of the 156 petitions from 1678 to 1782 she examined, only around 10 were denied, difficult, or resolved through compromise.

[83] Pérez de Herrera, *Amparo de pobres*, 67, 55.

committed at all. Nothing could be easier and, thus, more dangerous. It was the "very destruction of the Republic," it was contagious and, once tried (like anything good), impossible to resist.[84] The seventeenth-century magistrate Mateo López Bravo declared that "the supreme reason for all vices is *ociosidad*."[85] For Gutiérrez de los Ríos, ocio was "vice and injustice, the school and office of evil with which kingdoms and republics lose their soul and their body. . . . Ociosos are enemies of all virtue, their works and occupations are eating, drinking, gluttony, gambling, robbery, adultery, fornication, incest, sodomy, fighting, laziness, carelessness, betrayal, gossip and all sorts of evil."[86] Preachers, too, joined the chorus. They admonished, insulted, and barked (the image of the preacher as disciplinary sheepdog is common) to persuade their listeners to give up their idle ways.[87]

Given all the threats assailing Spain by the time most of these treatises were written, the tone is striking. One imagines legions of vegetating bodies, children going hungry as listless parents ignored them, artisans in a drunken stupor unable to pick up their rusting tools, confidence men roaming city streets in search of dupes. As with the question of the incompatibility of nobility and labor, it is worth pointing out that this preoccupation with idleness and knavery was not confined to Catholic Spain. The literature of roguery in England also projected an image of massive, evil, and dishonest inactivity. The 1563 Statute of Artificers in England began with a preamble complaining that laborers "waste much part of the day . . . in late coming unto their work, early departing therefrom, long sitting at their breakfast, at their dinner and noon-meat, and long time of

[84] Pedro de Valencia, "Discurso contra la ociosidad" (1608), in *Obras Completas*, vol. 4, pt. 1, ed. Rafael Gonález Cañal (Universidad de León, 1994), 159–161.

[85] Mateo López Bravo, *Del rey y de la razón de gobernar* (1616), in *Mateo López Bravo: Un socialista español del siglo XVII*, ed. Henry Mechoulan (Madrid: Editora Nacional, 1977), 166.

[86] Gutiérrez de los Ríos, *Noticia general*, 263.

[87] Smith, *Preaching in the Spanish Golden Age*, 112. Two French scholars have made an interesting suggestion regarding the anti-ocio writings in Spain, according to which *dejamiento* can be interpreted both as idleness (*dejando de hacer*) and in the religious sense of a mystical abandonment to God, the sort of spiritual excess of the *alumbrados* that the church, especially the Jesuits, fiercely opposed. The moralists' fixation on ocio, according to Alain Milhou and Anne Milhou-Roudié, who use the writings of Baltasar Gracián (1601–1658) as their chief example, therefore may be linked to a more fundamental obsession with heresy. They quote Melchor Cano's Inquisition testimony against Bartolomé Carranza, the archbishop of Toledo, in which the Dominican scholar said the ideas of the defendant (also a Dominican) about inner prayer offered "excuses for the enemies of work to give in to the indolence and relaxation of this prayer and contemplation. . . . Such praise, if heard by idlers, of whom there are many now, enemies of work and Christ's Cross, easily would move them to believe this preaching is better because it is more restful." See Alain Milhou and Anne Milhou-Roudié, "El pecado de pereza en el Criticón: 'dejamiento' sin obras," in *Estado actual de los estudios sobre el Siglo de Oro*, ed. Manuel García Martín (Universidad de Salamanca, 1993), vol. 2, 683–691. Carranza was imprisoned in 1559 and died in forced reclusion in 1576. Cano made a point of saying the idlers were *holgazanes y holgazanas*, of whom there were *muchos y muchas.*

sleeping after noon."[88] John Smith said colonists in Jamestown "would rather starve and rot with idlenes than be perswaded to do anything for their owne reliefe without constraint."[89] An alarmed Thomas Mun, a director of the East India Company, wrote that England was losing ground to the Dutch because of "the general leprosie of our Piping, Potting, Feasting, Factions, and mis-spending of our time in idleness and pleasure."[90] An Anglican bishop preached against "idle Gallants" who

> spend half the day in sleeping, half the night in gaming, and the rest of their time in other pleasures and vanities, to as little purpose as they can devise, as if they were born for nothing else but to eat and drink, and snort and sport . . . yet they neither sow, nor reap, nor carry into the barn, they neither labour nor spin, nor do anything else for the good of human society: let them know, there is not the poorest contemptible creature that crieth oysters and kitchen-stuff in the streets but deserveth his bread better than they.[91]

This does not sound like the England that Spain should be ashamed not to have been. To the credit and satisfaction of the English, however, they sounded the alarm early enough to stem the tide of pleasure, and they were confident things would have been much worse had they been Catholics.

There also were those whose complaints about ocio were less moral than they were economic. I refer here to the seventeenth-century arbitristas, many of whose assessments were repeated by the eighteenth-century reformers who are the subject of part 2. Among the best known were Martín González de Cellorigo, Pedro Fernández de Navarrete, Sancho de Moncada, and Lope de Deza. There were also many, many more obscure men whose proposals to right Spain's course, often ridiculed by contemporaries (among them Cervantes), were sometimes bizarre but often reflected an acute understanding of the errors and calamities of the previous century. For them, ocio generally was a systemic problem—in essence, unemployment. The economy was stagnant not because people were lazy but because there were no jobs. Solutions lay in a better tax structure, the establishment

[88] Cited in Edmund S. Morgan, *American Slavery, American Freedom: The Ordeal of Colonial Virginia* (New York: W. W. Norton, 1975), 62.

[89] Karen Ordahl Kupperman, *Settling with the Indians: The Meeting of English and Indian Cultures in America, 1580–1640* (Totowa, N.J.: Rowman and Littlefield, 1980), 123. Kupperman points out that the average workday in England and North America at the time was no more than six hours.

[90] Berry, *The Idea of Luxury*, 102–104, citing Mun's *England's Treasure by Forreign Trade*, published in 1664 but written some thirty years earlier.

[91] Bishop Richard Sanderson, quoted in Timothy Hall Breen, "The Non-Existent Controversy: Puritan and Anglican Attitudes on Work and Wealth, 1600–1640," *Church History* 35 (1966): 282. Breen's argument is that Christopher Hill and other historians were wrong when they argued that Puritanism was more conducive to work and industry than was Anglicanism.

of factories and schools, improvements in agriculture, a more coherent trade policy, emigration controls, and recovery of the bygone spirit of the Catholic Monarchs, to name a few. The *ilustrados* of the eighteenth century were their heirs, and they paid them tribute by republishing many of the earlier works.[92] Arbitristas also pointed to personal weaknesses in Spaniards that made indolence all the easier. Fernández de Navarrete, for example, wrote that Spaniards thought themselves too good for mining: "They are of such haughty heart (*tan altivo corazón*) that they do not settle for such servile work."[93] Such self-criticism often was followed by material explanations, however. A glut of cheap and shoddy imports had left Spaniards no choice but to give in to their worst vices, many wrote, and their vanity had led them to turn their back on work and spend their money on frivolities. Spaniards were "melancholy," said the political writer Luis de Salazar y Castro in 1687.[94] They were "the most disorderly people in the world," said another witness to the waning of the Spanish Hapsburgs.[95]

Religious holidays to relieve their melancholy and perhaps to indulge their disorderliness epitomized the problem, and they were a ubiquitous theme of anti-ocio literature, though they seemed to embody both the good sort of ocio (religious devotion) and the bad. The Count-Duke in 1628 received a *memorial* with the following complaints, in which we find all the leitmotifs: the foolish aping of the nobility, the laziness, the religious excess, the inferiority to other nations:

> There is hardly a place left without devotions to saints whose sacred days and traditions are commemorated with superfluous expenses, merriment, and amusements, with bullfights, jousting, and many other festivities, competing in this manner as other nations do over which is more skillful. With all the time spent on fiestas there is little time left to learn to be good journeymen or to work in their trades and support themselves. As they have more than fifty fiestas, more than in Rome, which makes them lazy even on work days, they never recover what they spend, thus following the example of the nobles, with whom they wish to compete.[96]

[92] The bibliography on the arbitristas is huge. The best general overviews in Spanish are Juan Ignacio Gutiérrez Nieto's essay, "El pensamiento económico político y social de los arbitristas," in *Historia de España*, ed. Ramón Menéndez Pidal, vol. 26, pt. 1: *El Siglo de Quixote: Religión, filosofía, ciencia* (Madrid: Espasa Calpe, 1986), 235–351; and Jean Vilar Berrogain, *Literatura y economia: La figura satírica del arbitrista en el Siglo de Oro* (Madrid: Revista de Occidente, 1973). In English see J. H. Elliott, "The Decline of Spain," and "Self-perception and Decline in Early Seventeenth-Century Spain," in his *Spain and Its World*, 217–240, 241–261.

[93] Pedro Fernández Navarrete, *Conservación de monarquías* (Madrid, 1626), discurso 21.

[94] Cited in Miguel Herrero García, *Ideas de los españoles del Siglo XVII* (1927), 2d ed. (Madrid: Edición Gredos, 1966), 100. Salazar lived from 1658 to 1734.

[95] Miguel Alvarez de Osorio y Redín, *memorial*, BN ms 6659.

[96] Untitled *memorial*, BN VE 99–49, ff. 21v–22r. The Biblioteca Nacional catalogue suggests the author was Sancho de Moncada, whose work was republished in the mid-eighteenth century.

But there were others, such as Camós, firm believers in the contribution of the mechanical arts to the well-being of the republic, who nonetheless were adamant about the sacred nature of feast days. For them there was no contradiction between the two, as there would be for economic writers, whose dim view of holidays continued to ring bells for the reformers and historians who followed. Camós told of a poor shoemaker who could not improve his lot though he worked day and night, even on Sundays and on holidays. He suspected that his neighbor, a rich shoemaker who prayed and went to Mass and observed his days of rest, must have found buried treasure. But no, Camós wrote: The neighbor's treasure was simply the knowledge that by giving God his due all else would follow.[97] He perhaps was thinking of cases such as the tanners of Burgos, who in 1569 amended their ordinances to prohibit members from working on feast days and on Saturday nights, which apparently they were doing.[98]

Holidays were among the subjects of the *Relaciones topográficas,* and William Christian's memorable study of local religion leads one to the conclusion that feast days spoke less of individual lethargy than they did of collective tragedy; no fewer than 90 percent of the 745 corporate vows (not all of them entailing nonworking days) listed in the survey arose in response to a natural disaster.[99] Giving up a day to prayer and thanksgiving probably was perceived by working people, especially by day laborers and peasants (the bulk of Christian's subjects), as an economic sacrifice, not a vacation. Such vows were perpetually binding, and violations could bring ruin on oneself and one's neighbors. In Puertollano (Ciudad Real), for example, when a reaper tried to harvest grain on the feast day of the local Virgin, "at the first sweep that he made in the grain the sickle turned against his hand and stuck to it in such a way that he could not reap anything."[100] Surely there were many such men who braved God's wrath as they struggled for their daily wage and for whom the distinctions in a 1579 treatise would have made little sense. If it was a matter of life and death, go ahead and work, the treatise said, and if the cart breaks down in the middle of the road, or the horse's shoe falls off, then fix it. "But when the need can wait another day, and the work is purely servile, it seems that one should not perform the labor on a feast day; and this means ploughing and digging and building a house for the poor, except if they cannot do it any other day because they are poor and they have to earn their bread on work days."[101] Was not that everyone?

[97] Camós, *Microcosmia,* 226.
[98] AMB HI 1325.
[99] William A. Christian Jr., *Local Religion in Sixteenth-Century Spain* (Princeton University Press, 1981), 32.
[100] Ibid., 42.
[101] Juan de Pineda, *Diálogos familiares de la agricultura cristiana,* Biblioteca de Autores Españoles, vol. 163 (Madrid: Atlas, 1963), 204.

Church and lay authorities recognized the predicament, as they had since early Christianity.[102] During the reign of Philip II, the synod of Toledo in 1581 addressed the problem, and the city of Toledo (whose archbishop was primate of the Spanish church), commenting on its abundance of holidays—in the late sixteenth century it observed thirteen work-free feast days in addition to all those ordered by Rome and the diocese—told the king's surveyors that still others were not observed "because of the necessity of the poor."[103] The church may well have allowed parishioners to work on feast days to ease their hardship, but it may also have been anxious to get a grip on a religious calendar slipping out of its hands. Long after Pius V implemented the reforms of the Council of Trent, a 1642 papal bull from Urban VIII reduced the number of general obligatory feast days to thirty-four and allowed people to work on some of them. Still, that was not enough: Juan de Cabrera, a Jesuit in Madrid, in an early eighteenth-century political treatise suggested, given the burden that holidays still imposed on the poor as evidenced by widespread violations of the calendar, that they be further limited in number. "We will never lack for reasons to celebrate and venerate the Saints with such holidays," he wrote, "but they must be satisfied with our desire for the good of the republic and with our reining in indolence and the problems it causes."[104]

The prevailing vision today of workers in early modern Spain is indebted to the writings of contemporary moralists and dramatists and to the Enlightenment figures who followed them and who had every reason to depict the artisanal class as woefully lacking in discipline. It is judgmental, paternalistic, partial, simple, and often wrong, yet it has survived virtually intact. Fiestas and ocio form a crucial part of that image. The examples are legion; to cite just one, the early twentieth-century Augustinian who edited the *Relaciones topográficas* from Cuenca remarked that one reason agriculture was in such deep trouble in the sixteenth century was people's affinity for religious holidays: "The tenacity with which people cling to their customs, even if they lead to economic hardship, is well known," he wrote.[105] Common sense would tell us there is a gulf between the unnamed and unrepentant laggards who apparently would let their children starve

[102] Constantine granted an exemption to agricultural workers, but it was repealed in 910 by Emperor Leo Philosophus. See A. H. Lewis, *A Critical History of the Sabbath and the Sunday in the Christian Church* (Plainfield, N.J.: American Sabbath Tract Society, 1903), 171.

[103] Christian, *Local Religion in Sixteenth-Century Spain*, 172. Joseph Townsend, a late-eighteenth-century Protestant traveler from England, said there were ninety-three fiestas a year in the archdiocese of Toledo, not counting local holidays (*A Journey Through Spain . . .* [London, 1792]), vol. 2, 226). One of his principal sources was Pedro Rodríguez de Campomanes, who used the same figure in his writings, and the number was often repeated in twentieth-century historical accounts.

[104] Padre Juan de Cabrera, *Crisis política determina el mas florido imperio* (Madrid, 1719), 263.

[105] Zarco-Bacas y Cuevas, ed., *Relaciones de pueblos*, vol. 1, xlvii.

rather than miss a holiday, and men such as Alonso Ortiz, who told his wife that "God led me to be a tanner," or the farrier Juan García Sierra, who believed that grace lay in his hands. It is bad enough that these people suffered the occasional indignities of their own era, but they have been forced in subsequent centuries to play roles in other people's mistaken productions about the history of Spain.

The Vile and Mechanical

Finally, does it appear that Spanish artisans in the sixteenth and seventeenth centuries suffered exclusion or scorn because of the nature of their work? Was it true that "most Spaniards preferred to beg or die of hunger rather than devote themselves to an occupation held to be dishonorable"?[106] There are few cases from which to choose. Personal testimony is scarce, and there was no agreed-upon ranking of crafts and occupations, which is precisely my point. Yet we have always been told that workers were unhappy:

> In a society where standards were set by the landed aristocracy there were few prospects for laborers and artisans. The Spanish working class of the sixteenth century, confronted by a prosperous nobility whose estate was a magnet for manufacturers and merchants, had visible evidence for the view that work was degrading. In the absence of an identifiable middle class, possible entry to which might have acted as a stimulus, the tenant and the craftsman lost confidence in work as a means of progress.[107]

A second example, whose similarity perhaps points to the widespread assumption that such circumstances were self-evident, was provided by Ruth Pike: "Spanish society of this period believed that manual labor was degrading, and workers, confronted by a prosperous nobility whose status was eagerly coveted by wealthy commoners, had visible evidence of this viewpoint. Therefore, craftsmen lost confidence in the dignity of their labor and in work as a means of advancement."[108] These statements, representative both in their assurance and their lack of documentation, are quite remarkable. It is known what craftsmen thought. It is known that in the

[106] Antonio Domínguez Ortiz, "Notas sobre la consideración social del trabajo manual y el comercio en el Antiguo Régimen," *Revista del Trabajo,* no. 7–8 (July–August 1945), 676.

[107] John Lynch, *Spain 1516–1598: From Nation State to World Empire* (Oxford: Blackwell, 1991), 149. This is a revised version of Lynch's 1965 *Spain under the Habsburgs,* in which the quote appears in vol. 1, 108.

[108] Ruth Pike, *Aristocrats and Traders: Sevillian Society in the Sixteenth Century* (Ithaca, N.Y.: Cornell University Press, 1972), 130.

past they had confidence in "the dignity of their labor" but, alas, no more. Confidence, however, does not seem to be a quality lacking in the petitioners and litigants who appear in these pages. They lacked money; sometimes they lacked a job. But the despair that we can imagine befalling unemployed craftsmen with families to feed was not a hopelessness arising from their status; it was the result of life's vicissitudes. Their words do not make them sound like people who thought their destiny was eternal degradation. If it had been their social status, their identity, their existence as workers that had condemned them to misfortune, then complaining would do no good. The very fact that they were petitioning, explaining, or scheming indicates that they saw their situation as anomalous, or at least as one with a possible solution.

As for a hierarchy whose rungs craftsmen could not climb, it does not seem to have been that formidable in a republic in which the ideals of distributive justice were the common currency. It is true that practitioners of one craft might think themselves superior in all ways to practitioners of another craft, but the manic concern for classifying all occupations that began with the Greeks and flourished through the late Middle Ages had ebbed by the seventeenth century and certainly was not internalized by craftsmen themselves. In times of crisis, craftsmen of all sorts could be one job away from hunger or vagabondage. Theater presents ideal types who inhabit separate worlds that only occasionally collide on stage. Guild ordinances also described starkly separate crafts. Alguaciles struggled to ensure that craftsmen did not cross boundaries. Economic historians differentiate those who made from those who sold. But on the street, none of this seemed to matter very much.

Every occupation, however, had its bad rap. Tailors, to cite one example, were said to cut pieces of cloth too large and then take the excess fabric home. They also were considered weak and effeminate (the tailor in "A Midsummer's Night Dream" was named Starveling), which partially explains the anti-ruffles, back-to-basics thinking behind sumptuary laws. In Quevedo's *Sueños*, tailors were shoveled into Hell and were said to be the best fuel around. The shoemaker Andrés de Mercado would not have disagreed with that: after his daughter denounced him to the Inquisition in 1612 for allegedly having destroyed an image of the Virgin, it turned out during testimony that he and an acquaintance, the tailor Gregorio Ruiz, had gotten into a sort of pissing match over the virtues and defects of their respective trades. Mercado said that shoemakers were robust and strong, like him, and tailors were sissies. The tailor then pointed out that it was big strong men who had crucified Christ. That's right, Mercado said, "And I'm man enough to crucify thirty Christs." Back came the winner: shoemakers were always Jews. To which Mercado, compounding his many problems, asked, Was it not honorable to be a Jew?[109] Cervantes, whose exemplary novel *El licenciado vidriera* was almost entirely devoted to repeating all the clichés about all occupations, showing you could trust no one, in his *Trabajos de Persiles y Sigismunda* granted tailors the right to be known as poets: "It is possible for an artisan to be a poet, because poetry is not of the hands but of the mind, and the soul of a tailor is no less capable of poetic composition than that of a field marshal."[110]

Shoemakers, as we saw earlier, were accused of using an insufficient number of soles, and the Italian Tommaso Garzoni (and Suárez Figueroa, his Spanish translator and editor) said one had to watch them carefully because "they sew badly, with big stiches, they don't fit the shoe properly to the foot, so they are either narrow or wide, they lie a lot, and above all they charge too much."[111] In Hell, Quevedo identified shoemakers by their smell. Locksmiths, too, were untrustworthy, because they could copy and pick locks; the Burgos and Seville locksmiths, aware of the prejudice against them, included sections in their ordinances prohibiting unauthorized key molds.[112] Watchmakers, who often shared jobs with locksmiths, were "extremely honorable and useful," yet they also were known to take forever to return clocks to their owners, claiming they were doing all sorts of necessary repairs, and no sooner did the owners have the clock back but it ceased to run once again.[113]

But suspecting craftsmen and vendors of dishonesty clearly is not the same as shunning them for who they are. Mistrust is not the same as scorn. Widespread prejudice against notaries and alguaciles, which also was frequent, had less to do with rank than with a healthy distrust for middlemen, tax collectors, and law-enforcement officers who took advantage of the poor. Popular sayings may have perpetuated certain occupational stereo-

---

[109] AHN Inq. leg. 41.4. Mercado came from a family of shoemakers and tailors. He excused his comments by saying he must have been drunk or crazy. I do not know the resolution of the case. Américo Castro, in *De la edad conflictiva,* 2d ed. (Madrid: Taurus, 1963), 193, reported that it was tailors who were said to be Jews. See part 2 for a discussion of the theory that certain crafts were despised because they were performed by conversos or moriscos.

[110] Cited in Green, "On the Attitude toward the Vulgo," 195. Green says Cervantes might have been ironic but also points out that he was speaking only of possibilities in a culture that proclaimed the equality of souls. If he were to have asked his artisan friends for a preliminary sonnet for *Don Quijote,* Cervantes wrote, "I know that they would give them to me, and of such a kind that they would not be equalled by the verses of those who have greatest fame in this our Spain."

[111] Garzoni, *Plaza universal,* 337v; Garzoni, *La piazza universale,* vol. 2, 1031.

[112] Garzoni, *Plaza universal,* 202v; "Ordenanzas del oficio de cerrajero de la ciudad de Burgos" (1567), *Boletín de la Institución Fernán González,* no. 207 (1993): 231; Vicente Romero Muñoz, "La recopilación de ordenanzas gremiales de Sevilla en 1527," *Revista de Trabajo,* no. 3 (March 1950), 230. In a paper presented to the 2001 meeting of the Society for Spanish and Portuguese Historical Studies, Professor Fred Bronner of Hebrew University reported that locksmiths in Peru were considered vile because they made false locks.

[113] Garzoni, *Plaza universal,* 284–285v.; Garzoni, *La piazza universale,* vol. 2, 762–763.

types, but, as far as I can tell, discrimination against an entire class of people because of the job they performed did not exist. Sweeping statements such as Pere Molas Ribalta's in 1970 that "the most miserable occupation of [Barcelona] was that of cobbler," followed by the comment that cobblers' plight was "similar in all cities," is typical of a determination at all costs to detect exclusion.[114] Virtue (or vice) lay in the person, not in the station. In this sense, there was no parallel in Spain to the ritual pollution of Germany, where a wide variety of occupations including hangmen, brothel-keepers, gravediggers, shepherds, barbers, millers, and linen weavers were shunned to the point that their dishonor was contagious. Though Maravall wrote that in Spain, "the 'vileness' of occupation was transmitted through inheritance, through 'bad blood,'" in the absence of evidence, I must conclude he was wrong.[115]

To be sure, there were occupations more problematic than others, those that repeatedly showed up at the bottom of normative hierarchies and whose practitioners were likely to be portrayed disparagingly by contemporary writers. Contempt for sailors, in the opinion of one historian, was a large part of the reason Spain's navy collapsed in the seventeenth century. Though Olivares and Philip IV declared that sailors were not to be excluded from the ranks of the hidalguía, David Goodman argues that the *desprecio* did not abate, which led to low morale and ultimately compromised Spain's military campaigns.[116] Barbers often are assumed to have been vile, even though they won their ordinances from Isabel and Ferdinand in 1500, were allowed to open shops, bleed, use leeches, and pull teeth, and were subject to examinations by their masters. Surgeons were held in much worse regard, and in fact were prohibited in 1787 from poaching on barbers' shaving tasks.[117] Gallows-building is another exam-

---

[114] Pedro Molas Ribalta, *Los gremios barceloneses del siglo XVIII: La estructura corporative ante el comienzo de la Revolución Industrial* (Madrid: Confederación Española de Cajas de Ahorros, 1970), 62. Though most cobblers probably were indeed very poor, Molas illustrates their low status by saying they were subservient to master shoemakers and nearly all considered *pobres miserables* for tax purposes, neither of which indicated the implied structural disdain and certainly did not extend to all cities. Molas is an example of a historian of the Spanish eighteenth century who extrapolates backward. For a study of the relationship between shoemakers and cobblers in Milan, see Elisabetta Merlo, "El trabajo de las pieles en Milán en los siglos XVII y XVIII: entre el divorcio y la unión corporativa," in *El trabajo en la encrucijada. Artesanos urbanos en la Europa de la Edad Moderna*, ed. Victoria López and José A. Nieto (Madrid: Los Libros de la Catarata, 1996), 179–202. The article was published originally in *Quaderni Storici* 80 (1992): 369–397. Luis Tramoyeres Blasco, *Instituciones gremiales: Su origen y organización en Valencia* (Valencia: Imprenta Domenech, 1889), 298–303, also discusses the relationship between shoemakers and cobblers.

[115] José Antonio Maravall, *Poder, honor y élites en el siglo XVII* (Madrid: Siglo Veintiuno, 1979), 103.

[116] David Goodman, *Spanish Naval Power, 1589–1665. Reconstruction and Defeat* (Cambridge University Press, 1997), 241–261.

[117] Antonio Carreras Panchon, "Las actividades de los barberos durante los siglos XVI al XVIII," *Cuadernos de historia de la medicina española,* no. 13 (1974): 205–218.

ple of an activity assumed to be vile: in Germany, an entire guild of carpenters shared the job so no individual was stained, and municipal festivities were held around the site to rid it of dishonor.[118] In Segovia, where carpenters also were responsible for the scaffold, the guild in 1645 reminded the corregidor that whenever a hanging was to take place, "the corregidores, to honor and favor the masters and journeymen of this occupation, have always permitted, and indeed ordered, that the scaffold be built at night so as not to be seen by anyone." Since time immemorial, the guild said, this was the way things had been done. The problem was that the corregidor was telling the guild to *dismantle* the scaffold in the Plaza Mayor, which the carpenters said was not their job, and even if it were, they would not touch it during daylight. As in Germany, the job was carried out by all guild members at once, but in Segovia there was no contagion. The job was dishonorable, but the men who performed it were not. Indeed, they said, they were worthy of honor and favor (*honra y merced*).[119] Carpenters never appeared on anyone's list of despised trades after the law of 1417, and their role as firefighters probably led them to be regarded as essential contributors to the common good. Taking stock of the lives and property Zamora had lost as the result of fires, the city council there in 1515 established a firefighting force of citizen master carpenters (*carpinteros maestros vecinos*) "to avoid and remedy this, and for the good governance of the said city, as other cities in these kingdoms have done and ordered for their common good." Carpenters nominated for the job were exempt from royal and city taxes and billeting obligations and would receive one dead bull, skin included, each time the bulls were run.[120]

It is nonetheless true that there were limits to what artisans and merchants could do. At least in theory, they were excluded from holding public office in many places. An Inquisition questionnaire asked witnesses if the subject or his ancestors had been convicted by an Inquisitorial court "or committed any other infamy that prevents him from holding an honorable and public office."[121] Infamy prevented one from holding office; at least in theory, so did mechanical occupations. The equivalence between work and infamy is implied, though still problematic. Queen Juana had to

---

[118] Kathy Stuart, *Defiled Trades and Social Outcasts: Honor and Ritual Pollution in Early Modern Germany* (Cambridge University Press, 1999), 125–127; Roper, *The Holy Household*, 37.

[119] AMSeg 1157–92–1.

[120] María del Carmen Pescador del Hoyo, "Los gremios de artesanos de Zamora," *Revista de Archivos, Bibliotecas y Museos* 78 (July–December 1975): 669–678. Carpenters also were esteemed in Zamora (and probably elsewhere) because they built the structures necessary for civic and religious celebrations. María del Carmen Pescador del Hoyo, "Los gremios de artesanos de Zamora," *Revista de Archivos, Bibliotecas y Museos* 77 (January–June 1974): 83–101.

[121] AHN Inq. de Mexico, libro 1056, cited in María Elena Martínez López, "The Spanish Concept of 'Limpieza de Sangre' and the Emergence of the 'Race/Caste' System in the Viceroyalty of New Spain" (Ph.D. diss., University of Chicago, 2002), 290.

remind city councilmen in Santa Marta (Mexico) that their jobs were mutually exclusive with running grocery stores "and other vile occupations."[122] At least eight times between 1584 and 1669 Zaragoza (part of Aragón) excluded from public office those with Moorish blood and those who had had a workshop (*público o secreto*) or whose father or brother had.[123] Philip II in 1580 ordered authorities in Santo Domingo to ensure that journeymen in mechanical or low trades not be named alguaciles.[124] In Calahorra (Rioja), municipal jobs were off-limits to mechanical craftsmen, including Blas Pérez, whose 1629 appointment to an Hermandad post was annulled by the *alcalde mayor* because he was a blacksmith.[125] Salamanca merchants could not serve on the city council.[126] In Segovia in 1648, nobles who controlled the municipality passed a law prohibiting cloth manufacturers, merchants, traders, notaries, attorneys, or their sons, from being regidores.[127] The Cortes in 1570 asked that member-cities not elect regidores who were not hidalgos or did not have clean blood, "nor anyone who has had an open store, selling wholesale or retail, or who has been a mechanical journeyman or a notary or procurator."[128] (Notaries frequently were scorned; the Cortes in 1579–82 took aim at them again, this time complaining that they had become so numerous that they were of suspect lineage "and many have been traders and worked with their hands.")[129] But, as I. A. A. Thompson has written, "forced to choose between honor and business, individuals did not always choose honor." Like noble Frenchmen, Spaniards learned to straddle the two realms. They entered and left the worlds of politics and commerce as it suited them, and fellow regidores and hidalgos would look the other way.[130]

---

[122] The 27 October 1530 *cédula* was signed by the queen but in fact came from her son, Charles V. See Richard Konetzke, ed., *Colección de documentos para la historia de la formación social de Hispanoamérica, 1493–1810*, 5 vols. (Madrid: CSIC, 1953–1962), vol. 1, 136. Three years later, Charles V found it troubling that settlers in Cuba inevitably elected "tailors and butchers and other similar people" to the post of alcalde (ibid., 148).

[123] José Ignacio Gómez Zorraquino, "Ni señores, ni campesinos/artesanos. El gobierno de los ciudadanos en Aragón," in *Burgueses o ciudadanos en la España moderna*, ed. Francisco José Aranda Pérez (Cuenca: Universidad de Castilla-La Mancha, 2003), 366–367. Similar rules existed in neighboring Huesca and Jaca. The author's principal argument is that wealthy merchants had long managed to evade such rules.

[124] *Cédula*, 26 May 1580, in Konetzke, ed. *Colección de documentos para la historia*, vol. 1, 523.

[125] Milagros García Calonga, *El poder municipal de Calahorra en el siglo XVII* (Amigos de la Historia de Calahorra, 1998), 92.

[126] Thompson, "The Nobility in Spain, 1600–1800," 230.

[127] Henry Kamen, *Spain in the Later Seventeenth Century, 1665–1700* (London: Longman, 1980), 262.

[128] Domínguez Ortiz, "Notas sobre la consideración social," 675; also cited in José Antonio Maravall, *Estado moderno y mentalidad social* (Madrid: Alianza, 1972), vol. 2, 490.

[129] Cited in Casey, *Early Modern Spain*, 168.

[130] Thompson, "The Nobility in Spain, 1600–1800," 230. Engaging directly in industry was more risky, and nobles therefore tended to be linked to more indirect forms of administration and/or investment.

So, some occupations were regarded as better than others, for good reasons or not, and some tasks were considered completely undesirable. Lists of permissible wages and prices were frequently issued, indicating the relative value of occupations: in 1627 in Seville, for example, common laborers were paid 3 reales a day, hosiers 5, hatters 6, and master carpenters 8. (Grape pickers were paid 1½ reales unless they were women, who earned just 1 real.)[131] Wool and silk workers often occupied the better-paid rungs of the occupational ladder, and their subsequent prestige can be inferred from the fact that they often assumed leadership roles in protests.[132] When taxes were assessed, larger and more powerful guilds might be responsible for collecting from the smaller guilds (inevitably abusing their authority), reflecting the existence of some sort of ranking. But there was no fixed hierarchy, and guilds subservient in one city might have authority in another. Hatters supervised rope makers (*cordoneros*) in Madrid, while the reverse was true in Zamora. Hosiers and tailors, tanners and shoemakers, and weavers and dyers throughout Castile litigated over who could inspect whom, and the frequency with which guilds fought one another in court or argued over who should have precedence in Corpus Christi processions attests to their conviction that they were at least on equal ground. In Mexico City in 1533, the first craftsmen in the Corpus procession were the shoemakers, followed by blacksmiths, carpenters, barbers, silversmiths, and tailors, but that order changed quickly; four years later, the wealthy silversmiths occupied first place.[133] The first contingent in Mexico City were the vegetable growers (*hortelanos*), a custom also followed in sixteenth-century Toledo. In eighteenth-century Seville it was the city's confraternities that opened the march, and the tailors followed directly behind them. Even inter-craft divisions such as those that separated shoemakers from cobblers, or hatters from those who fixed old hats, did not necessarily imply superiority and inferiority. In Zamora, for example, rural tailors who specialized in clothes made of rough cloth for simple folk

[131] AMSev Sec. I, Privilegios, caja 183, exp. 207, "Tasa general." Artisans were sometimes paid by the piece and sometimes by the day.

[132] Two examples of this can be seen in Zaragoza: Pablo Desportes Bielsa, "Entre mecánicos y honorables. La 'élite popular' en la Zaragoza del siglo XVII," *Revista de Historia Jerónimo Zurita*, no. 75 (2000): 55–74; and in Andalucía: Antonio Domínguez Ortiz, *Alteraciones andaluzas* (Madrid: Narcea, S.A., 1973).

[133] "Copia paleográfica de los antiguos Libros de Cabildo del Exmo. Ayunto de Esta Capital," 6 vols. (Mexico, 1849), Newberry Library, Ayer ms. 1143, vol. 2, 136; Richard Konetzke, "Las ordenanzas de gremios como documentos para la historia social de Hispanoamérica durante la época colonial," *Estudios de historia social de España* 1 (1949): 509; Dubravka Mindek, *Fiestas de gremios ayer y hoy* (Mexico: Consejo Nacional para la Cultura y las Artes, 2001). Guilds' participation in processions both civic and religious is often taken as a sign of their prominence, but a very interesting recent study argues that the Bourbon viceroys of Mexico used lavish processions essentially to run the guilds into bankruptcy. See Linda A. Curcio-Nagy, *The Great Festivals of Colonial Mexico City: Performing Power and Identity* (Albuquerque: University of New Mexico Press, 2004), 103–104.

and traditionally had been exempt from examinations (as had certain similar weavers and cobblers) protested in the 1590s that the "city tailors" were trying to control their craft and impose examinations, all to the detriment of the poor. After the usual round of appeals and hearings, the city council found with the aggrieved parties, who boasted that they made clothes "not found in any other part of the kingdoms." From then on, each would inspect its own.[134]

A writer in the late sixteenth century had an interlocutor say that some occupations were "totally prohibited by our Church," while others, such as pastry chefs and wine cellar keepers, were "tolerated."[135] Though undoubtedly there were few pastry chefs who ended up as bishops, nothing was totally prohibited in early modern Spain, which is not to say that everything was allowed or nothing was prohibited. Maravall referred to *deshonra legal* and to the "stain of infamy"; Domínguez Ortiz spoke of "legal infamy."[136] But honor was not always a matter of law, and stains could be washed. Readers may recall the citation from Jacques Le Goff, in which the medievalist said he had tried to come up with a list of reviled professions in medieval Europe and concluded that just about everyone would have to be on it. It depended on one's maxims, one's source, and one's community. There were lists to suit all prejudices. A royal hunting ordinance from 1592, to cite one example, admitted that "we have been informed that there have been difficulties in the declaration of [which] mechanical journeymen" were prohibited from hunting on work days. Difficulties in establishing criteria? Most likely. To clear up the matter, the crown decreed that the list should include tavern keepers, wine-cellar owners, pastry cooks, innkeepers, butchers, "and other journeymen of similar occupations and vile and low trades."[137] A religious seminary in Quito was admonished in 1603 for admitting and ordaining "sons of mechanical journeymen and of lesser sorts than are appropriate."[138] The Order of Santiago in 1653, in a reworking of its 1560 statutes, ended its list of barred candidates by saying: "And by vile and mechanical occupations we mean silversmiths or painters who earn their living at those occupations, embroiderers, stonemasons, inn keepers, tavern keepers, notaries who are not

---

[134] María del Carmen Pescador del Hoyo, "Los gremios de artesanos de Zamora," *Revista de Archivos, Bibliotecas y Museos* 78 (July–December1975): 610–613.

[135] Pineda, *Diálogos familiares de la agricultura cristiana*, 204. The reference probably was to practitioners of those occupations assuming high positions in the church.

[136] Maravall, *Poder, honor y élites en el siglo XVII*, 14, 120; Domínguez Ortiz, "Notas sobre la consideración social," 676.

[137] *Cédula*, 20 July 1592, from *Recopilación de las reales ordenanzas y cédulas de los bosques reales* (Madrid, 1687). My thanks to Suzanne Walker for showing me this document.

[138] *Cédula*, Philip III to the bishop of Quito, 30 August 1603. See Konetzke, ed., *Colección de documentos*, vol. 2, pt. 1, 98.

employed by royalty, public solicitors, or other occupations similar to these, or inferior to these, such as tailors and other similar types who live by working with their hands."[139] In Aragón the military orders also rounded off their list of excluded members with "and other similar types who live by working with their hands."[140]

Even ignoring the catch-all endings of these prohibitions, the lists pose problems. First, the tanners, everyone's favorite candidates for a vile and mechanical trade, are missing. Pastry cooks? These were the people who explained to Madrid authorities that allowing members to maintain two shops would be "useful and advantageous for the provisioning of the republic and its good government because the more stores, the more abundance and the cheaper the supplies, and masters and journeymen will benefit from selling."[141] Butchers, we saw earlier, were sometimes held in particularly high esteem. As for stonemasons, they staged a protest (*un motín*, according to the chronicler) at the construction site of El Escorial after town authorities threatened to whip their Vizcayan comrades (just to frighten them, the alcalde said). Partly because northerners regarded themselves as hidalgos, the chronicler Fray José de Sigüenza wrote, "they rose up and were up and armed most of the night." The next day they went on strike, persuading the rest of the journeymen to do the same, and then marched on the jail to free the Basques and kill the alcalde. The authorities gave in, everyone went back to work, "and with the same ease with which they had mutinied, they happily put down their arms."[142] These do not sound like despised laborers. Or, if they were despised, they certainly did not hold back because of it.

When historians point to exclusionary rules, they most often are examining elite organizations (especially military orders) and eighteenth-century guilds. Neither teaches us much about the status of work in the sixteenth or seventeenth centuries. Furthermore, the excruciating detail with which the Order of Santiago, for example, spelled out those who were not to enter, including a broad range of merchants and financiers, as well

[139] L. P. Wright, "The Military Orders in Sixteenth- and Seventeenth-Century Spanish Society: The Institutional Embodiment of a Historical Tradition," *Past and Present*, no. 43 (1969): 65. The seventeenth-century rules are in Francisco Ruiz de Vergara, *Regla y establecimientos de la Orden y Cavallería del glorioso Apostol Santiago* (Madrid, 1655), 57v.

[140] Pere Molas Ribalta, "El exclusivismo en los gremios de la Corona de Aragón: Limpieza de sangre y limpeza de oficios," in *Les sociétés fermées dans le monde iberique (XVI–XVII siècles)* (Paris: CNRS, 1986), 75. Molas does not give a date for the rule.

[141] AHN CS, libro 1214, 24 April 1629.

[142] Fray José de Sigüenza, *La fundación del monasterio de El Escorial* (Madrid: Aguilar, 1963), 73–74. Workmen building the cathedral of Granada in 1553 also went on strike, winning their demands after a three-day standoff. Rafael Marín López, "El cabildo eclesiástico granadino y las obras de la catedral en el siglo XVI," *Chronica Nova*, no. 22 (1995): 222–223. Stonemasons frequently were itinerant; it is perhaps for that reason that they were included on lists of undesirable types.

as artisans as highly regarded as silversmiths, makes one suspect the rules were not being put into practice. Maureen Flynn found that purity of blood (*limpieza de sangre*) was required in noble and clerical confraternities but not in popular ones, which led her to question the plebeian origins for pressures for limpieza. On the contrary, she said, "the common people were exceptional in upholding in their admissions' procedures their professed aspiration to promote harmony among all Christians."[143] What was true for religious confraternities was also true of craft guilds. Though requirements of limpieza and an ancestry clean of vile or mechanical trades began appearing in Castilian guild ordinances in the eighteenth century (they existed earlier in Valencia or Catalonia), examples from the sixteenth or seventeenth century are so rare that it is safe to say they practically did not exist. In one of the very few cases I have found, the *cordoneros* of Zaragoza in 1550 specified that no master could employ an apprentice who was a Moor, a Jew, or a slave.[144] Exclusion based on blood was not, however, the same as that based on occupational ancestry. The former was more prevalent in general, it was more prevalent in the eighteenth century than earlier, and it was vastly more important to the elite professions than to humble people.

Nonetheless, membership bars are simply assumed to have been there, always and everywhere. Maravall, for example, in an essay in an anthology devoted to studying exclusion in Spain, affirmed:

> If, since the society of orders began, the poor worker was excluded from the distinction, dignity, and riches that brought honor in the first modern centuries, it is easy to show he also was subject to a form of *marginación* that worsened his already sad situation. Moreover, he was attributed with explicit, regulated, formalized dishonor, a legal dishonor that affected not only the vile occupations but to some degree all of them, because the worker was confused with the poor and vice-ridden, with the *miserable* from whom he should remain distant, he was seen as a possible and even presumed delinquent.[145]

The assumption of such exclusion, of "formalized dishonor," comes from an overly close reading of treatises, which most often condemned such practices. Treatise writers' defense of the lowest craftsmen could suggest many things: that they were arguing with prior writers, not protesting an

---

[143] Maureen Flynn, *Sacred Charity: Confraternities and Social Welfare in Spain, 1400–1700* (Ithaca, N.Y.: Cornell University Press, 1989), 23.

[144] AHN CS libro 3958, cap. 22.

[145] José Antonio Maravall, "Trabajo y exclusión: El trabajador manual en el sistema social español de la primera modernidad," in *Les problèmes de l'exclusion en Espagne (XVI–XVII siècles)*, ed. Augustín Redondo (Paris: Publications de la Sorbonne, 1983), 144. The very fact that there are anthologies (this is not the only one) devoted to exclusionary practices is indicative of the historiographic problem.

actual state of affairs; or that exclusion did exist but they believed it was not indicative of a character trait among Castilians that prized ephemeral status over the common good; or that it did exist and they believed it was indeed indicative of character but was the fault of outsiders, generally the French or (in the case of eighteenth-century writers) the Hapsburgs. In short, these are difficult witnesses. On the one hand, working with one's hands supposedly was the basis for social punishment; on the other, it was cause for praise, adulation, and gratitude. The very vocabulary of exclusion and labor—*trabajo, vil, mecánico, bajo*—meant different things to different people. The social vocabulary of the nobility in early modern Spain, I. A. A. Thompson has written, was entirely incoherent; the same was true for the lower end of the spectrum.[146] Exclusionary discourse could help define boundaries for whatever reason, sometimes with great success, but it was not necessarily descriptive of worth any more than the language of poverty necessarily described need, though both were sometimes the case.[147] Nor did it mean that vertical mobility was out of the question, though it might take one or two generations. Blaming Castile's questionable disdain for labor on the old barriers against noble businessmen, a unique affinity for sloth, or a ranking system that identified both those occupations off-limits to the better sort and those craftsmen off-limits to good society is not a fruitful line of argument. Assumptions regarding hurdles waiting to be breached, rules deserving to be cast asunder, and dignity ripe to be restored are, I believe, part of a narrative that has less to do with how working people actually lived, labored, and spoke that it does with how their history was subsequently written.

[146] Thompson, "Hidalgo and Pechero," 57. Spaniards were equally sloppy with jurisdictional definitions: *sala, comisión,* or *junta* all could refer to the same entity. The languages of honor, reputation, law, and custom also were confused.

[147] Velázquez's decade-long effort to join the Order of Santiago is an instructive example of the language of vileness being used to thwart upward social mobility. The artist had to declare he painted solely to please the king, not to earn a living, and his petition required two papal dispensations before prospering. See Jonathan Brown, *Images and Ideas in Seventeenth-Century Spanish Painting* (Princeton University Press, 1978), 103–110.

PART TWO

LAS LUCES

Prologue

WORK IN THE EIGHTEENTH CENTURY

The seventeenth century and Charles II's reign ended with a wave of disturbances triggered by poor harvests, high prices, unemployment, and devaluation. The so-called Oropesa Riot in Madrid, named after the first minister, Manuel Joaquín García Alvarez de Toledo, count of Oropesa, began on 28 April 1699 after the prices of meat, oil, and bread all rose. Protesters marched to the royal palace, demanded that the corregidor be sacked, and attacked Oropesa's house. Several were killed when troops fired on the crowd. Silk workers and members of other guilds in Toledo, meanwhile, knowing of the Madrid riots, wrote the corregidor in July that they could not go on:

> When we see what little or nothing is achieved by the Poor man who, after intolerable labor to earn his money can do nothing with it, not even fill himself with bread, which is the greatest calamity to befall the poor in this life . . . no one should be surprised if, in order to prevent such misfortune, he were to use all those means allowed him by natural law, and even those that are not. The People, sire, does not mean to become enraged nor cause disturbances or scandal, although it has a great example in Madrid, because the people of Toledo bears its suffering and is obedient.[1]

Though historians' longtime assumption that the late seventeenth-century economy was stagnant appears to have been exaggerated, life was not easy for those who worked with their hands, and in many ways the econ-

---

[1] AHM CS leg. 7225, doc. 65. 14 July 1699. The corregidor managed to placate the guilds.

omy was profoundly unhealthy. Landownership in much of the country was highly concentrated and would remain so until the twentieth century. Those who might want to buy land were halted by myriad restrictions including municipal and church ownership, noble entailment, common access, and special jurisdictions.[2] Infrastructure was lacking, and production was dispersed and ill-equipped to compete with foreign manufactured goods. Spaniards blamed fate and themselves, but above all they blamed foreigners, and particularly the French, whose detestable influence they detected everywhere. French merchants were said to sell Spaniards articles they did not need and could not make, they invested nothing, and then they repatriated their sizable profits. Valencian leaders went to far as to claim in 1684 that "in order to ruin Spain the French have managed with cunning to induce laziness of spirit into Spaniards, to deaden their hands for laborious tasks, and to take from them their money and substance by sending all their wool to France."[3] A *memorial*, probably written in the 1680s, said foreigners "seek the ruin of this kingdom with obsessive malice. Like leeches they suck, squander, and bleed this political body, weakening it and sapping its strength."[4]

Protectionist measures were approved repeatedly in Aragón and Castile throughout the seventeenth century, often at the request of guilds, but mostly they were ignored. The glovers of Zaragoza, for example, filed a petition with Don Juan José of Austria, Charles II's half-brother (and viceroy of Aragón and Catalonia), reminding him that "in times past, when foreign gloves did not enter the kingdom, an infinite number of widows and young ladies and other people were occupied sewing gloves, with which they provided for their homes." The guild complained that imports "undermine the spirits of many journeymen, leading them to shut their shops, and they cheat many other people who work in the said workshops," adding that the French aspired to "destroy the hands of the natives."[5] At the same time, a report urging a renewed ban on imported brocade, silk, wool, and "other diverse and useless merchandise" claimed that in Toledo thousands of men and women, masters and apprentices, once had worked in the silk trade but had been reduced to begging. After a 1678 ban on im-

[2] James Simpson, *Spanish Agriculture: The Long Siesta, 1765–1965* (Cambridge University Press, 1995), 64.
[3] Cited in Henry Kamen, *Spain in the Later Seventeenth Century, 1665–1700* (London: Longman, 1980), 188.
[4] BN VE 180–40.
[5] BN VE 209–145. The document is not dated. Henry Kamen has called Don Juan José, a great military hero, "one of the most significant figures in the history of Habsburg Spain" (*Spain in the Later Seventeenth Century*, 329). In his fight against Queen Mariana, Juan José had his power base in Aragón, and it was from there that he launched his first coup in 1669. Soon after, he retreated to Zaragoza. He launched a second, successful coup in 1677 and died two years later. See also Ignacio de Asso y del Río, *Historia de la economía política de Aragón* (1798)(Zaragoza: CSIC, 1947), 236–239.

ports, artisans had begun recovering, the report said. From just 85 masters the number grew to 158, and the number of looms went from 170 to 790, "and reliable sources even say there were 900." But "today [in 1684] the workshops are back to ruin because the law is not being observed."[6]

The War of the Spanish Succession, which broke out after the death of Charles II, who left no heir, lasted fourteen years, pitting France and Spain against England, the Netherlands, and the Holy Roman Empire. It resulted in the Bourbons, in the person of Philip V, Louis XIV's grandson, taking the Spanish throne from the Hapsburgs. In 1716, after Castile imposed itself on Catalonia, which had supported the losing side, Spain for the first time became a politically united nation. A new dynasty was in place, one of whose objectives was (or would later be presented as) undoing the damage of two hundred years of Hapsburg rule and ruinous imperialism. The ministers of the eighteenth-century Bourbon monarchs—Philip V was followed by Ferdinand VI, Charles III, and Charles IV—all undertook reforms affecting industry, commerce, taxes, labor, social welfare, and trade with America, with varying degrees of success and imagination. At least five nationwide censuses were conducted in the eighteenth century. No longer confident that gold and silver could keep Spain afloat, though it continued arriving on a regular basis at the port of Cádiz, the ministers instead sought advice from experts, both national and foreign, and implemented policies directed by the crown. They advocated a mix of industrial innovation, commercial protectionism, and development projects fueled as much by pragmatism as by enthusiasm for the new economic science.

Among the most important of the economic measures during the waning decades of the Spanish Hapsburgs was an attempt to stimulate industry under the guidance of the Real y General Junta de Comercio, created by royal decree on 29 January 1679. The chief minister at the time was Juan José, who earlier had established a similar organ in Aragón. After several fits and starts, and armed with the 1682 edict declaring nobility to be compatible with industry, the Junta began establishing enterprises throughout Castile, particularly import substitution industries such as textile mills and luxury manufactures. But costs were high, sales were low, infrastructure was still lacking, and skilled tradesmen were scarce. One later crown official, complaining that the Junta was inoperative, wrote that its leaders "had no practice in commerce, had not previously lived in the areas most suited to their mandate, and had not the slightest notion of manufacturers or vendors."[7]

[6] BN VE 203–18.

[7] The count of Torrehermosa, 27 October 1720, in Antonio Valladares de Sotomayor, ed., *Semanario erudito, que comprehende varias obras inéditas, críticas, morales, instructivas, políticas, históricas, satíricas y jocosas, de nuestros mejores autores antiguos y modernos* (Madrid, 1787), vol. 30, 37. In 1730, a few years after Torrehermosa wrote these lines, the Junta was reorganized

Though it was explicitly granted independence at least twice during the reign of Charles II, throughout its existence the Junta continually fought with the Council of Castile for jurisdiction over guilds and commerce, with the Council insisting, in language recalling earlier guild litigation, that the guilds were legal corporations subject to the king, not industrial organizations. The dispute was mirrored in the sometimes ill-defined status of workers; they were still members of the republic and vassals of the king fulfilling their obligation to the common good, but they also began being referred to as *individuos* whose hands had the potential to create objects that would result in wealth. Efforts by the Junta to exert its authority over guilds were further torpedoed by the guilds themselves, which resented and often resisted such measures as prohibiting one guild from selling another's products or interfering with their ability to inspect products for sale, both of which resulted in litigation. Later in the eighteenth century, the Junta frequently advised the monarchs to simply eliminate guild ordinances deemed unnecessary.

We have seen that seventeenth-century artisans often described themselves as poor and that many complained their craft was endangered because of poaching by competitors and because of hard times in general. Though guilds were hardly as rigid as they were later described by reformers and historians, it is clear that examination fees and overhead costs prevented many journeymen from ever becoming masters. As markets collapsed, many were unable to work at all.[8] Merchants and rich masters gradually gained control over production in many urban sectors, making it impossible for guilds to guarantee their members supplies or employment, and many artisans ended up unemployed or as wage-earning employees.

This, very roughly, was the situation when Pedro Rodríguez de Campomanes (1723–1802), *fiscal* of the Council of Castile and later count of Campomanes and one of the key figures of the Spanish Enlightenment, in

for at least the fourth time: William J. Callahan, "A Note on the Real y General Junta de Comercio, 1679–1814," *The Economic History Review* 21 (December 1968): 519–528. Catalan merchant networks were able to take advantage of many of the structural inadequacies of regional Castilian markets during the eighteenth century: see Jaume Torras, "The Old and the New: Marketing Networks and Textile Growth in Eighteenth-Century Spain," in *Markets and Manufacture in Early Industrial Europe*, ed. Maxine Berg (London: Routledge, 1991), 93–113. See also José A. Nieto Sánchez, "'Nebulosas industriales' y capital mercantil urbano: Castilla la Nueva y Madrid, 1750–1850," *Sociología del Trabajo*, nueva época, no. 39 (Spring 2000): 85–109, for an interesting discussion of rural industrial efforts in New Castile, largely operated by women, whose very success was key in preventing the implantation of larger mercantile efforts.

[8] Many recipients of charity at Madrid's Santa y Real Hermandad del Refugio were unemployed artisans, though their exact occupation was rarely noted. Callahan estimated that in 1783 a carpenter would have spent 20 percent of his earnings on bread and an unskilled laborer 40 percent. See William Callahan, *La Santa y Real Hermandad del Refugio y Piedad de Madrid, 1618–1832* (Madrid: CSIC, 1980), 109, 15.

1765 successfully urged the crown to lift price controls on grain and implement a degree of commercial freedom. Predictably, especially as they followed an infusion of specie from America, the measures led to inflation. In March 1766 a wave of riots took place throughout the country, chief among them the so-called Esquilache riot in Madrid, recently termed "perhaps the most important political event in eighteenth-century Spain." Charles III, who had assumed the throne in 1759, responded to the disturbances with carrots and sticks, mostly the latter, applied by his newly named chief minister, the count of Aranda.[9]

Campomanes, whose interests and activities ranged widely, published two tracts on labor—*Discurso sobre el fomento de la industria popular* (1774) and *Discurso sobre la educación popular de los artesanos* (1775)—as disorganized as they are famous.[10] His overriding aims, to encourage rural industry and instill what we might call a work ethic, confronted two obstacles: the alleged dishonor of many crafts, and the guilds themselves. In the latter, he chose an easy foe. Philip V in 1703, possibly to reinforce economic stability, had issued an edict requiring all artisans to belong to a guild, indicating many did not.[11] The barriers they posed to industrial development may have existed once (though less than is assumed), but they certainly had disappeared by the late eighteenth century.[12] Nonetheless, Campomanes urged that guild ordinances, which for him and his supporters epitomized the particularist and noxious nature of corporative au-

[9] The riots were named for Leopoldo de Gregorio, marqués de Esquilache, the Italian (né Squillace) minister responsible for the grain policy and other economic reforms. See Stanley J. Stein and Barbara H. Stein, *Apogee of Empire: Spain and New Spain in the Age of Charles III, 1759–1789* (Baltimore: Johns Hopkins University Press, 2003), 81–115, for a brilliant dissection of the riots, which the authors describe as a "ritual mobilization of elites under stress" orchestrated by dissident sectors of the Council of Castile opposed to the reforms. The Steins also describe Campomanes's crucial role in blaming the uprising on the Jesuits, who were shortly expelled from Spain and the colonies. Also on the riots, see Jacinta Macías Delgado, ed., *El motín de Esquilache a la luz de los documentos* (Madrid: Centro de Estudios Constitucionales, 1988). See Francisco Sánchez-Blanco, *El Absolutismo y las Luces en el reinado de Carlos III* (Madrid: Marcial Pons, 2002), for a critical look at Charles III and the impact and content of the reforms implemented during his reign. In a similar vein, see the essays in Equipo Madrid, ed., *Carlos III, Madrid y la Ilustración* (Madrid: Siglo Veintiuno, 1988).

[10] Pedro Rodríguez de Campomanes, *Discurso sobre la educación popular*, ed. F. Aguilar Piñal (Madrid: Editora Nacional, 1978); and *Discurso sobre el fomento de la industria popular* (Madrid, 1774). On Campomanes, see Concepción Castro, *Campomanes: Estado y reformismo ilustrado* (Madrid: Alianza Editorial, 1996); Vicent Llombart, *Campomanes, economista y político de Carlos III* (Madrid: Alianza Universidad, 1992); and Laura Rodríguez Díaz, *Reforma e ilustración en la España del Siglo XVIII: Pedro Rodríguez de Campomanes* (Madrid: Fundación Universitaria Española, 1975). For an admiring contemporary bibliographic sketch, see Juan Sempere y Guarinos, *Ensayo de una biblioteca española de los mejores escritores del reynado de Carlos III*, vol. 2 (Madrid: Impr. Real, 1785), 42–107.

[11] *Novísima Recopilación*, libro 8, ley 5, tit. 23.

[12] However, Nieto argues that in rural areas the guilds (or their remnants) successfully collaborated with local industrial efforts to halt larger enterprises: Nieto Sánchez, "'Nebulosas industriales.'"

thority over labor, be rewritten, though the content of those ordinances often was unknown to him or misunderstood. His criticisms, in short, responded to material reality to the same degree as royal edicts on labor and vile occupations were based on prevailing prejudice or practice.

The first European monarch to abolish guilds was Prince Pierre Leopold of Tuscany, who issued his decree on 3 February 1770. He was followed by Turgot in 1775, though the measure in France was immediately made meaningless by the minister's dismissal (but reimposed in 1791). Joseph II abolished the Austrian guilds in 1786. Spain would have to wait until 26 May 1790, although it is essential to keep in mind that abolitions and enactments in early modern Spain often meant very little in practice. Spokesmen for change, both inside and outside the Spanish royal court, were united in their commitment to economic recovery but did not all agree on what to do about the guilds. Some, such as Campomanes, who was less concerned by restraints on freedom than with impediments to production and competition with the crown, suggested reforming them but allowing them to survive, replacing one sort of control with another. Others, such as Antonio de Capmany and Francisco Romá i Rosell, defended guilds. Both, not coincidentally, were Catalans. Romá i Rosell, in whose opinion Catalonia had prospered precisely because of its guild protections, admitted that European public opinion was not on his side. But opponents of guilds generally pointed to aberrations in their operations, not general practice, he said, adding for good measure that anti-guild arguments in the rest of Europe were anyway inapplicable to a country whose products could not possibly compete on the open market.[13] His countryman Capmany was the author of an eloquent appeal in 1778 "in defense of mechanical labor." He saw guilds as civic instruments, "organs of harmony" that offered working people a sphere of political action and existence, a way of understanding their own interests and behaving like citizens. It was not the *art* of silversmithing that afforded honor, he said, but rather the silversmiths *guild;* and if work had acquired a bad reputation, only the guilds could restore it. They also protected artisans from the cruelties of the market: "Where this political and productive system of crafts is lacking, all arts are daughters of the moment or of chance; one plague, one war, one bad harvest, and not a trace of industry remains." He went on: "The solitary artisan, dispersed or itinerant, neither calculates nor plans nor fears. He hears and understands nothing, he takes his work, suffers and is mute, because he does not

---

[13] Francisco Romá i Rosell, *Las señales de la felicidad de España y medios de hacerlas eficaces* (Madrid, 1768), 162. Though such an argument would land him in a typical contradiction (both defending and attacking guilds), Campomanes noted admiringly that prosperity in Catalonia was due in large part to the honor afforded to the manual trades (*Discurso sobre el fomento de la industria popular,* 68n4). Observations on Castile's and Catalonia's differing economic aptitudes were a commonplace.

know where the work comes from and because he has no representation, or power, or means to be heard."[14]

The usual reasons for getting rid of guilds, as put forth already in 1762 by Bernardo Ward, a royal adviser, were that they caused useless expense by artisans, closed the doors to outsiders, discouraged ambition, and impeded progress: "The spirit that generally prevails in these bodies is that of vanity, idleness (*ociosidad*), and monopoly," Ward wrote, adding, "they are against liberty."[15] Gaspar Melchor de Jovellanos (1744–1811), generally regarded the greatest thinker of the Spanish Enlightenment, was in favor of abolishing them altogether; like Adam Smith, he saw them as impositions on workers' free disposition of their labor power and the cause of higher prices, monopoly, and urban advantage over smaller towns. Unlike Smith (but like Campomanes), he favored some state control.

The new arbiters of production, in Campomanes's vision, would be the Sociedades Económicas, also called the Amigos del País or Patriotic Societies. Their predecessors were groups of noblemen and clergymen who began meeting informally to study science, cultural affairs, and economics. In the Basque town of Azcoitia, for example, such a group was gathering every night of the week already in 1748: Mondays were devoted to mathematics, Tuesdays to physics, Wednesdays to history, Thursdays and Sundays to concerts, Fridays to geography, and Saturdays to current events.[16] The first Economic Society was established in 1765 when a group of Basque noblemen, inspired by the French physiocrats, obtained permission from the king to form a society to "cultivate the inclination and taste of the Basque Nation toward the Sciences, Letters, and Arts; correct and polish its customs; abolish idleness and ignorance and their calamitous consequences;

[14] Antonio de Capmany [Ramón Miguel Palacio, pseud.], *Discurso político económico . . .* (1778) (Madrid: Almarabu, 1986) 48, 51. A nearly identical essay by Capmany, "Discurso político económico sobre la influencia de los gremios en el estado, en las costumbres populares, en las artes, y en los mismos artesanos," was published in *Semanario erudito, que comprehende varias obras inéditas, críticas, morales, instructivas, políticas, históricas, satíricas y jocosas, de nuestros mejores autores antiguos y modernos,* ed. Antonio Valladares de Sotomayor (1787), vol. 10, 172–224. Despite the date, the historian Fernando Díez believes the latter essay was a first draft of the former. See Fernando Díez, "El gremialismo de Antonio de Capmany (1742–1813). La idea del trabajo de un conservador ingénuo," *Historia y política: Ideas, procesos y movimientos sociales,* no. 5 (2001/1). Capmany also wrote an economic history, *Memorias históricas sobre la Marina, Comercio y Artes de la antigua ciudad de Barcelona,* in 1779. He was close to the Junta de Comercio, a member of the Royal Academy of History, and later a representative in the Cortes of Cádiz. He dedicated the *Discurso* to Campomanes, "who has put in movement innumerable hands once idle."

[15] Bernardo Ward, *Proyecto económico en que se proponen varias providencias, dirigidas a promover los intereses de España con los medios y fondos necesarios para su plantificación* (1762) (Madrid, posth. 1779), 190–191. Ward (d. 1779), a native of Ireland, was a member of the Council of Castile and the Junta de Comercio and director of the San Ildefonso glass factory.

[16] Manuel Dánvila y Collado, *Reinado de Carlos III* (Madrid: Real Academia de la Historia, 1894), vol. 6, 401. Also cited in Jean Sarrailh, *La España Ilustrada de la segunda mitad del siglo XVIII* (Mexico City: Fondo de Cultura Económica, 1985), 231.

and solidify the union of the three Basque provinces of Alava, Vizcaya, and Guipúzcoa."[17] Madrid's organization was founded in 1775. By the end of the 1780s, there were around sixty nationwide, in all major towns and cities with the notable exception of Barcelona. Most would not survive the decade.[18] The societies, whose members were usually educated and often noblemen, set up "patriotic schools" for children, artisans, women, and farmers; sponsored experimentation with new agricultural techniques; published works on industries and crafts; invited foreign experts to help local efforts; and offered prizes for essays and technological advances.

The societies form a crucial component of the celebratory view of the reign of Charles III and the men whom Spanish historians call the *ilustrados*. Benjamin Franklin, then living in Paris, was aware of their development and arranged to receive their reports.[19] In the words of Capmany, the societies would "surely confirm the famous Republic of Plato, where philosopher peoples are governed by philosophers."[20] For one Madrid participant, they were "the stairway along which the tears of the poor can reach the throne."[21] Their name, Amigos del País, spoke of their dedication to the common good: "The Basque Society of Amigos del País is a patriotic body united with the only goal of serving the Patria and the State by perfecting Agriculture, encouraging Industry and extending Commerce."[22] In Zaragoza the objective was to "give whatever occupation possible to the voluntary vagabonds, ociosos, and beggars who are the ruin of the Republic."[23] Far to the south, "the object of the Patriotic Society of Jeréz will be the same as that of the Kingdom's other [societies]: its tasks,

[17] Cited in Sarrailh, *La España Ilustrada,* 242.

[18] Madrid's in fact continued at least until 1875, when it celebrated its 100th anniversary, but it appears to have been completely insignificant. Already in 1786 the crown asked Jovellanos to write a report on the "decadence" of the societies. See "Dictamen," in Gaspar Melchor de Jovellanos, *Obras,* vol. 2, ed. Cándido Nocedal, Biblioteca de Autores Españoles, vol. 50 (Madrid, 1859), 57. In 1789, Juan Sempere y Guarinos, though calling the establishment of the societies one of the "most notable and glorious events" of Charles III's reign, also expressed disappointment that they had not done more, for which he blamed members' personal ambition, partisan judges, city councils, and, especially, priests (*Ensayo de una biblioteca española de los mejores escritores del reynado de Carlos III,* vol. 5, 135–151).

[19] Franklin's correspondent in Madrid, William Carmichael, who was John Jay's secretary, sent the reports to Paris with a French official in October 1781. In January 1782, Franklin told Carmichael he in turn would send Campomanes a copy of the transactions of the American Philosophical Society; Campomanes was elected a member in 1784. See *The Papers of Benjamin Franklin,* ed. Leonard W. Laboree, vols. 34–36 (New Haven: Yale University Press, 1998–2001).

[20] A (then) unpublished piece, cited in Sarrailh, *La España Ilustrada,* 233. I do not know if it has been published since.

[21] Manuel de Aguirre, cited in Elena Maza Zorrilla, *Pobreza y asistencia social en España* (Universidad de Valladolid, 1987), 101.

[22] Cited in Sempere y Guarinos, *Ensayo de una biblioteca española de los mejores escritores del reynado de Carlos III,* vol. 5, 160.

[23] Cited in José Alvarez Junco, "La Sociedad Aragonesa de Amigos del País en el siglo XVIII," *Revista de Occidente,* no. 69 (December 1968): 304.

labors, and projects will be devoted to nothing other than public happiness [and to populate] the Patria with useful inhabitants."[24] To be useful was to be happy. To be happy was to be prosperous and productive. "I do not use happiness in a moral sense," Jovellanos said, explaining his choice of words in a speech. "I understand it here as that state of abundance and comfort to which all good government and its individuals should aspire."[25] Implicit in the reformers' words was the link between enlightenment (*luces*) and labor.

The language and social relationships of labor I traced in part 1 had survived more or less intact; to misquote Locke, the eighteenth-century Enlightenment's voice was that of reason confirmed by inspiration.[26] The old republic guided by moral considerations met up with new economic demands in the context of a monarchy equipped with new political tools. The adjustment would be made by zealous reformers wielding a new vocabulary. Or would it? Perhaps the old was not quite as rigid as it appeared, and perhaps the new was not quite as innovative as it has been described. Policy makers, after all, came from a political culture with a long tradition of resisting *novedades*.

[24] Article 1 of the society's statutes, in Manuel Ruiz Lagos, *Historia de la Sociedad Económica de Amigos del País de Xerez de la Frontera* (Jerez de la Frontera: Centro de Estudios Históricos Jerezanos, 1972), 17; report, 1 October 1786.

[25] "Discurso sobre los medios de promover la felicidad del principado," in *Obras*, vol. 2, 439.

[26] John Locke, "Of Property," *The Second Treatise of Government.* (New York: Bobbs-Merrill, 1952), 19. Locke was referring here to our self-imposed limits on the use of God's gifts.

CHAPTER THREE

The New Thinking

My primary interest in writing this book is to trace what happened to a world and a discourse and how they came to be portrayed. In this second part I start by looking at aspects of three things—craft, the law, and the market—in the seventeenth and eighteenth centuries, setting words from the two eras alongside one another to find attitudes in the earlier period that later were deemed inadequate or harmful. I cannot pretend to present a comprehensive view of eighteenth-century Spanish thought, whose influence I suggest altered the perspective of modern Spanish historiography. The two sets of words from the seventeenth and eighteenth centuries do not always mesh nicely or even correspond to one another, and there are times one drowns out the other. But because these notions of science, law, and the economy were fundamental to reformers' explanations for the need to change work practices, and because those very same notions were proudly proclaimed and defended by the artisans whose practices, lifestyle, and organizations had become the source of such shame, they seem to be good places from which to examine the shift.

It is a truth undisputed in Spanish historiography that the value of labor and of those who performed it underwent an irrevocable transformation in the later eighteenth century both in word and in fact. One of the most convenient dividing lines separating the traditional from the modern was the publication of Campomanes's two pamphlets on labor and the attempt to implement policies in accordance with the new ideas. From then on, people would be put to work in the name of national progress. It should be clear by now that I believe this view reflects two important misunderstandings. First, labor before what Richard Herr called the eighteenth-century revolution was performed (or was supposed to be performed) with the same civic spirit that the *ilustrados* and their historians claimed as their creation and discovery. The common good and public utility were not children of the Enlightenment. Second, labor after that dividing line was no more dignified—in fact, it was a great deal less so for many people. The base of the republic was still getting stepped on, only without the small comfort of living in a world that saluted its crucial and even blessed function. Additionally, the practical reforms reflecting the new ideas were largely ineffective, though that is not necessarily a statement of the sincerity or wisdom of the ideas behind them.[1] Nonetheless, the language of discovery has survived, and in order to understand how work in early modern Spain came to be interpreted, we must take the reformers at their word. In rejecting the old forms of labor and labor's place in the commonwealth, the Spanish Enlightenment essentially created its own past.

Science and Perfection

There was no treatise, no lawsuit, no petition that did not proclaim utility to be the final judge of the worth of artisans, vendors, and their products. This was true both in the seventeenth century and in the eighteenth, though the word would acquire slightly new connotations in the latter era, a time of "the cult of utility."[2] "The more useful, the more honorable," wrote the Spanish intellectual considered to have been the first to promote the new forms of thinking, Benito Jerónimo Feijóo. He went on: "I venerate for his own sake and for his own merit he who serves the Republic usefully, be he illustrious or humble; and likewise I venerate the occupation with which he serves the Republic, gauging my appreciation by its utility."[3]

The common good was infinitely more important than private gain in the early modern era, and craftsmen tried to justify whatever it was they were doing (or not doing) by pointing to its utility and the degree to which it contributed to the common good. After the terrible plague of 1650, which particularly affected southern Spain, Madrid's shoemakers were unable to travel to Seville to buy leather, and the tanners had taken advan-

---

[1] Here I address the reformers only insofar as they talked about labor. I do not analyze their more general diagnoses of Spain's problems or the success or failure of their policies on manufacturing and trade.

[2] Jean Sarrailh, *La España Ilustrada de la segunda mitad del siglo XVIII* (Mexico City: Fondo de Cultura Económica, 1985), 182.

[3] Benito Jerónimo Feijóo, "Honra y provecho de la agricultura," in *Teatro Crítico Universal*, vol. 8, discurso XII (1739), ed. Giovanni Stiffoni (Madrid: Clásicos Castalia, 1986). In the same essay, the Benedictine monk and academic made the remarkable suggestion that *labradores* from around Spain gather at the royal court to offer their opinions on how to promote agriculture.

tage of the shortage to raise their prices. Vendors, who were authorized to sell only to certain people at certain times, petitioned to have these limits extended because "it is useful and advantageous to the public good that [sellers] at all hours, seven days a week, be allowed to sell soles and leather in their shops, particularly for the poor."[4] Earlier in the century, Madrid shoemakers punished for repairing shoes in their shops insisted that "making and working on shoes in workshops is of great use and advantage to the republic because of all the work there is."[5] Likewise, pastry chefs, it will be recalled, said that multiple (and illegal) shops were "very useful and advantageous for the provisioning of the republic and for the republic's good government, because the more stores there are the more abundance there is and costs will go down and journeymen and masters will benefit and sell more."[6] Utility, then, was associated with lots of business, the more the better, and especially with businesses that catered to the poor.

In the hands of early modern moralists, utility often evoked simplicity, a value once prized but now sadly lacking. This was particularly obvious in sumptuary legislation. The lamentation over the "disorder" arising from the multiplication of allegedly frivolous occupations devoted to conspicuous consumption is reminiscent of treatises that extolled old-time hard labor in the fields. In his defense of price controls on bread, for example, Melchor de Soria railed against fancy clothing, "which not only costs a great deal but makes men weak, and they flee from working the fields and dedicate themselves to easier, less necessary occupations in the republic."[7] Don Quixote, lecturing goat herders on the bygone Golden Age, yearned for a time when village girls wore just what they needed, when silk had not become a martyr to fashion, and when idle curiosity did not drive women to wear "strange and peculiar inventions."[8] This no-frills approach was exemplified by Marco Antonio de Camós, writing in 1592: "By chance did the old breeches [*calzas*] of forty or fifty years ago, smooth and close to the skin, not cover and protect without forty inventions? If one bolt of taffeta

---

[4] AHN CS Libro 1236, January–February 1651. Cervantes echoed the "useful and advantageous" (*util y provechoso*) mantra in "Rinconete y Cortadillo" when Rinconete comments on Cortadillo's ability to use scissors well. See *Novelas Ejemplares* (Madrid: Espasa Calpe, 1996), vol. 1, 211.

[5] AHN CS Libro 1200, 21 January 1610. The five defendants further said they couldn't survive on their work alone and could not afford a proper shop. Rich masters, they said, had engineered their arrest.

[6] AHN CS Libro 1214, April 1629.

[7] Melchor de Soria, *Tratado de la justificación y conveniencia de la tassa de el pan* (1627), ed. Francisco Gómez Camacho (Madrid: Fundación Banco Exterior, 1992), 95. A frequent complaint about fancy dress and excess in general was that it made men effeminate, an argument originating with the Romans, for whom luxury signified personal over civic interest. See Christopher J. Berry, *The Idea of Luxury: A Conceptual and Historical Investigation* (Cambridge University Press, 1994), chap. 3.

[8] Miguel de Cervantes, *El ingenioso hidalgo Don Quijote de la Mancha*, vol. 1, chap. 11.

was sufficient then for the fanciest *calzas*, then why do we need four or five today?" The excess, not only in clothes but in the guilds that produced them, was such that the poor Augustinian prior was forced to admit that "the Moors and the Turks appear more sensible to me in this matter, as they never change their fashions."[9] Aristotle surely would have applauded the recent *pragmáticas*, he concluded.

In an admission that Charles V's and his own edicts had been ineffective, Philip II in 1593 offered a sort of amnesty, along the lines of inner-city gun exchanges, saying men would have until the following year to turn in their prohibited outfits, with an extra year tacked on for women. Soon afterward, Philip III banned a long list of trimmings on furniture, carriages, and windows, and he also prohibited elaborate jewelry and silver-work so that "our subjects not spend their money on superficial and excessive things but rather save for useful and necessary things."[10] The monarchs' ceaseless campaign may have had economic motivations, as they said, but the cost of decorative velvet and silk trim was not pushing Spain into bankruptcy. Such faulty reasoning in fact would have dire consequences for certain sectors of the economy. In Seville, six hundred silk workers were laid off in the wake of a sumptuary law in 1648 described by Antonio Domínguez Ortiz as a "calamity."[11] Among the chief targets of the sumptuary laws were the *pasamaneros*, the decorative braid or passementerie makers, and the *cordoneros*, who did similar work, especially on hats, and who eventually merged with the hatters after much litigation. In 1600 there were 12 *pasamanero* masters in Madrid, and in 1618 there were 120.[12] According to the guild, it had 160 masters and journeymen in 1625, who had lots of work decorating clothing and other things, but membership had shrunk to just 40 in 1640, in part because of sumptuary laws.[13] A prohibition in February 1623 on elaborate collar work by *pasamaneros* and embroiderers caused "shock" in the court, a chronicler reported, adding that few had dared expose themselves to public humiliation by venturing outdoors with their skimpy neckwear. The crown must want to entomb women in their houses, the writer surmised. The following month, in honor of the Prince of Wales's visit to the capital, the prohibition was lifted.[14]

Proponents of sumptuary laws pointed to the uselessness of the items produced and, by extension, of those who made them. If artisans themselves

---

[9] Marco Antonio de Camós, *Microcosmia y govierno universal del hombre christiano* (Barcelona, 1592), 224–225.

[10] "Pragmática y nueva orden cerca de las colgaduras de casas . . . ," 3 January 1611.

[11] Antonio Domínguez Ortiz, *Alteraciones andaluzas* (Madrid: Narcea, 1973), 98.

[12] AHN CS Libro 1514. As with all guild lists, these numbers are not entirely reliable.

[13] AV 3.420.1. The decline was reported in response to a military levy the guild wanted to avoid, so it probably was exaggerated.

[14] Antonio de León, "Noticias de Madrid," BN ms 2395.

identified their contribution to the common good by pointing to the objects they made, then I think it is fair to implicate the worth of the artisans in the condemnation of luxury goods. For critics, labor and the products of labor had a purpose that had been made a mockery of. Craft had become synonymous with excess; it had abandoned its mission of providing useful and necessary things for the republic's inhabitants and instead had become part of the vice so antithetical to Aristotle's commonwealth of moderation. Even a champion of artisans such as Mateo López Bravo was forced to say, "Following the example of ancient Greece, we must harshly punish the inventor, the manufacturer, the vendor, and the trafficker of new things."[15]

The virtues and drawbacks of luxury were the basis of much debate among eighteenth-century intellectuals, with most *philosophes* deciding that its economic advantages far outweighed its moral dangers. Bernard Mandeville, in *The Fable of the Bees*, famously argued that luxury was the inevitable outcome of prosperity, a bad thing, to be sure, but one that could be controlled by wise government and prudent men. His contemporary, Jean-François Melon, said to have "gallicised Mandeville," in his *Political Essay on Commerce* also pointed to luxury's stimulating and dynamic effects and its creation of wealth and sociability.[16] In Spain, too, there were economists who realized the futility of attacking the trades and who detected science amid the velvet tassles. Miguel Dámaso Generés, for example, in 1793 exemplified the marriage between the late-eighteenth-century enthusiasm for science and the earlier guild culture when he asked:

> In what physical system can we find greater intelligence or more philosophical *luces* or mechanical knowledge than in machines that spin gold and in the looms of *pasamaneros* and silk makers? What more complicated demonstration exists than that resulting from a problem concerning a clock's inner workings? What could be more demanding than making velvet with Chinese flowers?

Generés, an Aragonese Jesuit, also noted the multiplier effects of the luxury trades. Even negative (i.e., unreasonable) repercussions of a passion for wealth "are accompanied by a great good to society because money passes through the hands of everyone," he said.[17] Lorenzo Normante y

---

[15] Mateo López Bravo, *Del rey y de la razon de gobernar* (1627), in *Mateo López Bravo: Un socialista español del siglo XVII,* ed. Henry Mechoulan (Madrid: Editora Nacional, 1977), 260.

[16] Berry, *The Idea of Luxury,* 136, citing A. Strugnell. See also Albert O. Hirschman, *The Passions and the Interests: Political Arguments for Capitalism before Its Triumph* (Princeton University Press, 1997).

[17] Miguel Dámaso Generés, *Reflexiones políticas y económicas sobre la población, agricultura, artes, fábricas y comercio del Reino de Aragón* (1793), ed. Ernest Lluch and Alfonso Sánchez Hormigo (Zaragoza: Institución Fernando el Católico, 1996), 132, 153. Generés (1733–1801) left Spain in 1767 after the expulsion of his order and lived the rest of his life in Italy.

Carcavilla, a prominent member of the Zaragoza Economic Society and a champion of the new secular morality, set off a furor when he not only attacked sumptuary laws but seemingly defended greed and opulence while dismissing controls as attempts "to enchain citizens' liberty."[18] In a calmer fashion, Jovellanos told the Junta de Comercio, "Fashion at every instant is producing new inventions, creating new manufactures, disfiguring old ones, altering their formulas, changing their names, and maintaining in continuous motion not only the hands but also the ingenuity of the industrious. Who is capable of stopping consumers' taste for novelty?"[19]

A member of Madrid's Economic Society, Juan Sempere y Guarinos, wrote a *History of Luxury* that began by stating that luxury, "the use of things not necessary for subsistence *out of vanity or voluptuousness,* is bad; it is a detestable vice." Elsewhere he elaborated: "All excess in the use of pleasures and comforts is bad, no matter how much the philosophy of this century tries to disfigure vice with the mask of virtue, calling gluttony delicacy, profusion sumptuosity, and luxury magnificence." But he also pointed out that banning luxury trades was tantamount to condemning artisans to "idleness and desperation," a problem of particular interest to Sempere y Guarinos, a lawyer, who a few years earlier had won a prize for an essay concluding that the poor were poor because they refused to work. He concluded by saying he did not even have to resort to foreign writers such as Montesquieu, Hume, or Melon to prove his point. Instead, he pointed to Francisco Martínez de la Mata, "an excellent Spanish economist" whose mid-seventeenth-century writings recently had been rediscovered and promoted by Campomanes.[20] Martínez de la Mata's "Fifth Discourse" was entitled "In which it is proved that vassals' and monarchs' excessive and superfluous expenses do not impoverish them; and it is proved that poverty is the result of abusive trade with foreigners."[21]

[18] Lorenzo Normante y Carcavilla, *Discurso sobre la utilidad de los conocimientos Económico-Políticos y la necesidad de su estudio metódico. Proposiciones de Economía Civil y Comercio. Espíritu del Señor Melón en su Ensayo político sobre el Comercio* (1786), ed. Antonio Peiró Arroyo (Zaragoza: Diputación General de Aragón, 1984); and William Callahan, "Utility, Material Progress and Morality in 18th Century Spain," in *The Triumph of Culture: 18th Century Perspectives* (Toronto: A. M. Hakkert, 1972), ed. Paul Fritz and David Williams, 362–364.

[19] Gaspar Melchor de Jovellanos, "Informe dado a la Junta General de Comercio y Moneda sobre el libre ejercicio de las artes," in *Obras*, vol. 2, ed. Cándido Nocedal, Biblioteca de Autores Españoles, vol. 50 (Madrid, 1859), 33. His purpose in posing the rhetorical question was to point out the uselessness of craft ordinances.

[20] Juan Sempere y Guarinos, *Historia del luxo y de las leyes suntuarias de España* (Madrid, 1788), vol. 1, 22; vol. 2, 19; vol. 2, 9; vol. 2, chap. 12. Emphasis in the original. He cited Martínez de la Mata's "Memorial en razón del remedio de la despoblación, pobreza y esterilidad . . . ," contained in *Memoriales y discursos de Francisco Martínez de Mata* [*sic*], ed. Gonzalo Anes (Madrid: Editorial Moneda y Crédito, 1971). The Anes collection includes Campomanes's comments on Martínez de la Mata, which also had been published as an appendix to Campomanes's *Discurso sobre la educación popular.*

[21] Martínez de la Mata, *Memoriales y discursos,* 137.

Campomanes himself often seemed confused about the utility of crafts, or even what he meant by utility, though it usually had more to do with material satisfaction than with social harmony, more with usefulness than with goodness. Utility in his hands usually implied prosperity and, especially, activity, but he exhibited as much concern for Christian rectitude as he did for economics. Indeed, his moralistic pronouncements at times are hardly distinguishable from those of the previous century. The useful poor should be put to work, just as fallow land should be cultivated; political economy was the useful science; the scorn allegedly endured by certain artisans was not useful because it discouraged industry. Luxury goods "provide no utility at all to society and should be banished," he said, but at the same time sumptuary laws harmed local trades and destroyed craftsmen. The solution was to ban the consumption of luxury goods, but not their production, a compromise reflecting new notions of trade.[22]

In their frequent visits to courtrooms, artisans proclaimed the utility and the artistry of their craft, which they did not see as mutually exclusive, and they often also pointed to its transformations, the results of learning and innovation. They drew links between the products they made, their possession of the skills necessary for producing them, and the well-being of the republic that consumed them.

One guild that left frequent tracks through legal records was that of the tailors, the *sastres*. In Madrid they were the dominant craft; in 1625, there were some 280 in the capital. (According to José Nieto's calculations, the trade reached a peak in mid-century, with 368 masters, by 1706 was back to 298, and then rose again to reach 420 in 1757.)[23] But tailors' litigiousness was more than a question of their numbers; it reflected mounting subdivision of the clothing trades in the seventeenth century. The number of occupations exceeded the number of guilds, and guilds scrambled to keep up. Depending on the city, there could be organizations of tailors, hosiers, secondhand-clothing dealers, hatters, hat trimmers, embroiderers, stocking makers, cape makers, cap makers, hood makers, doublet makers, braid makers, ribbon makers, and jerkin makers. As more tasks were delineated and more garments invented, more lawsuits were filed over who could make what and who could inspect whose shops. Rulings often were con-

[22] Pedro Rodríguez de Campomanes, *Discurso sobre la educación popular,* ed. F. Aguilar Piñal (Madrid: Editora Nacional, 1978), 56, 198–200. He perhaps was thinking of the Dutch, whose capacity to make luxury goods and sell them to others also was remarked upon admiringly by the English (Berry, *The Idea of Luxury,* 107).

[23] José A. Nieto Sánchez, "Labour, Capital and the Structure of the Textile Industry in Seventeenth-century Madrid," in *Occupational Titles and Their Classification: The Case of the Textile Trade in Past Times,* ed. Herman Diederiks and Marjan Balkestein (Göttingen: Max Planck Institut, 1995), 217–229. See also María del Carmen González Muñoz, "Datos para un estudio de Madrid en la primera mitad del siglo XVII," *Anales del Instituto de Estudios Madrileños* 18 (1981): 149–185, for a study based on the same sources.

tradictory, something that did not escape the notice of the latest weary court to inherit the disputes. Earlier, we looked at litigation between Segovia's tailors and hosiers as each used custom and law to their advantage. Now let us return to those guilds, still fighting over the right to make breeches, to see how they each understood the development of their respective craft.[24]

In the summer of 1623, Madrid's hosiers provided an appeals court with a list of nine questions they would put to their witnesses, who numbered around thirty. The hosiers were hoping the weight of custom would help overturn a 1597 verdict that had gone against them. Did the witness know, for example, that, notwithstanding that prior verdict, "for ten, twenty, thirty, forty, fifty, sixty, one hundred and more years, and for so long that no man can remember the contrary, the occupation of hosier in all ways has been and is distinct from that of tailors, the latter occupying themselves with the waist up, and the former with the waist down?" Did they know that "for the sake of the best government of the Republic and the most appropriate (*más político*) attire, it is all for the best and necessary that only hosiers make *calzones?*"

Many of the witnesses were remarkably old, if not the better to remember, at least the more to remember. Pedro de Lucuriaga, who stated his age as one hundred, said he had been a tailor for the past eighty-six years, "and the occupation of hosiers had always been distinct and separate, [and] he had never wanted to take their occupation away because by right it is and was theirs." As in Segovia, one of the points of contention was the making of *greguescos,* and here we see how vulnerable crafts were to changing fashions. Lucuriaga recalled that "Don Juan de Austria, when he returned from Flanders to the court more than forty years ago, brought *la invención de los calzones* and he brought his hosier, who made them and trimmed them, and this witness knew him but cannot remember his name, and after this invention arrived, the first one in [Madrid] to make them was Valmasada, a hosier who lived in Valdara's house." Witness Francisco López, a ninety-two-year-old tailor, also remembered that once Don Juan's hosier began making *greguescos* in Madrid, Valmasada and all the other hosiers followed suit, and he explained that one invention was followed by another. When soldiers returned from the Alpujarras uprising (1568–1570) by the moriscos, for example, they had modified their breeches the better to ride horseback. All these additions and modifications to breeches were and always had been the territory of the hosiers, the witnesses said. Alonso Farina, who was fifty-five, had been working as a doublet maker since he was

---

[24] AHN CS leg. 51.046. Similar disputes between tailors and hosiers occurred in France; see James R. Farr, *Hands of Honor: Artisans and Their World in Dijon, 1550–1650* (Ithaca, N.Y.: Cornell University Press, 1988), 61n173.

thirteen; he said he remembered his father telling him time and again that hosiers and tailors had always been distinct. When he visited tailors' workshops to make his doublets he never saw them cutting breeches, he said. Other witnesses reported that in Valencia and even in Brussels and Antwerp, the jobs also were distinct.

The problem, witnesses agreed, was that fashions had changed and fewer men now were wearing breeches, leaving the hosiers with little to do and unable to support their families. Trousers (*calzas*) at some point in the sixteenth century were divided into two parts: what we would call breeches (*calzones* or *greguescos*), and the lower part, covering the legs (*calcetas*). This was not only a bad thing for the hosiers, the hosiers said; it was a bad thing for everyone. They wrote to the king on 4 December 1622 (their third such petition) telling him they were in dire straits because "in Castile they had always made *calzas* and Your Majesty's grandfather, who is in Heaven, never allowed anyone to speak with him if he was not wearing *calzas*, and when Don Juan de Austria arrived from a naval battle, even though His Majesty was anxious to see him, he would not grant him an audience until he donned *calzas*." Alas, they said, that was no longer the case, for even Philip IV himself no longer wore them, and if within just one year the king were to require *calzas* for a wedding or a fiesta or a baptism, there would be nobody to make them. Despite the hosiers having won verdicts in Valladolid, Segovia, Burgos, Zaragoza, and Valencia, they said, the greedy tailors in Madrid continued elbowing their way onto the territory of others, with the families of more than two hundred hosiers at stake. The tailors, it should be noted, disputed this figure, claiming there were no more than twenty hosiers left in Madrid anyway. (The hosiers in reply produced a notarized list of 149 men.)

Allowing tailors to make breeches not only would ensure poverty for the redundant men, it would be a disservice to the population, according to the hosiers' witnesses, because the tailors didn't know what they were doing. "It is most fitting for the Republic," López said, "that only hosiers make *calzones* because they make them better and more proportioned and with less cloth than the tailors and they are longer-lasting and use fewer pieces, because when a tailor makes them they come out very different and ugly and with many pieces." Furthermore, tailors already were allowed to make a long list of clothing: capes, jerkins, doublets, cassocks, mantillas, and overcoats, to name just a few listed by Philip III's own hosier in a 1611 petition included in the proceedings: "I humbly implore Your Majesty to order the tailors to be content with dressing a man from the belt up, as that gives them plenty to do."

Just as tailors and hosiers fought over how their respective crafts should be defined, so did artisans who worked with metal. One such case pitted the Madrid *doradores,* who gilded weapons and objects of art, against the painters, who didn't consider themselves to be in the same league as other artisans to begin with.[25] In 1613, the gilders began drawing up new ordinances, which they described as "very necessary for the republic and very useful." The ordinances included tasks the painters considered theirs. For reasons unclear to me, the city of Madrid had approved the ordinances but the crown prosecutor had objected, and the issue wound up in court.

The painters' lawyer sued two of the gilders, trying to discredit them at the outset: They were "so-called examiners . . . who call themselves examiners by virtue of ordinances they say were confirmed by Your Highness, and . . . a so-called provision issued by Your Highness." From there it got worse. Did the painters' witnesses know, for example, that one of the gilders' witnesses, Alonso de Avila, "says he is a painter but in fact he just paints the green parts of carriages, which any apprentice can do because it is so simple, besides which he is not even a member of the painters guild and earns very little money because he is distracted and useless and his usual activity is to wander around the capital paying no attention to his job nor showing up at his home, for which reason he is so poor that he cannot support himself?" Did they know that Thomas de Velasco "is no more than a grinder of colors who pesters painters and pharmacists for day work and is everywhere considered an ordinary man of little wealth or understanding?" Did they know that "the occupation of gilder consists of no science, making an examination unnecessary, because it is nothing more than preparing and applying gold, which can be learned very quickly and is such an easy job that anyone could learn it by just watching?" Did they know, in case one wasn't listening, that the art of painting is superior to that of gilding? And that the king employed gilders only if he couldn't get a painter? The gilders, whose ordinances finally were allowed to stand, stood remarkably firm in the face of this artisanal trash talk. It is baseless to say one occupation is superior to another, they replied, once the verdict was in and the two groups were picking away at appeals. "The lawsuit is not about which occupation is better but rather about each one doing his own job."

In Seville a few years later, gilders became entangled with swordmakers, who told the city council in May 1637 they wanted to update their ordinances.[26] Like hosiers and tailors, swordmakers were subject to the vicissitudes of fashion and technique. "As times have changed, with new practices and the continual exercise of the craft, [our] ordinances are lacking and defective with regard to bronzing and burnishing," the guild said. Many techniques were not even mentioned in their rules, making the city inferior to places such as Granada and Murcia, an unusual case of one city admitting its inferiority vis-à-vis another. From now on, they said, sword-

---

[25] AHN CS leg. 24.783.
[26] AMSev Sec. X Actas, escr. 2, tomo 121.

makers should be examined in the arts of burnishing and bronzing "so their work can be as perfect as that to which other parts of these kingdoms are accustomed." It took the gilders less than two weeks to get the news and complain. Burnishing and bronzing, they said, was what they did. The swordmakers' claim that these tasks were by rights theirs "disturbs the said ordinances [of the swordmakers] and confuses one occupation with another. . . . If the swordmakers want to bronze and burnish, they can do so by taking exams administered by the gilding inspectors." The city council took a second look at the swordmakers' petition to change their ordinances and, after a debate, decided to keep them as they were.

These were essentially intellectual property disputes. Eighteenth-century writers would have argued that artisans could not be "in possession" of knowledge because knowledge belonged to everyone equally, but guilds linked their struggle to retain control over their craft precisely with the safeguarding of artistic knowledge. It is not surprising that guilds fought for their economic survival; historians have less often noticed that they perhaps were doing something else as well, and that their struggle was not necessarily opposed to technical progress. Despite Campomanes's frequent assertions that ordinances effectively annulled the possibility for change in crafts, guilds in fact recognized the need to adapt in accordance with fashions and with the influx of new materials and changes in taste.[27] They simply did not wish to grant new markets to their competitors. They invariably based their refusal on utility and the common good, which did not necessarily contradict the economic and scientific principles invoked a century later by the organs effectively appointed to replace them, the Economic Societies.

One of the greatest concerns of eighteenth-century reformers was that Spain was scientifically backward. Campomanes, for one, attributed the problem in part to the multiplicity of guilds, which he said impeded the development of crafts, something that would seem to be disproven by their very multiplicity, which indicated change (albeit at the cost of excessive specialization).[28] José Clavijo y Faxardo (1726–1806), a scientist and the publisher of a 1760s periodical called El Pensador, who also worried that Spain lagged behind, told the story of how Adam decides to return to Earth. He first visits Asia and Africa and recognizes nothing. He then goes to Italy,

[27] "Technical or professional aspects of the arts should not be subject to ordinances because they are continually changing as occupations advance or decline" (Campomanes, Discurso sobre la educación popular, 56, 159).

[28] S. R. Epstein and James Farr also both see the appearance and disappearance of guilds as signs of their capacity to adapt to changing technologies: S. R. Epstein, "Craft Guilds, Apprenticeship, and Technological Change in Preindustrial Europe," in Journal of Economic History 58 (September 1998): 684–713; James R. Farr, "On the Shop Floor: Guilds, Artisans, and the European Market Economy, 1350–1750," Journal of Early Modern History 1 (February 1997): 24–54.

France, England, and Holland and again finds them so different he begins to wonder if God perhaps had created an entirely new Earth. But then he visits Spain, and finally is relieved: "Now this I recognize!" he cried. "It's exactly how it was when I left it!"[29] Though craftsmen might have protested—recall the insult that a particular job was so easy anyone could learn it just by watching—the assumption in the late eighteenth century was that tradition and science were antithetical. A claim like that of the hosiers in 1581 that making *calzas* and *greguescos* "requires and contains particular science" would not have been taken seriously.[30] Nor would the assurance with which townspeople in El Toboso responded to Philip II's questionnaire in 1576, telling the monarch that what the town made better than any other place were "vats for storing wine or oil or whatever one wants, and in making them there is a great deal of skill and science in the said town."[31] The empiricism of guildsmen was not the sort of empiricism reformers needed, and in their opinion what artisans called science was no such thing. Though Campomanes proclaimed that "the State is, in essence, a large family," such sentimental moments occurred rarely, and he was perfectly willing to throw off the weight of useless old relatives.[32] The traditional way of doing things—imitation and routine, according to him—must be replaced with a new critical spirit of experimentation that would reap greater fruits. The problem had two explanations. Either, as Campomanes said, fathers were simply teaching sons. Or, as his contemporary José Cadalso believed, Spain's artistic decline was the fault of "the repugnance that all sons have toward following their father's career," a commonplace also found in Francisco Bruna's essay on the mechanical arts, reproduced, interestingly enough, in the appendices to Campomanes's *Discurso sobre la educación popular,* according to which, "Arts in Spain are never hereditary."[33] Either way, knowledge —real knowledge—was not being passed on. Once again contradicting himself, Campomanes opined that it was the carelessness of fathers and masters (elsewhere he blamed what amounted to a traditional caste system) that had condemned crafts to disdain.[34]

[29] José Clavijo y Faxardo, *El Pensador* (1763) (Las Palmas: Universidad de Las Palmas de Gran Canaria, 1999), 388.

[30] ARCV Pleitos Civiles Pérez Alonso (F) 270.2.

[31] Carmelo Viñas y Mey and Ramon Paz, eds., *Relaciones de los pueblos de España ordenadas por Felipe II* (Madrid: Instituto Balmés de Sociología, 1949). For some reason the identical reply appears in the Cuenca survey: Eusebio Julián Zarco-Bacas y Cuevas, ed., *Relaciones de pueblos del Obispado de Cuenca hechas por orden de Felipe II,* 2 vols. (Cuenca: Biblioteca diocesana conquense, 1927), vol. 1, 146.

[32] Pedro Rodríguez de Campomanes, *Discurso sobre el fomento de la industria popular* (Madrid, 1774), 186.

[33] José Cadalso, *Cartas marruecas* (1793), ed. Joaquin Marco (Madrid: Planeta, 1985), letter 24; Francisco de Bruna, "Reflexiones sobre las artes mecánicas," in Pedro Rodríguez de Campomanes, *Apéndice a la Educación Popular* (Madrid, 1776), vol. 3, 297.

[34] Campomanes, *Discurso sobre la educación popular,* 89.

So the Economic Societies, symbolic of a movement more pedagogical than executive, took it upon themselves to instruct artisans. In Zaragoza, Normante y Carcavilla published an essay recalling a scene in 1781 in which an Illustrious Citizen wisely had persuaded artisans to study mathematics, adding, "The number of Nobles who have instructed the people in their true interests is not small."[35] Apparently believing there was no honor without a prize and that education was not its own reward, the Societies also sponsored contests. As Campomanes wrote, "How many of our artisans' useful discoveries are drowned and die with them? It is only natural that this happen as long as inventors are not given *prizes* to publicize the discoveries to the benefit of the arts."[36] As an example, at a meeting of the Real Sociedad Económica de Amigos del País of Tárrega (Lleida), the gentlemen members admired a succession of prizewinning handicrafts produced by the girls at the local Patriotic School and then moved on to the inventions, including a machine to crumble clumps of earth, another that wound silk, and a third that shelled hemp. The society heard a speech by the *alcalde mayor* celebrating their activities, "the useful ocupation of the members for the entire year," and then presided over a raffle of a pair of oxen, generously donated by the count of Carpio to the poorest and hardest-working farmer in the town. Also receiving prizes were women and girls especially gifted at embroidery and weaving. As the prizes were announced and handed out, all were treated to a concert, "a moving and tender experience for all present." The organizers now had "a basis for hoping the time will come when laziness (*desidia*) will be banished from this land, and in its place Agriculture, Arts, and Industry will flourish, for that is the only objective of this Junta de Amigos."[37]

If traditional guild practices were considered unscientific, there also was something contrary to the Enlightened mind about the compatibility of science and "secrets," so often referred to by craftsmen who were proud that they had mastered them. The meaning of "secret," which appeared in hundreds of ordinances, might appear self-evident, but it is not. In fact, in the sixteenth and seventeenth centuries there was a growing number of "books of secrets" on the mechanical arts.[38] Ordinances, which contained a mind-numbing amount of technical detail, were read aloud in public squares and at town meetings. Artisans were constantly litigating over the borders of their guilds' jurisdictions, and in the course of litigation secrets

---

[35] Normante y Carcavilla, *Discurso sobre la utilidad,* 18.

[36] Campomanes, *Discurso sobre la educación popular,* 62. Emphasis in the original.

[37] AHN CS Libro 5290. Pamphlet published in Madrid, 1779. It is unclear why, if the oxen were to go to the poorest farmer, a raffle was even necessary unless there was competition for that honor.

[38] William Eamon, *Science and the Secrets of Nature: Books of Secrets in Medieval and Early Modern Culture* (Princeton University Press, 1994).

get spilled. When the silk twister Cristóbal de Balboa went before the Seville city council to request that his out-of-town papers be accepted in his new home, he said he had been examined in Ecija on the "arts and secrets" of his craft.[39] His counterparts in Toledo boasted in their ordinances that "the art of silk is useful and has many secrets . . . and because of the quality and secrets of the said art, no matter how deft a man may be, he cannot master them except through long practice and the passage of time."[40] Though autobiographical artisans may not have made many specific references to their labor, "the theme that lent itself most clearly to assertive statements of class identity . . . involved the defense of popular knowledge against claims of the superiority of 'higher' learning," according to James Amelang.[41] It was not that seventeenth-century artisans believed there was magic in the art of carpentry (though some may have) but rather that there was power in their art. It was the power of what they had inherited and what they could pass on, the power of their place in a community and even in history. For Aristotle, secrets could not be scientifically known, and for centuries they were regarded as being beyond investigation, what we might call superstition. In this regard, the sixteenth and seventeenth centuries marked a change; secrets could be known, but they still carried special weight. By the eighteenth century, boasts of mastery of "secrets" could easily be dismissed as irrational foolishness.[42] I don't believe Cristóbal de Balboa meant what we mean or what critics and historians of the eighteenth and nineteenth and twentieth centuries meant by "secret," that is, something that is mine, not yours. Rather, secrets amounted to the "science and perfection" that guilds invoked as their object, and in principle they were not antithetical to market transparency.

The Madrid turners in 1654 said their regulations would ensure "the perfection, strength, and preparation" of their works because "it aids the common good of this Republic if all that concerns this said occupation be

---

[39] AMSev Sec. X, Actas, 2a. escr., tomo 122, 14 June 1638.

[40] *Ordenanzas para el buen régimen y gobierno de la muy noble, muy leal e imperial Ciudad de Toledo* (Toledo: José de Cea, 1858), 236.

[41] James Amelang, *The Flight of Icarus: Artisan Autobiography in Early Modern Europe* (Stanford University Press, 1999), 212.

[42] Even in the eighteenth century, however, one of the objectives of the Madrid Economic Society was to "write reports to improve popular industry and occupations, the secrets of the arts, and machinery to aid production; and to help with education." See Alberto Bosch, *El Centenario: Apuntes para la historia de la Sociedad Económica Matritense* (Madrid: Impr. y fundición de M. Tello, 1875), 197. Pamela O. Long, in *Openness, Secrecy, Authorship: Technical Arts and the Culture of Knowledge from Antiquity to the Renaissance* (Baltimore: Johns Hopkins University Press, 2001), argues that craft manuals helped create a "border area" between learned men and mechanical practitioners. The "proprietary attitude" of the latter toward their work was later adopted by scientists, Long says, a process by which the mechanical arts were transformed, first being made suitable for philosophical endeavors, and then being appropriated (244–250).

of the required quality."[43] Madrid gilders said a particular rule was "appropriate and necessary for the good of the republic so that works be performed with the goodness and perfection required."[44] Hatters wanted to ensure that their products were "perfect and well finished, healthy (*sanos*) and without seams."[45] The Burgos city council, as it approved the ordinances of the laborers guild, remarked that the public good would benefit from "perfect materials and proper designs."[46] By making good shoes or forging fine swords or producing beautiful cloth, craftsmen were doing their part to keep their community healthy. Condemnations such as the preacher Luis de Granada's of the "disorderly appetite of many who want their things to be the best and very well created and refined, including house, clothing, books, pictures, and other similar treasures," generally were ignored.[47] The aim of perfection, in fact, rather than discouraging innovation, may have encouraged it. Though my study cannot offer quantitative data to support such a claim, it would be a logical outcome of the data I do have, which concern the positive and useful aspects of the guilds as described by members themselves. Self-serving though it may be, their testimony must have made some sense, despite simultaneous evidence that barriers imposed by guilds also hindered production reforms. Such a position furthermore bolsters arguments by economic historians in other parts of Europe who refute the prevailing view of guilds' negative influence by pointing to unintended pricing and quality-control benefits.[48]

Guilds saw themselves as guardians of both secrets and the common good. Ordinances and examinations guaranteed perfection so as to protect guild members and their community from unfair competition and deception. Fraud hurt the poor, misled one's neighbors, and violated morality. When Enrique de Villena described the fierce moral struggle within the artisan trying to choose virtue over vice, one of the temptations put before him by the forces of evil was "falsifications and deceits he could

---

[43] AV 2.309.31.

[44] AHN CS leg. 50.965, caja 2.

[45] AHN CS leg. 705.

[46] AMB Actas 6 Jan. 1609.

[47] Luis de Granada, *Guía de Pecadores* (Barcelona, 1625), book 1, part 2, f. 173.

[48] For recent work rejecting the view that late medieval craft guilds impeded technological innovation, see Epstein, "Craft Guilds, Apprenticeship, and Technological Change"; Farr, "On the Shop Floor"; John Munro, "The Symbiosis of Towns and Textiles: Urban Institutions and the Changing Fortunes of Cloth Manufacturing in the Low Countries and England, 1270–1570," *Journal of Early Modern History* 3 (February 1999): 1–74; Heather Swanson, "The Illusion of Economic Structure: Craft Guilds in Late Medieval English Towns," *Past and Present*, no. 121 (1988): 29–48; and Heather Swanson, *Medieval Artisans: An Urban Class in Late Medieval England* (Oxford: Basil Blackwell, 1989). For a critical view of the standard interpretation of French guilds, see Gail Bossenga, *The Politics of Privilege: Old Regime and Revolution in Lille* (Cambridge University Press, 1991).

commit in his occupation."[49] When Virgil lauded rural laborers by exclaiming, "Theirs is . . . a life that knows no fraud," he was describing a world of harmony and perfection that seventeenth-century city dwellers had not necessarily given up on.[50] Campomanes, however, apparently had. In his vision of factory labor, in which individual crafts would be merged into one collective enterprise, the whole of which would be superior to the parts, he described what would happen to perfection:

> It is of little importance in a textile factory if woolens are not well prepared, if carding is not perfect or if the threads do not correspond to the type of cloth or the weave of wool. [All the various crafts] to some degree are entirely distinct occupations, but out of their progressive and systematic union comes the perfection of wool manufacture.[51]

How did one demonstrate perfection before Campomanes's time? Madrid's cabinetmakers in the 1660s said their opponents in court, the carpenters, were not really carpenters at all because they were "without ordinances, without art, without examinations."[52] Without those attributes, one was nothing. I will return to ordinances, and we will see they meant something quite different to seventeenth-century artisans than they did to eighteenth-century reformers. Here I would like briefly to discuss masters examinations, which were both symbols and tools of guilds' power over their members and of their relation to the city council, as cities at times tolerated or even encouraged craft deviations (codified in examination rules) that the guilds perceived as threats.

Many ordinances indeed itemized the exact steps over which a journeyman would have to show mastery in producing a given object, giving credence to Campomanes's and others' claim that crafts had disintegrated into rote imitation. But examinations also were the clearest articulation of the idea that only skilled craftsmen could (and should) make good products for a healthy republic. I have found no more eloquent statement of the vital importance of examinations than a petition by Zaragoza's guilds written sometime during the reign of Charles II, probably just after 1674, when an Aragonese Cortes committee set up by Juan José de Austria had recommended a series of trade regulations including the prohibition of imports and the abolition of guild-supervised examinations. Though the

---

[49] Enrique de Villena, *Los doze trabajos de Hércules* (1483), ed. Margherita Morreale (Madrid: Real Academia Española, 1958), 79.

[50] Virgil, *Georgics*, vv. 458ff, cited in Paul Freedman, *Images of the Medieval Peasant* (Stanford University Press, 1999), 215.

[51] Campomanes, *Apéndice a la Educación Popular*, vol. 2, vi.

[52] AHN CS Libro 3948. The carpenters clearly did have ordinances, so it is unclear to me what the basis of the claim was.

guilds of Zaragoza carried more political weight than their Castilian counterparts, their document still deserves extensive quotation here.

"Two poles, Your Excellency, have fundamentally assisted monarchies: Arms and Letters is the one and Commerce and Arts is the other," the guilds began, pointing to the examples of Venice, Genoa, and Holland.[53] "Within a small, sandy stretch, [Holland] works with hoes and ploughs, supports powerful armies, and maintains bustling cities with its commerce and its journeymen." Spain, of course, once had claimed similar accomplishments, but that was no longer the case. The fault for that, the guilds said, had nothing to do with their examinations and everything to do with imports. Imports had blinded Spaniards with their apparent but deceptive authenticity and had made it impossible for the country's best artisans to tap the "treasure flowing through their veins." The "ancient use and custom of examinations, so praiseworthy and beneficial to your republics," in contrast, had been on the books since 1528 when Charles V had ruled that "it [was] just and reasonable and very necessary that journeymen of all occupations and arts be skilled, wise, and expert." It was in accordance with civil law, canon law, and common law everywhere that journeymen be examined, they said, and without examinations they had no doubt that misery would spread, artisans would have to beg, and only the unskilled would be left to cobble together society's needs. Imports would flood the market, "because with no account, mark, goodness, quality, rule, form, or manner, each journeyman would try to rig and confuse what they make, using materials other than those proper and necessary for the conservation of the monarchy." To those who might argue that the market would straighten things out, promoting true craftsmen and discarding the false, the guilds replied that the useless and unskilled would so outnumber their betters that the outcome would be hopeless. In short, eliminating examinations would result in "a chaos of confusion and a labyrinth so pernicious to the Republics that it would be the cause and origin of alterations and tumults."

Examinations proved an artisan had learned his craft. Could he learn more than one? Since the reign of the Catholic Monarchs, there had been laws prohibiting one person from performing two jobs. When Isabel and Ferdinand in 1500 issued regulations for the cloth and wool trades, they explicitly ordered shearers, dyers, weavers, and dressers to stick to one task; if they were caught moonlighting they would be fined and their tools would be taken from them. In 1537 and again in 1548, the Cortes asked Charles V to prohibit shoemakers from working as tanners, a request he complied with in 1552. In 1560 Philip II ordered that shearers not work as tailors and vice versa, and in 1591 bakers were prohibited from selling bread. It is unlikely that any of these rules were obeyed; there were few common

[53] BN VE 209-137.

people who did not perform more than one craft, especially in rural areas, as we saw earlier. Diego Pantoja of Cáceres, for example, who petitioned to emigrate to America in 1595, boldly stated on his application that his occupation was "tanner and shoemaker," which almost surely was illegal.[54] Francisco Ximénez Franco, of Trujillo, announced he was a "shoemaker and *labrador* and not among the prohibited," presumably a reference to conversos.[55] The tailors and the hosiers guilds clearly were performing each other's jobs and often ended up merging (as did the rival hatters and *cordoneros*), and in fact Madrid's Alcaldes de Casa y Corte in their general civic rules regarded the two as one and the same.[56] The father of one of literature's most famous pícaros, Cortadillo, was both a tailor and a hosier.

Guilds, when they stood to gain, sometimes argued in favor of allowing members to expand their repertoire. Depending on the case, the practice might offer smaller towns a wider array of skills, it could provide better and cheaper goods to consumers, it was the way things had always been done (which the *Relaciones topográficas* would seem to confirm), or it was in concordance with guild ordinances, city laws, or royal edicts. In any case, the assumption was that one person was capable of doing two things; indeed, the prohibitions assumed the same thing. In the various disputes described above, the two jobs were fairly similar (at least they appear so to us), but the principle underlying the assertion is, I believe, broader. People can be taught new skills. Indeed, sometimes they should be taught new skills. Such a notion is not surprising if we find it in the eighteenth century: Clavijo y Faxardo, for example, noted that

> the principle aim of men should always be to do the job they have been given. But once that is accomplished, what harm is there in the Minister discovering defects in the cultivation of the land so as to correct them for the good of the State, or in the farmer learning those Laws favorable to him so as to thwart the ambition of the powerful man intent upon stealing his wealth?"[57]

But we find it much earlier, making it necessary to question the depiction of Spain as a society of static orders and occupational rigidity. Identity was

[54] AGI Indiferente General leg. 2102 exp. 39. The prohibition against one person exercising both crafts, in the *Nueva Recopilación*, Libro 7, tit. 2, law 1, was lifted by Charles IV on 6 June 1791.

[55] AGI Indiferente General, leg. 2055, exp. 75 (1574).

[56] For example they merged in Teruel; see Carlos Luis de la Vega y de Luque, "Historia y evolución de los gremios de Teruel," in *Teruel*, vol. 77–78 (1987); and in Valencia (see BN VE 209–74). In Seville the clothiers were subsumed under the tailors, but a tailor still had to pass a special examination to work both trades. In Mexico City at least until the 1560s the two were in one guild, as were gilders and painters, two crafts that spent a great deal of time in peninsular courtrooms defending their particularity. For the Alcaldes' rules, see, for example, AHN CS Libro 1205.

[57] Clavijo y Faxardo, *El Pensador* (1763), 185.

not necessarily synonymous with occupation. If one could have an aptitude for a particular skill, or a hankering to learn a new one, then there was no inherent virtue or vice in the occupation itself. If the vast majority of humble Spaniards worked outside the guild system, which they did, generally performing different and multiple tasks according to their material needs and the time of year, then the notion of impassable barriers is further undermined.

Many early modern Spanish treatises on labor suggested people had particular "inclinations" and aptitudes that made them able to learn some things better than others, as if there were some sort of inner being impelling them toward one craft or another. Juan Luis Vives advised early in the sixteenth century that the poor "be asked if they know a trade; those who know none, if they are of an appropriate age, should be instructed if possible in that which most attracts them (*aquel a que tengan más inclinación*); and if not, in that which is closest."[58] "Inclination" also was the criterion for Antonio de Guevara, for whom it was "reckless and perhaps even frivolous to advise anyone to get married, learn to read, go to war, become a priest, learn a trade, or become a courtier, because no one should be bound by what someone else says, but rather they should follow their own inclinations." It would be no less than a sin, he added, to counsel someone inclined to weave to paint instead.[59] Huarte de San Juan suggested to Philip II that there should be a law "that a carpenter not work in the fields, nor the weaver as an architect, nor should a jurist cure people nor a doctor argue in court. Rather, each should exercise only that art for which he has natural talent and leave the rest," an argument that could be interpreted as restrictive but at the same time suggests that inner capacity, not external rules, should govern human activities.[60] Much later, Campomanes retained the same criterion: "The inclinations of the young are different, and each one will advance more if he is allowed to choose the art toward which he is inclined."[61]

All the talk of inclination, "possession" of a skill, the notion that an occupation required science and could achieve perfection, and that an artisan had the obligation, as a craftsman and as a member of the body politic, to do the best and most skilled job he could and provide the republic with what it needed, in some ways moved early modern workers onto the dis-

---

[58] Juan Luis Vives, *Tratado del socorro de los pobres* (1526) (Valencia: Prometeo, 1929), 109.

[59] Antonio de Guevara, *Menosprecio de Corte y Alabanza de Aldea* (1539), ed. Asunción Rallo (Madrid: Cátedra, 1984), 134–136. See also Francisco Márquez Villanueva, '*Menosprecio de Corte y Alabanza de Aldea' (Valladolid, 1539) y el tema áulico en la obra de Fray Antonio de Guevara* (Santander: Universidad de Cantabria, 1999), 103. This passage earned the book a place on the Inquisition's Index of forbidden books.

[60] Huarte de San Juan, *Examen de Ingenios* (1575), ed. Guillermo Serés (Madrid: Cátedra, 1989), 149–151.

[61] Campomanes, *Discurso sobre la educación popular,* 108.

cursive plane occupied by debates over the liberal arts or even over the obligations of the nobility, whose ethic was based on the celebration of public virtue exercised in the name of the common good. I do not mean to equate an enterprising tailor with a leading nobleman, but the language is similar. The worker had a more limited space but also possessed the ability to transform himself, improve himself, and thus better serve the republic of which he was a member. He could do so by exercising his craft, which, at least as far as he was concerned, embodied both art and science.[62]

The Law of the Guilds

Ordinances were the manifestation of guilds' connection to the municipality and to the community. As I described them in part 1, they were written by guild members in conjunction with the city council, and in writing them guilds themselves functioned as if they, too, were tiny republics. Ordinances were regarded as laws, they contained knowledge, and they established the economic and social relationships craftsmen would have with their colleagues, their neighbors, and the authorities. They were the property of guilds, but their repeated public readings in a way made them also the property of the consumers of the goods being made or sold, with whom they embodied a pact. For many eighteenth-century thinkers, however, ordinances were the epitome of guilds' harmful nature. In addition to stifling the development of the arts, by their very existence they mocked the authority and jurisdiction of the state and the monarchy. Ordinances as documents were on the one hand unstable and subject to contradictory interpretations; on the other, they limited production and confined artisans' possibilities. On both counts, they were unacceptable.

Traditionally, Spanish monarchs managed guilds by managing their ordinances. We also have seen that cities, at least in theory, oversaw the amendment of ordinances and established their authenticity with the public readings. Municipal records are full of petitions from artisans and their guilds resisting moves by cities or their agents to control the content and enforcement of ordinances. Casting doubt on a guild's possession of true and good ordinances was the standard way for any city or plaintiff to attack

[62] Pamela H. Smith, in her study of what she calls "artisanal epistemology," cites a mid-sixteenth-century humanist "who marveled that an illiterate locksmith constructed and set into motion a model of the planets through his knowledge of astronomy, and that an unlearned carpenter with no knowledge of mathematics could build a set of gears that was perfect in all proportions and measurements." Smith adds: "One might say that in their knowledge of the behavior of matter, early modern artisans were experts on natural processes," something that she says explains the rise of naturalism. See Pamela H. Smith, *The Body of the Artisan: Art and Experience in the Scientific Revolution* (University of Chicago Press, 2004), 7.

a guild's credibility. The city council of Madrid, for example, suddenly announced in 1641 that it needed to see all the guilds' ordinances.[63] During the reign of Ferdinand VI, in the 1750s, the city fathers of Zamora complained to a sympathetic Council of Castile that there were no guild ordinances at all in that city and that therefore artisans did and sold whatever they wanted. The claim was spurious, and the city was forced to restate it: it turned out there were ordinances after all, but they were not good ones.[64]

Starting in the late seventeenth century, the crown's relationship with guilds and their ordinances was to a large extent (though not entirely) funneled through the Junta de Comercio. Charles II in 1683 gave the Junta sole jurisdiction (*conocimiento privativo*) over guilds, a ruling more or less maintained over the subsequent century, but the Junta frequently was challenged by the Council of Castile, and even by the Inquisition. The ensuing disputes, which are difficult to disentangle, reveal what each party thought the importance of labor and its organizations were. The Alcaldes de Casa y Corte, the royal judges in the capital, for example, were under the jurisdiction of the Council of Castile yet also traditionally had their own power over guilds, based principally on the fact that guild inspectors took their oath of office before them. Though in 1686 the king ruled that one of the Alcaldes should sit on the Junta, there still was rivalry between the two bodies; the Alcaldes complained in 1717 that guild veedores were no longer taking their oaths in their courtroom, but rather before the Junta.[65] Later in the century, by which time the Bourbon monarchs had established intendancies in newly formed provinces, the intendants and the corregidores, a post that survived the Hapsburg monarchy, similarly clashed over supervision of veedores' elections.[66]

In 1685, the Junta sent the king copies of "ordinances" for all guilds, large and small, asking the crown to publish and enforce them.[67] These new documents applied to all of Castile (not just to particular cities, as before) and stated only what each guild could make or buy, omitting all the

---

[63] AV 2.309.16.

[64] María del Carmen Pescador del Hoyo, "Los gremios de artesanos en Zamora," *Revista de Archivos, Bibliotecas y Museos* 75 (January 1968–December 1972): 194–195.

[65] Eugenio Larruga y Boneta, *Historia de la Real y General Junta de Comercio . . .*, 12 vols. (Madrid, 1779–1789), vol. 1, ff. 15. See also AHN CS leg. 7223.

[66] Larruga y Boneta, *Historia de la Real y General Junta*, vol. 5, ff. 132–133 for one such case from Palencia, in which the king ruled that the corregidor should preside over the election but the intendant, regarded as a commerce official, should have the last word on the appointment. The murky distinction is illustrative.

[67] AHN CS leg. 7223, AHN CS leg. 51, and AV 2.311.7; I am grateful to María del Carmen Cayetano Martín for the last. Some of these developments also are described, in a confusing manner, in Miguel Capella and Antonio Matilla Tascón, *Los Cinco Gremios Mayores de Madrid* (Madrid, 1957). The authors were a leader of the Madrid Chamber of Industry and the director of the Ministry of Finance archive, respectively.

usual provisions regarding matters such as membership requirements, examinations, shop policies, and meetings. In other words, they concerned the products of guild members' labor, not the members themselves. Guilds now had old ordinances and new ones, and the latter in theory left intact any provision in the former not explicitly altered.

In 1700, under the new Bourbon monarchy, Corregidor Francisco Ronquillo Briceño of Madrid announced he would enforce sections of the 1685 ordinances that made smaller guilds more vulnerable with regard to two things: payment of the alcabala tax (which was paid in a lump sum assessed on guilds as a whole called the *encabezamiento*) and elections of representatives to a new body called the Diputación, setting off litigation that lasted thirty years.[68] Starting in 1703, the smaller guilds protested that the way in which the ordinances were being applied (or not) benefited only the five powerful merchant guilds. The distinction between *gremios menores* and *gremios mayores* was a new one. The author of a crown-sponsored history of the Junta, Eugenio Larruga, for one, took issue with the Council of Castile's demarcation between these types of organization: "Before this, they all were generically called guilds or occupations [*gremios u oficios*], distinguished among themselves as artisan, merchant, or mechanical [*menestrales*], with greater or lesser reputation as liberal or mechanical according to the greater or lesser esteem of the materials with which they work." (The lack of precision on this last point is once again instructive.)[69] Elsewhere he specified, "The fact that they call themselves *mayores* is not a sign of honor or distinction with respect to the court's other guilds that are called or named *menores*."[70] At any rate, the smaller guilds in 1725, now referring to themselves as the sixty-two guilds "that join together in community" (*que hacen cuerpo de comunidad;* by the end of the process there appeared to have been fifty-nine), said merchants were "harming Your Majesty's devoted vassals who with their sweat and their labor gladly contribute whatever they can to his royal service," and they asked the crown to summon them all to draw up new ordinances, a request with which the crown complied. The basic issue was who would get to vote in the Diputación de Todos los Gremios de Madrid and how. "Laborers, wood workers, and others" in January 1728 wrote a petition saying, "each and every one has equal representation and a vote in everything pertaining to the common interests of

[68] Ronquillo Briceño also undertook economic reforms as corregidor of Córdoba. See José Ignacio Fortea Pérez, "The Textile Industry in the Economy of Córdoba at the End of the Seventeenth and the Start of the Eighteenth Centuries: A Frustrated Recovery," in *The Castilian Crisis of the Seventeenth Century: New Perspectives on the Economic and Social History of Seventeenth-Century Spain*, ed. I. A. A. Thompson and Bartolomé Yun Casalilla (Cambridge University Press, 1994), 151–153.

[69] Larruga y Boneta, *Historia de la Real y General Junta*, vol. 1, cap. 5.l: "Lo que ha sido la Junta desde el año de 1730 . . . ," f. 114v.

[70] Ibid., vol. 4, Libro 3, f. 1.

all the Communities called the Diputación." Deputies watch over "every-thing useful for the guilds [*todo lo que es utilidad de los gremios*], the state of their assets, and the progress of their common interests." The follow-ing month they insisted they were fighting for "an immemorial custom, and we have never heard the contrary to this inalterable Right for an equal voice, active and passive, by the communities of guilds making up the Diputación." Merchants, in contrast, argued that they contributed far more to the royal coffers than did the smaller guilds and therefore should have a greater voice; one vote per guild made no sense, they said. In April 1728, after sixteen days of raucous meetings, compromise ordi-nances were approved and sent to the Council of Castile. There apparently were appeals, because the royal decree was issued only on 19 November 1731. That same year, the Cinco Gremios Mayores withdrew from the Diputación.

It is unclear what happened to these new "ordinances." Either they dis-appeared or they were ignored. Throughout the century, guilds continued to have their own, linked to specific cities and periodically revised, causing new jurisdictional problems resolved with contradictory decrees. The Council of Castile repeatedly complained to the king about the Junta, which believed it had inherited the council's former ordinance-granting powers. In the 1760s, for example, the council said the Junta "had gone so far as to get involved in the approval of ordinances," leading to "universal disorder" among the guilds, which appeared only too happy to take ad-vantage of the confusion. Some *individuos* of the guilds (a new synonym for "member"), the king said later, dissatisfied with the council-approved ordinances, had turned to the Junta and drawn up new statutes, literally hiding the old ones. If that didn't work, they called themselves a confra-ternity and went to the ecclesiastical courts, "wandering from court to court, causing notable harm."[71]

In Larruga's account, the council considered its jurisdiction to be *mera política,* or organization, which it accused the Junta of poaching.[72] Lar-ruga's argument (and, presumably, that of the Junta) was, on the one hand, that civil governance of crafts, which recently had been classified into 103 categories covering animal, vegetable, and mineral, was "a long way from the rules of *mera policía* [*sic*] as it is closely connected and inter-twined with the most urgent questions of well-ordered commerce." If in-

---

[71] BN VE 1066/10, 17 February 1767. William Callahan reports on one such case, in which Madrid wig makers in 1766 petitioned both the Junta and the Council of Castile for new ordinances. The king split authority between these organs, resolving nothing (William J. Callahan, "A Note on the Real y General Junta de Comercio, 1679–1814," *Economic History Review* 21 [December 1968]: 519–528).

[72] This discussion is based on Larruga y Boneta, *Historia de la Real y General Junta*, vol. 1, ff. 90–103v.

deed the matter were just one of mere organization, why would the Junta bother with it? he asked. The answer was that the Junta was encharged with "everything pertinent to manufacturing and general commerce in the Kingdom, of which an essential and indispensable part is the government of the arts and offices." The council's complaints, he said, pointed to the fact that its members were not "keeping their eye on the higher goal so as to truly grasp that lofty political point (*aquel alto punto de política*) that must be our sovereign's objective." From that perspective, anything that contributed to material progress and happiness could, conceivably, belong to the Junta. Here we see Larruga blurring (unavoidably or not) the demarcation between production and consumption, between what we might call politics and economics. Making things (production, but also the organization of those who made them) was inseparable from trafficking them (commerce), except in the case of the lowest guilds, the *gremios mecánicos y menestrales*, whose matters Larruga agreed corresponded entirely to the council, as such craftsmen in no way participated in commerce.

But in another way, Larruga (and the crown) did establish a dividing line, which only complicated things more as all parties tried to sort out the political (or organizational) and the industrial (or commercial), a task the artisans' ancestors may well have thought absurd. The problem for eighteenth-century authorities was how to define the guilds and their members. Who would govern them indicated what they did; it indicated if they were political or economic actors. The crown was no help: in 1717, Philip V, after hearing complaints from the Alcaldes, ruled: "Despite the fact that veedores take their oath before [the Alcaldes] or at City Hall, the Junta has exclusive jurisdiction over all denunciations regarding manufacturing, commerce, and observance of the ordinances."[73] In 1767, Charles III declared that the Junta could *not* get involved in craft guilds' ordinances.[74] That was followed in 1770 by an ambiguous decree that appeared to leave governance of the *craft* up to the Junta but governance of the *guild* up to the council.[75] On 13 June of that year, Larruga wrote, the king divided guild matters into three sections—*comercio, política,* and *justicia*—corresponding to the Junta, the council, and the ordinary judiciary, respectively. "Ordinances that attend to the perfection and progress of the arts and handicrafts [*maniobras*]" belonged to the Junta; "ordinances that attend to the good government and *policía* of the guilds, either among their mem-

---

[73] Ibid., vol. 1, f. 37.

[74] *Cédula,* 17 February 1767, in Santos Sánchez, *Colección de pragmáticas . . . Carlos III,* 3d ed. (Madrid, 1803), 58; and Larruga y Boneta, *Historia de la Real y General Junta,* vol. 5, 106–109: "y que la Junta no debe mezclarse en lo respectivo a ordenanzas, negocios ni instancias de los Gremios menores ni menestrales."

[75] 24 June 1770. BN VE 1265–82, also Sánchez, *Colección de pragmáticas,* 171, and Larruga y Boneta, *Historia de la Real y General Junta,* vol. 5, f. 110. Larruga describes the edict in depth in vol. 1, ff. 103v–105, which is from where I am drawing.

bers [*individuos*] or with respect to others . . . and generally everything that does not concern the rules and perfection of the arts and *maniobras*" belonged to the council. So the objects being produced were being separated from those who produced them. Ordinary courts would attend to contract disputes, which the Junta had said it did not want. In 1807, Charles IV admitted that his father's edicts "had not been sufficient" and he issued yet another one, stating clearly this time (on the eve of the French invasion) that the Junta had authority over "all guild ordinances of commerce, the arts, and manufactures."[76]

By the time of his reign, it was clear, anyway, that the Junta was urging the monarch to scrap the guilds and their ordinances altogether. When a glover's widow was prevented by her husband's guild from keeping her shop, for example, the king, after consulting with the Junta, overturned not only the relevant ban in the glovers' ordinances but a similar one in all other ordinances.[77] He took similar action after a Madrid carpenter, Santiago Ximénez, was denounced by cabinetmakers for buying a type of wood off-limits to him.[78] After the Junta explained to the king that there was no need anymore for a guild of silk twisters, he declared the craft to be "free" to all people, women included, and instructed his officials to make sure the artisans stopped meeting as such.[79] On 17 March 1796, the monarchy simply abolished the guild.[80]

Around the same time as Larruga wrote his history of the Junta, Campomanes wrote his two pamphlets on labor, insisting that ordinances around the country be examined and then modified to correct what he already had identified as their grievous faults. In the spirit of the times, he appeared confident that scientific study could ascertain the truth and the *ilustrados* then would apply a rational remedy. Each guild would have a *socio protector*, sort of an enlightened big brother, who would report back to his Economic Society on the predictably lamentable state of his respective craft. The Council of Castile (an interested party regarding ordinances) asked the Real Sociedad Económica de Madrid to undertake the investigation, indicating the research took place after Campomanes's condemnation, not before. As one historian put it, the Economic Society was asked to "study the guild organization as a barrier in the way of economic progress."[81] That was exactly what it studied.

[76] BN R/34927, 9 September 1807.

[77] *Cédula*, 19 May 1790. The problem in this case apparently was that the glover was the widow's second husband and practiced a craft other than that practiced by the first husband.

[78] *Real órden*, 19 June 1799.

[79] *Cédula*, 29 January 1793.

[80] James Clayburn La Force Jr., *The Development of the Spanish Textile Industry, 1750–1800* (Berkeley: University of California Press, 1965), 107.

[81] Robert Jones Shafer, *The Economic Societies in the Spanish World (1763–1821)* (Syracuse University Press, 1958), 104.

The "class," or committee of the Madrid Economic Society devoted to guilds, began with twenty-one members and ended up with between forty-three and fifty-six (the reports vary). Starting in April 1776, they met once a week and slowly began drawing up their reports based on what the guilds told them about their organization and membership. They began with the capital's various woodworking guilds, whose masters' stubborn practice of limiting the number of journeymen and apprentices employed in each shop appeared to them as evidence they did not know where their own interests lay. Indeed, the woodworking ordinances were so *defectuosas* that the society decided there was nothing the *socio protector* could do until they were rewritten.[82] Tailors' ordinances also were rife with problems including monopoly, privileges, membership limitations, and expensive examinations, but the committee decided it would not be prudent to dissolve the guild because "the situation is not yet ripe for this revolution."[83] In similarly considering Toledo's cutlers, basing its study on ordinances that the guild had given to the Council of Castile, which then handed them to the society, the committee said the principal objective of these ordinances in particular and of all ordinances in general should be members' "subordination to fathers, to masters, and to the judiciary."[84] In its summary considerations, the committee weighed a host of broad questions concerning guilds, including whether they should even exist: "Is it advisable that they be dissolved and instead enjoy full and absolute freedom?" it asked, while acknowledging that their existence since time immemorial made elimination difficult. It understood that preservation of the arts was endangered if there was no "progressive and methodical instruction or if [craftsmen] were left with just purely traditional teachings, the only ones the state would count on in the absence of bodies whose legislation embodied *luces*." Particularly relevant to my interest in ordinances' role as a key device anchoring craftsmen's simultaneous position as bearers of specific manufacturing skills and as creative inhabitants of a republic, the committee wrote:

[82] Sociedad Económica de Madrid, *Memorias de la Sociedad Económica*, 5 vols. (Madrid: 1780–1795), vol. 2. This particular volume, a collection of reports, is not always paginated. For further documents on the Madrid organization, including the establishment of Patriotic Schools and debates on whether to allow women to become members, see Olegario Negrín, *Ilustración y educación: La sociedad económica matritense* (Madrid: Editora Nacional, 1984). On the "class" devoted to guilds, see Antonio Manuel Moral Roncal, *Gremios e Ilustración en Madrid (1775–1836)* (Madrid: Actas Editorial, 1998). Moral reports (187) that members of the class included three sculptors, two painters, two arquebusiers, three watchmakers, one framer, five architects, two machinists, one engraver, and the director of the Royal Coaches Workshop.

[83] 15 July 1786 report by Manuel Sixto Espinosa, cited in Alberto Bosch, *El Centenario: Apuntes para la historia de la Sociedad Económica Matritense* (Madrid: Impr. y fundición de M. Tello, 1875), 75. As an indication of how little was known about the guilds, Jovellanos in 1785 wrote that the tailors had not had ordinances before 1756 ("Informe dado a la Junta general de Comercio y Moneda sobre el libre ejercicio de las artes," 9 November 1785, in Jovellanos, *Obras*, vol. 2, 39.

[84] Sociedad Económica de Madrid, *Memorias*, vol. 2, 15–33.

The technical or professional aspect of the arts cannot be subsumed in a code of law because [laws] that prescribe rules for the employment of men's talents must necessarily be subject to continual variation, as it is impossible to account for the multitude of combinations of which human understanding is capable.[85]

Similar examinations of ordinances were under way around Castile, as local notables received their copies of Campomanes's works, part of a massive publicity campaign spearheaded by the author himself. The intendant of Granada received 360 copies of the *Discurso sobre el fomento de la industria popular,* for example.[86] After the Council of Castile sent all four volumes of the appendices of *Discurso sobre la educación popular* to the Zamora city council (the same that in the 1750s had complained about inadequate ordinances), the most notable men (*personas clásicas*) there decided they too wanted to establish an Economic Society, one of whose committees would "try to perfect all the occupations and arts of the Republic." Among its tasks: "It will carefully examine guild ordinances so that, once abuses that prevent liberty and the progress of the arts are verified, new ones can be proposed to the Council."[87] In Valladolid, the society's *socios protectores* also "examined guild ordinances, noting their defects and proposing reforms."[88] Zaragoza's Economic Society drew up a Guilds Plan in 1778.[89]

Campomanes was quick—too quick—to condemn guilds for including in their ordinances clauses excluding people who had performed (or whose ancestors had performed) certain (unspecified) vile jobs in the past. It was a "great oversight" that such clauses had been tolerated, he wrote, and such "odiousness and extravagance" should be eliminated immediately. The only such clauses I have found, and I have found very few, date from Campomanes's era, not from before, and I have found no indication they were enforced.[90] Campomanes also was adamant that ordinances did not properly provide for instruction of apprentices, which also was not the case. But his chief objection was that guilds had their own jurisdiction, or *fuero.* On the one hand, rigid regulations were said to stifle creativity and technical advances, an issue I already have addressed; on the other hand, particular laws that applied to just some people should not be allowed to exist on principle:

[85] Ibid., vol. 4. The class examined nearly eighty ordinances, according to Moral Roncal, *Gremios e Ilustración en Madrid,* 231–233.

[86] Sarrailh, *La España Ilustrada,* 252. Chapter 16 of the *Discurso sobre la educación popular* is a handy twenty-three-point summation of the book's "general axioms," undoubtedly designed to aid public digestion.

[87] AHN CS Libro 5271, p. 31.

[88] Jorge Demerson, *La Real Sociedad Económica de Valladolid (1784–1808)* (Universidad de Valladolid, 1969), 26. Demerson is quoting a 1788 report by Josef Mariano Beristain found at the Real Academia de Historia. Valladolid's society was established only in 1783.

[89] Introduction to Normante y Carcavilla. *Discurso sobre la utilidad,* 20.

[90] Campomanes, *Discurso sobre la educación popular,* 111. I return to this issue below.

Nothing is more contrary to popular industry than the erection of guilds and privileged jurisdictions, which divide people into small societies often exempt from ordinary justice. . . . The greatest damage lies in exclusive ordinances and the monopoly they encourage. If enlightened measures do not put a stop to this, each guild's actions will prevent the flowering of popular industry.[91]

He was wrong on several counts, and somewhat disingenuous. The particularity of guild ordinances, first, was contingent on a host of factors, and ultimately could be (and often was) appealed in ordinary courts. Guilds did not have their own judicial jurisdiction, though reading Campomanes might lead one to deduce they did. The horror evoked by the words privilege, monopoly, and barrier far exceeded the actual state of affairs of most crafts; and capacities such as electing their own inspectors—"an intolerable abuse," he declared—were anyway being challenged by city councils.[92]

By arguing, with some logic, that society could not function if everyone answered to a different law, he removed all possibility for specific regulations, be they for guilds or for any other organization. But he ignored the fact that Bourbon Spain was not governed by universal law. Though from the start the dynasty made clear that it wanted to impose "uniformity of the same laws, uses, customs, and tribunals," that objective had not been achieved.[93] Law in seventeenth-century Spain, as we have seen, was often confused with custom. It was not followed if judged contrary to the common good and frequently was appealed, often with inconsistent results. Despite its obvious powers, the Hapsburg monarchy found law to be something that had to be defended time and again, a situation the Count-Duke attempted unsuccessfully to remedy. The Bourbons, in a sense, tried to implement Olivares's plan. Nonetheless, by the second half of the eighteenth century, laws still amounted to royal decrees, which could be particular, ambiguous, and contradictory, with which Campomanes had no general problem. What he did have a problem with was guilds armed with weapons, which sometimes worked, with which to challenge municipal and royal authorities, whom he accused of not paying close attention. "Nobody is concerned about improving these bodies except when there are denunciations or complaints," he complained, "and thus they do what they want in a sort of languid anarchy."[94] Guilds must not be able to draw up ordinances without approval from "legislative authority," he said.[95] If he meant city councils, that was already the case. To remedy the problem, the

---

[91] Campomanes, *Discurso sobre el fomento,* 108.

[92] Campomanes, *Discurso sobre la educación popular,* 151.

[93] *Autos,* 29 July 1707, cited in Pablo Fernández Albaladejo, *Fragmentos de Monarquía* (Madrid: Alianza Universidad, 1992), 354.

[94] Campomanes, *Discurso sobre la educación popular,* 152.

[95] Ibid., 155.

Council of Castile should approve all guild ordinances, he said. In fact, except when the Junta de Comercio interfered, it already did, and had done so since the reign of Charles V.

Campomanes was not alone in using the universality of law as an argument in favor of undermining guilds. One of the many treatises he reproduced in the appendices to the *Discurso sobre la educación popular* was by Francisco de Bruna, a member of the Council of Finance and a Seville magistrate. In his essay, which Sempere described as "short but containing grand principles," Bruna returned to the differences between law and custom:

> Customs have a greater role than laws in increasing the Arts because the latter cannot descend to such particularity nor can they be efficient without customs. In this matter, the purpose of laws should be only to remove impediments and ensure the security and liberty of the artisan. All else is the task of magistrates, not laws. In this regard I consider three points: first, the horror of laziness and idleness [*ocio y holgazanería*]; second, the removal of bums [*vagos*], correcting them with hospices that cannot be perpetual; third, honor, interest, and emulation. I do not think manufacturing laws should go beyond this, or they would lose their natural majesty.[96]

Jovellanos—a poet, playwright, critic, jurist, statesman, and economist, and at one point the president of the Madrid Economic Society—looked upon all regulatory laws with suspicion, and guild ordinances were no exception.[97] In his view, the state should encourage education and infrastructure aimed at economic progress, but the details should be left to the private sector and economic societies. Like Bruna, he figured custom would take care of most things. For example, there was no need for a law prohibiting women from becoming barbers because no woman would ever dream of such a thing, he said. Jovellanos agreed with Campomanes that *socios protectores* could ensure enlightened supervision of the crafts. But because labor power is the worker's property, he believed, it would be wrong to limit its disposition in any way, and such a violation of principle would lead to harm in practice. His opposition to restrictions on craftsmen also bore similarities to that of the Madrid Economic Society, cited above, when it rejected the notion of a law imposing itself on art. The Zamora city council in 1776, we saw, referred to "abuses that prevent liberty." Jovellanos as a young man had read Locke, and liberty, too, was his main concern. "Let us with one blow break the chains that oppress and weaken our industry

---

[96] Sempere y Guarinos, *Ensayo de una biblioteca española de los mejores escritores del reynado de Carlos III*, vol. 1, 30; Bruna, "Reflexiones sobre las artes mecánicas," in Campomanes, *Apéndice a la educación popular,* vol. 3, 298.

[97] "Informe dado a la Junta General de Comercio y Moneda sobre el libre ejercicio de las artes," 9 November 1785, in Jovellanos, *Obras,* vol. 2, 33–41.

and let us restore once and for all the liberty we desire, on which our hopes for prosperity and growth are pinned," he wrote in a discussion of guilds. Original sin had obliged humans to work; Jovellanos turned that obligation into a right, any restriction of which served "to defraud man's most sacred property, the most inherent to his being, the most necessary for his preservation." No law can require us to renounce our natural rights, and yet that is exactly what guild ordinances did by, for example, barring women from certain jobs or men in villages from becoming masters. Furthermore, the fraud was committed not only against artisans but against consumers, who lost their "reciprocal right" to freely select the maker of their goods. The liberty he advocated, he reassured his readers, would not "defraud the public of its security," which it still could claim before courts of law.

From the perspective of guild members, the word "fraud" traditionally had signified what happened when their rules were not obeyed or when products from outside were allowed in. In part 1 we saw guilds arguing that a community had a right (though that word was not used) to expect certain goods of a certain quality, and if a guild did not respect that expectation, it defrauded its neighbors. Jovellanos left that sort of public fraud behind, as did Campomanes: "Those who form a corporation are individuals [*particulares*]. And just as an individual is not owner of what belongs to the community [*al común*] . . . a guild comprises individuals who, while they are associated in an occupational or artistic body, have acquired no exclusive right with respect to the public."[98] In Locke's words, they had enclosed property, the products of their labor, from the common.[99] Craftsmen no longer could defend their particular law by saying it protected the common interest, and at the same time their own labor power and its product were now deemed part of the public domain. While "individual" guild members now had no claim on the public sphere and could not presume, with their ordinances, to act as guardians of the common good, their labor power was regarded as something that must be made available to everyone under equality of conditions. What had been sheltered in the realm of the particular now lost its privilege and became public.

The assurance with which the reformers spoke of themselves can be distracting: "Not all centuries are enlightened," Campomanes commented in 1764. "There are some dominated by custom, when pure imitation rules, and reason and discourse are neglected."[100] Their self-conscious project made it difficult and perhaps uninteresting for them to observe the mul-

[98] Campomanes, *Apéndice a la educación popular,* vol. 2, 166.
[99] John Locke, "Of Property," *The Second Treatise of Government* (New York: Bobbs-Merrill, 1952), 20.
[100] Concepción de Castro, *Campomanes: Estado y reformismo ilustrado* (Madrid: Alianza Editorial, 1996), 303. The citation is from "Respuesta fiscal sobre abolir la tasa . . ."

titude of relationships contained in, for example, guild ordinances, whose simultaneously restrictive language and celebration of the common good and public utility appeared to be the antithesis of the new economic forms of thinking. The differences, though, were not as absolute as are sometimes thought; even Jovellanos could remark at the end of the century that "he who measures his utility by moral good is more just than he who measures by physical good."[101] In fact, the language of utility and the common good survived nearly intact from the sixteenth century, but the reformers had new objectives and in general were ill-equipped, as they looked at their country's past, to detect the coexistence of regulation and freedom, of hierarchy and negotiation.

The Marketplace

If liberty defined artisans' labor power, as Jovellanos said, it also defined the ideal state of the market for producers, vendors, and buyers.[102] *The Wealth of Nations* was translated into Spanish in 1794 (with omissions and alterations) by José Alonso Ortiz, a Valladolid magistrate, but many of the leading figures of the reform movement by then already had read it as well as other economic works from the rest of Europe, and indeed had been writing their own. Vicente Alcalá Galiano, a leader of the Segovia Economic Society, called the author "*el profundo Político Smith.*"[103] Campomanes used the expression "political economy" already in 1750; Montesquieu's *Spirit of the Laws* (1749) was banned in Spain in 1756, meaning it had arrived; Jovellanos read Smith at least three times and did not have to wait for the translation.[104] The Basques, the first to establish an Economic Society, were especially important in maintaining contacts with French intellectuals and policy makers and providing translations of their works for colleagues around the country. Educated Spaniards' embrace of change

[101] Jovellanos, *La Ley Agraria* (1794), cited in John H. R. Polt, *Jovellanos and His English Sources: Economic, Philosophical and Political Writings,* Transactions of the American Philosophical Society, vol. 54, pt. 7 (Philadelphia: American Philosophical Society, 1964), 23.

[102] I am not separating vendors from producers because most artisans were both and because both, depending on what they sold or made, often are said to have been living on the edge of the republic.

[103] Cited in Richard Herr, *The Eighteenth-Century Revolution in Spain* (Princeton University Press, 1958), 54. The translation is *Investigación de la naturaleza y causas de la riqueza de las naciones,* 4 vols. (Valladolid, 1794); see Robert Sydney Smith, "The 'Wealth of Nations' in Spain and Hispanic America, 1780–1830" *Journal of Political Economy* 65 (April 1957): 104–125.

[104] Campomanes: in the title of *Bosquejo de política económica española,* which Llombart says is the first use of the term in Spain (Vicent Llombart, *Campomanes, economista y político de Carlos III* [Madrid: Alianza Universidad, 1992], 50). Montesquieu: Antonio Elorza, *La ideología liberal en la ilustración española* (Madrid: Editorial Tecnos, 1970), 70; Jovellanos: Smith, "The 'Wealth of Nations' in Spain and Hispanic America," 108.

was a wide one, though with particularities. It was wide enough that, according to Richard Herr, political economy "was a subject for polite conversations."[105] But the new doctrine—"the science of the citizen and the patriot," in the words of Jovellanos—bore stark similarities to the old.[106] Spaniards were not quite ready to abandon the common good for individual happiness, even if maximation of the latter was said to bring about the former.

Significantly, the Economic Societies were interchangeably called Economic Societies, Patriotic Societies, and Societies of Friends of the Country. The seal of the organization in Jeréz, for example, showed two men laden with crops and tools and a walled, medieval town in the background. Below them were the words EL PATRIOTISMO. "Overcoming obstacles and hardships, they do not rest until they bring abundance and happiness to the Patria," the society explained in its articles of incorporation. A few years later, when the organization was showing early signs of decay, members attributed the troubles to "ignorance of patriotism and Society and economics and the usefulness they bring to the state and to individuals." One solution was to offer economics classes at religious institutions, "because the voice of religious authority makes the greatest impression on our spirits," a statement in passing that tells us much about the world of the reformers.[107] God and economics were not incompatible, and instruction could dissolve nearly all obstacles.

Economics was a question of doing good for a collective entity. Though this entity was now called the *patria,* not the republic, the moral considerations and debates aired for centuries in town squares, universities, and pulpits had not been left behind in the rush to embrace science, reason, and commerce. In 1571, the Dominican friar Tomás de Mercado had written, "Not to know in business what is just and what is unjust is not to understand anything, for that is the first thing a Christian must know about any business in order not to lose the eternal good while dealing with worldly goods."[108] A healthy body politic required justice, which could not be served through material abundance. Two hundred years later, the organic requirements were somewhat different. Smith declared commerce a guarantee of a healthy constitution, and a Spanish merchant declared:

---

[105] Herr, *Eighteenth-Century Revolution in Spain,* 56. According to Jonathan Israel, British empiricism completely eclipsed other strains of the Enlightenment as they entered the Iberian peninsula (*Radical Enlightenment: Philosophy and the Making of Modernity, 1650–1750* [Oxford University Press, 2001], 528–540).

[106] Polt, "Jovellanos and His English Sources," 16.

[107] Manuel Ruiz Lagos, *Historia de la Sociedad Económica de Amigos del País de Xerez de la Frontera* (Jeréz de la Frontera: Centro de Estudios Históricos Jerezanos, 1972), 31, 49.

[108] Tomás de Mercado, *Suma de Tratos y Contratos* (1571), ed. Nicolás Sánchez Albornoz (Madrid: Instituto de Estudios Fiscales, 1977), 14. Mercado lived in Seville and thus had a privileged view of Spain's commercial prosperity.

"Commerce, in the opinion of the most informed authors, is the blood of the nation's body politic. It can even be seen as the spirit that gives it life." Businessmen no longer were lions lying in wait or the hungry wolves of Mercado's day. Instead, they were part of the "conduit from whence spills forth opulence and common utility." The common good was still, implicitly and explicitly, rhetorically and otherwise, the goal. What had changed was how to get there.[109]

Before briefly examining the content of the new political economy in Spain, I want to return to the marketplaces of the seventeenth century, where, in full view and within earshot of one another, craftsmen and vendors fought with authorities and one another over who could sell what, where and when they could sell it, and how they should make it. How explicitly did buyers and sellers have in mind the moral precepts of treatises? Take the small example of the stonemason Francisco García de Dueñas, who in 1649 was denounced to the Inquisition by several of his neighbors in Madrid. Among other things, he was said to have commented that priests could make mistakes, that it was the church, not Christ, who had ordered Christians to fast, and that it would be far better for the church to give alms to the poor than to dress up the Virgin Mary in jewels and expensive clothes. García de Dueñas, who could read and write, added to his problems by announcing that he had lots of books at home that proved he was right. When it came time to respond to the accusations, one of the questions he put to his witnesses said a great deal:

> Do they know that [the prosecution witness and hatter] Miguel de Barrios is a capital enemy of the said Francisco García Dueñas . . . because the said Miguel de Barrios bought a beaver hat for much less than it was worth, and he sells hats of one class as if they were another, deceiving those who buy them, and Francisco García Dueñas told him he was a bad man and not a Christian, and they quarreled, and Miguel de Barrios said he swore to God he would have his revenge.
>
> And do they know that when [García de Dueñas] told [Barrios] that he had to rectify his deceit in selling one class of hat as if it were another, he said he would give him a book, and the book he promised was by Fr. Juan de Santo Tomá, on the explanation of the doctrine of matters of conscience.[110]

---

[109] Juan Antonio de los Heros Fernández, "Discursos sobre el comercio . . . ," in Antonio Valladares de Sotomayor, ed., *Semanario erudito, que comprehende varias obras inéditas, críticas, morales, instructivas, políticas, históricas, satíricas y jocosas, de nuestros mejores autores antiguos y modernos,* vol. 26 (Madrid, 1787), 146, 183. De los Heros was director of the Cinco Gremios Mayores.

[110] AHN Inq. 202.27. García de Dueñas was sentenced to two years' banishment from Toledo and Madrid. Richard Mackenney's book on Venetian tradesmen includes similar Inquisition tales, including one of a goldsmith who said it would be better to give alms than to keep oil lamps and candles burning before the images of the saints, and a practical grocer who suggested "better to use the oil to fry fish." See Richard Mackenney, *Tradesmen and*

García de Dueñas's source, the Dominican John of St. Thomas (1589–1644), was an outstanding seventeenth-century Thomist scholar and ended his days as confessor to Philip IV. His theological and philosophical writings devoted to the work of Aquinas were widely read—even, it would appear, by a Madrid stonemason.

The greatest of Spain's public marketplaces was Madrid's Plaza Mayor, and if one were to give physical existence to theories of work and commerce, this is where one would do it. In 1620, the Council of Castile dictated how city council members should control the Plaza Mayor and exactly when they should patrol it.[111] They were to ensure that price controls were enforced and that they were announced (*pregonados*) at the appropriate times, not only in the Plaza Mayor but also in four nearby plazas. (*Pregones* could be read out in as many as twenty-five plazas, intersections, gates, and bridges.) If no new prices were set that day, vendors could assume the previous price was in effect. Councilmen explicitly were prohibited from accepting money, presents, or merchandise from vendors. If fines were levied against vendors for disobeying price controls, one-third would go to the court, one-third to poor prisoners, and one-third to the person who denounced the violation. It was a lucrative business, and indeed the resultant fraud and extortion led the Council of Castile to later recommend that corporal punishment, not fines, be imposed.[112]

Fair prices and fluid trade were among the most important means of maintaining a republic's dignity and civic peace, and officials spent an extraordinary amount of time trying to ensure commercial harmony. Madrid's corregidor, for example, squabbled in 1667 with the Alcaldes de Casa y Corte over, of all things, asparagus.[113] The crown's highest authority in the city explained to the queen regent (the matter reached the monarch) that "in matters of government and for the benefit of the republic, I have worked to see that [the republic] is supplied at moderate prices." As part of that policy, he had recently ordered asparagus sellers who were charging excessive prices to move their stalls from the Puerta del Sol to the Plaza Mayor, where they could be better controlled. He had killed two birds with one stone in so doing, he reported, clearing a public thoroughfare of loose women and shiftless men who shared disreputable habits. "Considering that the asparagus sellers did not announce their wares with the appropriate publicity, but rather had them hidden in crates behind their stalls," he had ordered them to move, "with very positive ef-

---

Traders: The World of the Guilds in Venice and Europe, c. 1250–c. 1650 (London: Croom Helm, 1987), 177–178.

[111] AV 3.404.37.

[112] Similar payments to those who denounced fraud existed elsewhere in Spain (AMB Hi 1392 and AHN CS leg. 7137, doc. 1), and in Mexico.

[113] AV 3.405.23.

fects for *la causa publica*." The effects on his career were not nearly as positive; the asparagus vendors protested and the alcaldes ordered his arrest, prompting his appeal to the queen regent.

The asparagus vendors preferred being down the street in the Puerta del Sol. Where vendors sold was of immense concern to them for obvious economic reasons but also for reasons of tradition. Likewise, sales sites were of interest to authorities for motives of public order and public health. Women who sold fowl (*gallineras*), for example, got into trouble over the matter of eviscerated birds, live versus dead birds, and smelly birds, the latter of which led to the women being booted down to Lavapiés. Naturally, they appealed:

> For more than forty years the said guild [of *gallineras*] has had the use and custom in this city of Madrid of *la zapatería vieja* [the area where used shoes were sold, on the east side of the square] from 15 May of each year until St. Michael's Day, when the Plaza Mayor is cleared for three bullfights. . . . And this city assigned the said guild its site because it is appropriate and cool. . . . And it is in the interest of the said guild and the good government of the republic that the said guild be in the said street for the benefit of the fowl and game, and if this were not so the game would rot because of the dust and the summer heat, and both the republic and the said guild would suffer great harm.[114]

Vendors of used items, especially hats and shoes, were near the bottom of the business world, not necessarily because of any inherent stigma but because they were a constant annoyance to other guilds. They were prohibited from dealing with new objects, and there are endless examples of alguaciles sniffing out new bolts of cloth, or a piece of leather with which a cobbler could surreptitiously make new shoes. While it is no doubt true that creating a new object was cause for greater admiration than repairing an old one, it is no less true that used-clothing dealers were taxpayers, litigants, and vecinos just like these who handled and made new items. They might have had less prestige, but at the same time they often were praised because they especially served the poor, which every petitioner naturally pointed out. A series of disputes between *sombrereros de nuevo* and *sombrereros de viejo* in the Plaza Mayor illustrates how problems of the marketplace could stir up theoretical issues first raised in far distant and quieter arenas and how the geography of commerce was more than a matter of being in the shade or getting better customers. Exactly how many secondhand and new hatters there were is hard to say, as sometimes one group was distinguished from the other and sometimes not (yet another indication that the crafts hierarchy was a contingent one.) In 1625, there were

---

[114] AV 2.245.21. See also AHN CS Libro 1226.

fifty-seven hatters listed in a Madrid *donativo* record book (probably the two guilds combined), and most gave 4 reales (equal to two-thirds of a day's wages in Seville two years later).[115] In 1636, the hatters guild was assessed 900 reales (whether in copper or silver we do not know) for a donativo, the same as the carpenters and just less than the locksmiths, which would seem to indicate things were going well for them.[116] But in 1659, the secondhand and new hatters (separately) were excluded from a Madrid donativo for being too poor, although they may have ended up paying something anyway. Forty-two of 113 guilds that year also were excluded for being too poor.[117]

In 1613, the *sombrereros de viejo* successfully appealed to the Council of Castile against the corregidor and recovered their right to sell fixed-up hats by the gallows.[118] This may not appear to be the most appealing of spots to set up shop, but the hatters claimed it was the tradition, and the council agreed, ordering custom to be maintained (*se guarde la costumbre*). It is worth emphasizing that craftsmen who essentially patched hats for a living had merited the attention of the highest magistrates in the land and won. But the issue was back in court seven years later when the corregidor, after complaints by the *sombrereros de nuevo* and arrests by the alguaciles, again ordered them to move away from the gallows. In their appeal this time, their lawyer argued there was "no cause or reason to innovate":

> The plaza should be the site of necessary occupations of ordinary commerce, and there are no better examples than my clients, who benefit poor and needy, honest people who avail themselves of the convenience of the sale and repair of old goods. It is both useful and advantageous that they remain in the said site, where locals and outsiders can seek them out for their needs. My clients are honest, needy, poor people who support their homes and their families with the said trade, and they have worked in the said site since time immemorial.

As *sombrereros de viejo* were being denounced by the alguaciles and seemingly consistently vindicated by higher authorities, there were simultaneous suits against the hatters for trying to pass off rotten (*podridos*) hats as new ones, and skirmishes over an allegedly fifty-year-old custom of hanging a sort of blanket over their stalls. Apparently it was not just the city that wanted the hatters away from the gallows, for in 1641 the owners of the houses next to the Casa de la Panadería (present-day municipal offices on the north side of the square) complained that in fact the used-hat dealers

---

[115] AGS CG leg. 3251, Libro 86; BN VE 208–45.
[116] AGS CG leg. 3251, Libro 61.
[117] AV 2.315.32.
[118] AV 2.245.27. See also AHN CS Libros 1218 and 1267.

were not gathering by the gallows at all but were trailing down Calle de Amargura (Bitterness Street, so called because prisoners would be escorted there), also on the north side, and generally getting in the way of business and pedestrians. This was not just a nuisance but a fraud, the neighbors said: "They thus cheat people who can distinguish the old from the new only by the stands they are sold in, not by their quality." So much for the hatters' argument that location was crucial for serving the people. But decades later, in 1681, the secondhand hatters were again (or still) reported using the northwest corner of the plaza, keeping it clean and well-lit at night to ward off vagabonds.

These disputes illustrate a few ways in which artisans cohabited in two worlds, described by Michael Sonenscher as the world of legal argument and the world of the bazaar.[119] It was the realm of order and the realm of flux, but there was order to this realm of flux, and a great deal of legality. Throughout, exchange relations—production, consumption, and sales— were conducted according to standards and principles that were well known and articulated by all concerned and cannot be designated by us as mere tradition any more than guild ordinances could be deemed *mera política.*

Logically, the countless craft rules and the ensuing litigation drove late-eighteenth-century economists to distraction, though not all of them were willing to go as far as Smith and Jovellanos in recommending the guilds' disappearance. Though merchants themselves might rail against the *gremios menores* and their ordinances, they also stood to lose from wholesale deregulation. "The liberty that Commerce requires cannot be understood as absolute. It must be subject to rules appropriate to the constitution of the state," cautioned the director of the Cinco Gremios Mayores, who was not prepared to entirely give up the world he was losing.[120] He, like the rest of his generation, had somehow to work with an extraordinary and often contradictory array of imperatives involving ambition and enterprise, faith and form, and the specific and the general, along with the state's simultaneous duty of justice to each inhabitant of the republic and to the *patria* at large. The path between the physical marketplace of downtown Madrid and the abstract marketplace of Adam Smith was littered with obstacles.

If there was a divide between the old rules of commerce and the new, the same was true of the rules of morality. Though Jovellanos promised that liberty would not lead to fraud, there were many who harbored doubts, most notably the clergy. There were many reasons for mutual dis-

---

[119] Michael Sonenscher, *Work and Wages: Natural Law, Politics and the Eighteenth-Century French Trades* (Cambridge University Press, 1989), 30.

[120] Heros Fernández, "Discursos sobre el comercio," vol. 26, 227–228.

trust between crown and church in eighteenth-century Spain, a relationship in which the former had the advantage. The church had immense landholdings, but its earnings were heavily taxed. The 1753 concordat confirmed the crown's capacity to appoint bishops and archbishops. The Jesuits were expelled in 1767, after the Esquilache riots. There were stark social and political differences within the church—notable clergymen, in fact, were members of some Economic Societies, while others supported the Inquisition's ban on certain books providing the underpinning of the reforms—further undermining its ability to oppose the crown. But though the ministers of Charles III and Charles IV opposed the church as an institution on many fronts, they were believers. (The same cannot be said for some of the writers of the period.) In other words, secularization was not on the agenda. The obligation to work was as much a Christian precept as it was an Enlightened one. Campomanes, who died a Franciscan tertiary, sought the secular virtue of which J. G. A. Pocock has written with respect to English-speaking eighteenth-century Protestants; Jovellanos was as scandalized as any clergyman at the immorality of contemporary theater.[121] But while some reformers and priests, and the monarchs themselves, were able to find a compromise between Christian virtue and commercial wealth, between the republic and the marketplace, others could not.

Some of the most ferocious opposition to the reforms came from the charismatic traveling preachers who, in Charles Noel's words, had "a keen sense of evil, and an equally sharp sense of virtue."[122] Theirs was a "perverse century, a damned century, a century of error," Diego José de Cádiz declaimed.[123] The English traveler Joseph Townsend caught Fray Diego's act in Cartagena: Every evening, Townsend reported, the Capuchin preached to more than ten thousand people, some of whom assembled in the main square before sunrise to assure themselves of good seats. Like any good celebrity, the preacher had bodyguards to "prevent his clothes from being torn from his back for relics."[124] Though requiring protection from the masses, Diego and his *compadres* were fearless when it came to confronting

[121] J. G. A. Pocock, *The Machiavellian Moment: Florentine Political Thought and the Atlantic Republican Tradition* (Princeton University Press, 1975), chap. 14.

[122] Charles C. Noel, "Missionary Preachers in Spain: Teaching Social Virtue in the Eighteenth Century," *American Historical Review* 90 (October 1985): 887. See also William Callahan, "Utility, Material Progress, and Morality in 18th-Century Spain," in *The Triumph of Culture: 18th-Century Perspectives*, ed. Paul Fritz and David Williams (Toronto: A. M. Hakkert, 1972), 353–368; and Francisco Sanchez-Blanco, "La situación espiritual en España hacia mediados del Siglo XVIII vista por Pedro Calatayud: Lo que un Jesuita predicaba antes de la expulsión," *Archivo Hispalense*, no. 217 (1988): 15–34.

[123] Cited in José Alvarez Junco, "La Sociedad Aragonesa de Amigos del País en el siglo XVIII," *Revista de Occidente*, no. 69 (December 1968): 308.

[124] Joseph Townsend, *A Journey through Spain in the Years 1786 and 1787, with Particular Attention to the Agriculture, Manufactures, Commerce, Population, Taxes, and Revenue of That Country; and Remarks in Passing Through a Part of France*, vol. 3 (London, 1792), 147–148.

the crown. They had no hesitation about naming names of godless merchants and ministers—Diego's lips "were purified with a burning coal," according to a contemporary—resulting in frequent appearances before secular and church authorities, who warned them to temper their language.[125] But these were mild risks to run for men who clearly believed that novelties were undermining the foundations of Christian society. Their "missions" could last weeks, engulfing cities, towns, and villages in enthusiasm and fear. Pedro de Calatayud, who in mid-century introduced Spain to the cult of the *corazón de Jesús,* was famous for organizing nighttime processions that included *asaltos,* assaults in which unsuspecting sinners would be jumped upon with loud warnings of the imminent destruction of their morally corrupt world. The economic language of the reformers was understood by this sector of the church to be an endorsement of greed and injustice. Though preachers at times seemed obsessed with sexual behavior and family relations, they were equally worried about business. They did not confine their appearances to churches; they preached anywhere they could, including in marketplaces, which many of them regarded as the site of some of the greatest sinning. The rich were damned, that was clear, but the poor, too, were endangered: Calatayud, in particular, warned craftsmen against cheating their customers.

Not surprisingly, Calatayud also spoke out in favor of the just price, a concept whose origins lay in Roman law. Aquinas had developed a subjective theory of value combining Augustine's idea that human want determined value and Aristotle's notions of use value and exchange value, placing the problem of price within the larger context of universal justice: "If the price exceeds the quantity of value of the thing, or conversely if the thing exceeds the price, the equality of justice is destroyed."[126] For Mercado, the just price was part of natural law, "written in our soul and in the

---

[125] William J. Callahan, *Church, Politics, and Society in Spain, 1750–1874* (Harvard University Press, 1984), 64. In one of the most famous such episodes, the Economic Society of Zaragoza protested to the Council of Castile after Diego José denounced Lorenzo Normante y Carcavilla to the Inquisition for his views on luxury. The modern editor of Normante's essays comments that Normante is better known today for Fray Diego's assault than for his own ideas, which the editor suggests is only fair.

[126] Thomas Aquinas, *Summa theologica,* II, II, qu. 77, cited in John W. Baldwin, *The Medieval Theories of the Just Price: Romanists, Canonists, and Theologians in the Twelfth and Thirteenth Centuries* (Philadelphia: American Philosophical Society, 1959), 72. On the just price, see also José Barrientos, "El pensamiento económico en la perspectiva filosófico-teológica," in *El pensamiento económico en la Escuela de Salamanca* (Universidad de Salamanca, 1998), 103–108; José Barrientos, *Un siglo de moral económica en Salamanca (1526–1629),* 2 vols. (Universidad de Salamanca, 1985); Marcia L. Colish, *Medieval Foundations of the Western Intellectual Tradition 400–1400* (New Haven: Yale University Press, 1997), 330–332; J. Gilchrist, *The Church and Economic Activity in the Middle Ages* (London: Macmillan, 1969), 58–62, 116–118; Francisco Gómez Camacho, ed., *Luis de Molina: La teoría del justo precio* (Madrid: Editora Nacional, 1981); and Marjorie Grice-Hutchinson, *Early Economic Thought in Spain, 1177–1740* (London: George Allen and Unwin, 1978), 81–122.

law of nature."[127] Its counterpart in positive law was price ceilings, which in Spain (and elsewhere) had existed for hundreds of years and affected hundreds of items. The monarchy in 1502 said it was enforcing price ceilings on grain because "all the wheat is in the hands of resellers or people who do not need it, and they hold back the said wheat, giving rise to disorderly prices that severely trouble the poor and miserable." Seventy years later, Philip II appealed to his Christian subjects in reiterating that disobeying price controls was tantamount to violating one's conscience and committing a sin against one's neighbors.[128] Most moralists, theologians, and political commentators of the sixteenth century defended price ceilings. One exception was Luis de Mejía y Ponce de León, the creator of Doña Ocio, who published a treatise against Philip II's grain price ceilings in 1569.[129] Mercado two years later published a defense of the laws in reply to Mejía, saying a republic would be most cruel with its citizens were it to leave the price of wheat up to merchants.[130] Another well-known treatise on the subject was by the humanist Pedro de Valencia: when harvests fall short and immoral merchants hold back their product only to sell it later at inflated prices, he wrote, "God is gravely offended and the poor suffer and die, and the Republic suffers grave injury, becoming weak and missing its most willing members, who are like its feet and hands, carrying the weight and suffering the hardships."[131] Complaints about high prices induced by hoarding, such as in the case of an egg-seller in Madrid who had "the use and custom on Fridays and other days when there is a shortage of eggs to hide and conceal them in various places and take them out little by little for her business," typically followed a formula in which the culprit was said to have "shown no fear of God or justice and seriously harmed and damaged the republic."[132] Sellers who exceeded established prices were punished and their goods were seized. A woman in Seville, for example, who sold cherries and plums above the set price was sentenced to two hundred lashes.[133]

---

[127] Tomás de Mercado, *Suma de Tratos y Contratos* (1571), ed. Nicolás Sánchez Albornoz (Madrid: Instituto de Estudios Fiscales, 1977), 45.

[128] Angel García Sanz, "El contexto económico del pensamiento escolástico: El florecimiento del capital mercantil en la España del siglo XVI," in *El pensamiento económico en la Escuela de Salamanca*, ed. Francisco Gómez Camacho, 27; *Nueva Recopilación*, Libro 5, tit. 25, ley 6.

[129] Luis de Mexía y Ponce de León, *Lakonismos* (1569). Mejía's name is frequently spelled Mexía.

[130] Mercado, *Suma de Tratos y Contratos,* vol. 1, 261.

[131] Pedro de Valencia, "Discurso o memorial sobre el precio del pan" (1605), in *Obras Completas*, ed. Rafael González Cañal (Universidad de León, 1994), vol. 4, pt. 1, 32–33. See also Melchor de Soria, *Tratado de la justificación y conveniencia de la tassa de el pan* (1627), ed. Francisco Gómez Camacho.(Madrid: Fundación Banco Exterior), 1992.

[132] AHN CS leg. 42.482, exp. 188.

[133] Francisco de Ariño, *Sucesos de Sevilla de 1592–1604* (Seville: Ayuntamiento de Sevilla, 1993), 6 May 1597.

The ceiling on grain prices was lifted on 11 July 1765 after several decades' worth of consideration. Proponents of the measure argued that liberalization would revitalize the economy and would be good not only for large merchants and growers but also for the common people, who, despite the price ceilings (or, according to some, because of them), were frequent victims of scarcities and price spikes. Among the measure's chief champions were the Junta de Comercio, the marquis of Esquilache, and Campomanes, the last arguing that the *tasa,* or ceiling, violated property rights and that only the market would ensure distributive justice.[134] Among its opponents were the church hierarchy, city councils, and intendants, who predicted public disturbances as prices rose and were proven right the following year when the Esquilache riots occurred. Nor was the Council of Castile ever entirely convinced of the merits of liberalization. In subsequent years, the poor remained vulnerable to bad harvests and speculators, and production did not increase as expected. Many towns maintained their granaries, or *pósitos,* to make up for shortfalls. Though all remaining price controls on food were lifted in June 1767, they were reimposed in 1772; the *tasa* finally was restored in 1804, a year of disastrous harvests and plague.

Debates over prices, both in the eighteenth century and before, were implicitly linked to those over the role of labor and laborers in the republic. First, price included labor; already in 1553 the neo-scholastic Domingo de Soto had suggested that labor was one of several factors involved in calculating price.[135] At around the same time as Soto, Cristóbal de Villalón, explaining how to calculate a just wage, said one must measure the republic's need of a particular craft and then the scarcity or abundance of those who performed it. "The silversmith is worth more than the digger (*el cavador*), though the latter works harder, because there are more diggers than silversmiths. . . . Industry also raises the price; therefore the master who designs the work is worth more than the apprentice who makes it."[136] Gutiérrez de los Ríos in 1600 described added value when he wrote that "with labor, craftsmen give being and estimation to things that do not possess them, and they give being and greater quality to pearls and precious stones."[137] Martínez de la Mata, celebrated by Campomanes, in the 1650s got even closer to describing a labor theory of value:

---

[134] Campomanes's best-known writing on the subject is "Respuesta fiscal sobre abolir la tasa y establecer el comercio de granos," of 10 September 1764. See also Llombart, *Campomanes, economista y político de Carlos III,* chap. 5.

[135] Domingo de Soto, *De la justicia y del derecho* (1556) (Madrid: Instituto de Estudios Políticos, 1968), vol. 3, book 6, 544–545.

[136] Cristóbal de Villalón, *Provechoso tratado de cambios y contrataciones . . .* (Valladolid, 1541), 19v.

[137] Gaspar Gutiérrez de los Ríos, *Noticia general para la estimación de las artes . . .* (Madrid, 1600), 261.

Peasants do not give the fruits of the earth more being than that which Nature gave them. While they are in their possession, they are worth little. Passing to the hands of *fabricantes,* their estimation grows from one to a hundred
because intrinsic value is formed from the benefits which, *en la fábrica,* are
given to all through whom they pass, until they reach the consumer, who pays
the price that sustains the Republic.[138]

In a world in which producers usually were sellers, it was logical that concrete labor was both the key to establishing an equitable price and the ul-
timate source of value. Over time, however, classical political economy
overtook neo-scholastic considerations, and utility (from the buyer's perspective) came to replace labor as the critical determinant of exchange
value. The law of supply and demand implicitly reflected what was valued—that is, what had utility—and labor increasingly was abstracted from
the actual physical exertion involved in making a commodity. Labor in the
abstract created value, enabling exchange. To cite Smith, "The real value
of all the different component parts of price . . . is measured by the quantity of labor which they can, each of them, purchase or command."[139]
Second, the people doing the buying and the selling (and the making)
of the foods and commodities of daily life were those often considered by
historians to have been outside the realm of politics and decent social in-
tercourse, yet it was their protests, their purchasing power, their skills, and
their ability (or not) to maintain themselves in a somewhat dignified fashion that impelled theologians and royal officials to come up with laws, wage
schedules, and price lists to ensure economic justice. The exchange of
products and of labor power took place in the same discursive, moral, and
physical realm, in which collective considerations outweighed individual
ones, and that fact changed less over time in Spain than is usually thought.
Indeed, in this regard there was a profound disjuncture between the language of Smith and Locke and the language of the *ilustrados.* If Valentín
de Foronda, a well-born Basque businessman and political reformer, could
celebrate commerce in 1787 by exclaiming that it "transforms ferocious
spirits into sweet dispositions, cruel hearts into soft natures, and savage
men who obey neither limits nor laws into tranquil and docile citizens,"
then it should be clear that sociability still trumped self-interest, both on
moral and on efficacious grounds.[140] Foronda might as well have been cit-

[138] Martínez de la Mata, *Memoriales,* 98.

[139] Adam Smith, *An Inquiry into the Nature and Causes of the Wealth of Nations,* ed. R. H. Campbell and A. S. Skinner, 2 vols. (Oxford: Clarendon Press, 1976), vol. 1, 67; Ronald L. Meek,
Studies in the Labor Theory of Value (New York: Monthly Review Press, 1956), chap. 1.

[140] Valentín de Foronda, *Miscelánea o colección de varios discursos . . .* (Madrid, 1787), 21–
22. For more on Foronda (1751–1821), later a Spanish consul to the United States and a
member of the American Philosophical Society, see José Manuel Barrenechea, *Valentín de
Foronda, reformador y economista ilustrado* (Vitoria: Diputación Foral de Alava, 1984); and An-

ing Cicero, for whom cities and commerce "led to a softening of men's spirits and a sense of shame; the result was that life became less vulnerable, and through giving and receiving, through sharing out abilities and advantages, we came to lack nothing."[141]

Membership in the Spanish republic may have depended less on what one owned than on how one lived and what one did, and what one did could still be a matter of vindication. Values, in both senses of the word, may have been quite different than they were elsewhere, though simultaneous (and competing) discourses could and did exist in Spain, each offering a slightly different vision of virtue and worth. There was room for Aristotle, Jesus, and Machiavelli as well as for Locke and Smith. Stated objectives and outcomes were not always in accordance with each other because the languages of science, the law, and the marketplace did not always fit, in the sense that we would have them match material circumstances or historical developments. But overall, the eighteenth-century narrative of the behavior, obligations, and possibilities of the lowest members of the Spanish republic was a story whose preface and argument remained focused on the collective. To the degree that it did not, it was not true. To the extent that subsequent accounts failed in the same manner, they have told the wrong story.

---

tonio Elorza, *La ideología liberal en la ilustración española* (Madrid: Editorial Tecnos, 1970), chap. 6.

[141] Cicero, *On Duties,* ed. M. T. Griffin and E. M. Atkins (Cambridge University Press 1991), book II, 15, p. 68.

CHAPTER FOUR

The New Work Ethic

Spanish dramatic works of the Golden Age rarely, if ever, feature crafts-men or artisans as protagonists. When they appear, they are mere *pícaros*, idle rogues, comic relief in a corrupt urban landscape. They are not peo-ple. In the works of Cervantes and Lope de Vega and Calderón de la Barca, people who worked honestly with their hands for a living—with the obvi-ous and meaningful exception of farmers and peasants—were conspicu-ously absent.[1] As elsewhere in Europe, they began appearing on stages in the later eighteenth century, encouraged from the wings by Campomanes, Jovellanos, and others who were convinced that their real-life counterparts needed educating.

In 1784, a Madrid jury chosen by Campomanes gave the playright Cán-dido María Trigueros one of the prizes in a competition to celebrate the birth of the twin princes Carlos and Felipe (who soon died) and the sign-ing of the 1783 Peace of Versailles. Trigueros's *Los Menestrales* was a light look at amorous mix-ups and deceptions. The hero of the play is Justo, the anti-noble, upright, hardworking, virtuous new man, an honest and faith-ful tailor who is in love with Rufina. She in turn is seduced by Rafa, who pretends to be a nobleman but really is an unhappy shoemaker anxious to escape his fellow "victims of sweat and scorn." After much ado about noth-ing, all ends well, Justo marries Rufina, and the audience learns that every-one should stick to his or her own class. Don Juan, the host of the onstage celebration that is the finale, and sounding suspiciously like Campomanes,

---

[1] On the ideological function of peasants in the *comedias*, see Noël Salomon, *Lo villano en el teatro del Siglo de Oro* (Madrid: Editorial Castalia, 1985), especially 221–268.

declares that shoemakers, too, can be noble as long as they are *honrados.* "One of the best *comedias* we have," in the words of Juan Sempere y Guarinos, the play "ridicule[s] those who wish to appear more than they are."[2] The happy resolution of the disorder set in motion by pretense is one befitting the "great attention taken by the Government and the enlightenment of a philosophical century which, despite present-day ignorance, will one day be the era most honored by the human race," Trigueros commented in his prologue. The play closed after eleven days.[3]

Though it may have failed in its didactic and dramatic objectives, the work nonetheless is useful to us in that it focused on a substantial change (or a desired substantial change) in attitudes toward labor. Proponents of reform in the late eighteenth century believed (or said they believed) that craftsmen until then had aspired only to live a life of leisure. In fact, as we have seen, not only was that not necessarily true, but thinkers in the previous era also had praised men such as Justo. No matter: there was a stated conviction that something new was occurring, that old habits were being cast aside, and erroneous ideas were being repaired.

Much as the second half of part 1 was an attempt to shine light on artisans inhabiting seventeenth-century Castilian cities whose political and moral boundaries were to a large degree defined by republican discourse, this section focuses on craftsmen in the eighteenth century emerging from an age when, so we are told, work was despised. In both cases, the objective is to bring theory together with practice, or at least place the discourse of work and antiwork in the workplace and with the workers. After considering the campaigns to put both the poor and the rich to work, I finally turn to the issue that inspired this book in the first place, the exclusion of vile and mechanical workers from membership in a community. The chapter to some degree describes a paradox: eighteenth-century reformers decried the alleged ill repute of labor even as they themselves denigrated it, in a sense creating a problem in order to fix it. They relied on images and tropes familiar to any sixteenth-century parishioner while at the same time insisting they were building a new world. They attacked the old hierarchies of labor, which in fact were never firm, while around them new or revived exclusionary rules were being put into practice in a society suddenly confronted with multiple challenges to traditional structures. As they harnessed a familiar vocabulary to a carriage they hoped would quickly

[2] Juan Sempere y Guarinos, *Ensayo de una biblioteca española de los mejores escritores del reynado de Carlos III,* vol. 6 (Madrid: Impr. Real, 1789), 96. Trigueros's writings included a multitude of plays, poems, and scientific articles that, Sempere noted, were written "hastily."

[3] Cándido María Trigueros, *Los Menestrales* (1784), ed. Francisco Aguilar Piñal (Universidad de Sevilla, 1997), 89. The modern editor of the play suggests that one of the reasons for its failure was the propaganda campaign waged by the forty or so poets who lost the competition and then "flooded the capital with ill-intentioned and satirical verses" criticizing the play, in part for its instructional nature (37).

transport them to a more prosperous future, the reformers' praise for labor and their rejection of idleness had a new purposefulness characterized by a rejection of sin, an embrace of civic virtue, and a pressing desire to increase production.

The Restoration of Dignity

The deregulation of labor can be said to have begun in 1682 with Charles II's law allowing nobles to engage in commerce and industry as long as they themselves did not perform certain tasks. The latter caveat was lifted in 1770, and during the following twenty years there was a stream of edicts concerning labor, many of them repetitive. On 30 April 1772, guilds were ordered to admit qualified foreigners; on 12 January 1779, guilds were ordered to admit qualified women; on 18 March 1783, the most famous of the edicts lifted the qualification of "vile" from a host of occupations, allowing nobles to engage in them;[4] and on 2 September 1784, craftsmen with unclear parentage were allowed to join guilds. Edicts on women were reissued in 1784, 1789, and 1790;[5] edicts on foreigners (except Jews, who still could be legally banned) were reissued in 1777 and 1797.[6] It is generally thought that because of these edicts by Charles III and Charles IV, occupational prejudices lost their sway. But historians of Spanish labor often have made the mistake of assuming that restrictions from the eighteenth century were continuations from the previous era. "Vile and mechanical" was not a new concept, to be sure, but it gained new

[4] *Novísima recopilación*, libro 8, ley 8, tit. 223.

[5] The impetus for the 1779 *cédula* allowing women into guilds was opposition by Valencia's combined guild of *cordoneros, pasamaneros, y botoneros* (rope makers, braid makers, and button makers, formerly separate crafts) to the establishment of a school for girls. Presumably, the school was designed to replace the guild insofar as teaching was concerned. Following a recommendation by the Council of Castile, the king prohibited that and any other guild from interfering in such efforts to teach girls and women "to make buttons or any other craft appropriate to their sex and womanly strengths . . . thus ensuring that their hands not be idle and that men's hands be dedicated to agriculture and other more strenuous operations or in the service of weapons or the navy." See Eugenio Larruga y Boneta, *Historia de la Real y General Junta de Comercio, Moneda y Minas y Dependiencias Estrangeros y Colección Integra de los Reales Decretos, Pragmáticas, Resoluciones, Ordenes y Reglamentos* . . . , 12 vols. (Madrid 1779–1789), vol. 9, 388–390. Implementation of the decree in America seems to have lagged; a 19 November 1799 consulta from the Council of Indies urged the king to support the petitions of women in Mexico who were being harassed by guilds in their respective crafts. The council and colonial authorities, apparently to facilitate measures against the guilds, suggested that their ordinances possibly had not received royal approval back in the sixteenth century. See Richard Konetzke, ed., *Colección de documentos para la historia de la formación social de Hispanoamérica, 1493–1810*, 5 vols. (Madrid: CSIC, 1953–1962), vol. 3, pt. 2, 767–771.

[6] These and other laws can be found in Santos Sánchez, ed., *Colección de pragmáticas, cédulas, provisiones . . . en el Reynado del Señor Don Carlos III*, 3d ed. (Madrid, 1803), and a similar volume for the reign of Charles IV.

prominence in the Age of Enlightenment. In fact, prejudices concerning occupation and race (broadly defined) gained virulence.

The periodical *El Censor* in 1787 published a dialogue between a commoner and a noble in which the former proudly declared, "*Soy nuevo . . . soy cabeza, no miembro*" ("I am new . . . I am the head, not a member").[7] But Campomanes was rather taken by the old organic metaphor and approvingly cited Martínez de la Mata's observation that "the head is the principal member that sustains the rest."[8] Other champions of mechanical labor whose work is discussed below also stressed the harmonious nature of human society, much as writers had two hundred and four hundred years earlier. Limbs had their proper place, and should not be interchanged with heads. In the words of Antonio Javier Pérez y López, whose 1781 treatise on work and honor is and was widely cited, society is "a kind of chain in which each link is joined to the next in such beautiful proportion that the links sustain one another reciprocally."[9]

Equilibrium, then, was a good thing. So, too, was decency, a version of the same proposition. The rhetoric of dignity and the new man sometimes rang out in meeting halls as local Patriotic Societies awarded prizes to industrious pupils and farmers, but the rhetoric most often detected was that of sin and vice. Work was still good because it removed the possibility of *ocio*, that mother of all evils: "Honest occupation will correct the willful or barely decent habits of many," Campomanes advised.[10] Jovellanos, speaking at an awards ceremony in Madrid in 1785, commented eloquently about how the spinning school's female pupils would benefit from their experience:

Its utility and importance are especially evident in its influence on public habits. Who could deny this influence, with these innocent creatures before us? Consider for a moment the benefits they have received from us; consider the evils from which we have preserved them; see in them religious instruction replacing the grossest ignorance, honest work replacing clumsy idleness,

[7] *El Censor: Obra periódica, comenzada a publicar en 1781 y terminada en 1787*, ed. José María Caso González et al. (Oviedo: Instituto Feijóo de Estudios del Siglo XVIII, 1989). Discurso no. 163 (26 July 1787).

[8] Pedro Rodríguez de Campomanes, *Discurso sobre la educación popular* (1775), ed. F. Aguilar Piñal (Madrid: Editora Nacional, 1978), 47.

[9] Antonio Javier Pérez y López, *Discurso sobre la honra y la deshonra legal* (Madrid, 1781), 69. The Great Chain of Being was a common metaphor; the attorney general of the Parisian Parlement, Antoine-Louis Séguier, in the seventeenth century proclaimed the nation's corporations to be "links in a great chain, of which the first lies in Your Majesty's hand, as chief and sovereign administrator of everything that constitutes the corps of the nation." Cited in Clare Haru Crowston, *Fabricating Women: The Seamstresses of Old Regime France, 1675–1791* (Durham, N.C.: Duke University Press, 2001), 177.

[10] Pedro Rodríguez de Campomanes, *Discurso sobre el fomento de la industria popular* (Madrid, 1774), 176.

emulation replacing indolence, modesty replacing shamelessnes. In a word, see them placed from the roads to vice onto the path to virtue.[11]

The *ilustrados* were sure mechanical laborers suffered from *desprecio,* or scorn, and were condemned to a life of sin, and they treated them appropriately. Campomanes, following the Spanish Academy, defined *mecánico* as *bajo,* which he then, momentarily forgetting the bodily metaphor, mistook for scorn. If one is low, one must be vile. It is an estimation that corresponds poorly to the body politic described by artisans themselves in previous years. Likewise, when Campomanes expressed concern that humble theatergoers would take Lope de Vega's plays to heart and emulate the noble or shiftless characters they saw on stage, he demonstrated scant knowledge of the lives he intended to improve upon.[12] At least in this regard, the man who preached scientific investigation was curiously ignorant.

Though in many ways the corrective language of the eighteenth century was not distinct from previous language, there is one important difference: the reformers were faced with an economy in need of repair, and they possessed the political tools to impose and implement policies to that end. Treatise writers of the sixteenth and seventeenth centuries to a large degree were less concerned with policy than with ideas, though clearly there was no sharp dividing line between the two. At any rate, the *ilustrados* could try to put into practice what their ancestors had merely discussed.

The obvious place to start if one wanted to create a new workforce was with the poor, a moral and economic problem that only seemed to increase as the useful population declined. I remarked elsewhere that Campomanes's writing on the subject was almost entirely taken from the past. In the appendices to *Discurso sobre la educación popular,* he reproduced huge chunks of text by Cristóbal Pérez de Herrera, Miguel de Giginta, and Juan de Robles, the most prominent sixteenth-century writers on poverty. He and his contemporaries, like their predecessors, took excruciating care to distinguish the true poor from the false poor, the deserving from the undeserving, and good charity from bad charity, classifying beggars and their ilk into various categories, each meriting different grades of attention. Campomanes had four types of beggars; José del Campillo, a reformist minister under Philip V, had three types of poor people; Bernardo Ward

---

[11] Gaspar Melchor de Jovellanos, "Discurso pronunciado en la Sociedad económica . . ." in *Obras,* vol. 2, ed. Cándido Nocedal, Biblioteca de Autores Españoles, vol. 50 (Madrid, 1859), 32.

[12] Campomanes, *Discurso sobre la educación popular,* 251. The title of Lope's play *La pobreza no es vileza* could lead the unlearned to believe that poverty bestows honor and that the mechanical arts are dishonorable, he wrote. Campomanes's citation of the dictionary is on the same page.

had two.[13] The Madrid Economic Society in August 1781 issued a call for papers on four topics—alms, customs and labor, begging by women and children, and cleanliness—and summarized the general aim of the competition as the promotion of measures to help the "true poor." Of the nineteen entries, fifteen concerned alms. The contestants, like better-known essayists, all turned back in history to the language, categories, and debates they knew best.[14]

Most everyone agreed that more jobs were needed and that the poor had to be educated, both in attitudes and in skills, and that institutions such as workhouses could accomplish both objectives. Particularly after the fright of the 1766 Esquilache riots, workhouses were a solution to the swarms of "unprofitable subjects," as Joseph Townsend referred to the poor of Alicante, who soon were denied their alms and put under one roof where, he reported, "they are well fed and do little work at present. But when they shall have been reconciled to the idea of confinement, their diet will be administered with a more sparing hand, and their labor will be rendered more productive."[15] In Campomanes's words, "the well-directed work of men and the useful employment of their arms is truly a mine."[16] Early to bed and early to rise, the better to work twelve-hour days (or longer), he recommended elsewhere. If an item requires eight days to manufacture but takes sixteen, then money has been lost. The solution was to eliminate holidays and bad work habits, adopt strict schedules, and impose punishments when necessary.[17] Workhouses offered all that and more. After centuries of proposals for turning the idle poor into a useful

[13] For an overview of the various proposals and their authors see Rosa María Pérez Estévez, *El problema de los vagos en la España del Siglo XVIII* (Madrid: Confederación Española de Cajas de Ahorros, 1976), 301–336. See part 3 for a discussion of Ward's and Campillo's works and the possibility that one plagiarized from the other.

[14] Real Sociedad Económica de Amigos del País, *Colección de las memorias premiadas y de las que se acordó se imprimiesen sobre . . . el ejercicio de la caridad y socorro de los verdaderos pobres . . .* (Madrid, 1784). The assignment for the essay on customs and work, which garnered just one respondent, was: "If general dedication toward work and the endeavor and effort that each person should devote to improving themselves and moving ahead in their profession or occupation and to administering their property or promoting and favoring the perseverent and industrious is the only practical way in civil society [*el orden civil*] to conserve good habits, public decency, and culture where they exist and to introduce them where they do not." The only submission, which answered in the affirmative, was seventeen pages long and began with the story of Adam and Eve.

[15] Joseph Townsend, *A Journey through Spain in the Years 1786 and 1787, with Particular Attention to the Agriculture, Manufactures, Commerce, Population, Taxes, and Revenue of That Country; and Remarks in Passing Through a Part of France* (London, 1792), vol. 3, 183–185.

[16] "Oración gratulatoria," 16 September 1775, in Alberto Bosch, *El Centenario: Apuntes para la historia de la Sociedad Económica Matritense* (Madrid: Impr. y fundición de M. Tello, 1875), 191. In a similar vein, the English Quaker John Bellers complained of "The labor of the poor being the mines of the rich." Cited in Karl Polanyi, *The Great Transformation: The Political and Economic Origins of Our Time* (Boston: Beacon Press, 1957), 105.

[17] Campomanes, *Discurso sobre la educación popular,* 170–171.

resource—for blending punishment, training, education, shelter, rescue, and reform in differing proportions—it finally was a reality and there were no (or far fewer) bothersome theologians complaining that economics was eclipsing Christian charity. The recollections of a joiner in Valladolid attest to the shadow cast by the new institutions:

> They rounded up all the *vagos,* both boys and married men who mistreat their wives, and they issued an edict ordering all women to work and not gather thistles, alfalfa, ears of grain, or gleanings under punishment of confinement, where they would be made to spin, because the serge makers complain that no one will spin and they say they'll give the women work, and also the men.[18]

According to William Callahan, some twenty-five cities founded work-houses by the end of the eighteenth century. There the poor were told charity was theirs but they had to earn it. Some of these institutions were huge: Barcelona's had 960 inmates and Madrid's more than 1,600.[19] In Cádiz, Townsend observed eight hundred people working at forty-five looms and fifteen stocking frames along with a sea of spinning wheels, workbenches, and other smaller work stations.[20] For the count of Florida-blanca, chief minister of Charles III and Charles IV, workhouses ensured that charity would be controlled by the state, not individuals. Relying on the latter, or, worse, on the mendicant orders, was "prejudicial and dangerous" because confusion inevitably arose over who was deserving and who was not. Such "promiscuous charity" amounted to "a contempt of public authority," in the view of the count.[21]

Ambivalence over the respective roles of the state and the (private) economy in this new world where each man perhaps was on his own, but perhaps not, also was reflected in the inextricable relationship between education and work. The logo of the La Bañeza Economic Society (in the mountains of León) featured a boy working a warp frame saying, "I learn and I am helped" (*Aprendo y soy socorrido*); Madrid's motto was "Help by teaching" (*Socorre enseñando*).[22] A disproportionate number of the poor, of course, were very young, and attention to this problem bore a particular discursive imprint. Unemployed youths were potentially dangerous; the boys caused one kind of trouble, the girls could cause another. Fortunately

[18] Ventura Pérez, *Diario de Valladolid* (1885) (Valladolid, 1983), 501. The edict was announced 13 June 1779.

[19] William J. Callahan, *Honor, Commerce, and Industry in Eighteenth-Century Spain.* (Boston: Baker Library, Harvard University, 1972), 60–63.

[20] Townsend, *A Journey through Spain,* vol. 2, 350.

[21] October 1788 memorial to Charles III, in William Coxe, *Memoirs of the Kings of Spain of the House of Bourbon,* 3 vols. (London, 1813), vol. 1, 356–358.

[22] Valentina K. Tikoff, "Assisted Transitions: Children and Adolescents in the Orphanages of Seville at the End of the Old Regime, 1681–1831" (Ph.D. diss., Indiana University, 2000), 17–18.

they were malleable, but it was essential to get to them quickly. In a 1726 letter to the Council of Castile, Seville's governor recommended that a poorhouse be established (the proposal would take a century to bear fruit) to serve, among others, children at "the most dangerous ages." He was supported by the city council, which commented on the "ruin to honest living at such risky ages" which resulted from "too much liberty."[23] Decades later, the city's Economic Society, which also urged that a poorhouse be built, pointed to "the common passions to which youth is most inclined," including "haughtiness, pride, vanity, ire, vengeance, tenacity, etc."[24] Yet the degree to which education and work could and should be combined was not clear. One small example can be found at Los Toribios, a Seville institution for boys, many of whom were sent out to work in crafts workshops, a practice also followed in many workhouses that contracted out. In the late eighteenth century, however, a school administrator called for an end to it: the boys "will never become masters [because] they learn just one step and nothing else. He who learns to be a tailor or a hatter or a shoemaker will never know anything other than these pieces . . . and the same is true of the brazier or gilder, who has no science beyond his buttons or tacks."[25] Apprenticeship was not what it had been, though there had been no complaints in the past that an apprentice hatter learned only to make hats, not shoes. In deploring the allegedly low level of instruction offered by the guild structure, judged to be wholly inefficient, this administrator, like Campomanes, was preparing the way, deliberately or not, for labor practices that sacrificed art for science, with science apparently having acquired a quantitative meaning.

There were few more irritating thoughts for late-eighteenth-century economic reformers than that urban women were not working enough. The fault lay with the women themselves, the guilds, and, of course, France. The director of the Madrid Economic Society calculated that the capital city was populated by sixty-five thousand women, twenty-five thousand of whom lived in idleness. If each were to spin six ounces of material a day, he figured, thirty million ounces could be produced in a working year of two hundred days.[26] Similarly, Ward believed there were one million idle women in all of Spain, not counting the wives of all the Spanish soldiers abroad, who he recommended should do more handicrafts. (Allowing children of five or six years old to be breadwinners would be an incentive for people to marry, he further reasoned, which in turn could

---

[23] AHN CS leg. 34, doc. 7, cited in Tikoff, "Assisted Transitions," 12.
[24] Tikoff, "Assisted Transitions," 15.
[25] Archivo Histórico de la Diputación Provincial de Sevilla, Hospicio, leg. 1, doc. 24, cited in Tikoff, "Assisted Transitions," 228.
[26] Cited in Callahan, *Honor, Commerce and Industry*, 64.

alleviate the population shortage.)[27] Returning to the old lament, Campomanes compared the strapping peasant women of northern Spain who worked in the fields, carried heavy tubs of butter, and sold fresh fish in the market, to the women of central and southern Spain, who lived "in profound repose, in misery," perhaps, he said, because they were more vulnerable to the pernicious influence of the Moors. Nuns and priests could be especially helpful in encouraging women to improve themselves, he thought, teaching them to read and perform honest occupations.[28] Those who might feel "false compassion" for women's lot, thinking that household tasks were time-consuming, would be making a big mistake: "[Such people] don't notice that women rise late and maids spend as much time fixing themselves up as their mistresses do, they take long siestas and long walks on work days, dress as luxuriously as their mistresses, and generally have the custom of idling away most of the day and the night."[29] By specifically making women part of the problem, Campomanes was carrying on a long tradition of dismissing or ignoring women's domestic existence and activities, easing the way for taking control of such untenable frivolity. The fact that southern women in particular were singled out for abuse (though southerners in general were not treated fondly by the Asturian) also signals that gender provided a convenient way of discussing the vast regional, economic, and cultural disparities in Spain. It also brought the subject back to conspicuous consumption, a crime often attributed especially to women: Mandeville had scoffed at the laborer's wife who would "starve herself and her husband to purchase a second-hand gown and petticoat that cannot do half the service because forsooth it is more genteel."[30] In eighteenth-century France, too, polite, civilized behavior associated with women was counterposed to a more desirable, hardy patriotism.[31] Though Campomanes appeared to blame women for their own inactivity and weakness, two sins that imperiled the new national project, Jovellanos at least blamed society, which he said had chosen to see women solely as objects of

[27] Bernardo Ward, *Proyecto económico en que se proponen varias providencias, dirigidas a promover los intereses de España con los medios y fondos necesarios para su plantificación* (1762) (Madrid, posth. 1779), xvi, 10. Campomanes believed that teaching small children to read and write was harmless as long as they were still too young to hold a job, and it had the added advantage of keeping them busy. "If I thought [literacy] was incompatible with popular industry, I would be the first to prohibit it," he assured his readers (Campomanes, *Discurso sobre la educación popular*, 113–114).

[28] Campomanes, *Discurso sobre la educación popular*, 207–218.

[29] Pedro Rodríguez de Campomanes, *Apéndice a la Educación Popular* (Madrid, 1775), vol. 2, 126.

[30] Bernard de Mandeville, *The Fable of the Bees, or Private Vices, Public Benefits* (London, 1714), 105.

[31] David Bell, *The Cult of the Nation in France: Inventing Nationalism, 1680–1800* (Cambridge, Mass.: Harvard University Press, 2001), 149–150.

pleasure, thus depriving them of their liberty and depriving society of the products of their labor.[32] In fact, according to at least one study of eighteenth-century rural industry, women were not only very busy working but were key to the success of development efforts in New Castile, efforts whose existence may have escaped the notice of officials and historians precisely because the labor was feminine.[33]

For Campomanes, the key to reviving the Spanish economy lay in the establishment of "popular industry," by which he meant occupations and enterprises that would reduce the gap between rural and urban, provide villages with goods available only in cities or abroad, remove the restive poor from the cities, and bring some wealth to depressed areas. Peasants, both men and women, spent a great deal of the year doing very little, he believed, and combining their agricultural pursuits with industrial ones would make for a far more productive economy. He similarly advocated, as we have seen, schools and manufacturing efforts in the cities. But in specifying that the new workforce should above all comprise women, the poor, the unemployed, beggars, children, and vagrants, one is hardpressed to see how he was honoring mechanical labor. On the contrary, it would appear that a new underclass was being proposed for what was, in essence, protoindustrialization. The jobs would be so simple even women and children could perform them; it was "sedentary work not worthy of the name 'occupation.'"[34] This new dignity was a dubious distinction.

Economic reformers all recognized the structural defects of the Spanish economy: there simply was no work. But it was no less true that the poor were assumed to be lazy, every bit as much as Doña Ocio's subjects had been. Indeed, the weariness of the language with which eighteenth-century intellectuals treated the subject makes one wonder if they weren't conscious of the echo and if it wasn't making them feel a bit indolent themselves. "Given that divine and human law obliges us to help the true poor, the nation as a whole [*el voto común*] cries out that the healthy should be corrected and put to work," Campomanes told the Madrid Economic Society.[35] Normante y Carcavilla suggested that friendly priests, "after teaching the holy mysteries, should encourage love for methodical work and inspire horror against the capital vice of ociosidad."[36] In his periodi-

---

[32] Gaspar Melchor de Jovellanos, "Informe . . . sobre el libre ejercicio de las artes," in *Obras*, vol. 2, 34–36.

[33] José A. Nieto Sánchez, "'Nebulosas industriales' y capital mercantil urbano: Castilla la Nueva y Madrid, 1750–1850," *Sociología del Trabajo*, nueva época, no. 39 (Spring 2000): 88–89. Campomanes was aware of the efficient sexual division of labor in Novés (Toledo), but his writings indicate he assumed it was the exception.

[34] Cited in Ricardo Krebs Wilckens, *El pensamiento histórico, político y económico del conde de Campomanes* (Santiago de Chile: Universidad de Chile, 1960), 252.

[35] "Oración gratulatoria," 16 September 1775, cited in Alberto Bosch, *El Centenario*, 193.

[36] Lorenzo Normante y Carcavilla, *Discurso sobre la utilidad de los conocimientos Econó-*

cal publication, Clavijo y Faxardo declared, "the evils about which I have most reflected these days are laziness, idleness, negligence, and indolence, all of which can be restated as *pereza*, their true mother."[37] José Cadalso protested that "for every Spaniard who works in a mechanical art, there are endless more who wish to shut their shops and go north to Asturias or to the mountains to claim their *hidalguía*."[38] Such complaints recall the formulaic debates among sixteenth-century moralists as they devised hierarchical schemes of the mechanical and liberal arts and crafts, or the sermons that pointed to the Creation and the Fall as evidence that we were put on this Earth to labor, or the glosses of Cicero and Aristotle in treatises devoted to describing workers' place in a perfect republic. The new voices may have been more cold-blooded—"If a man is without an occupation, he is dead as far as the state is concerned," Nicolás de Arriquíbar wrote— but the horror of inactivity and the categorical condemnation of those who practiced it did not spell a new work ethic as much as it did a redeployment of economic and moral categories.[39]

When the historian Jean Sarrailh described Spain's urban denizens as people who "lived in profound ignorance, led a mediocre existence, and had nothing but gross or reprehensible distractions," he took his portrait from the reformers' depictions.[40] In the style of those who love humanity but cannot stand people, Campomanes generally glorified work while spending as little time as possible with those who actually performed it, who were simply indecent, according to their alleged champion: "Their scant cleanliness makes it easy to confuse them with beggars or vagabonds," he wrote. Apprentices should be instructed in Christian morals, "civil knowledge" (but guilds must not hold meetings on public affairs or "get involved in things that are not their concern and which they do not understand"), and hygiene, this last point being of particular concern; artisans routinely left their houses in the morning dirty, uncombed, unwashed, and with ripped clothing. They or their mothers and sisters should learn to mend and darn "in the same color." In short, work was scorned because workers were disgusting; they were disgusting because they were scorned.[41]

One of the most objectionable of their habits was spending money on

---

mico-Políticos . . . , ed. Antonio Peiró Arroyo (Zaragoza: Diputación General de Aragón, 1984), 22.

[37] Joseph Clavijo y Faxardo, *El Pensador* (1763) (Universidad de Las Palmas de Gran Canaria, 1999), 363. The quotation is an exercise in synonyms: *ociosidad, holgazanería, negligencia,* and *indolencia,* followed by *pereza.*

[38] José Cadalso, *Cartas marruecas* (1793), ed. Joaquin Marco (Madrid: Planeta, 1985), 54.

[39] *Recreación política* (Vitoria 1779), cited in Callahan, *Honor, Commerce and Industry,* 58.

[40] Jean Sarrailh, *La España Ilustrada de la segunda mitad del siglo XVIII* (Mexico City: Fondo de Cultura Económica, 1985), 79.

[41] Campomanes, *Discurso sobre la educación popular,* 98–100. The quotation in parenthesis is from 157.

vulgar entertainment, such as the plays by Lope that Campomanes believed filled their heads with erroneous ideas. There were those who thought the theater served as an escape valve that reduced the possibility of rowdiness in other, more economically delicate arenas. But the more moralistic of the reformers saw little to praise in foolishness and fantastic heroes. Instead, they saw theater as a potential school. Campomanes told masters to prohibit their apprentices, sons, and journeymen from going to bullfights or the theater on work days, partly because it would teach the wrong things, partly because it was a waste of money.He also protested against the widespread custom of using Mondays to sleep off the hangover from Sunday. Outlining appropriate theatrical diversions for the common people, Jovellanos laid out an astonishing program: he wanted theater "where one can see continual and heroic examples of reverence toward the Supreme Being [and this was no reference to the French Revolution] and the religion of our fathers; love of *patria*, sovereign and constitution; respect for hierarchy, law and authority; conjugal fidelity, paternal love, tenderness, and filial obedience."[42] Indeed, that does sound like work.

I alluded in part 1 to Campomanes's concern with the plethora of religious holidays, which he conveyed to Townsend, whose report has found its way into so many modern English-language histories of Spain. Campomanes in *Discurso sobre el fomento de la industria popular* listed ninety-three fiestas in the archbishopric of Toledo. Not all of them required parishioners to lay down their tools, but they were time-consuming nonetheless. As in previous centuries, piety and labor had to be weighed against each other. On the one hand, the conservative church was armed with stories right out of William Christian's sixteenth-century villages: a best-selling catechism reported that a woman in Asturias who baked on the day of San Lorenzo opened her oven only to find that the *tortas* had turned into bricks, which were on display at the local church as a cautionary tale.[43] On the other hand, the religious calendar was still judged by many to be out of control. The author of the report on the Junta de Comercio mentioned earlier wrote that Zamora's artisans spent one-third of their year occupied in fiestas, guild duties, prison time, confraternities, and meetings to grant powers of attorney for lawsuits.[44] (It is worth noting that his observations were

---

[42] Gaspar Melchor de Jovellanos, *Espectáculos y diversiones públicas*, ed. Guillermo Carnero (Madrid: Cátedra, 1997), 201. Jovellanos was a close friend of Trigueros, the author of *Los Menestrales*, and frequently loaned him books.

[43] Pedro de Calatayud, *Cathecismo práctico y muy util . . .* (Valladolid, 1747), 212. This catechism was recommended by four archibishops and a dozen bishops and was reprinted at least eight times in the eighteenth century. See Charles C. Noel, "Missionary Preachers in Spain: Teaching Social Virtue in the Eighteenth Century," *American Historical Review* 90 (October 1985): 882.

[44] Eugenio Larruga y Boneta, *Memorias políticas y económicas sobre los frutos, comercio, fábricas y minas de España . . .* 45 vols. (Madrid, 1787), vol. 35, 172.

written some two decades *after* the crown had outlawed craft guilds' confraternities, which, of course, in theory had been illegal ever since Charles V did exactly the same in 1552.) The Segovia Economic Society successfully persuaded the bishop there to reduce the number of religious holidays, enabling artisans to "usefully occupy their time instead of wasting their days, giving in to reprehensible ocio."[45]

It was not just the poor, however, who were to be put to work; the rich also had to do their share. Criticizing the Spanish nobility had a long pedigree, starting in the Middle Ages when alarmed writers warned that warriors were losing their manhood and getting flabby. It was thought that nations tend to weaken as a result of what Quevedo, in "España defendida," called "malicious peace," an idea whose origins went back at least as far as Aristotle and which enjoyed a revival during the reign of the Catholic Monarchs. Chronicles of the conquest of Granada, among many other sources, remarked on the problem: "Destiny was already at work devising causes that might rouse our princes, who were asleep with idleness and long peace, . . . so they might erase the dishonor of Spain and the manifest shame of all the Christian religion," wrote Elio Antonio de Nebrija in his *Guerra de Granada.*[46] Treatise writers had long taken it upon themselves to remind the useless sons of the nobility (assuming they were even reading) that they were shirking their obligation not only to their forefathers' good name but to the republic. Likewise, underlying the unpopular reforms proposed by the Count-Duke in the 1630s was Olivares's belief that nobles were selfish, disobedient, and lazy, and that they needed to contribute more. What was new in the eighteenth century was the blatantly economic edge to such arguments. More than political morals was at stake; there was a lot that needed doing. Among the many *utilidades* of the Economic Societies, according to at least one contemporary, was that they would keep noblemen honestly occupied rather than ociosos, their natural inclination.[47] Foreigners, of course, had long commented on the failings of the Spanish aristocracy, more on which in part 3; in one late example, the Englishman William Beckford in 1840 regarded them as a "scurvy, ill-favored generation" who, unless they pulled themselves together, would be on "all fours before the next century is much advanced."[48]

Arguments and laws in favor of putting the nobility to work brought together two overlapping exclusionary discourses—rank and occupation—

[45] Sempere y Guarinos, *Ensayo de una biblioteca española*, vol. 6, 4.

[46] Cited in David A. Boruchoff, "Historiography with License: Isabel, the Catholic Monarch, and the Kingdom of God," in his *Isabel la Católica, Queen of Castile: Critical Essays* (New York: Palgrave MacMillan, 2003), 235.

[47] Sempere y Guarinos, *Ensayo de una biblioteca española de los mejores escritores del reynado de Carlos III,* vol. 5 (Madrid: Impr. Real, 1789), 142.

[48] Cited in Mario Ford Bacigalupo, "An Ambiguous Image: English Travel Accounts of Spain (1750–1787)," *Dieciocho* 1 (Fall 1978): 122.

in the context of economic recovery. The reason why nobles did not want to work, many argued, was because of the old prohibitions against engaging in vile tasks. One such writer was a Galician professor of theology, Pedro Antonio Sánchez, who wrote a *memorial* under the pseudonym of Antonio Filántropo and presented it in December 1782 to the Madrid Economic Society, which sent it on to the Council of Castile.[49] The reason his countrymen were so poor, weighed down with debts, literally going hungry, and lacking sufficient clothing, he said, was that social prejudices prevented them from working at useful occupations such as tanning. It was not sloth that stopped them, he was careful to point out. But as things stood, if they were to commence tanning, their neighbors would shun them, their relatives would hate them, and their children would be vilified and unable to pursue careers in the church or in government. The background to the Sánchez *memorial* is worth comment. Charles III on 8 May 1780 had granted a series of privileges and exemptions to tanners in an effort to revive the industry. When those measures did not produce the desired effects, the Madrid Economic Society stepped in to study the matter and found that the reason the sector was in a slump was "the disregard with which manual laborers in general and tanners in particular were looked upon." That discovery led indirectly to the publication of the *memorial*.[50] One must ask why, if disregard toward workers in general and tanners in particular was the tradition since time immemorial, no one had noticed it earlier and why there had been no crisis before. How was it that anybody ever became a tanner? The Madrid Economic Society and the crown in the 1780s framed their effort to revive a (conjuncturally) stagnant sector not in structural economic terms but by blaming discriminatory social practices. Such a strategy offered them an opportunity to educate (or reeducate) both the victims of those practices and their perpetrators.

At around the same time, Antonio Javier Pérez López, a jurist in Seville, published a tract exemplifying the ambiguous and ultimately illogical position of the reformers vis-à-vis the nobility. On the one hand, they criticized an irrational hierarchical system that enforced idleness as the only alternative to vile activities; on the other, they were compelled (for pragmatic reasons as well as by their nature) to praise the nobility, its traditions, and its honor (and the very notion of honorability), and furthermore to use the language of nobility and privilege in celebrating the virtues of their

---

[49] Pedro Antonio Sánchez, "Memoria anónima bajo el nombre de Don Antonio Filántropo, sobre el modo de fomentar entre los labradores de Galicia las fábricas de curtidos," in *Colección de los escritos del Dr. D. Pedro Antonio Sánchez* (Madrid: Imprenta de M. Minuesa, 1858). Also in Sociedad Económica de Madrid, *Memorias de la Sociedad Económica*, 5 vols. (Madrid: A. de Sancha, 1780–1795).

[50] María del Carmen Pescador del Hoyo, "Los gremios de artesanos en Zamora," *Revista de Archivos, Bibliotecas y Museos* 77 (July–December 1974): 487–488.

opposite. Pérez López, after the usual arguments against alleged prejudices against allegedly vile occupations, concluded both that artisans deserved special honor and that nobility of blood was an excellent thing. (It was he who was cited earlier describing society as a chain "in which each link is joined to the next in . . . beautiful proportion." If the links were all equal, however, "shocking anarchy" would ensue.) Much of his treatise was devoted to dissecting what he argued were misinterpretations and misunderstandings of the various laws on vileness, an idle pursuit if there ever was one, for popular prejudice is hardly the result of a law, nor would it disappear if the law were reworded.[51] In a similar vein, Antonio Arteta de Monteseguro, a cleric and member of the Economic Society of Zaragoza, in 1781 published a prizewinning pamphlet on the mechanical arts that, despite the usual long historical buildup (in this case going back to Noah) and the citations to Plato, argued that all people are basically equal and that no one should be excluded from public office for reasons of blood or status. "Is it not a declared injustice and contrary to reason that [artisans] be excluded from public posts, depriving them of an honor they are owed?" he asked. His concern, as Sempere put it in his summary of Arteta's work, was "true nobility": "Wise men insist and argue that the spirit of true nobility is not incompatible with the exercise of arts called mechanical. Legislation has opened the door to honorable artisans to practice honorable jobs in the Republic."[52] A similar appreciation of "true nobility" can be detected in Capmany's work. Artisans should be honored, he said, adding that the guilds were the most appropriate vehicle for that: "The people will then have signs, bearing, and a style of life fitting to an honorable people. There will be no confusion with the nobility (because guilds make citizens known for what they are and what they are worth). People will know that within their sphere there is honor and virtue, and they will try to maintain them." And, he added, "the distinctions of orders in a nation are more influential than one might think in conserving the spirit of each one."[53]

In general, then, eighteenth-century writers blamed the nobility's lethargy on ill-advised legal impediments, though a royal and municipal

[51] Antonio Javier Pérez y López, *Discurso sobre la honra y la deshonra legal* (Madrid, 1781). The essay has been described as "a concrete, rationalizing effort with an eminently conservative base" (Antonio Elorza, *La ideología liberal en la Ilustración española* [Madrid: Edición Tecnos, 1970], 88).

[52] Antonio Arteta de Monteseguro, *Disertación sobre el aprecio y estimación que se debe hacer de las artes prácticas y de los que las exercen con honradez, inteligencia y aplicación* (Zaragoza, 1781), 61; Juan Sempere y Guarinos, *Ensayo de una biblioteca española de los mejores escritores del reynado de Carlos III*, vol. 1 (Madrid: Impr. Real, 1785), 146.

[53] Antonio de Capmany (pseud. Ramón Miguel Palacio), *Discurso político económico en defensa del trabajo mecánico de los menestrales y de la influencia de sus gremios en las costumbres populares, conservacion de las artes y honor de los artesanos* (Madrid, 1778; repr., Madrid: Almarabu, 1986), 13.

official, Miguel de Zavala y Auñon, sensibly had pointed out already in 1732 that nobles who expressed reluctance to get involved in business were simply being foolish: "What else is being a businessman than buying and selling, than having dealings and sales that produce profits? Who in Spain does not do that?"[54] Even the Madrid Economic Society, certainly not the site of debates to make the crown uncomfortable, in October 1783 announced a prize to the person who best argued against the institution of entailed estates, yet another obstacle in the way of enterprising noblemen, whose utility to the republic now was weighed in new units of measure.

At the same time, while arguing against noble privilege, the *ilustrados* proposed rewarding deserving artisans with privileges of their own. Partly as a result of these and similar pieces of advice, Charles III on 18 March 1783 issued what, in the eyes of historians, became the centerpiece of the reformist legislation:

> I declare that not only the occupation of tanner but also the arts and occupations of blacksmith, tailor, shoemaker, carpenter, and others like these are honest and honorable, that their practice vilifies neither he who exercises it nor his family, nor does it prevent artisans or mechanics who exercise them from occupying municipal posts in the Republic in which they live, nor do arts and occupations prevent one from enjoying the privileges of hidalguía.

(As with previous such lists, note the indeterminate "and others like these.") Antonio Domínguez Ortiz in the 1940s called the edict "truly revolutionary." Gonzalo Anes has said it "contributed to the dignification of occupations considered mechanical."[55] Such opinions are widely shared. Some have remarked that there was a contradiction in simultaneously honoring the lower crafts while maintaining the social hierarchy, to which I would reply that the crafts were not bereft of honor to begin with and that hierarchy responds to deeper structures than vileness.[56] The law essentially reiterated those of the late seventeenth century. Though it may have provided an extra push toward creating an elite entrepreneurial class, there was no rush by noblemen to go into business. Those who wanted to already had, and those who truly were holding back because of public regard were unlikely to be dissuaded by an edict. As for public offices, deci-

[54] Miguel de Zavala y Auñon, *Representación al Rey Nuestro Señor D. Phelipe V . . .* (1732), 151. Zavala was a permanent *regidor* in Badajoz and a member of the Council of Castile.

[55] Antonio Domínguez Ortiz, "Notas sobre la consideración social del trabajo manual y el comercio en el antiguo régimen," *Revista del trabajo*, no. 7–8 (July–August 1945): 680; Gonzalo Anes de Castrillón, "Pedro Antonio Sánchez y la honradez de los oficios," *Torre de los Lujanes*, no. 25 (1993): 170.

[56] Javier Guillamon Alvarez, *Honor y honra en la España del siglo XVIII* (Madrid: Universidad Complutense, 1981), 24–26; Callahan, *Honor, Commerce and Industry,* 52–55; Antonio Elorza, "La polémica sobre los oficios viles en la España del siglo XVIII," in *Revista de trabajo*, no. 22 (1968): 69–78.

sions regarding the ability of the vile and mechanical (or anyone else) to hold those positions were made by cities and towns, and they varied from place to place. Spain certainly was not alone in preventing or discouraging propertyless or common men from holding municipal office and had no need of a late medieval edict to enforce class privilege. Officeholding anyway was a complicated affair; sometimes the aristocrats who ran cities excluded mere hidalgos from their sanctum, sometimes they did not. It is true that in many towns artisans were ineligible for office, as we saw in part 1, but this was not a rule that was necessarily followed. At stake always were local, political interests.[57]

The edict apparently did not have much of an effect either in America, or it was misunderstood. In 1804, after a zealous tax collector in León, Mexico, found it in a collection of overlooked orders, the viceroy of New Spain alerted the crown and asked for instructions. Soon after, officials in New Granada, noting that people there preferred being ociosos to working at low trades, also asked that the 1783 *cédula* be implemented. In response, the Council of Indies prosecutor (*fiscal*) issued an order on 24 January 1807 referring to the largely negative consequences the edict had had in Spain, where, he said, erroneous notions of upward mobility had caused endless confusion, and he recommended that the edict not be applied to the Indies. Referring to an edict of 4 September 1803 essentially undoing the damage of the 1783 law, the *fiscal* said that declaring certain occupations free of vileness was one thing, but enabling their practitioners to attain high honors was quite another. Therefore, though the king had reiterated that the arts and occupations of "blacksmith, tailor, shoemaker, carpenter, and others like these are honest and honorable," the edict "neither removed artists and *menestrales* from their class nor did it make any allusions to their not being ineligible for those distinctions for which their occupations have always been an impediment." If the multitude of mixed-bloods in America, carriers of "original vice" who often were "blacksmiths, shoemakers, and other mechanicals," were to find out that they were eligible for honors, "disturbances and harmful consequences for the State" would ensue.[58]

Along with the 1783 edict, another innovation often pointed to as evidence of Charles III's eagerness to eliminate barriers to enterprise was the Order of Charles III, usually regarded as a special honor for noblemen who

[57] For a very interesting examination of the complex relationship among municipal elites that rejects the usual dichotomies, see José Ignacio Fortea Pérez, "Los abusos del poder: El común y el gobierno de las ciudades de Castilla tras la rebelión de las Comunidades," in *Furor et rabies: Violencia, conflicto y marginación en la Edad Moderna*, ed. José Ignacio Fortea Pérez et al. (Santander: Universidad de Cantabria, 2003): 183–218.

[58] Konetzke, ed., *Colección de documentos para la historia*, vol. 3, pt. 2, 813, 832–834. I am grateful to Rafael Tarragy, of the University of Minnesota, for pointing this out to me. I regret that I was unable to locate the 4 September 1803 edict.

engaged in commerce, though the law itself says nothing about such an objective. Established on 19 September 1771 upon the birth of the king's grandson, the new order was declared to be under the special protection of the Virgin Mary and the Immaculate Conception, to which Charles III was especially devoted. A total of no more than 260 men, divided into two classes, were to become members. They were to have exhibited special love and service for the monarch; no other requirement was mentioned.[59] The honor may have been an attempt to make businessmen out of nobles, but of course it also created nobles out of businessmen. Indeed, the campaign to put nobles to work carried no implicit criticism of a caste, simply recognition of an economic need. Campomanes, who himself was named a member of the Order of Charles III in September 1782, denied he had any interest in undermining the social order, suggesting at one point that a small number of artisans whose work was particularly good or esteemed might be named "honorary citizens."[60] The 1783 edict, in fact, provided that families who during three generations managed a commercial or industrial enterprise could attain noble rank. Leveling, in other words, was not the objective (though, to be fair, no historian has ever made that claim); rationalization was. Privileges were fine, but, like alms, they had to be earned. As Jovellanos remarked, nobility was an arbitrary state; it was not established by nature.[61]

Trigueros, author of *Los Menestrales,* shared the widespread opinion that, historically, Spain was especially lax in forcing its nobility to get its hands dirty. They did better even in Egypt, he wrote:

> The dwellers of the Nile in ancient times
> would punish idleness like other crimes.[62]

His Don Juan was the prototype of the new, enlightened noble; the character's final speech in *Los Menestrales* summarized the official ideology on the matter:

[59] *Novísima recopilación,* libro 6, ley 12, tit. 3; and in Marcelo Martínez Alcubilla, ed., *Códigos antiguos de España* (Madrid: J. López Comancho, 1885), vol. 2, 1, 175.

[60] Campomanes, *Discurso sobre la educación popular,* 112. The expression was *ciudadanos honrados,* an expression which in Aragón referred explicitly to those who did not work with their hands and were part of the lower aristocracy. See José Ignacio Gómez Zorraquino, "Ni señores, ni campesinos/artesanos. El gobierno de los ciudadanos en Aragón," in *Burgueses o ciudadanos en la España moderna,* ed. Francisco José Aranda Pérez (Cuenca: Universidad de Castilla-La Mancha, 2003), 365.

[61] Gaspar Melchor de Jovellanos, "Discurso sobre los inconvenientes de fundar un Montepío para los nobles de la Corte, in *Obras,* vol. 2, 14.

[62] "Oda filosófica," in Nigel Glendinning, *A Literary History of Spain: The Eighteenth Century* (London: Ernest Benn, 1972), 2.

Dejad esos delirios, la nobleza
se funda en la virtud y en el trabajo.
Al sudor destinados nacen todos;
el que busca con él lo necesario
cumple con su deber, y es hombre bueno,
digno por tal de ser reverenciado . . .
Todos de un solo tronco ramas somos.
No hay más noble que el que es buen ciudadano,
y el que más útil es, es el mas noble,
en bajo esté o en alto: tales grados
de las necesidades son secuela:
mas tan bueno es el alto como el bajo.[63]

"We are all branches of the same tree," he told his humble listeners. We all have a job to do, all jobs are equally important, and "there is no one more noble than a good citizen." Don Juan and his like-minded brethren, who always had had a relationship of mutual need with the crown, now were to be its business partners.

There were other eighteenth-century social critics, however, who had no use for a class they regarded as parasitic. For them, the task was not as simple as de-vilifying tanning but rather to abolish altogether the traditional system of orders which, using the criterion of the day, served no utility. The 1787 dialogue in *El Censor* quoted earlier was remarkable not only because of the content ("*Soy nuevo*") but because of the disrespectful tone and the use of the informal second-person pronoun (*tu*). "I'm the first of my line, you're the last of yours," the commoner tells the nobleman, who replies: "Your father was a tailor, your grandfather a shoemaker, your great-grandfather a tanner." Yes, the impudent new man responds, "I'd not trade them for a perfidious father, an adulterous grandfather, and a thieving great-grandfather." "I was born noble," insists the aggrieved aristocrat, to which he is told: "Good thing you told me, I wouldn't have noticed." But such cheek was not tolerated widely, and after the French Revolution, two years after these lines were written, not at all. Through fits and starts, *El Censor*—"anti-noble, egalitarian, and protoliberal," in the opinion of Francisco Sánchez-Blanco—lasted from 1781 to 1787, when it was finally silenced.[64]

---

[63] Trigueros, *Los Menestrales*, 194–195. These lines were not uttered at the play's few performances, according to the editor, diminishing the play's didactic purpose.

[64] Francisco Sanchez-Blanco, *El Absolutismo y las Luces en el reinado de Carlos III* (Madrid: Marcial Pons, 2002), 321.

The Revival of Exclusion

In this atmosphere of putting everyone to work for the sake of the *patria* there was no room for excuses based on arbitrary, traditional, irrational, or unjust prohibitions and prejudices. Such rules, we have seen, were offered as the reason for the indolence of people both rich and poor, who were said to prefer remaining inert rather than risk the social consequences of engaging in vile labor (though no one has explained why a laborer would refuse to work at a specific craft because it would preclude his son from entering a university residence [*colegio mayor*] or joining a noble military order). These arguments by now should be familiar to readers. They had been around for literally hundreds of years, and for hundreds of years they rarely if ever were supported by evidence from town halls or courts of law. I suggest that eighteenth-century royal ministers and writers turned back to vileness because it was a convenient way of explaining and addressing an economic problem. To them, it explained why people didn't work, and it pointed the way to ensuring that they did.

But reformers also turned to vileness because, ironically, to some extent it began to reflect the true state of affairs. Though barriers among classes always can be ambiguous, it is also true that in periods of social stress, such distinctions sharpen. Such was the case starting in the late seventeenth century, both in America and in Castile, as two related criteria of differentiation were invigorated (and overlapped) precisely when men supposedly were remaking themselves into new, modern creatures: occupation (or social class), and that outstanding marker of Spain's peculiar heritage, purity of blood (*limpieza de sangre*), which itself combined considerations both religious and racial.

The seventeenth and eighteenth centuries were a time of intense economic and existential anxiety for the nobility, hidalgos, and anyone else concerned about social status. As elsewhere in Europe, old categories were under attack. Critics of the aristocracy became braver. Wealth was more difficult to attain and hold on to, and as a result privileges became all the more important even as their meaning grew more unclear. The Inquisition's requirements for familiars began including occupational barriers in 1604.[65] The military orders of Alcántara, Calatrava, and Santiago incor-

[65] In 1604, the Suprema ordered tribunals not to accept butchers, shoemakers, bakers, and in general anyone who had been involved in mechanical or vile trades or who descended from such inviduals. See María Elena Martínez López, "The Spanish Concept of 'Limpieza de Sangre' and the Emergence of the 'Race/Caste' System in the Viceroyalty of New Spain" (Ph.D. diss., University of Chicago 2002), 272n7. Jean-Pierre Dedieu found inquisitorial instructions from 1575 excluding those who had certain vile occupations in their past from becoming ministers, but he says it did not yet indicate a general trend. The instructions were modified (presumably becoming more restrictive) in 1728. Jean-Pierre Dedieu, "Limpieza, pouvoir et richesse: Conditions d'entrée dans le corps des ministres de l'inquisition Tribunal

porated them by 1600, and as the seventeenth century wore on, they drew up longer and more precise lists of people whose membership they would not entertain. The Order of Santiago until 1653, for example, admitted wholesale merchants but after that date adopted the more stringent criteria of Calatrava and Alcántara. (At the same time, however, the sale of *hábitos* offered the crown a source of badly needed money, and dispensations were granted for a number of failings and impurities; those given for low occupations accounted for 6 percent of the total under Philip III but rose to 32.2 percent under his son. The body was less exclusive as a result, but the numbers attest to the growing desirability of membership.)[66] María Elena Martínez López's examination of novitiate records of the Franciscan Order of colonial Puebla (Mexico) shows that by the late seventeenth century, candidates often were claiming racial purity as well as a past free of low offices and mentioning their parents' professions, which they did not do before.[67] As elite groups tried to keep workers out, workers themselves closed ranks. As the economy contracted in the seventeenth century, it became harder to take master's examinations, apprenticeships grew longer, outsiders who wanted to join a guild faced more obstacles, and the family tree of prospective members became an issue. For our purposes, then, two sets of exclusionary practices gained importance: limits placed by guilds on membership, and limits placed by other arenas (social, political, or religious) on access by practitioners of certain crafts. Together they add up to the category of *limpieza de oficios*. Social status and impurity now were linked.

Slippage between racial and occupational categories of exclusion, confusing cause and effect (which were, in fact, confused), was evident both in the seventeenth and eighteenth centuries and in the subsequent historiography. One of Campomanes's explanations for Spanish society's low regard toward certain occupations was that they traditionally were performed by Jews (or *conversos*) or Muslims (or *moriscos*), an assessment echoed by many of his contemporaries and ever since.[68] In other words, Jews (for example) made a job vile. When Pedro Berindoaga traveled to a

---

de Tolède—XVIe–XVIIe siècles," in *Les sociétés fermées dans le monde iberique (XVI–XVIIIe s.)* (Paris: CNRS, 1986), 173.

[66] Elena Postigo Castellanos, *Honor y privilegio en la Corona de Castilla: El Consejo de las Ordenes y los Caballeros de Hábito en el s. XVII* (Soria: Junta de Castilla y León, 1988), 134, citing a 1982 work by Martine Lambert Gorges; L. P. Wright, "The Military Orders in Sixteenth- and Seventeenth-Century Spanish Society: The Institutional Embodiment of a Historical Tradition," *Past and Present*, no. 43 (1969): 61–62; José Antonio Maravall, *Poder, honor y élites en el siglo XVII* (Madrid: Siglo Veintiuno, 1979), 108–111.

[67] The documents are in the John Carter Brown Library. Martínez López, "The Spanish Concept of 'Limpieza de Sangre,'" 388–397.

[68] Campomanes, *Apéndice a la Educación Popular,* vol. 3, 27. See also "Reflexiones sobre las artes mecánicas," by Francisco de Bruna, in the same volume.

town in Toledo on behalf of the Madrid Economic Society, of which he was a member, to find out why the wool industry there had collapsed, he reported back that peasants looked down on workers at the new woolens factory because wool workers traditionally had been Jews.[69]

It could also be the other way around. Pere Molas Ribalta wrote:

> Certain occupations were considered inferior and therefore despised. For Capmany, 'certain provinces of Spain' regarded as vile the occupations of blacksmith, tavern keeper, boilermaker, pewter worker, etc. According to Domínguez Ortiz, these occupations, because of the repugnance they inspired, were in the hands of foreigners. For the same reason, many blacksmiths, shearers, butchers, and innkeepers were mulattoes and gypsies.

According to this account, then, Gypsies and foreigners took jobs previously classified as vile; they did not cause those jobs to become vile. Vileness was inherent to the job for no apparent reason.[70] I have found practically no causal links between race/religion and occupation in contemporary guild ordinances, lawsuits, or *memoriales*. (One example in part 1 showed a tailor saying that shoemakers were always Jews, which they were not.) Yet this is one of the most enduring of explanations for Spaniards' aversion to manual labor. Américo Castro, for one, wrote that what he called Spain's "inferiority complex" was not the fault of Philip II or of the empire but rather of "the valuational criteria of the Old Christians, who did not want to tarnish their *honra castiza* by cultivating intellectual and technical pursuits which since the end of the fifteenth century were considered abominable because they pertained (because they were *perceived* as pertaining) to the Hebrew-Hispanic and Morisco-Hispanic castes." Science, the art of creating wealth, and technical efficacy, he said, were "characteristic of the Hebrew-Hispanic

---

[69] William J. Callahan, "La estimación del trabajo manual en la España del siglo XVIII," *Revista chilena de historia y geografía*, no. 132 (1964): 61.

[70] Pere Molas Ribalta, *Los gremios barceloneses del siglo XVIII* (Madrid: Confederación Española de Cajas de Ahorros, 1970), 126–127, citing Antonio Domínguez Ortiz, *La sociedad española en el siglo XVIII* (Madrid: CSIC, 1955), vol. 1, 217. Note once again the use of "etc." and the circular citation. There is no explanation for the internal quotation marks. Javier Guillamon Alvarez repeated the same assertion, though citing Gonzalo Anes citing Domínguez Ortiz and confusing matters by saying, "'people in southern Spain would rather go hungry than sweep streets, carry water, and perform other such tasks' perhaps because in previous centuries slaves and foreigners had performed these jobs." These internal quotes presumably come from Anes/Domínguez Ortiz. See Javier Guillamon Alvarez, *Honor y honra en la España del siglo XVIII* (Madrid: Universidad Complutense, 1981), 125. Postigo also cites Domínguez Ortiz (though another work of his) when she avers: "There were few profes-sions considered 'infamous' by civil law, and there were a few more regarded as such by public opinion" (Postigo Castellanos, *Honor y privilegio en la Corona de Castilla*, 140). The original Domínguez Ortiz reads: "The professions considered infamous by Law were very few: *comediante*, hangman, and a few others; public opinion also scorned butchers, tanners, and others similar to those" (Antonio Domínguez Ortiz, *Las clases privilegiadas en el Antiguo Régimen*, 3d ed. [Madrid: Ediciones Istmo, 1985], 286).

caste."[71] Similarly, the nineteenth-century writer Francisco Martínez de la Rosa described the 1609 expulsion of the moriscos by saying they were "the most useful, active, and industrious vecinos, who had inherited traditions of irrigation and agriculture from their parents as well as knowledge of the arts and crafts, practiced almost exclusively by them."[72] Certain jobs and certain functions were necessarily in the hands of certain people.

Late medieval and early modern Spain not infrequently is described as being in the grip of racism and paranoia. Though there is no question that racism and paranoia existed, entry to organizations often was subject to racial or religious restrictions, and many people lost their lives or otherwise suffered because of their religious beliefs or race, it is nonetheless also true that the Spanish state was not a monolithic entity. There was disagreement within educated circles, many of whose members were not conversos, on the justice and utility of limpieza statutes.[73] Castilian society, always highly pragmatic, tolerated both anti-Semitism and coexistence between Christians and Jews. Like treatises that criticized counterproductive hierarchies of labor, contemporary critiques of limpieza have been understood as exceptions signaling widespread acceptance; in fact, as with the alleged rules on vile and mechanical artisans, they may well signify the opposite. There were no general limpieza statutes, though some local exclusionary laws regarding officeholding were enforced. Most often, they were rules of particular (usually elite) organizations, and as such they often were not observed. As we (or Campomanes) look back, divisions between Old and New Christians may appear more stark than they really were, a result, in part, of inquisitors' insistence that Christians and conversos had radically distinct religious and social practices and identities. An explanation for occupational exclusion that privileges conversos, furthermore, may reflect historians' interest in conversos more than it reflects the true contemporary weight of conversos as a category. Limpieza frequently served as a placeholder for power and status, not race or religion. Accusations of having Jewish heritage, indeed, could and did take place even when there was not the remotest possibility that the subject or anyone he knew was a Jew. "Proving" one's cleanliness was not cheap; it required money and contacts. It was proof of one's economic resources and connections, not one's bloodline.[74]

---

[71] Américo Castro, *De la edad conflictiva*, 2d ed. (Madrid: Taurus, 1963), 26, 44. *Honra castiza* was Castro's term for authentic, pure, or primal honor.

[72] Francisco Martínez de la Rosa, *Bosquejo histórico de la política de España desde los tiempos de los Reyes Católicos hasta nuestros dias*, 2 vols. (Madrid: M. Rivadeneyra, 1857), vol. 1, 55.

[73] Henry Kamen, "Limpieza and the Ghost of Américo Castro: Racism as a Tool of Literary Analysis," *Hispanic Review* 64 (Winter 1996): 19–29; Henry Kamen, "Una crisis de conciencia en la Edad de Oro en España: Inquisición contra 'limpieza de sangre,'" *Bulletin Hispanique* 88 (July–December 1986): 321–356.

[74] Claude Chauchadis, "Les modalités de la fermeture dans les confréries religieuses es-

Attempts to exclude certain racial or religious groups can, on the one hand, be seen as an effort to preserve the honor of the craft at a time when it apparently was under attack or was perceived as such; on the other hand, it is a tacit admission that the craft was racially integrated and that the presence of blacks or Jews or mixed-bloods suddenly became a problem. Guilds began excluding those descended from Jews and Muslims only at the end of the seventeenth century, if at all.[75] In eighteenth-century Cartagena, for example, carpenters specified that apprentices and journeymen "must be of good customs and clean of all *mala raza*." The same was true of some vendors and pastry cooks. It was not true, however, of locksmiths, chandlers, tanners, and a long list of other occupations there.[76] Laborers in Seville's cathedral stated in 1784 that "neither black nor mulatto nor morisco" could be a member of the Confraternity of Nuestra Señora de la Granada.[77] In the province of Cádiz, shoemakers in 1745 approved ordinances stating that masters should gather every December to choose six men who would then choose inspectors. The six should be "of good life and habits, hard-working, meritorious, and with clean blood."[78] A study of 141 guild ordinances in Seville from the fifteenth to the eighteenth centuries found that only 1 before 1566 excluded a group a priori from membership (the linen and wool weavers, who excluded slaves). From 1566 to 1699, a small minority (all from the textile trades) excluded blacks, Jews, Moors, slaves, mulattoes, and conversos. Only in the eighteenth century do we begin frequently seeing the requirement that prospective members be Old Christians.[79]

Guilds' barriers on the basis of ethnicity or religion do not seem to have

---

pagnoles (XVI–XVIII siècles)," in *Les sociétés fermées dans le monde iberique*, argues that limpieza was simply one of a series of economic and cultural requirements to join a *colegio mayor*, a confraternity, or a cathedral chapter; see also Stafford Poole, C. M., "The Politics of 'Limpieza de Sangre': Juan de Ovando and his Circle in the Reign of Philip II," *The Americas* 55 (January 1999).

[75] An exception was Córdoba, a city of unusual racial diversity, where blacks, mulattoes, slaves, and former slaves generally were prohibited from becoming apprentices, and certainly from becoming masters. José Ignacio Fortea Pérez, *Córdoba en el siglo XVI: Las bases demográficas y económicas de una expansión urbana* (Córdoba: Monte Piedad y Caja de Ahorros de Córdoba, 1981), 361. The Córdoba cathedral was also the first to implement a limpieza statute: John Edwards, "The Beginnings of a Scientific Theory of Race? Spain, 1450–1600," in *From Iberia to Diaspora: Studies in Sephardic History and Culture*, ed. Yedida K. Stillman and Norman A. Stillman (Leiden: E. J. Brill, 1999), 181. Valencia's shoemakers in 1597 also excluded blacks, slaves, and *moros*. See Luis Tramoyeres Blasco, *Instituciones gremiales: Su origen y organización en Valencia* (Valencia: Imprenta Domenech, 1889), 183.

[76] Eduardo Cañabata Navarro, *Ordenanza [sic] de los gremios de Cartagena en el siglo XVIII* (Murcia, 1962).

[77] AAS Sec. III.1.6, Hermandades, caja 12, no. 6 (1784).

[78] AHN CS Sala de Gobierno, leg. 645.

[79] Antonio Miguel Bernal, Antonio Collantes de Terán, and Antonio García-Baquero, "Sevilla: De los gremios a la industrialización," *Estudios de Historia Social*, no. 5–6 (1978): 100–101 and 137–139.

included Gypsies, perhaps because it went without saying that such a people, who were not only ethnically different but apparently inherently shiftless, should not be admitted, or perhaps because there were other exclusionary laws to take care of them. There was a long tradition in Spain of either expelling Gypsies or of limiting their movements and forcing conformity, each successive attempt attesting to the failure of the last.[80] Scattered among the many expulsions and exclusions were edicts banning Gypsies from working as blacksmiths, an itinerant trade (along with locksmith) in which they specialized. In 1612, blacksmiths living in the Triana district of Seville complained they should not be included in the most recent ban because they were vecinos, had steady jobs, and owned their own homes, and therefore, by definition, were not really Gypsies.[81] A century later, on 30 June 1717, Philip V issued the latest *pragmática* prohibiting Gypsies from performing any job other than farming, "especially blacksmithing." Punishment for violating the law was exile; failure to leave the kingdom was punished with eight years in the galleys.[82] Immediately after the *pragmática* was issued, Seville's (non-Gypsy) blacksmiths excluded New Castilians (another name for Gypsies) but allowed them to be farriers. Nonetheless, the problem continued; the guild asked the city council in 1765 to do something about the invasion of "suspicious and bad-living people" who, most importantly for the city, did not pay the alcabala tax.[83]

The Bourbon monarchs' interest in economic recovery was such that there was a place even for Gypsies. An official at the Cádiz shipyards reported in 1749 that there were as many as a thousand employed there after having been impressed.[84] Many of the boys wanted to become carpenters, he said, but found their way blocked by the guild, which admitted only Old Christians and prohibited the admission of anyone of *mala casta de gente*. Campomanes later told Townsend there were more than ten thousand Gypsies in Spain and that they had suffered unjust incarceration

---

[80] See Marcelo Martínez Alcubilla, ed., *Códigos Antiguos de España* (Madrid: J. López Comancho, 1885), vol. 2, 1875–1881, for a series of such laws from the fifteenth through the eighteenth century; and Angus Fraser, *The Gypsies* (Oxford: Blackwell, 1992), 161–169.

[81] *Memorial*, AMSev Sec. IV, Escr. 16/42. "So many Gypsies, so many smiths" was a saying in Hungary, according to a frankly racist account: John Hoyland, *A Historical Survey of the Customs, Habits, and Present State of the Gypsies; Designed to Develope the Origin of this Singular People and to Promote the Amelioration of their Condition* (London, 1816), 49.

[82] This and other laws and documents on Gypsies can be found in María Helena Sánchez Ortega, ed., *Documentación selecta sobre la situación de los gitanos españoles en el siglo XVIII* (Madrid: Editora Nacional, 1976). Sánchez Ortega's dates are unreliable, and she does not provide full archival citations.

[83] Bernal, Collantes de Terán, and García-Baquero, "Sevilla: De los gremios a la industrialización," 139.

[84] Fraser, *Gypsies*, 165–166. According to Fraser, between nine thousand and twelve thousand Gypsies were captured and sent into labor in 1749.

in the past.[85] A more enlightened approach to the problem was his own: in 1768 he ordered the establishment of *poblaciones cerradas,* to be inhabited by Gypsies with no criminal record, who could be taught useful skills in order to become like everyone else. Those who did not qualify were to be sent to America.[86] Ward in 1779 also favored ethnic cleansing followed by "a useful and Christian life" in America. Floridablanca, in turn, who noted elsewhere that it made no sense to accuse Gypsies of sloth while at the same time refusing to let them work, issued a *pragmática* in 1783 declaring that Gypsies did not belong to an "infected race," in return for which they lost the names *gitanos* and New Castilians and were prohibited from speaking their language, wearing their own dress, or wandering as they used to. The law, "by which your majesty extinguished the very name and race of those called Gypsies," he later told Charles III, "has had the same object of converting into useful and industrious persons so many thousands of those who were lost in licentious idleness and vice."[87] Nevertheless, though in principle Gypsies were now allowed to perform any job they wanted and any guild that refused to admit them would be fined, authorities discovered both that guilds ran that risk if it meant being free of Gypsies, and that the Roma's desire for assimilation was confoundingly low.

The paradigm of the vile and mechanical laborer was a useful one for eighteenth-century reformers both in the inner circles of the monarchy and in the Economic Societies. They pointed to old prejudices and then wiped the stain away with edicts, clearing the way for the creation of a new workforce that was trained, docile, well behaved, patriotic, devout, and clean. It is sometimes confusing to follow the vileness argument as it turns on itself. Campomanes and his cohorts took pains to deny there was any national laziness gene—workers would if they could, but they could not—though at the same time they devoted inordinate amounts of time to condemning ocio. Treatises, as always, can be deceptive. A comment by Pedro Antonio Sánchez in his *memorial* on tanning, for example, that guilds, rather than exclude members because of their vile and mechanical back-

---

[85] Townsend, *A Journey through Spain,* vol. 3, 308. A royal edict on 24 July 1751 on ociosos warned that all male vagabonds and *malentretenidos* over the age of twelve would be sent to the shipyards or to the army (Larruga y Boneta, *Historia de la Real y General Junta,* vol. 9, 267–269).

[86] In the past, Gypsies were routinely shipped to North Africa but not to America, which they were forbidden from entering (though Philip II in 1581 ordered Peruvian colonial officials to round up those who had emigrated "under cover" and were causing confusion among the Indians. *Cédula,* 11 February 1581 [Konetzke, ed., *Colección de documentos para la historia,* vol. 1, 532]). Passengers to America had to prove they were not descendants to the second degree of converted Jews or Muslims or of any person condemned by the Inquisition; again, that did not mean that conversos did not manage to emigrate.

[87] October 1788 *memorial* to Charles III, in William Coxe, *Memoirs of the Kings of Spain of the House of Bourbon,* 3 vols. (London, 1813), vol. 1, 362; Sarrailh, *La España Ilustrada,* 514.

ground, should instead exclude the descendants of adulterers, fornicators, drunks, men of bad faith who broke contracts, and ociosos, could lead us to believe that guilds in fact did exclude the vile and the mechanical, which was hardly ever true.[88] Two of his co-essayists at the Madrid Economic Society, brothers and master watchmakers, wrote an essay whose denunciations are similarly misleading:

> A career in the arts in Spain is a disaster because of its narrowness and disorganization and because of the scarce esteem in which it is held. Entry is difficult, passage is obscure, and the objective is cumbersome and replete with misery. Ultimately even the most outstanding and admirable master ends up in eternal oblivion. A not inconsiderable reason for this is that those who most commonly devote themselves to the profession of the arts are those of great misfortune and little means, because the better sort look upon the arts with horror because of the scorn and lowliness they have unjustly acquired.[89]

The picture admittedly is tangled: a craft is maligned for its own sake, and therefore nobody wants to enter it and those who do are maligned. At the same time, in order to make a craft less maligned, certain groups are excluded, indicating it is their presence that maligns the craft and once they are excluded the craft will be restored to its original goodness. Meanwhile, if a maligned occupation is exclusively in the hands of certain groups, which perhaps was why it was maligned in the first place, then the rest of us will be saved the indignity of working in them. No single part of this scenario actually existed in its pure form, as best I can tell.

In the Indies, too, various categories of exclusion took on heightened importance in the late seventeenth and eighteenth centuries; and as they did, they were collapsed. Religion, race, and occupation all increasingly were matters of purity and impurity. Though racial and ethnic combinations in America obviously were more complex than those in the Iberian peninsula and the two contexts are not analogous, still there is evidence that something changed in the Age of Enlightenment, and the attitudes behind those changes formed part of the transatlantic trade. Social and racial disturbances and challenges by new waves of immigrants eager to make money and displace established elites threatened the moral fabric of colonial society, it was said. Upward mobility by tradesmen may not have been easy, but it was possible, and the new exclusion also was part of the struggle by the successful to ensure that not too many of their old friends followed them.

[88] Sánchez, "Memoria anónima bajo el nombre de Don Antonio Filántropo," 52–53. Why the sons of drunkards should be punished for their fathers' sins was not explained.

[89] "Memoria de los señores Don Felipe y Don Pedro Charost," 20 July 1782, in Sociedad Económica de Madrid, *Memorias de la Sociedad Económica*, vol. 4.

As one example of the tendency to close ranks, Ann Twinam in her work on illegitimacy in colonial Spanish America found that whereas royal officials until 1760 generally were willing to grant illegitimate American petitioners the honor they requested, after that date standards of proof were far more demanding and officials had heightened scruples. The number of petitions for legitimation increased dramatically in the 1780s and 1790s, perhaps triggered by the 1778 Royal Pragmatic on Marriages, which gave parents and royal officials the authority to prevent marriages that crossed natal and racial boundaries. Elites, she says, were increasingly uneasy about the "ambiguous barriers of race and birth that had previously established their precedence and that were now under challenge. Their response was heightened discrimination."[90]

There also are indications that in Peru and Mexico some guilds' racial restrictions grew more intense, though others' remained the same or continued absent. (Apparent tolerance also may have indicated simply a shortage of skilled laborers.) Lima's silver- and goldsmiths in 1778 added a provision to their ordinances not included in the 1633 version explaining that because of the "very recommendable" nature of their art it was essential that apprentices be sons of "honorable fathers of good customs," though they made no mention of race or of occupational ancestry.[91] Mexico City's cloth makers approved ordinances in 1592 that made no mention of race; in 1676, similar ordinances were approved in Puebla for cloth weavers (*tejedores de paños*) based on the prior ones with modifications, including a race ban. Justifying the addition, guild inspectors told colonial authorities the king would lose tax revenues if "*mulatos, mestizos, negros o chinos*" made cloth because "many people" would choose not to engage in that occupation. In a subsequent section, the word *indios* was added to the list. The *fiscal* responded by saying the ban was out of the question, particularly as concerned Indians.[92] Lima's blacksmiths (who also worked as locksmiths) in July 1552 asked the city to prohibit blacks from opening shops because it would invite insults over the fabrication of "false keys and other things." The city complied, ordering that no free or enslaved black nor any other slave or former slave could work without a Spanish journey-

[90] Ann Twinam, *Public Lives, Private Secrets: Gender, Honor, Sexuality, and Illegitimacy in Colonial Spanish America* (Stanford University Press, 1999), 336. The law, and a flurry of related petitions in the late eighteenth century, can be found in Konetzke, ed., *Colección de documentos para la historia.*

[91] Francisco Quiroz Chueca and Gerardo Quiroz Chueca, eds., *Las ordenanzas de gremios de Lima (s. XVI–XVIII)* (Lima, 1986), 149–154.

[92] Genaro Vásquez, ed., *Legislación del trabajo en los siglos XVI, XVII y XVIII. Relación entre la economía, las artes y los oficios en la Nueva España* (Mexico City: Departamento Autónomo del Trabajo, 1936), 111–119. The story also appears in Richard Konetzke, "Las ordenanzas de gremios como documentos para la historia social de Hispano-américa durante la época colonial," in *Estudios de historia social de España* 1 (1949).

man, and the provision was incorporated into the guild's ordinances. But a century later, the blacksmiths said it had never been enforced, the result of the opposition of the *oidor,* an important royal judge. Serious troubles (*gravísimos inconvenientes*) and a plague of bad or false keys over the past one hundred years had ensued, they said. Because blacks were working as masters, Spaniards shunned the occupation, and it was "unjust that such people exercise the said occupations nor is it decent for the republic." The ordinances, with the ban, were reconfirmed in the summer of 1634. But one of the city's alcaldes commented that the ban was incorrect "because this is not a question of honor" and because "vile persons" (such as blacksmiths, one assumes) could not exclude blacks and slaves. The version of the ordinances read aloud by the town crier in April 1636 does not appear to have included the restrictions requested by the blacksmiths. The issue continued alive, however. The viceroy, the count of Salvatierra (a former governor of Seville), in 1649 referred the matter to the courts, which in 1653 recommended that the ban be implemented.[93]

Despite the fact that many guilds prohibited Indians, mixed-bloods, and blacks from becoming masters, it also is clear that many guilds ignored their own rules in the sixteenth and seventeenth centuries. Evidence of such disobedience came on 17 July 1706, when the Lima *audiencia* ruled that no "*negro, zambo, mulato* [or] *indio neto*" could traffic, trade, open a shop, or sell goods on the street "because such people are untrustworthy and unforthcoming and it would not be decent for them to be side-by-side with others in these occupations, for which reason they should dedicate themselves to mechanical occupations, as they are suited only for such activities."[94] As in Spain, the prestige of a craft seemed to demand the absence of certain racial groups, though the prohibitions, the more adamant the more they were repeated, indicated their presence.

Aside from questions of race or blood, occupational anxiety also was palpable in late seventeenth-century Spain. The *memoriales* sounded familiar. When sculptors, for example, wanted to separate from carpenters in 1679 and become a *colegio* rather than a guild, they insulted the carpenters by saying the latter were manual laborers whose job required no intelligence. At another point, they claimed that while sculptors could paint, painters certainly could not sculpt.[95] Painters also wanted special consideration. In

---

[93] Quiroz Chueca and Quiroz Chueca, eds., *Las ordenanzas de gremios de Lima,* 111–118. Mexican silk workers in 1584 included a ban on black and mulatto masters in their ordinances, which also was struck down by judicial authorities (Vásquez, ed., *Legislación del trabajo,* 56–58).

[94] Jorge Juan and Antonio de Ulloa, *Noticias secretas de América,* ed. David Barry (London, 1826), 423, note inserted by the editor.

[95] Pere Molas Ribalta, "El exclusivismo en los gremios de la Corona de Aragon: Limpieza de sangre y limpieza de oficios," in *Les sociétés fermées dans le monde iberique,* 74; BN VE 142–21.

part, this was an old story; Diego de Velázquez in the early seventeenth century had insisted on his pedigree, famously painting himself with the cross of Santiago in *Las Meninas*.[96] In a *memorial* (probably directed to Juan José of Austria), the *profesores de pintura* (the term they preferred to masters) reminded authorities of the "incomparable credit and luster" painting had enjoyed throughout the centuries. It had been the pastime of kings and wise men and a guarantee of immortality. Anticipating one of the usual objections, they admitted they used their hands to create their art but added, "that is nothing compared to the immensity of the theory therein contained." Anticipating another, they pointed out that selling their paintings "[did] not offend their nobility because the action of receiving is admitted in such noble Sciences as Jurisprudence and Medicine." Finally, they reminded authorities that the Council of Finance in 1633 had freed painters of the obligation of paying the alcabala, "which clearly proves their ingenuity, hidalguía, and excellence."[97] One hundred years later, the painters were still at it: the Real Academia de San Fernando in 1784 had to referee disputes between artists and craftsmen over closed-shop rules adopted by guilds of painters in Majorca, Catalonia, Zaragoza, and Valencia.[98] In the same vein, the farriers in the king's stables, as we saw earlier, protested their inclusion in a 1691 sumptuary law by saying they were deeply saddened that the *pragmática* likened theirs to "occupations that by their nature are mechanical and of the lowest degree, while the supplicants' is Art and even Science."[99] In Madrid, the makers of doors and windows (*portaventaneros*) went to court to claim theirs was a liberal art because it required "anticipation," which seems to have meant something akin to inspiration. At any rate, they thought themselves better than carpenters. The issue in the 1708 suit (the latest of many) was similar to those throughout the early modern period: the *portaventaneros'* ordinances said they could make doors and windows of pine, a wood the carpenters claimed as their own, and they demanded the right to administer examinations. Artists, the *portaventaneros* sniffed, did not need examinations, unlike carpenters, who had an occupation that was *materialísimo*. Arguing in terms reminiscent of those later used by Jovellanos and others who fought guild ordinances by saying they restricted creativity, the *portaventaneros* said examinations were precise things

[96] See Jonathan Brown, *Images and Ideas in Seventeenth-Century Spanish Painting* (Princeton University Press, 1978), 103–110, for a description of Velázquez's attempts to join the Order of Santiago.

[97] BN VE 141–14. Representatives of the humbler trades employed the opposite tactic in their petitions in the sixteenth and seventeenth centuries, emphasizing they *did* pay alcabalas and therefore were worthy of respect as contributors. For more on painters' defense of the nobility of their art, see Juan José Martín González, *El artista en la sociedad española del siglo XVII* (Madrid: Cátedra, 1993), 77–83.

[98] Glendinning, *A Literary History of Spain*, 11.

[99] BN VE 210–128.

circumscribed by rules appropriate to material pursuits. Art could not be thus confined. Carpenters did not disagree with the definition but said it was "ridiculous" and an insult to include *portaventaneros* among the liberal arts.[100] Again, the point is not that two guilds were fighting over jurisdiction but rather the nature of the terms invoked at this relatively late date, particularly given that *portaventaneros* in the past had never run the risk of being confused with artists. In similar terms, a 1719 manual for architects (republished in 1760) decried the "confusion between the intellectual speculation of Art with the materiality of exercise" and went on to declare architecture free of contagion (*contagio*) by the mechanical arts.[101] Mexico's silversmiths in 1774 described themselves to the king as "individuals of distinguished birth, clean blood and good habits, related to families of distinction and character."[102]

These are all examples of elite (or allegedly elite) crafts, but sudden concern for rank also can be found among the lower crafts as the eighteenth century progressed. In 1721, for example, administrators of the San Telmo orphanage in Seville began requiring applicants to submit documentation attesting not only to their purity of blood but also to a family background free of low and vile trades. Administrators of the Seafarers Guild, to which San Telmo pertained, argued that they simply were adopting the criteria then in use for controlling emigration to America, though they had never shown such discrimination in the past and I have been unable to find any evidence that such a rule was in effect. They also may have been concerned that mechanical ancestors might prevent their wards, future naval pilots, from entering the maritime officer corps, though pilots' examinations did not include testimony regarding occupational ancestry.[103] Those whose exclusion was now required in order to ensure that the school not "suffer any dishonor in common regard" included the sons of hangmen, town

---

[100] AHN CS libro 3949. The Council of Castile issued a compromise ruling.

[101] Theodoro Ardemans, *Ordenanzas de Madrid, y otras diferentes, que se practican en las ciudades de Toledo, y Sevilla con algunas advertencias a los Alarifes . . .* (1719) (Madrid, 1760), 4–6.

[102] Konetzke, "Las ordenanzas de gremios," 512.

[103] Testimony by four witnesses at the examinations, two of whom had to be pilots, concerned birthplace, "good customs," absence of vice, and experience as a pilot. See Federico de Castro y Bravo, *Las naos españolas en la carrera de las Indias. Armadas y flotas en la segunda mitad del siglo XVI* (Madrid: Editorial Voluntad, 1927), 102–103; Carla Rahn Phillips, *Six Galleons for the King of Spain: Imperial Defense in the Early Seventeenth Century* (Baltimore: Johns Hopkins University Press, 1986), 132–133. A modern study of sixteenth-century mariners on Spanish ships (many of them not Spaniards) makes no mention of occupational ancestry; indeed, it stresses that many of the men were not who they said they were and furthermore knew nothing of their own family (Pablo E. Pérez-Mallaína, *Spain's Men of the Sea: Daily Life on the Indies Fleets in the Sixteenth Century,* trans. Carla Rahn Phillips [Baltimore: Johns Hopkins University Press, 1998]). A seventeenth-century manual stated that to be admitted as a pilot one had to "prove one was not among the prohibited," a probable reference only to Jews or Muslims (Joseph de Veitia Linage, *Norte de la contratación de las Indias Occidentales* (1672) (Buenos Aires: Comisión argentina de fomento interamericano, 1945), 617).

criers, coach drivers, mule drivers, tanners, butchers, fish cleaners, pastry chefs, tavern keepers, cobblers, actors, dancers, fruit sellers, "and any other occupation that bars entry into the sacred religions," a possible reference to the theoretical inability of those people to occupy certain ecclesiastical offices.[104]

Also in eighteenth-century Seville, two members of the shoemakers confraternity went to court to complain that the confraternity was not abiding by chapter 14 of its ordinances, which specified that to open a shop, a master shoemaker must be a confraternity brother and an "Old Christian without a trace of Jew, Berber, mulatto, Gypsy, or the newly converted; and must not have committed crimes that are punishable or infamous; and he, his parents, and his grandparents must not have been punished by any court; and he must be of good life, opinion, and habit."[105] (A Madrid shoemakers confraternity in 1785 had similar, though less stringent restrictions. Applicants would be received as brothers if they were "not quarrelsome, depraved, a criminal, or guilty of infamy, and if [they were] Old Christian and younger than fifty-one years old.")[106] Despite the membership criteria, the Seville complaint stated, entry was being granted to those "whose fathers exercised low and vile occupations such as, according to common opinion and censure, butchers, fish cleaners, slaughterhouse workers, tavern keepers, pastry chefs, and others who are similar to these." Note, first, the ubiquitous indeterminate nature of the list and, second, that chapter 14, at least as described by the plaintiffs, says nothing about the vile and mechanical trades. Perhaps to remedy the inconsistency, certain members of the confraternity gathered on 2 February 1766 and voted that confraternity examiners should not administer tests to anyone whose father was not a shoemaker himself or "of another decent occupation, excluding those who are sons and grandsons of vile and low occupations." The *fiscal* of Seville objected to this move as divisive and said there had been no quorum. The shoemakers responded by having nearly all (if not all) members ratify the vote. Their lawyer, Antonio Ezquibel, then launched a bold (though ultimately unsuccessful) argument: though the *fiscal* might say the prohibition violated city ordinances, in fact there was nothing in the latter that said sons of those who had practiced vile trades *could* be admitted. In fact, far from upsetting things, the measure actually would promote civic

[104] Tikoff, "Assisted Transitions," 128–131. Similar rules were suddenly imposed in a prominent Madrid orphanage for girls (William J. Callahan, *La Santa y Real Hermandad del Refugio y Piedad de Madrid, 1618–1832* [Madrid: CSIC, 1980], 144–146).

[105] AAS Sec. III.1.6, leg. 207. This case is, I believe, unusual in that the confraternity appears to have had many of the responsibilities held elsewhere by guilds. In an earlier suit between the guild and the confraternity, a lawyer clarified the difference between the respective organizations by saying, "They are separate bodies and therefore have distinct heads" (AAS Sec. III.1.6, leg. 14).

[106] AHN CS leg. 613.

peace because the city's requirement that guilds meet every year to pick their officials specified that those elected should be wise and knowledge-able in their occupation, "and it is clear that legislators wanted to exclude those from vile occupations because [they] are presumed not to be good people but prone to acts of wickedness." As there was no record of having admitted such people in the past, doing so now would be a novelty and would expose the confraternity, "so useful and necessary to the public," to being governed by hateful people. Obviously, the restriction was new, though the confraternity might argue (disingenuously) that previously it had been assumed. It meant shoemakers with vile and mechanical back-grounds had in fact been joining the guild and/or its confraternity, and furthermore that shoemakers did not consider themselves to be vile, though others apparently did.

Yet another guild that suddenly acquired airs was that of the Toledo dy-ers, whose 1732 ordinances excluded sons of "infected fathers . . . and [those practicing] the vilest occupations." In 1749, the guild expelled a journeyman after the organization discovered "he was the son of a man practicing an occupation reputed as low in Spain." In 1748, Toledo's braid makers specified which were the vile and mechanical occupations off-lim-its to the ancestors of prospective members: they were butchers, shoe-makers, tavern keepers "and others of equal lowliness."[107]

These cases contribute to the argument that guilds showed new interest in the eighteenth century in delimiting their territory, often using mark-ers of ancestry or race, to ensure that their prestige was greater than that of their competitors. But though their rejection of certain people as low or vile does not mean manual labor per se was despised, reformers blurred the two, as have historians. In one such example, William Callahan pointed to the town of Horche (Guadalajara) to make his case: crown officials in the early 1780s insisted that workers at a local cloth manufactory be ad-mitted to the Horche town council, which was dominated by *labradores,* the majority of the population. Earlier, town leaders had ordered three of the workers into the local militia and refused to allow workers from elsewhere to transfer there to make up the difference. In 1781, the workers sent the Council of Castile a *memorial.* Town leaders, they complained, "look upon those who dedicate themselves to the commendable object of the manu-facture of wool with a sort of disdain and contempt . . . as if industry and agriculture were incompatible, as if both did not reciprocally contribute to the people's happiness, as if there were something inherently vile or shameful in the making of cloth." The Council of Castile reprimanded the

[107] Pere Molas Ribalta, in *Historia de España,* ed. Ramón Menéndez Pidal, vol. 28: *La tran-sición del siglo XVII a1 XVIII: Entre la decadencia y la reconstrucción* (Madrid: Espasa Calpe, 1993), 646. Molas Ribalta cites Eugenio de Larruga.

leaders for regarding the workers' jobs as "vile occupations, making them ineligible for the *honoríficos* of the Republic," that is, seats on the town council, and told a Guadalajara official, Francisco Dueñas, to ensure that a worker was elected to the Horche council. The town council replied that the petitioners and their colleagues spent much of their time in the local tavern and furthermore had worked as swineherds, oil and fish mongers, and similarly dishonorable jobs, and therefore anyway were ineligible. When Dueñas arrived, he told the locals that the notion of *oficios bajos* "was of the past, not the present," but they were not moved. He remained for at least a month, finally telling the Council of Castile that the elections would take place. Unfortunately, none of the workers were elected to important posts, and Dueñas was ordered to return. Finally, democracy triumphed and a wool worker was elected to an important post, which remained in the workers' hands until 1787, at which point the *labradores* wrested it back. Once again the workers complained, and this time they could point to the 1783 edict, though it did them no good. The town was divided, and it would apparently remain so. Callahan reports that in 1794 the town council was still resisting orders to admit workers.[108]

In this and similar conflicts the language of vileness seems very well-timed. There is no good explanation why petitioners suddenly used that discourse to condemn exclusionary attitudes except that they thought they would find an audience in Madrid. When Berindoaga went to Toledo on behalf of the Madrid Economic Society he reported back that "the opinion of dishonor with respect to the manual trades is so extended and entrenched that there are few people who do not suffer from this illness among the common people and even among the upper classes."[109] The *desprecio* paradigm enabled the Economic Society to treat the ailment with strong, rational medicine. But though they certainly knew the cure, we cannot conclude that Berindoaga or his colleagues correctly diagnosed the illness. When villages resisted the presence and advances of transplanted workers, labor probably was not the issue. Instead, the principal problem was that they were outsiders, and therefore by definition untrustworthy. Ostracism of imported wage laborers such as the ones in the examples above had far more to do with community than with categories of labor, no matter how true those categories appeared to the *ilustrados*.

Reconstruction of one's past in early modern Spain and its colonies often was an arbitrary undertaking. Defendants in Inquisition trials some-

[108] Callahan, "La estimación del trabajo manual," 66–71; and Callahan, *Honor, Commerce and Industry*, 51–52. Callahan cites "Memoria de Francisco Ventura, Gerónimo Cortés, fabricantes de Horche," 21 March 1781 (AHN Consejos leg. 895, exp. 39). I have drawn entirely from Callahan's accounts.

[109] Callahan, *Honor, Commerce and Industry*, 45. I particularly like the word "even."

times were required to supply an autobiographical sketch of themselves; the vast majority told the court they had no idea who their grandparents were or where they were from. Such ignorance naturally was greatest in common people, who had little reason to construct family trees. Yet as pressure mounted to ward off challenges from darker, less Christian, or less established vassals, this same society showed an increasingly frenetic interest in genealogy. Guilds and other corporate entities evidenced a sudden preoccupation with their members' ancestors, a matter of little or no concern in the past. Historians have been too willing to believe that such interest was of a long-standing nature and that the issue really was occupational ancestry, when in fact it was something else. The discourse of work, not-work, and antiwork was deployed and redeployed in the eighteenth century by the state and by individuals, both elite and common, in different ways and to different ends. Though the former was concerned about the rationalization of the workforce, both its body and its soul, and the latter were concerned about social status and survival, all used refurbished idioms of virtue, purity, ocio, duty, and vileness. They took what had been a largely rhetorical and metaphysical concept and transferred it to the physical and economic world.

PART THREE

"THE PROBLEM OF SPAIN"

Prologue

THE SHORT NINETEENTH CENTURY AND THE EMPIRE

Charles III died in 1788. "Spaniards!" Jovellanos cried out to his audience at the Madrid Economic Society. "See here the greatest of all the gifts bestowed on you by Charles III. He planted seeds of light in the nation to enlighten you, and he cleared the paths of knowledge."[1] The king was succeeded by his son, Charles IV, whose reign coincided with the French Revolution, the wars with France, and the Napoleonic invasion in 1808. After his abdication, the throne was occupied by Napoleon's brother, Joseph. Charles IV's ministers initially continued the reforms instigated under the previous reign, but the 1789 revolution jolted the chief minister, the count of Floridablanca, in a decidedly conservative direction. Newspapers and periodicals were shuttered, the Inquisition was called upon to halt the inflow of revolutionary materials from France, and the lively atmosphere of political and intellectual debate in Spain's cities came to an end. Some of the most notable of the movement's leaders went into exile. In the words of Raymond Carr, enlightenment now was government property.[2] Floridablanca was replaced with the more conservative count of Aranda, who in turn was replaced by Manuel Godoy, who presided over an increasingly factionalized government and society from 1792 to 1808. A year after Godoy's appointment, Spain and France were at war. Those who supported the French Revolution were called *afrancesados;* after Napoleon, they also

[1] Gaspar Melchor Jovellanos, "Elogio de Carlos III, leído en la Real Sociedad Económica de Madrid, 8 November 1788," in *Obras,* vol. 1, ed. Candido Nocedal, Biblioteca de Autores Españoles, vol. 46 (Madrid, 1858), 311–317.
[2] Raymond Carr, *Spain, 1808–1975,* 2d ed. (Oxford University Press, 1989), 72.

would be known as traitors. Nineteenth-century liberals and their heirs would continue to bear that burden.

The Hapsburg monarchs had regarded the Indies as among their many kingdoms; the Bourbons saw them more as possessions and since the early eighteenth century had sought to make the relationship between Spain and its American empire more profitable. The famed Bourbon reforms in America—Spain's last-ditch effort to centralize control, revive trade, increase revenue, and combat corruption—ultimately had contrary effects. They instilled resentment on the part of the American elites at the same time as they pointed the way to the possibility of internal changes engineered locally. Free-market economic reforms also, of course, were inspired by a rhetoric of progress and enlightenment that would prove dangerous in the wrong hands. The changes exacerbated tensions that had been growing throughout the century. In Paraguay the *comunero* revolts, from 1721 to 1735, pitted creoles crying democratic slogans against colonial authorities; in Quito, thousands participated in the 1765 tax revolt known as the *rebelión de los barrios;* and in Peru, the lower classes revolted in the enormous peasant rebellion in 1780 led by the second Tupac Amaru.

One of Philip V's leading ministers, José del Campillo, in 1743 proposed a vast reorganization of the colonial government, noting that Great Britain and France were making huge profits off their Caribbean sugar islands, in contrast to Spain. To remedy the situation, he urged a general inspection followed by the liberalization of trade regulations, the appointment of intendants, and land grants for Indians. He also warned that the church had far too much power and wealth. Few if any of the proposals bore fruit. After the British seizure of Havana and Manila in 1762 (much of the Seven Years' War, from 1756 to 1763, was fought in the colonies), however, Charles III sent an envoy to implement some of the old proposals. The inspector, José de Gálvez, spent from 1765 to 1771 on tour. A francophile lawyer from Málaga who later was named minister of the Indies as a reward for his labors, Gálvez overhauled colonial tax collection and customs, set up a militia system, and established a new viceroyalty in Buenos Aires. He and similar envoys in the late eighteenth century profoundly distrusted the Americans and deprived them of bureaucratic representation, which previously had been available to them through the purchase of office; out of a total of 754 viceroys and other high officials in Spanish America, just 18 were creoles.[3] John Lynch has described this gradual exclusion as Spain's second conquest of America.[4] At the same time, Charles III's government gradually ended port monopolies, allowing greater numbers of Spaniards

---

[3] Antonello Gerbi, *The Dispute of the New World: The History of a Polemic, 1750–1900* (1955), trans. Jeremy Moyle (University of Pittsburgh Press, 1973), 183.

[4] John Lynch, *The Spanish American Revolutions 1808–1826*, 2d ed. (New York: W. W. Norton, 1986), chap. 1.

to participate in American trade. In 1774, the crown legalized trade between Mexico and Peru, though authorities still tried to ensure that intercolonial commerce did not compete with Spanish products; and in 1778, the Cádiz monopoly was abolished and all Spanish ports were permitted to trade with almost all parts of America. The few remaining restrictions were eliminated in 1789.[5] But increasingly after the American Revolution, the colonies regarded the United States, not Spain, as their chief trading partner. In 1803, with political and economic arguments in hand, Simón Bolívar went to Europe to seek aid for his explicitly republican independence movement. The following year, the Haitians won their freedom from the French.

At home, meanwhile, Spaniards revolted against the French invaders on 2 May 1808, an event immortalized by Goya in his paintings *May 2, 1808: The Charge of the Mamelukes,* and *May 3, 1808: The Execution of the Defenders of Madrid.* For the philosopher Miguel de Unamuno, writing in 1895, May 2 was "in all ways the symbolic date of our regeneration."[6] Spain's famous guerrilla warfare against Napoleon's army (the war created the neologism) inspired admiration around the world. The so-called War of Independence (known to the English, who played a large part in winning it, as the Peninsular War) was crucial in creating a mythic national spirit maintained and cultivated throughout the nineteenth century by subsequent liberal and republican political formations and their historians.

With the throne occupied by Joseph Bonaparte, Spanish patriots immediately organized *juntas* in nearly every province and in America, finding themselves suddenly able to put into practice the innovative ideas of the past several decades. In the absence of Ferdinand VII, Charles IV's son, who was in the custody of the French, they regarded themselves as the country's only legitimate government, descendants of both the sixteenth-century *comuneros* and the Enlightenment. The central *junta,* one of whose leaders was Jovellanos, called for the convocation of the Cortes, the ancient representative assembly that had last met during the reign of Charles II.[7] They opened in January 1810 in Cádiz, capital of the Spanish Atlantic trade, and in 1812 the country belittled by much of Europe for being

---

[5] On Spanish trade policy and reforms during the reign of Charles III, see Stanley J. Stein and Barbara H. Stein, *Apogee of Empire: Spain and New Spain in the Age of Charles III, 1759–1789* (Baltimore: Johns Hopkins University Press, 2003).

[6] Miguel de Unamuno, *En torno al casticismo* (Madrid: Colección Austral, 1972), 17. Today 2 May is a holiday in Madrid, but it is not the national holiday along the lines of 4 July in the United States or 14 July in France; that privilege is reserved for 7 December, the date the current constitution was approved in 1978.

[7] Jovellanos had been forced to leave Madrid during the Godoy years but used his time wisely in Asturias in the 1790s, writing his masterpiece, *Informe de la ley agraria,* a radical exposition on free trade and agrarian reform. Charles IV invited him back to court in 1797, but he spent from 1801 to 1808 in prison. On his release, unlike some of his former colleagues, he declined to form part of Joseph's cabinet. He died in 1811.

chained to an absolutist, reactionary past enacted the continent's first modern constitution, providing for popular sovereignty, fundamental liberties, and the separation of church and state, the last leading in 1812 to the seizure of ecclesiastical community properties. Colonial reforms, however, were postponed, an error on the part of the *peninsulares*. In the decade after Bolívar's successful uprising in Caracas on 19 April 1810, a chain of similar revolts took place throughout Spanish America, and by the end of the decade virtually all the colonies had won their independence.

After Napoleon's defeat put Fernando VII on the throne, the king's first act was to nullify the Constitution of Cádiz. The first of Spain's many military revolts took place in 1820; unlike those to follow, it was of a liberal bent and restored the constitution. Three years later, Fernando struck back and displayed his reactionary character, which was unswayed until the end of his reign, in 1833, and which Goya so pointedly depicted in his royal portraits.

Spanish politics throughout the rest of the nineteenth century were marked by sharp instability, and, uniquely among European nations, by the coexistence of fervent liberalism and staunch antiliberalism.[8] A succession dispute between Ferdinand VII and his brother Charles was the excuse for the Carlist Wars in the 1830s and 1870s, essentially conflicts between extreme conservative Catholics and liberals. After Ferdinand, the throne was variously in the hands of his daughter, Isabel II, who enjoyed support from the liberals; two regency governments; an Italian (Amadeo, in 1871); and a restoration monarchy. There were several military coups and a short-lived republic. Politically, there were sharp movements back and forth between the liberal and conservative factions, the latter primarily representatives of the Catholic church, the armed forces, and the powerful landholding class.

During their years in power, the liberals managed to get much of the church and the aristocracy's land disentailed, though once the land was put on the market it often ended up in the same hands, and no meaningful agrarian reform ever was enacted. A strong antimonarchical, republican movement developed in the 1860s, resulting in the so-called September Revolution in 1868, causing Isabel to flee to France. The revolution was a reference point for later liberals and an event that happened to coincide with the first serious Cuban revolt. A five-year experiment with an unsteady constitutional monarchy followed. Spain's first republic lasted from 1873 to 1874 and was succeeded by the Bourbon Restoration of Alfonso XII, who died unexpectedly, and Alfonso XIII, born after his father's death. For

[8] This point is made in Jesús Millán and María Cruz Romeo, "Was the Liberal Revolution Important to Modern Spain? Political Cultures and Citizenship in Spanish History," *Social History* 29 (August 2004): 285.

nearly fifty years, the central government under the Bourbons continued to alternate between left and right, the two giants of the respective sides being Práxedes Mateo Sagasta (1827–1903) and Antonio Cánovas del Castillo (1828–1897). In general, the liberals, who represented an urban political class with virtually no social base in a country with unfathomable geographic and economic imbalances, were unable to impose their reform program in the face of the united front of the landholding class, the church, and a restless army suspicious of anyone not Castilian.

Throughout the middle part of the century, the only economic growth to speak of took place in the Catalonian textile industry, railroad construction (largely inadequate), and mining, shipbuilding, and metallurgy in the northern regions of Asturias and the Basque Country. Government debt, the result of military outlays, was huge. The Junta de Comercio continued to exist during the early part of the century, though crafts guilds were abolished (again) during the reign of Isabel II. Spain, even compared to other southern European countries, remained poor and underdeveloped. In 1860, 76 percent of the population was illiterate; by 1910, 50 percent of all people over ten years of age were illiterate. The relative prosperity of Catalonia and the Basque Country fueled regional patriotism among their inhabitants: the Basque Nationalist Party was founded in 1894, and Catalonia similarly witnessed a surge in cultural nationalism that included celebrations of its language and countryside. In both regions, a bourgeois nationalist movement and working-class sentiments dovetailed with sympathies for independence from Madrid. Anarchism found fertile ground in rural southern and eastern Spain starting in the 1880s, as did socialism. As Spain's cities finally began to be the site of industrial development, radical working-class movements emerged around the turn of the century. Ironically, given the subject of this book, that is where I leave things.

A new movement of intellectuals arose, strongly influenced by the work of a minor German philosopher, Karl Christian Friedrich Krause (1781–1832), arose in the latter part of the nineteenth century. Calling for *regeneración*, these philosophers, poets, historians, educators, journalists, and novelists together loosely formed what would later be known as the Movement of 1898, named after the year Spain lost its last colonies. Cuba's Ten Years' War began in 1868, signaling the beginning of the end. After several more attempts, the island's final, successful revolt began in 1895. Spain, politically unstable and verging on bankruptcy, responded ineptly, first with inadequate concessions, then with military repression, and ultimately with catastrophic economic policies. The war ended with Spain's (and the Cubans') defeat at the hands of the United States, which had entered the war after the *Maine* blew up in February 1898. The Filipino war for independence began in 1896, also ending in 1898 with a U.S. triumph.

In Spain, there were protests, mutinies, and despair. Tens of thousands of demoralized, bewildered troops returned home after years of hunger, mosquitos, disease, and heat prostration. An estimated one hundred thousand Spanish soldiers died in Cuba, around half of those sent; thousands more lost their youth in appalling conditions.[9] International capitalism suffered a deep depression at the turn of the century; Spain suffered doubly.

The first chapter of this final section is devoted, first, to the image of Spain over a period of several centuries, the product of a complex set of relationships between Europe and Spain and Spain and its colonies. It then treats two imperial phenomena in particular: the relationship between peninsular Spaniards and America before the wars of independence and the reaction at home to the defeats of 1898. Beyond their political and military aspects, these two matters also concern work, or the absence thereof. Antipathy toward work was present in explanations of the twin disasters; it formed part of the discourse of peninsular Spaniards toward creoles and indigenous subalterns, and it also formed part of the excruciating self-criticism, pessimism, and lament that characterized the late nineteenth-century "disaster literature." Chapter 6 returns to my argument that the Enlightenment provides the key moment for understanding how our age has read the early modern age. Finally, I offer some observations about how the history of Spain has been written and the role labor has played in that historiography, with some broader considerations on reading the past that I hope will also be useful to those whose focus extends beyond Spain and its empire.

---

[9] Louis A. Pérez Jr., *Cuba between Empires, 1878–1902* (University of Pittsburgh Press, 1983), 75.

CHAPTER FIVE

A Nation Punished

They were "a poor, lazy, idle, dirty, ignorant race of semi-savages," a text-book instructed U.S. schoolchildren.[1] "They" were Spaniards, not Indians or Cubans or Filipinos. The empire had struck back. At the start and again at the end of the nineteenth century, the monarchy that had colonized much of the world saw its dominions vanish.

The principal theme of this chapter is the intersection of work, empire, national character, and historiography. Such a theme should not be taken as a multistep formula of causes and effects but rather as a framework of influences that to some degree helps explain how Spain's past and its history have been conceived so narrowly. There have been so many strictures on thought and imagination, so many debts to pay.

Spain's image of itself was inextricably bound up with others' image of Spain, be they competitors or subalterns. As a kingdom, a nation, and a people, Spain had been the object of derision, jealousy, stereotyping, and hatred ever since the conquest of America. At the same time, Spaniards always had been self-critical, most notably in the early seventeenth century, when arbitristas flooded royal councils with suggestions on how better to stand up to the country's enemies, irrigate the land, ensure fiscal stability,

[1] Samuel Whelpley, *A Compend of History,* cited in Richard Kagan, ed., *Spain in America: The Origins of Hispanism in the United States* (Urbana: University of Illinois Press, 2002), 23. A recent article indicates that U.S. textbooks' presentation of Spanish history has not improved much over the years, a failure the author attributes to the small number of universities that employ professors of Spanish history. See William Phillips Jr., "Images of Spanish History in the United States," *Bulletin of the Society for Spanish and Portuguese Historical Studies* 27 (Summer–Winter 2002): 40–49.

and spur population growth. For hundreds of years, as its enemies characterized Spain, so Spain characterized itself, its colonized vassals, and the Spaniards who emigrated to govern them. Fighting wars and battling heresies, Spaniards at home and abroad long had been devising formulas to distinguish themselves from other Europeans and from their colonies. Work and its opposites, not-work and antiwork, were among the components of these characterizations. The question of the historiography and image of Spain as it related to Spaniards' capacity for or antipathy toward labor is complicated by the fact that Spain as an imperial nation and, ultimately, as an imperial nation represented as a failure, both absorbed others' image of it and imposed its image onto its colonies. Those imposed images would then recross the Atlantic.

These images and their metamorphoses lead us to consider two things: what I call national character and what I call nationalism. National character, which can comprise cultural stereotypes, innate qualities, or self-imposed myths, exists prior to nationalism and does not necessarily entail linkage to political or administrative entities, though it can. Nationalism, in contrast, must engage with or refer to those entities. There was something in their national character, Spaniards told themselves, that impeded Spain from becoming a proper nation. The educated protagonists of this book often referred to patriotism, or to the *patria*; I understand them to mean nationalism or nation, as I am defining it, that is, an enterprise that extends beyond individuals (sometimes defined, in the context of nationalism, as citizens) to encompass a collective project, often predicated on the elements of national character.[2] Readers may want more precision, but the linguistic exercise would distract from my primary purpose, and the lack of precision on the part of contemporaries is warning enough to stay away. Nor do I want to enter into an exploration of when and how something called "Spain" emerged and if it was a nation. It is worth a reminder at this point that this book anyway deals largely with Castile, not with what we know today as Spain, though for convenience and out of respect for the usage of the times I am using the latter term. Travelers' puzzled and disapproving descriptions were largely applied to Castile, not Catalonia, which they easily recognized as another country: "Activity is the basis of the Catalan character," one admiring French traveler wrote, while Christopher Hervey proclaimed Catalonia to be "the best part of all Spain."[3] Campo-

[2] David Bell, *The Cult of the Nation in France: Inventing Nationalism, 1680–1800* (Cambridge, Mass.: Harvard University Press, 2001), 42–43, discusses the difference between *nation* and *patrie* in eighteenth-century France. The terms were more interchangeable in Spain.

[3] Alexandre Laborde, *A View of Spain* (London, 1809), cited in William J. Callahan, *Honor, Commerce, and Industry in Eighteenth-Century Spain.* (Boston: Baker Library, Harvard University, 1972), 37; Hervey cited in Mario Ford Bacigalupo, "An Ambiguous Image: English Travel Accounts of Spain (1750–1787)," *Dieciocho* 1 (Fall 1978): 128.

manes and other economic boosters often pointed to Catalonia as the anti-Castile, though praise for that region's industrious character necessarily entailed praise for its relatively powerful craft guilds, leaving the champions of a free market in somewhat of a bind.

This chapter covers some three hundred years of international relationships, often traveling back and forth in time and across more than one ocean. The point of such a complex journey is to figure out the connections among the allegedly natural attributes of the Spanish people that condemned them to shun labor, the political structures amid which this inborn character developed, and the manner in which both were recorded. What interests me are the qualities Spaniards ascribed to themselves, those ascribed to them by others, and those that they, in turn, ascribed to the inhabitants of their colonies, and how those qualities helped or hindered a national, economic, and imperial project. The development of the notion of what it meant to be Spanish was an intrinsic part of the process by which Spain ruled its colonies, and imagining what it meant to be Spanish ran parallel to imagining what it meant to be Indian (or mestizo or creole). The discourse of labor, in short, was also a discourse of empire, both triumphant and failed.

National Character

Throughout part 2 we saw that writers and reformers in the sixteenth, seventeenth, and eighteenth centuries used similar words to describe social problems and their remedies. I have argued that the dawn of the Enlightenment spelled no radical change of attitude regarding labor, as historians often have said, but rather a new set of economic and political needs and possibilities. The earlier period was characterized by praise for labor and vilification of indolence just as the later period was; the later period, in turn, was just as reliant on moral notions as the earlier period, though with different ends.

Clearly, however, the world looked different in 1775, the year Campomanes published *Discurso sobre la educación popular,* from the way it did in 1526, when Juan Luís Vives wrote his treatise on poverty, offering remedies that were among Campomanes's starting points. Social and moral problems appeared less broad, less general, as national boundaries solidified and patriotism shared the stage with Christian solidarity as a motive for social acts, though in Spain the two impulses were never separate. Throughout Europe, writers exhibited a veritable obsession for defining national characters; and starting in the later eighteenth century, Spaniards had a growing sense that that is what they were: Spaniards.

This sense of nation was quickened by the looks of disparagement cast their way from France. Frenchmen, long ruled by Bourbons, did not have a high opinion of the newly acquired monarchy on the other side of the Pyrenees, and the list of French abuse and stereotyping of Spain in the eighteenth century is nearly endless. With the usual caveat of using literary sources, one is obliged to cite a famous passage from Montesquieu's *Persian Letters*, published in 1721:

> When a man possesses some special merit in Spain, as, for example . . . that of owning a long sword, or that of having learnt from his father to strum a jangling guitar, he works no more; his honor is concerned in the repose of his limbs. He who remains seated ten hours a day obtains exactly double the respect paid to one who rests only five, because nobility is acquired by sitting still.[4]

Spanish intellectuals respected Montesquieu and did not like being what María Carmen Iglesias has called his "political anti-model," though they themselves had spent several hundred years wondering if they had not brought their own misfortunes on themselves.[5] Another figure they admired greatly, Benjamin Franklin, later praised the Spanish Economic Societies, but previously he had shared the prejudices of his future French hosts. "Our tradesmen," he wrote gloomily to a friend, "are grown as idle and as extravagant in their demands when you would prevail on them to work as so many Spaniards."[6] Voltaire's Candide suffered only misfortune when he ventured into the Hispanic world. Spaniards could and did dispute characterizations of themselves as lazy by pointing to their history: laggards did not conquer America. But they had to counter more than just the commonplace of indolence. Spaniards also were averse to learning, it was said. They "neglect nearly equally agriculture, the arts, the sciences, commerce, and warfare," in the opinion of an early eighteenth-century Frenchman.[7] Returning to the *Persian Letters*, "Glance at one of their libraries, with romances on the one side and the schoolmen on the other, and you would say that the arrangement had been made, and the whole collected, by some secret foe of human reason." In the opinion of Casa-

[4] *The Persian Letters of Montesquieu*, ed. Manuel Komroff (New York: Library of Living Classics, 1929), 153.

[5] María Carmen Iglesias, "Montesquieu and Spain: Iberian Identity as Seen through the Eyes of a Non-Spaniard of the Eighteenth Century," in *Iberian Identity: Essays on the Nature of Identity in Portugal and Spain*, ed. Richard Herr and John H. R. Polt (Berkeley: University of California Press, 1989), 143.

[6] Benjamin Franklin, Letter to Richard Jackson, 2 December 1762, quoted in H. W. Brands, *The First American: The Life and Times of Benjamin Franklin* (New York: Anchor Books, 2002), 333.

[7] Michel-Antoine Baudrand, *Dictionnaire géographique universelle*, cited in Paul Ilie, "Exomorphism: Cultural Bias and the French Image of Spain from the War of Succession to the Age of Voltaire," in *Eighteenth-Century Studies* 9 (Spring 1976): 377.

nova, "the men of Spain dwell mentally in a limited horizon, bounded by prejudice on every side." The women, he noted, were more intelligent, though equally ignorant.[8]

Most famously, a French writer who probably otherwise would have gone unnoticed launched a challenge in 1782 in the *Encylopédie méthodique.* "What is owed to Spain?" asked Nicolas Masson de Morvillers. "After two centuries, after four, after ten, what has it done for Europe?" Spain, he concluded, was "possibly the most ignorant nation in Europe." Excluding a few admitted geniuses such as Cervantes or Calderón, "Where are her mathematicians, her physicians, her naturalists, her historians and her philosophers?"[9]

The question *¿Qué se debe a España?* hit home more than any other previous insult. A furor ensued; Charles III demanded an apology and the Spanish Academy soon convoked a contest to provide "an apology or defense of the Nation." The winner was Juan Pablo Forner (1754–1797), a satirist with a reputation for a hot temper and a mean tongue. His work, a vindication of Spanish culture, was entitled *Oración apologética por la España y su mérito literario.* In it, he returned Masson's favor by dismissing European Enlightened thought altogether and proclaiming that self-knowledge, not scientific knowledge, was what counted, more or less proving the Frenchman right and provoking *El Censor* and other liberal publications to attack both Masson and Forner.[10] Others responded in more tempered ways; Juan Sempere y Guarinos, for one, assembled his multivolume collection of writings of the Spanish Enlightenment in response to Masson's challenge.

At issue in the dispute, which swept up just about everyone writing in Spain in the late 1780s, was how Spaniards should think about themselves given what others thought about them. The *ilustrados* embraced the new ideas, but they were not prepared to accept Spain's assignment to a negligible place on the edge of the Continent. The history of Spaniards' unhappy relationship with their past and their resistance to foreigners pointing out their failings was a long one, of course. The celebratory prose of the sixteenth century and earlier recounting the admiration Spain had

---

[8] *The Memoirs of Jacques Casanova: An Autobiography* (London: Venetian Society, 1928), 62.

[9] The Masson affair is recounted in every history of the Spanish Enlightenment. See, for example, David T. Gies, "Dos preguntas regeneracionistas: '¿Qué se debe a España?' y '¿Qué es España?' Identidad nacional en Forner, Moratín, Jovellanos y la Generación de 1898," *Dieciocho* 22 (Fall 1999); Richard Herr, *The Eighteenth-Century Revolution in Spain.* (Princeton University Press, 1958), 220–230; François López, *Juan Pablo Forner et la crise de la conscience espagnole au XVIII siècle* (Université de Bordeaux, 1976); and Francisco Sánchez-Blanco, *El Absolutismo y las Luces en el reinado de Carlos III* (Madrid: Marcial Pons, 2002), 349–371.

[10] See Jorge Cañizares-Esguerra, "Eighteenth-Century Spanish Political Economy: Epistemology and Decline," *Eighteenth-Century Thought*, no. 1 (2003): 295–314, for an analysis of Forner's epistemology.

always caused in others, starting with the inevitable Romans, smacked of defensiveness. One such volume started off by announcing "The region of Spain, about which this Book is written, is the leader and head of all the other regions of the world."[11] The land was fertile, the fruits delicious, the air mild, the inhabitants brave, the women beautiful. Beyond the tedious lists of their ancestors' heroic accomplishments lay the notion of Spain as a nation with a coherent past fueled by an essentialist Spanish spirit virtually impossible to vanquish. Such literature also signaled the beginning of the two-Spains problem—the one open to the ideas of outsiders, the other perfectly content to remain pure and impenetrable to heresies, both religious and intellectual—and the more difficult and interesting problem of how to balance the two and reconcile their consequences. When Forner spat that Spain had no use for the malignant sophists across the border, he exhibited xenophobia and patriotism, but there also was anguish.

On both sides of the English Channel, climate was a powerful influence in eighteenth-century explorations of national character. A diffuse category embracing weather, landscape, and other geographic features, its relative weight among other factors was disputed, but it was always present, reflecting new scientific concerns and anxiety over the relationship between Europe and the rest of the world. On the one hand, it would seem to have condemned whatever people or nation was being scrutinized to a given set of attributes, a given character. After all, one can't do much about the weather. Sloth, to take the attribute that concerns us, was thought to be a logical outcome of heat, be it humid (in America) or arid (in Castile). The *Grand dictionnaire géographique, historique et critique* commented in 1740, for example, that Spain's climate produced indolence, "the distinctive character of the Spanish Nation."[12] On the other hand, meteorological determinism inevitably collided with observations that different people seemed to thrive in different ways under similar circumstances, the result, perhaps, of their relative ability to overcome climate. It also undermined the notion that all human beings, wherever they lived, shared some basic human nature. Even in the hands of those most concerned with the weather, the national character debate also included more social explanations for behavior, ranging from the impact of imports to the humiliation of servitude. Europeans' explanations for Spaniards' idiosyncrasies and Spaniards' pronouncements on those of the Americans thus straddled nat-

---

[11] Pedro de Medina, *Libro de grandezas y cosas memorables de España* (1548), ed. Angel González Palencia (Madrid: CSIC, 1944), 7. For seventeenth-century examples of the genre of the *laudes Hispaniae*, see Fr. Benito de Peñalosa y Mondragón, *Libro de las cinco excelencias del español* . . . (Pamplona, 1629); and Rodrigo Méndez Silva, *Población general de España* . . . (Madrid, 1645). For the eighteenth century, see Fr. Benito Jerónimo Feijóo, "Glorias de España" (1730), Biblioteca de Autores Españoles, vol. 56 (Madrid: 1952), 194–230.

[12] Cited in Ilie, "Exomorphism," 376.

ural and political causes. Weather may not have been negotiable, but character was.

Travel accounts and works of natural history multiplied and became bestsellers in the eighteenth century, and America obviously was a center of attention. George Louis Leclerc, count of Buffon, in 1747 wrote in his *Histoire naturelle* that the American climate was naturally conducive to degeneration and backwardness. Montesquieu, one of the chief proponents of climatological influence, in *The Spirit of the Laws* asserted that people who lived in warm climates were "as timid as old men."[13] For David Hume (1711–1776), however, "physical causes" (air and climate) were of far less importance than "moral causes" (political and social organization) in accounting for differences in character; in fact, he wrote, "I am inclined to doubt altogether of [the former's] operation in this particular." Yet national borders, which he counted as "moral causes," allowed him to usefully distinguish among peoples: "The Languedocians and Gascons are the gayest people in France, but whenever you pass the Pyrenees, you are among Spaniards."[14] The Romantic philosopher and historian Johann Gottfried von Herder (1744–1803) left room for both human will and the environment in the creation of the *volksgeist:*

> As a mineral spring draws its components, healing powers and taste, from the soil within which it came to be, so the ancient character of the peoples sprang from the features of the race, the climate, the way of life and education, from the early endeavors and attainments that became peculiar to this people. The customs of the fathers were deeply rooted, and they became the guiding light of the race.[15]

Migrations proved that peoples could and did eventually re-create themselves, though neither colonialism nor travel were activities Herder advised, as he thought people did not belong in each other's worlds and ultimately could not understand one another.[16]

Hispanophiles, though they often found themselves forced to discount the influence of the weather, also unfailingly insisted that the ancients had

---

[13] Georges Louis Leclerc, count of Buffon, *Natural History, General and Particular* (London: T. Cadell and W. Davies, 1812); Montesquieu cited in Henry Vyverberg, *Human Nature, Cultural Diversity, and the French Enlightenment* (Oxford University Press, 1989), 69. In Montesquieu's opinion, things got worse as one moved south.

[14] David Hume, "Of National Characters," (1748) in *Essays, Moral, Political, and Literary,* part 1, available at www.econlib.org/library/LFBooks/Hume/hmMPL21.html; Christopher J. Berry, *Hume, Hegel, and Human Nature* (The Hague: Martinus Nijhoff, 1982), chap. 6.

[15] Johann Goffried von Herder, *Further Reflections on the Philosophy of the History of Humankind,* in *On World History: Johann Gottfried Herder, An Anthology,* ed. Hans Adler and Ernest A. Menze (New York: M. E. Sharpe, 1997), 271.

[16] See Anthony Pagden, *European Encounters with the New World: From Renaissance to Romanticism* (New Haven: Yale University Press, 1993), 172–181.

remarked frequently on Spain's excellent conditions. Quevedo, who generally took a gloomy view of his countrymen (though not of their ancestors), noted that extreme heat canceled out extreme cold, an example of the triumph of Aristotelian moderation: "The cold does not make us phlegmatic and lazy like the Germans, nor does the great heat make us useless for labor like blacks and Indians."[17] The exiled Jesuit Juan Francisco de Masdeu, often considered Spain's first modern historian, whose projected nine-volume history of Spain turned into twenty volumes and never got past the Middle Ages, also addressed the respective roles of determinism, will, and the weather in shaping national character. Writing for an Italian audience, he said in the first volume, published in 1783:

> Intellectual faculty, taken generally, is vigorous in all climates. Climate can grant a mind greater inclination and greater facility for progressing in this art or that science; it can, for example, make one nation poetic by nature and another political; it can produce one disposition or another; but it cannot produce in the mind of a people a universal aptitude for everything nor extinguish all potential.

The Dutch are industrious, the English sublime, Spaniards sharp, the French methodical, Italians friendly, and Germans hardworking, and "it would appear indisputable that weather is the principal cause for these national differences."[18] That said, weather could not account for Spaniards' sloth for the simple reason that they were not slothful; on the contrary, they were great lovers (*amantísimos*) of industry.[19] As Spain's fortunes began to ebb, Masdeu wrote, countries whose battle wounds were still smarting had taken their revenge in calumny: "The Dutch, the English, the French, the Italians, and the Germans believed they had a right to say Spain was by nature a lazy, idle, and negligent nation, a nation of men neglectful of agriculture, unskilled in the arts, with no knack for business, simple administrators of foreign trade." In his own eighteenth century, Masdeu suggested, unwise readers had been swayed by texts from the pre-

---

[17] Francisco de Quevedo, "España defendida y los tiempos de ahora de las calumnias de los noveleros y sediciosos," in *Obras completas,* ed. Felicidad Buendía, 2 vols. (Madrid: Aguilar, 1969). As late as the mid-nineteenth century, the historian Modesto Lafuente proclaimed that in Spain "it would appear that all climates and all temperatures are concentrated." Cited in José Alvarez Junco, *Mater dolorosa: La idea de España en el siglo XIX* (Madrid: Taurus, 2001), 203. A history texbook in 1871 instructed children that Spaniards were "a synthetic race, capable of adaptation, like no other, to all climates and all customs, and of assimilation of all ideas." See Alfonso Moreno Espinosa, *Compendio de historia de España . . . ,* cited in Carolyn Boyd, *Historia Patria: Politics, History, and National Identity in Spain, 1875–1975* (Princeton University Press, 1997), 81. The French were similarly convinced that their weather was perfectly balanced; see Bell, *Cult of the Nation,* 95.

[18] Juan Francisco de Masdeu, *Historia crítica de España y de la cultura española* (Madrid, 1783), vol. 1, 54–58.

[19] Cited in Alvarez Junco, *Mater dolorosa,* 204.

vious century, the era of Spain's decline, and erroneously had extrapolated.[20] (In a similarly gracious move of giving critics the benefit of the doubt, the writer José Cadalso, one of Montesquieu's greatest admirers and whose *Cartas marruecas* was both an homage and a critique of the *Persian Letters,* said the acid-tongued Frenchman simply had been misinformed.)[21] On the same subject, the ever logical Antonio de Capmany pointed out that if indeed the weather were the great impediment it was made out to be, then it would do little good to import foreign artisans, as was being proposed in the late eighteenth century, to instruct the lackadaisical Spaniards. The Tatars who conquered China ended up Chinese, he added by way of illustration.[22] (Buffon, too, had surmised that Africans transplanted to Scandinavia eventually would become white.) Another Jesuit exile, Miguel Dámaso Generés, wrote in 1793 that if one paid attention to foreign writers,

> one would have to conclude that the deplorable state [of arts and manufacturing] in Spain resulted from the character and nature of its inhabitants, victims of a fatal genie that emerged from the heat of its climate, weakening them and obliging them to be lazy and listless, [a state encouraged by] their pride and romantic spirit and their ancient and fanatical inclination toward wandering knights.

Blame the government, not the weather, was his reply, echoing Hume's.[23]

But whether or not it was caused by climate, or to what degree, laziness was part of Spain's image and self-image. "There is no halfway creditable foreigner who is not amazed (or who does not mock, more to the point) the imponderable laziness of Spaniards, who are entirely oblivious to respectable matters and content with reprehensible inactivity," wrote José del Campillo (1693–1743), one of Philip V's most perspicacious reformist ministers.[24] The question was to what to attribute the laziness. Campillo's successors, while vowing to do something about the hordes of ociosos, found themselves at the same time denying that ocio was a national flaw.

[20] Masdeu, *Historia crítica de España,* vol. 1, 169–170.

[21] José Cadalso, "Defensa de la nación española contra la Carta Persiana LXXVIII de Montesquieu," in *Cartas Marruecas,* ed. Juan José Amate Blanco (Madrid: Plaza & Janés, 1984), 304–307.

[22] Antonio de Capmany (pseud. Ramón Miguel Palacio), *Discurso político económico en defensa del trabajo mecánico de los menestrales y de la influencia de sus gremios en las costumbres populares, conservacion de las artes y honor de los artesanos.* (Madrid, 1778; repr., Madrid: Almarabu, 1986), 17–18.

[23] Miguel Dámaso Generés, *Reflexiones políticas y económicas sobre la población, agricultura, artes, fábricas y comercio del Reino de Aragón* (1793), ed. Ernest Lluch and Alfonso Sánchez Hormigo (Zaragoza: Institución Fernando el Católico, 1996), 143.

[24] Cited in Rosa María Pérez Estévez, *El problema de los vagos en la España del siglo XVIII* (Madrid: Confederación Española de Cajas de Ahorros, 1976), 307.

There were parts of Spain where people once had worked as hard as in any foreign country, Bernardo Ward wrote in *Proyecto Económico,* even harder than in Holland or England.[25] In Capmany's opinion, foreigners who accused Spain of moral and political vices had never been to Spain, didn't speak the language, and couldn't spell Spanish surnames.[26] Campomanes, too, protested, effectively distinguishing unemployment from sloth: "According to the old song, Spaniards are lazy. It is a widespread error, spread by our enemies, and we have believed it. In fact, we see women and children idle in every town where there is no manufacturing, and because factories are so rare we attribute to the Nation the effect of not seeking steady work for these honest families."[27] Joseph Townsend, whose source for many of his observations was Campomanes himself, also corrected the stereotype: "We must not imagine that the Spaniards are naturally indolent; they are remarkable for activity, capable of strenuous exertions, and patient of fatigue. If, therefore, unemployed, this must be attributed to other causes."[28]

Unlike Townsend, most travelers did not have Campomanes as a guide. Sloth was part of the literature, and travelers saw what they expected to see: bad roads, horrific inns, and inert natives. "It would be incorrect to say that the roads were bad, for, to tell the truth, there were no roads at all," Casanova bravely recorded.[29] Spain was abnormal, foreign, dangerous, and dramatic. Spaniards themselves compared their country to the most exotic and irrational of locales: Pedro Antonio Sánchez, the Galician theologian who wrote a treatise on tanning, worried that "if time transmits only our errors and not our culture to our descendants, they most certainly will find us more barbarian than the Hottentots and the Canadians."[30]

[25] Bernardo Ward, *Proyecto económico en que se proponen varias providencias, dirigidas a promover los intereses de España con los medios y fondos necesarios para su plantificación* (Madrid, 1779), 105.

[26] Capmany, *Discurso político,* 17.

[27] Pedro Rodríguez de Campomanes, *Discurso sobre el fomento de la industria popular* (Madrid, 1774), 14.

[28] Joseph Townsend, *A Journey through Spain in the Years 1786 and 1787, with Particular Attention to the Agriculture, Manufactures, Commerce, Population, Taxes, and Revenue of That Country; and Remarks in Passing Through a Part of France,* 3 vols. (London, 1792), vol. 2, 241.

[29] *The Memoirs of Jacques Casanova,* 57.

[30] Pedro Antonio Sánchez, "Memoria anónima bajo el nombre de Don Antonio Filántropo, sobre el modo de fomentar entre los labradores de Galicia las fábricas de curtidos" (1782), in *Colección de los escritos del Dr. D. Pedro Antonio Sánchez* (Madrid: Imprenta de M. Minuesa, 1858), 52. The Hottentots were a frequent rhetorical recourse: Prime Minister Lord Salisbury of Great Britain in the late nineteenth century equated Irish unsuitability for autonomous representative institutions with that of the Hottentots; see Andrew Roberts, "Salisbury: The Empire Builder Who Never Was," *History Today* 49 (October 1999): 47. Rousseau also discussed them when describing humans in the original state of nature, in *Discourse on Inequality,* as did Diderot in his contributions to Raynal's ten-volume *Histoire philosophique et politique des établissemens et du commerce des Européens dans les deux Indes* (Geneva: J. L. Pellet, 1780).

Cándido María Trigueros, we saw earlier, noted that even Egyptians punished the idle rich.

Francesco Guicciardini, who came from Florence to the court of Ferdinand the Catholic in 1512, set the tone for subsequent ambassadors with his famous observations:

> Spaniards are considered subtle and astute, yet they distinguish themselves in no mechanical or liberal art. Nearly all the artisans at the king's court are French or from other nations. [Spaniards] do not work in commerce, considering it shameful, because they all have airs of being hidalgos. . . . Their artisans work when they must, and then they rest as long as their earnings last, and that is the reason why manual labor is so expensive.[31]

Guicciardini, who beheld no industry to speak of, was one of the first to comment that people who worked in Spain often were foreigners, taking it as a sign that Spaniards themselves were too lazy or too proud. A Welsh visitor one hundred years later, both more perceptive and probably more widely traveled, commented that the mutual contempt of Spaniards and Frenchmen could have originated in their mutual emigration, which he interpreted as a sign of economic opportunities in both places.[32] A century after that, an anonymous traveler published an account in Amsterdam depicting Spaniards as lazy, malicious, and violent, noting again that "they so scorn working that most artisans are foreigners." The only journey Spaniards could trouble themselves to make, he added, was to America.[33] Christopher Hervey in the eighteenth century wrote that he had met many Irish merchants in Spain and that "the true born Spaniard has generally too high a notion of himself to apply to commerce, and much less to the menial offices of life, which are mostly performed by the French and Italians."[34] The English naturalist Francis Willughby, a member of the Royal Society, reported that Spain was almost desolate because of

> 1. a bad Religion. 2. the tyrannical Inquisition. 3. The multitude of Whores. 4. The barenness of the soil. 5. The wretched Laziness of the people, very like the Welsh and Irish, walking slowly and always cumbred with a great cloke and long Sword. 6. The expulsion of the Jews and Moors. 7. Wars and Plantations.

---

[31] Cited in Antonio María Fabié, ed., *Viajes por España* (Madrid: Librería de los Bibliófilos, 1879), 199–201.

[32] The traveler was James Howell, who visited in the 1620s. See J. N. Hillgarth, *The Mirror of Spain, 1500–1700: The Formation of a Myth. History, Languages and Cultures of the Spanish and Portuguese Worlds* (Ann Arbor: University of Michigan Press, 2000), 80–81.

[33] José García Mercadal, ed., *Viajes por España*, 2d ed. (Madrid: Alianza, 1972), 226–248. The account was published in 1700. García Mercadel's compilation and translation of two thousand years' worth of travel commentaries has been reissued in six volumes by the Junta de Castilla y León (Salamanca, 1999).

[34] Cited in Mario Ford Bacigalupo, "An Ambiguous Image," 121.

"Laziness and sloth makes [Spaniards] poor," he went on to say, predictably remarking that the French performed most of the labor in Spain, so much so that if the king of France were to order all his subjects home, Spaniards would soon die of hunger.[35] So, Spaniards literally were lazy by nature, or they were lazy simply because it was easier. In either case, poverty was the entirely predictable result.

Willughby was not alone in thinking religion had a lot to do with it. The French sneered at Spain, but the Protestant Dutch and English hated the place. The Black Legend, that famous and enduring collection of myths and propaganda, was rooted in Spain's repression of the Dutch and the Indians in the name of a Catholic God.[36] It was about horror and fanaticism and cruelty, not laziness, but the two tales were not unrelated. Demonic Spaniards were able to perfect their indolence by having slaves and Indians perform their work for them, an injustice that spoke ill of their presumed piety (though the English and the Dutch also knew a bit about the slave trade). If the executors of Spain's imperial policies were unfathomably cruel, the architects of the policies in Madrid were said to be morally corrupt and incurably decadent. The three texts that established the basis for the Black Legend were bestsellers in the sixteenth century and subsequently: William of Orange's *Apologia* of 1581, an impassioned denunciation of Philip II's tyranny (and bigamy and infanticide) written after the king put a price on William's head; Antonio Pérez's *Relaciones*, published in London in 1594, in which the king's former secretary of state, who had fled the court after being accused of murder, repeated many of the Dutch leader's accusations and added some of his own; and Bartolomé de las Casas's *Brevísima relación de la destrucción de las Indias*, which ensured that Europeans would link tyranny on the Continent with the savagery committed against the Indians. The little book was written by the Dominican friar in 1543, published in Seville in 1552, and caused a sensation when it was translated into Dutch in 1578 and into English in 1583. The 1656 version in England, entitled *The Tears of the Indians: Being an Historical and True Account of the Cruel Massacres and Slaughters of Above Twenty Millions of Innocent People*, was translated by a nephew of the poet John Milton,

---

[35] Francis Willughby, *A Relation of a Voyage Made through a Great Part of Spain* (London, 1673), 493–497.

[36] The journalist Julián Juderías, a disciple of Marcelino Menéndez y Pelayo, coined the expression in 1914. For Juderías, perfect geography and climate had helped guide Spanish history, a project forged over centuries by a race of noble men whose spirit and goodness had been maligned by foreigners. The white legend he counterposed to the black was no more nuanced or scientific than its opposite, but unlike his sixteenth-century predecessors he understood that at least one terrible crime had been self-imposed: "The abominable, completely injust, and completely unscientific attitude—fruit of the indescribable ignorance of many wise men—that Europeans have and always have had toward us has had a deplorable and demoralizing influence on our spirit" (Julián Juderías, *La leyenda negra: Estudios acerca del concepto de España en el extranjero* [1914; repr., Salamanca: Junta de Castilla y León, 1997], 291).

John Phillips, who dedicated the publication to Cromwell.[37] It was reissued multiple times in England; as William Maltby has noted, it "had a way of reappearing during conflicts with Spain."[38]

America

Europe looked at Spain. Spain looked at the creoles and the Indians. The Americans looked back. Economically, discursively, and culturally, each of these three relationships resonated against the others. Arbitristas often complained that Spain had become the Indies of its Indies, a reference to the staggering expense of maintaining the empire. Quevedo, as usual, put it nicely: "Poor, we conquer distant riches; rich, the same riches conquer us."[39] One small such conquest can be seen in the fact that Spaniards who emigrated to America and returned with money (as many did) were, until the late years of the Franco regime, referred to as *indianos,* not necessarily a pejorative term. At least one description suggested that others might see the character of the Indians beneath the guise of their colonizers: in the nineteenth century, the English Protestant Hugh James Rose echoed the words of Las Casas, who, when he was not condemning his countrymen for their butchery, proclaimed the innocence and nobility of the Indians. Spaniards were simple children of Nature, similar to the Irish, Rose said, and he was sure that if they were given proper instruction they would grow up: "Were true religion offered to these people; were they taught something of the dignity of self-control, and the power of moral cul-

---

[37] Other translations were called "The Mirror of Spanish Tyranny" (Amsterdam, 1620), "The Tyrannies and Cruelties of the Spaniards" (Rouen, 1630), and "History of the West Indies, in Which the Goodness of That Country and Its Peoples and the Tyrannical Cruelties of the Spaniards Are Recognized" (Lyon, 1642). See ibid., 251.

[38] William S. Maltby, *The Black Legend in England: The Development of Anti-Spanish Sentiment, 1558–1660* (Durham, N.C.: Duke University Press, 1971), 13. It is worth noting that Spaniards never could (or perhaps never wanted to) compete with English invective. The late nineteenth-century reformer Joaquín Costa once remarked that as a Spaniard he detested the English, but as a man he revered them: quoted in H. Ramsden, *The 1898 Movement in Spain: Towards a Reinterpretation, With Special Reference to 'En Torno al Casticismo' and 'Idearium Español'* (Manchester University Press, 1974). Likewise, David Bell notes that while hateful anti-French literature from England always mentioned Catholicism, the French never mentioned Protestantism and generally distinguished the barbarian English from the good English (Bell, *Cult of the Nation,* 43–49). In one small but illustrative example, British prisoners of war in the early 1780s were brought to Seville from the Caribbean after the governor learned they were skilled in textile crafts. They were well treated and encouraged to remain as teachers, though they eventually went home in prisoner exchanges. See Valentina K. Tikoff, "Assisted Transitions: Children and Adolescents in the Orphanages of Seville at the End of the Old Regime, 1681–1831" (Ph.D. diss., Indiana University, 2000), 221–222.

[39] Quevedo, "España defendida." Shakespeare, too, had John of Gaunt say: "That England, that was wont to conquer others / Hath made a shameful conquest of itself" (*Richard II,* Act II, Scene 1).

ture in addition to education. . . . I believe that morality would have as firm a stronghold in Spain as in any other European country."[40] Las Casas could not have said it better.

The origin of the Black Legend in large part lay in America, and the evil and decadence that transpired there would be retold and retooled in Europe. The damage did not concern just Indians, however, but Spaniards themselves. Though Hume had believed that "the same set of manners will follow a nation and adhere to them over the whole globe," peninsular Spaniards were sure that Spanish manners had not, in fact, accompanied the emigrants.[41] Nature trumped society. There was something in the air, in the food, and above all in mother's milk that transformed robust Spaniards into lethargic creoles. The first generations of Spaniards to go to America all commented on the damp weather, the strange species, and the apparent inability of the land to nurture plants from home. The environment was both wild and weak. From the start, this did not bode well: the chronicler Gonzalo Fernández de Oviedo reported that Queen Isabel, on being told by Columbus that trees in Hispaniola had shallow roots because of the great rainfall, replied, "this land, where the trees are not firmly rooted, must produce men of little truthfulness and less constancy."[42] In the following two centuries, few accounts of the New World failed to include some sort of natural history. By the time of the Enlightenment, there were, to put it very simply, two schools of thought: America was the Garden of Eden; or it was a terrifying example of nature gone mad. Proponents of the former included creoles and many Jesuits who had lived in America before the 1767 expulsion and then moved to Italy; proponents of the latter included some of the era's best known natural scientists. Most infamously, there was Cornelius de Pauw, a Dutch cleric and naturalist at the court of Frederick II of Prussia, who in 1768–1769 published a three-volume tract indebted to Buffon declaring the New World to be a land of complete savagery.[43] His *Recherches philosophiques sur les Américains* affirmed that American natives were indolent, wicked, childlike idiots; it described Cuzco as "a heap of little huts"; and it returned to the very old matter of whether or not Indians were natural slaves. He saw Buffon's degeneracy bid and raised it, asserting that men in America were like women:

[40] Hugh James Rose, *Among the Spanish People*, 2 vols. (London: Richard Bentley and Son, 1877), vol. 1, 13. This travel account is remarkably sympathetic and wide-ranging.

[41] Hume, "Of National Characters."

[42] Gonzalo Fernández de Oviedo, *Historia general y natural de las Indias*, cited in Antonello Gerbi, *The Dispute of the New World: The History of a Polemic, 1750–1900* (1955), trans. Jeremy Moyle (University of Pittsburgh Press, 1973), 40.

[43] See Gerbi, *Dispute of the New World*, chaps. 3, 4, 6. Thomas Jefferson was familiar with Buffon, de Pauw, and the abbé Guillaume-Thomas Raynal's 1772 *Histoire philosophique*, a similar work, and his *Notes on the State of Virginia* was written expressly to refute the denigration of America therein.

vindictive, beardless, and even capable of producing milk. Transported to America, dogs ceased barking and camels lost their genitals.[44] De Pauw, not surprisingly, was a permanent point of reference for subsequent Spanish-American writers and patriots.

Laziness was an essential component of transatlantic descriptions. Indeed, laziness would appear to be an obligatory component of any colonizer's depiction of the colonized, a necessary justification for the colonizer's presence and authority, though ambitious creoles eventually would end up turning the tables by accusing Spaniards of the sin. The Laws of Burgos, the first Spanish code of Indian legislation, were promulgated in December 1512 and amended in July 1513 to compel the Indians to work nine months of the year.[45] The view that Indians were phlegmatic and prone to drunkenness also was reproduced in Juan de Solórzano's *Política indiana*, a seventeenth-century compendium of prior statutes and their justifications. In it, Solórzano cited a 1552 law from Guatemala: "[Indians] are said to be weak and lazy, and if they are not made to work for their own sustenance they will enjoy no order or progress, which would be in their detriment." Three years later, a similar law in Mexico stated that Indians had to be forced to work because they would remain idle if left to their own devices.[46] Much later, an eighteenth-century writer defended the *repartimiento*, the system by which Peruvian Indians were kept in effective perpetual servitude, by commenting, "if it were absolutely forbidden to supply the Indians with clothes, mules, and iron for farm tools, they would be ruined within ten years and would let themselves be eaten by lice, so lazy is their temperament and so prone are they to drunkenness."[47]

On the other side of the Pacific, meanwhile, a 1696 Spanish visitor to the Philippines said the natives were "so entirely addicted to [laziness] that if in walking they find a thorn run into their foot they will not stoop to put

[44] Cited in John D. Browning, "Cornelius de Pauw and Exiled Jesuits: The Development of Nationalism in Spanish America," *Eighteenth-Century Studies* 11 (Spring 1978): 293. Such fables led Feijóo to write an essay disputing them: "Fábulas de las batuecas y paises imaginarios," in vol. 4 of *Teatro crítico*, Biblioteca de Autores Españoles, vol. 142 (Madrid, 1961).

[45] A Catalan historian has made the point that "the central thread that runs throughout the empire's history is the capacity of its administrators to measure, fix, and mobilize the necessary quantum of labour at the exact social cost that would permit the continued functioning of the complex relations that composed colonial society" (Josep M. Fradera, "Spanish Colonial Historiography: Everyone in Their Place," *Social History* 29 [August 2004]: 372).

[46] Juan de Solórzano, *Política indiana*, 2 vols. (Madrid, 1647), vol. 1, 94–95. This is the first Spanish translation of the original work, *De indiarum iure*, released in six volumes between 1622 and 1639. (The translation generally is dated 1648; this copy, at the Newberry Library, is dated 1647.) Solórzano (1575–1655), who worked as a judge for nearly two decades in Peru and married a creole, was among those who rejected the notion that creoles had inherited Indians' vices.

[47] Concolorcorvo (pseud. Alonso Carrió de la Vandera), *El Lazarillo de ciegos caminantes desde Buenos Aires hasta Lima* (1773), cited in John Lynch, *The Spanish American Revolutions 1808–1826*, 2d ed. (New York: W. W. Norton, 1986), 8.

it out of the way that another may not tread on it." (The same visitor re-marked, though, that their lethargy had grown since the Spaniards' ar-rival.) A few years later, a Spanish friar, Gaspar de San Agustín, listed thirty negative traits of the Filipinos, among which: "Their laziness is such that if they open a door they never close it."[48] The modern Philippines' great na-tional hero, José Rizal, went so far as to write an essay on "The Indolence of the Filipinos" in which he pointed out that his countrymen, first, had been quite energetic before the Spaniards appeared and, second, that there was no point in a colonized people's exerting itself when it could hope to derive little or no benefit: on the contrary, "one who is not lazy must needs be a fool or at least an imbecile." He also pointed to the indo-lence of the Spaniards themselves:

> The pernicious influence of the rulers, surrounding themselves with servants and despising physical or manual labor as unworthy of the nobility and aris-tocratic pride of the heroes of so many centuries; those lordly manners that the Filipinos have translated into 'Tila ka Kastila' (you're like a Spaniard), the desire of the ruled to be the equal of the rulers, if not entirely, at least in man-ners—all these naturally produced aversion to activity and hatred or fear of work.[49]

Rizal's implicit observation that natives' laziness was a sign of recogni-tion of their own oppression had been made already in the 1730s by Jorge Juan and Antonio de Ulloa, naval officers and scientists dispatched by the Spanish crown to America to write a report on the colonies' infrastructure, commerce, and economy. Juan and Ulloa found it perfectly logical that the Indians were sluggish: "Just imagine that in Spain there were a regime un-der which the rich forced the poor to work for free—how anxious would they be to comply?" When Indians themselves stood to gain by working, the officials noted, they did so, but "as long as the benefit to them of work-ing or doing nothing is the same, it is no surprise that they are inclined more toward laziness than toward activity."[50] Innate national character, then, or the power of the weather, was set alongside other explanatory nar-ratives of behavior. Twin discourses of nature and politics worked with each other.

---

[48] Syed Hussein Alatas, *The Myth of the Lazy Native: A Study of the Image of the Malays, Filipinos, and Javanese from the 16th to the 20th Century and Its Function in the Ideology of Colonial Capitalism* (London: Frank Cass, 1977), 52–53.

[49] *Selected Essays and Letters of José Rizal*, ed. and trans. Encarnación Alzona (Manila: G. Rangel, 1964), 202–203. The previous quotation was from 207. The essay on indolence (here awkwardly translated) was published in installments in the summer of 1890. Rizal (1861–1896) was a physician, novelist, and scholar. He was executed by the Spaniards.

[50] Jorge Juan and Antonio de Ulloa, *Noticias secretas de América*, ed. David Barry (London, 1826), 285.

Spaniards were not alone in regarding colonized peoples as lazy.[51] Early English settlers were appalled by the spectacle of Indian women working themselves to the bone while their men apparently did nothing but hunt and fish, those occupations being deemed sport, not labor. (The English settlers themselves were described by their leaders and by contemporary writers as being as lazy as they said the Indians were.)[52] They also were sure the Indians' naturally indolent ways would change once they understood the advantages of efficient farming and industry. *New England's Prospect*, an early booster book, told prospective immigrants that the Indians were gentle, civil, and forthcoming, and, "being strangers to arts and sciences and unacquainted with the inventions that are common to a civilized people, are ravished with admiration at the first of any such sight."[53] But as the years went by, it became apparent to North American settlers that their own good, industrious example would not suffice. Franklin in 1753 admitted that "Little success . . . has hitherto attended every attempt to civilize our American Indians," though he seemed to think they were less unable than resistant. By the time *New England's Prospect* was reissued in Boston in 1764, the editor was forced to concede that "[the Indians'] immense sloth, their incapacity to consider abstract truth . . . and their perpetual wanderings, which prevent a steady worship, greatly impede the progress of Christianity."[54]

Despite such widespread attitudes among Europeans (or North Americans), the Spanish case was unique for two reasons. First, Indians from the start were codified as rational, free vassals of the king and therefore, at least in theory, were less dehumanized than colonial subjects elsewhere. They were inhabitants of the Republic of Indians, a parallel jurisdiction. Law after law after law instructed local officials to treat the Indians well, telling them the natives were free laborers, not slaves. "God created and made these Indians free," the Council of Indies reminded Philip II, though adding that by nature they were so lazy and so easily seduced by vice and drink that their former rulers would have them move mountains from one place to another just to keep them busy.[55] The benevolence was a fiction,

---

[51] One study, however, argues that the Dutch considered the Indians superior in all ways to the Spanish and saw in them a New World version of themselves. See Benjamin Schmidt, *Innocence Abroad: The Dutch Imagination and the New World, 1570–1670* (Cambridge University Press, 2001).

[52] Edmund S. Morgan, *American Slavery, American Freedom: The Ordeal of Colonial Virginia* (New York: W. W. Norton, 1975).

[53] William Wood, *New England's Prospect* (1634), ed. Alden T. Vaughan (Amherst: University of Massachusetts Press, 1977), 95.

[54] Introduction to ibid., 12. The Franklin quote is from Alden T. Vaughan, "From White Man to Redskin: Changing Anglo-American Perceptions of the American Indian," in his *Roots of American Racism: Essays on the Colonial Experience* (Oxford University Press, 1995), 26.

[55] *Consulta*, 15 August 1596, in Richard Konetzke, ed., *Colección de documentos para la historia de la formación social de Hispanoamérica, 1493–1810*, 5 vols. (Madrid: CSIC, 1953–1962), vol. 1, pt. 2, 44–45.

to be sure (made manifest by the laws' repetition), but it was a fiction that rang true. Learned Spanish Americans surmised that Indians were descended from Jews and/or Spaniards but had been transformed by the climate, or that they had been evangelized long before the arrival of the Spaniards but in the interim had been led astray. Similar theories were expounded in North America. Roger Williams was among those who detected Hebrew ancestors in his new neighbors' family tree; he also suggested they might have known Christianity in the past. North American Indians certainly were deemed capable of knowing Christ, in a Protestant manner, of course. As Karen Ordahl Kupperman points out, "no one in America could afford to trivialize the people who occupied the land."[56] The English needed the Indians too much to think they were savages. They also needed to lure immigrants from England, and therefore were obliged to present the Indians in a positive light, even if they did bear a disturbing likeness to the Irish. Like Spaniards, the English used the Indians to study themselves; they saw in them remnants of old Saxons or primitive Britons who could be civilized.

As the relationship between English colonists and Indians grew less complex and both more distant and more violent, the bodies of law in British America and Spanish America began to reflect the differing degrees of intermingling on the two continents. The laws of the Virginia colony and subsequent North American codes did not contemplate the Indians' integration; the natives were foreign "nations," admirable in some ways but generally repellent and hopelessly impervious to teaching. In contrast, pre-Hispanic systems of social stratification and honor basically survived the conquest, though in a simplified version. Indians in Spanish America whose ancestors had been in positions of religious or political authority were deserving of the same honors as descendants of Spanish nobility, the king instructed in 1697, not for the first time.[57] When the Mexico City potters guild excluded Indians, crown magistrates in 1681 declared such a practice to be "opposed to virtue," pointing out that half the city council members were descended from Indian *caciques*.[58] Indians in Cuba (and presumably elsewhere) were not to be referred to as people of *mala raza*.[59]

---

[56] Karen Ordahl Kupperman, *Indians and English: Facing Off in Early America* (Ithaca, N.Y.: Cornell University Press, 2000), 144; see also Karen Ordahl Kupperman, *Settling with the Indians: The Meeting of English and Indian Cultures in America, 1580–1640* (Totowa, N.J.: Rowman and Littlefield, 1980).

[57] *Real cédula*, 26 March 1697, in Konetzke, ed., *Colección de documentos para la historia*, vol. 3, pt. 1, 66.

[58] Manuel Carrera Stampa, *Los gremios mexicanos: La organización gremial en Nueva España, 1521–1861* (Mexico City: EDIAPSA, 1954), 227–228.

[59] Council of Indies, 25 March 1778, in Konetzke, ed., *Colección de documentos*, vol. 3, pt. 1, 437. Five years later, the Bourbon monarchy of Charles III declared that Gypsies were not a bad race either.

But if they were not of a bad race, perhaps they were of the same race, which complicated things. The English had no such problem.

Second, the Spanish case was unique because Spain itself was the subject of the colonizing discourse of sloth. Faulty national character was a concept very familiar, all too familiar, to Spaniards. It never was formally colonized by the rest of Europe, of course, but starting in the seventeenth century Spain saw a growing amount of its national wealth drift into the hands of the English, the French, and the Dutch who, as elsewhere, disparaged the natives as they appropriated their properties—though the romantic tint through which some Europeans viewed Spanish laziness was a luxury other colonized peoples rarely had. The old stereotypes and prejudices about lazy Spaniards thus were a perfect fit for a country ripe for economic subjugation. In the New World, meanwhile, the English disdain for the Spanish took on a new cast and a new cast of characters. One of the initial goals of English colonizers in America was precisely to save the Indians from tyrannous and papist Spaniards and somehow make the Indians more English, which meant both not-Indian and not-Spanish. Thus Spain's efforts to encourage work among the Amerindians (and complaints about the futility of such efforts) took place in a context in which Spain itself was being put to work (or not) by foreign capital.

The Spanish colonial discourse of laziness bore similarities to the domestic eighteenth-century economic writings we saw in part2. Ward's 1762 *Proyecto económico,* a series of enlightened recommendations on how best to encourage economic revival at home and abroad, had no trouble moving from Spanish ociosos to the Indians:

> [Indians] must be made into useful vassals. Even here in Europe, among the most cultured of Nations, the most useful men are those who are least enlightened [*los que tienen menos luces*], in other words, peasants, farmers, shepherds, and so on. It is not necessary that everyone in a monarchy have great talent; rather, the greatest number should work, and few should govern, and [the latter] need superior ability. But the masses [*muchedumbre*] need only bodily strength and docility to allow themselves to be ruled.[60]

Though others might regard Indians (whom he defined as anyone not *español puro*) as a nonentity (*una gran nulidad*), he disagreed, saying their nature was a great advantage in many ways precisely because they could potentially be made useful. Ward further suggested that Indians be allowed to wear clothes other than their traditional dress, which was mandatory. There was no doubt in his mind that Spanish clothes would add to their dignity and, more to the point, their utility.

---

[60] Ward, *Proyecto económico,* 259–260.

The idea would appear to have been taken directly from Campillo, author of a work probably plagiarized by Ward (though, given that *Proyecto económico* was published after Ward's death, it is hard to say who was responsible). Campillo's *Nuevo sistema económico para America,* written in 1743, emphasized the importance of increasing the flow of wealth from America to Spain and, as part of that project, of making the American workforce more productive by protecting it from corrupt colonial officials. Spanish dress, in addition to making Indians feel better about themselves and work harder, also would boost the textile trade, he pointed out, and would encourage Indians to speak Spanish. (Incessant orders from Madrid throughout the seventeenth and eighteenth centuries regarding language instruction point to the Indians' linguistic obstinance.) Those who engaged in vile trades, however, would have to retain their traditional clothes, an apparently punitive provision that possibly would not have passed muster in Spain thirty years later during the campaign to honor vile labor. If Indians' minds worked as Campillo predicted, they all would abandon the lower trades in order to wear Spanish clothes, leaving one to wonder just who would take over in their stead. Like later reformers, Campillo saw women as a particularly vexing problem. "The laziness and idleness of Indian women is notorious," he wrote, because (as everywhere else) *ocio* leads to vice, and women are those most easily seduced by vice. The fashion solution was particularly apt, then, as women's vanity (as everywhere else) would induce them to dress up and try to outdo one another: "Men's and women's strongest passion is to appear well before others. This is the State's richest mine, the origin of the desire of possession, and it is inseparable from industry," Campillo wrote.[61] In Guatemala at the turn of the century, the Patriotic Society also suggested that Indians be encouraged to wear European clothes and shoes (meaning the earlier plan still had not taken hold). "It's time we wake up," read a letter to the editor of the *Gazeta de Guatemala* in 1800:

> We must ensure that Indians and Ladinos are dressed, shod, eat, live, and imitate our customs. We must encourage this idea and make it real, offering our delicious fruits at a moderate price so their use is widespread. We are sure that

[61] José Campillo y Cosío, *Nuevo sistema económico para America* (1789 posth.), ed. Manuel Ballesteros Gaibois (Oviedo: Grupo Editorial Asturiano, 1993), chap. 9. The quotations are from 155 and 169. Jean Sarrailh (*La España Ilustrada de la segunda mitad del siglo XVIII* [Mexico City: Fondo de Cultura Económica, 1985], 18n) said Ward (or his publisher) also lifted sections of Campillo's *Lo que hay de más y de menos en España para que sea lo que debe ser y no lo que es* (1741) (ed. Antonio Elorza [Universidad de Madrid, 1969]), which does not seem as apparent. Elorza (15–16) believes Campillo was the author of the *Proyecto económico/ Nuevo sistema* text, but the care with which someone transformed one into the other, and the fact that both authors were dead by the time their respective books were published, makes certainty impossible. Campillo's *Nuevo sistema* version of the long Ward quotation directly above is on 131.

as soon as they enjoy these conveniences and are forced to work in order to obtain them and multiply them, we will see the disappearance of inaction, weakness, and *ociosidad*.[62]

Campomanes, we have seen, said he was determined to root out indolence and restore dignity to working people in Spain; I have argued that his language was taken from the neo-scholastic and moral philosophers of previous centuries and applied to a project of economic mobilization in which patriotic duty rhetorically supplanted devotion to the common good. Degradation of working people was an essential first part of the project of making them useful, followed by a campaign to mold them. They should be docile, well-dressed, punctual, and gramatically correct. So it was in America and the Philippines, whose wealth was essential for the survival of the monarchy.

A crucial aspect of the transatlantic discourse of laziness was the antipathy and distrust felt by peninsular elites toward their kinsmen on the other side, the creoles.[63] Already in the late sixteenth century, Spaniards were convinced that the strange physical conditions in America inevitably would corrode spirits and minds. How was it that emigrants became so defective? A fundamental part of the explanation was that as infants they fed at the breasts of Indian and black women. Milk transmitted character, a belief firmly in the camp of the nature lovers, as opposed to those who held with Hume's moral causes, and which was repeated throughout the colonial period: "He who suckles lying milk is a liar, drunken milk a drunkard, thieving milk a thief."[64] In Spain, blood transmitted stigma (though not always), which is not quite the same, though in one (possibly unusual) early Inquisition case from Teruel we find the belief that drinking a Jewish nurse's

---

[62] Cited in John D. Browning, "The Periodical Press: Voice of the Enlightenment in Spanish America," *Dieciocho* 3, no. 1 (1980): 13. Ladinos were mixed-bloods of Spanish and Indian descent. The word *ladino* also signifies the language spoken by Sephardic Jews.

[63] Travelers and officials began using the word *criollo* in the sixteenth century to denote those of Spanish blood who were born in America. Previously the term had applied to blacks born there. The multiple combinations among whites, Indians, Asians, and blacks inspired the famous Mexican *castas*, series of paintings illustrating as many as twenty-five different classifications of racial mixes and attesting to the enormous challenge of fixing identities in a world that would have none of it. "Creole" was one of those classifications and may not always have been applied only to racially "pure" Spaniards, although the two words often were used interchangeably. As an interesting aside, *morisco*, which in Spain referred to converted Muslims and their descendants, in the *castas* referred to the offspring of one Spanish parent and one mulatto (Spanish/black) parent. See Ilona Katzew, "Casta Painting: Identity and Social Stratification in Colonial Mexico," in *New World Orders: Casta Painting and Colonial Latin America, ed. Katzew et al.* (New York: Americas Society Art Gallery, 1996). For the art itself, see María Concepción García Sáiz, *Las castas mexicanas: Un género pictórico americano* (Milan: Olivetti, 1989).

[64] Reginaldo de Lizárraga, *Descripción breve de toda la tierra del Perú* . . . , cited in Bernard Lavallé, *Las promesas ambiguas. Criollismo colonial en los Andes* (Lima: Pontificia Universidad Católica del Perú, 1993), 48. Lizárraga (1545–1615) was a Dominican.

milk could transmit Jewish qualities to a baby.[65] Indians' refusal to accept Christianity was attributed in part to "a bad seed that has grown deep roots and has turned itself into blood and flesh . . . a vice that comes in the blood and is suckled as milk . . . [because] the customs of parents and ancestors are converted into nature and transmitted through inheritance to their children."[66] Turning the argument to the creoles' advantage, however, a Spanish American delegate to the Cortes of Cádiz claimed that milk also transmitted loyalty: "We Americans, as sons of Europeans, suckle from birth a love of the peninsula, and since childhood we call ourselves and regard ourselves as its children."[67]

Regardless of the intentions stated in emigration petitions, everyone agreed that once in America, Spaniards did not engage in low occupations. In 1629, Benito de Peñalosa, the Spanish author of one of the celebratory texts referred to earlier, complained that too many peasants were leaving for America, where they would abandon agricultural tasks; and he added that all mechanical occupations in America were performed by blacks, Indians, and mixed-bloods because emigrants refused to get their hands dirty.[68] At exactly the same time, but in an entirely different voice, Buenaventura de Salinas y Córdoba's *Memorial de las historias del Nuevo Mundo, Pirú,* a celebration of the New World, exclaimed of his fellow creoles: "The most marvelous thing is to see how early children acquire the use of reason and that they all have such spirit that not a single one of those born here is inclined to learn the mechanical arts and occupations that their parents brought from Spain because this Peruvian sky and climate elevates and ennobles them in spirit and thought."[69] "He who was but a laborer in Spain assumes the airs of a noble" in America, his fellow Peruvian chronicler Antonio de la Calancha wrote proudly.[70] Juan and Ulloa did not share the Peruvians' enthusiasm. They confirmed that those who had learned a trade in Spain soon ceased practicing it in America, leaving the lower, mechanical crafts for Indians and mestizos. They also were appalled by the

[65] John Edwards, "The Beginnings of a Scientific Theory of Race? Spain, 1450–1600," in *From Iberia to Diaspora: Studies in Sephardic History and Culture,* ed. Yedida K. Stillman and Norman A. Stillman (Leiden: E. J. Brill 1999), 186–187.

[66] Alonso de la Peña Montenegro, *Itinerario para párrocos de indios* (1668), cited in Jorge Cañizares-Esguerra, "New World, New Stars: Patriotic Astrology and the Invention of Indian and Creole Bodies in Colonial Spanish America, 1600–1650," *American Historical Review* 104 (February 1999): 67.

[67] Cited in Tamar Herzog, *Defining Nations: Immigrants and Citizens in Early Modern Spain and Spanish America* (New Haven: Yale University Press, 2002), 151.

[68] Peñalosa y Mondragón, *Libro de las cinco excelencias del español,* 170v.

[69] Cited in Lavallé, *Las promesas ambiguas,* 114. Salinas y Córdoba (1592–1653) was a Franciscan and the grandson of a conqueror.

[70] Cited in D. A. Brading, *The First America: The Spanish Monarchy, Creole Patriots, and the Liberal State 1492–1867* (Cambridge University Press, 1991), 330. Calancha, an Augustinian, was born in Peru. His 1639 chronicle was entitled *Chronica moralizada del Orden de S. Augustín* (Madrid: CSIC, 1972).

"tyrannical government" they found and minced few words on their return. As a result, their report remained unpublished until 1826. According to its English editor, a supporter of the independence cause (and, not
coincidentally, a merchant), Spain feared that release would "confirm the
tales that long ago had been published by the famed Bishop Las Casas, and
that foreigners would reproach the Spanish nation for having extermi-
nated the natives."[71] Juan and Ulloa pointed to two reasons for the deep-
seated hatred between *peninsulares* and creoles: the economic differences
between them, and the vanity of the latter. (The editor added an obvious
third reason, that creoles were denied offices.) According to the authors,
Spaniards generally arrived in America with little money but worked hard
and quickly acquired wealth. Right away, of course, we have a problem with
this characterization in that Spaniards are depicted as hard workers. In the
same vein, an English privateer at around the same time also contradicted
the prevailing view by noting that while

> in the British and French nations a pedlar is despised, and his employment
> looked upon as a mean shift to get a living, it is otherwise here, where the
> quick return of money is a sufficient excuse for the manner of getting it, and
> there are many gentlemen in Old Spain who, when their circumstances in life
> are declining, send their sons to the Indies to retrieve their fortune this way.[72]

Creoles, on the other hand, Juan and Ulloa said, referring to longtime residents in the New World, especially those who lived in the mountainous regions of New Granada, did absolutely nothing except envy the Spaniards
and exploit the Indians. At some point, of course, the newly arrived
Spaniards (now with money) would start doing as the Romans, at which
point the cycle presumably would repeat itself. If there was a gap between
longtime residents and *arrivistes,* there was a greater one between the latter and the descendants of the original conquerors, whose profound sense
of dispossession and nostalgia frequently was commented on by Spaniards.
Some of the privileges bestowed on the early conquerors by the crown
proved complicated. Creoles' theoretical inability to engage in certain
commerce had obvious drawbacks. Further, the requirement in 1552 that
governorships (*corregimientos*) in America be reserved for the first genera-

---

[71] Juan and Ulloa, *Noticias secretas de América,* viii.

[72] "Captain Betagh's Observations on the Country of Peru and Its Inhabitants, During his
Captivity," in *A General Collection of the Best and Most Interesting Voyages and Travels In All Parts
of the World,* ed. John Pinkerton, vol. 14 (London, 1813), 4. The captain's observations and
adventures are well worth the read. Harking back to our discussion in part 1 of law and custom, he noted that Spaniards' "effeminate disposition," phlegm, and stubborness were such
that "whatever settles amongst them into a custom obtains the force of an inviolable law, and
however absurd, however contrary to religion or virtue, however noxious to society, or fatal
to private peace, is not to be rooted out by art or force" (10–11).

tion and their heirs meant that laborers, tailors, and those who made or sold pots and pans were now occupying public office just because they had gotten there ahead of everyone else, which obviously violated officehold-ing rules.[73]

"The people of this land are different from before," a crown official wrote to the Council of Indies in 1567.[74] Another told the king, "You can not imagine the avarice, disorder, and laziness of Spaniards in [Mex-ico]."[75] America had changed them, and not for the better, despite what Salinas y Córdoba might think. The environment not only made them lazy; it made them untrustworthy and immoral. Echoing the luxury debates of Europe, critics opined that creoles' sartorial extravagance was an indica-tion of weakness and political corruption along with moral laxity.[76] Fran-ciscans would not allow secular clergy to work in Mexican Indian parishes, for example, because they mostly were creoles and therefore incompetent; the Jesuits did not want American-born instructors, who already in 1569 were called "inconstant and weak"; the Dominican Juan de la Puente in 1612 said, "The heavens of America induce inconstancy, lasciviousness and lies, vices characteristic of the Indians and which the constellations make characteristic of the Spaniards who are born and bred there."[77] In the words of a Spanish intendant in Peru,

> For appointments here, natives of the country are not suitable because they are extremely difficult to dissuade from the customary ways ingrained in them even in contravention of the laws; they lack that mode of thinking, at once pure, sincere and impartial, prevalent in Spain, and even Spaniards who live for some time in these parts come to acquire the same or worse customs. How can we possibly appoint to the office of subdelegate people who do not even know who their fathers are?[78]

A late sixteenth-century cosmographer wrote that Spaniards in America were "declining [*declinando*] to the disposition of the land." When creoles in the early seventeenth century demanded that their *encomiendas* (their control over Indian labor or rents) be made perpetual (largely as a means of survival, being that most were unwilling or unable to enter commerce, and mining and agricultural profits were siphoned off to Spain), one op-

---

[73] *Cédula*, 3 September 1552, in Konetzke, ed., *Colección de documentos*, vol. 1, 309.

[74] Cited in Lavallé, *Las promesas ambiguas*, 18.

[75] Oidor Juan de Salmerón to Charles V, quoted in Peggy K. Liss, *Mexico under Spain, 1521–1556* (University of Chicago Press, 1975), 107.

[76] Rebecca Earle, "Consumption and Excess in Spanish America (1700–1830)," working paper, Centre for Latin American Cultural Studies, University of Manchester, April 2003.

[77] J. I. Israel, *Race, Class and Politics in Colonial Mexico 1610–1670* (Oxford University Press, 1975), 88–94; Lavallé, *Las promesas ambiguas*, 198; cited in Brading, *First America*, 298.

[78] Quoted in John Lynch, *Bourbon Spain, 1700–1808* (Oxford: Basil Blackwell, 1989), 337.

ponent was the count of Miranda, a member of the Council of Indies, who advised his colleagues: "We must take into account that the population of the Indies are descendants of conquerors who, because they were born there and are the sons of Indians, have greatly declined [*declinado*] in value."[79] Such language, of course, comes straight out of the writings of the arbitristas, for whom there was no more pressing issue than the monarchy's decline. For them there was something natural, albeit no less disturbing, in the rise and fall of states, which could be attributed to acts of God and errors by men. The human body, the metaphor for the social body, also grew ill and declined as a matter of course. Possibly they thought there was something equally inevitable in the decline of those who had gone abroad.

From the time of discovery, mechanisms of control—whether governmental, religious, economic, or social—embodied increasingly precise notions of suitability for an activity, privilege, or station based on geography, blood (or milk), or race. It is difficult to disentangle the influences from the effects. Indeed, centuries of thinking of themselves in terms of the percentage of clean blood that coursed through their veins made Spaniards unlikely to try to disentangle them. There were few urban peninsular families without Jewish ancestors, and likewise there were few creole families with no Indian parentage. Adding to the mix, it was more difficult for creoles than for *peninsulares* to prove limpieza, so they more often bore the suspicion of not being Old Christians. At the best of times, it is difficult to prove one is not something; in Spain, people could use character witnesses to attest to their spotless past, but in America, where everyone was a newcomer, such friends were hard to find. People of mixed blood sometimes tried to pass themselves off as creoles, further complicating the racial burden, although the conflict was not, in principle, a racial one; both *peninsulares* and creoles could point to illustrious ancestors, and there was a tradition of regarding the offspring of Spaniards and mestizos as legal Spaniards. The terms of the dispute inevitably veered into questions of vice resulting from character, not just race, and character was inextricably bound up with geography. Again in principle, moving onto geographic terrain meant that virtues and vices were more widely available to everyone than if racial criteria were used.

Just as peninsular Spaniards defended themselves against Protestants and the French by pointing to their country's natural attributes, the creoles celebrated America's natural wonders, especially after Spaniards began wondering if exterior beauty did not in fact conceal something rotten, both in nature and in humans. Patriotism and *luces* combined to inspire a genre of homegrown natural histories of America. According to these writ-

[79] AGI Indiferente General leg. 1624, cited in Lavallé, *Las promesas ambiguas*, 56, 46.

ings, which began in earnest in the seventeenth century, the New World both resembled Europe and at the same time was much better. Lima and Mexico City were proclaimed to be the New Rome, the New Athens, the New Venice. The wild combination of colors and the lavish fashion and jewelry spoke of the region's grandeur, not its effeminate decadence. Calancha noted that creole children learned everything much more quickly than their European counterparts and were "so rapid in the use of reason that a twelve-year-old often reaches further than a man of forty in other kingdoms."[80] In 1618, the physician Diego Cisneros published a treatise on the climate and environment of Mexico City, applying the teachings of Hippocrates and Galen to demonstrate that Mexico and Castile actually were quite similar, right down to their diet.[81] Responding to the calumny from abroad that the warm Mexican climate could provoke lethargy, another Augustinian chronicler, Esteban García, pointed out that it also could inspire obedience.[82]

Of course, praising the environment made it difficult for the local elite to blame it for Indians' sluggishness, and attributing Indians' sluggishness to the humidity and the air suggested that Spaniards, too, could fall victim. Such contradictions have prompted Jorge Cañizares-Esguerra to propose that colonists at that point postulated "clear-cut racial distinctions and [constructed] separate bodies for Indians and Creoles (and, to a lesser degree, blacks)."[83] Indeed, he argues persuasively that the science of race was first articulated in colonial Spanish America in the seventeenth century, not in Europe in the eighteenth and nineteenth centuries, as is generally thought, precisely to address the problem of different responses to the same external influences.

Creoles found themselves in the contradictory and ultimately untenable position of vindicating both the indigenous empires and the Spanish empire that had conquered them. Americans sought defenses among the ruins, depicting themselves as the rightful heirs of Montezuma and Atahualpa. The Jesuit Francisco Javier Clavijero's *Storia antica del Messico* (1780), to cite one such example, described Mexico's past with so much patriotic fervor and indignation that the book was banned in Spanish. Nonetheless, Americans read it in Italian and embraced it. Of particular interest was Clavijero's praise for the Aztecs' economic accomplishments. His description of bygone (i.e., destroyed) trade networks, marketplaces,

[80] Cited in Brading, *First America*, 330.

[81] Israel, *Race, Class and Politics*, 91, citing Diego Cisneros, *Sitio, naturaleza, y propriedades de la ciudad de Mexico*.

[82] Israel, *Race, Class and Politics*, 91, citing *Crónica de la provincia Augustiniana del santísimo nombre de Jesús de Mexico*.

[83] Cañizares-Esguerra, "New World, New Stars," 37. See also Jorge Cañizares-Esguerra, *How to Write the History of the New World: Histories, Epistemologies, and Identities in the Eighteenth-Century Atlantic World* (Stanford University Press, 2001).

tribunals, and industrial ventures "told readers that at one time, before the coming of the Spaniards, that part of the world had been prosperous and self-sufficient, its trade dynamic and extensive, conducted honestly, according to a clearly defined set of laws." Speaking directly to de Pauw, Clavijero summed up: "This is how those peoples, of whose rationality certain Europeans have seen fit to doubt, governed themselves."[84] Even patriotic Argentines composed a new national anthem that proclaimed, "The Inca is roused in his tomb."[85]

Many creoles excluded from administrative posts were, of course, themselves caught up in the excitement of *las luces*. Though most blamed their region's alarming economic difficulties on Spaniards and the Bourbon monarchy and had nursed resentments and grievances against Spain for two centuries, they nonetheless followed the programmatic and discursive cues emanating from the peninsular Patriotic Societies. In Mexico, for example, a watchmaker in 1777 began publishing a short-lived monthly newsletter about his craft as part of an effort to contribute to "the instruction of our *patria*."[86] Members of the Patriotic Society in Guatemala City, where the economic situation was particularly dire, established a spinning school, complained that guild ordinances needed to be rewritten and enforced, and even became involved in a debate over the utility (or not) of classifying certain occupations as vile. Like their counterparts in Madrid, they were dedicated to improving the personal habits and hygiene of manual workers. Members also conducted surveys similar to those in Spain, discovering that in a population of one million there were hundreds of thousands of ociosos.[87] A representative from Buenos Aires in 1800 told Madrid authorities that he and his colleagues wanted "to banish idleness and beggary" by preparing boys for the crafts and girls for spinning tasks.[88] The Bogotá newspaper editor Jorge Tadeo Lozano, who later was executed by the Spaniards, wrote in 1801 that New Granada needed a

> patriotic body which would be dedicated to the reform of customs by means of good education and to introduce a good appreciation of industry and

[84] Browning,"Cornelius de Pauw and Exiled Jesuits," 304–305.

[85] Cited in Rebecca Earle, "Creole Patriotism and the Myth of the 'Loyal Indian,'" *Past and Present*, no. 172 (August 2001): 130.

[86] Browning, "Periodical Press," 8. The publication lasted for six issues.

[87] Robert Jones Shafer, *The Economic Societies in the Spanish World (1763–1821)* (Syracuse University Press, 1958), 206, 285, 339. The 1795 petition to the *fiscal* requesting that an economic society be founded in Guatemala is a remarkably compassionate piece of social analysis. See Hector Humberto Samayoa Guevara, *Los gremios de artesanos en la Ciudad de Guatemala (1524–1821)* (Guatemala: Editorial Universitaria, 1962), 224–226. "With *luces* we will be able to teach the ignorant (which, without insulting anyone, includes just about everyone)," the petition began by saying.

[88] Shafer, *Economic Societies,* 240.

arts. . . . The country in which the arts do not flourish is not capable of being less than crowded with beggars and corrupt people. . . . More contemptible is the noble who passes his days in shameful idleness than the artisan who professes however humble a craft.[89]

The motto of the Patriotic Society in Santiago de Cuba was simply "Rise and Work."[90]

As in Spain, work and patriotism were equated, but the consequences of such a pairing clearly were different. American Patriotic Societies, whose members lived in perpetual fear of social and racial protest, battled ocio by idle creoles, the lower classes, and lazy natives. Furthermore, they themselves were subject to slurs from the motherland, which they were only too happy to return. Though I am cautious about using literary sources, especially as their use has created so much of the historiographic problem regarding social exclusion, I nonetheless would like to point to one example from the eve of Mexico's War of Independence from Spain. The author of what is generally described as the first and last novel of colonial Mexico, ridiculing the preoccupations of social climbers there, presents the young picaresque protagonist deciding what to make of his life. His father figured it was better for the boy to be a bad artisan than a good vagabond, those apparently being the available options, and he made his decision known to the boy's mother, who was horrified. "My son, an artisan?" she asked. "May God prevent that! What would people say if the son of don Manuel Sarniento was apprenticed to a tailor, a painter, or a silversmith?" Well, her husband replied, they'd say don Manuel is a decent but poor man who wanted to teach his son a useful trade "without burdening the republic with yet another ocioso." When young Pedro's mother insisted that the boy hailed from noble stock, her husband replied that he still had to eat. The mother won, and her son was rewarded with a useless university education from whence he embarked on a series of failed ventures. It was an old story, here adapted to colonial circumstances.[91]

American patriotism, of course, almost by definition had a subversive ring to it. Colonial *ilustrados* had a choice as to which *patria* they would sacrifice themselves for by working hard, and one of them had an obviously more promising future than the other. Royal authorities may not have grasped the gulf, however. Witness the official description of a Mexico City fiesta organized in 1784 to hail the arrival of the same royal baby twins

[89] Ibid., 236–237.
[90] Ibid., 283.
[91] José Joaquín Fernández de Lizardi, *El Periquillo Sarniento* (1816) (Mexico: Editorial Stylo, 1942), vol. 1, 62. Lizardi (1776–1827), in addition to being a novelist, was a journalist and a political activist in the years leading to independence.

whose birth was the occasion for the dramatic production of *Los Menestrales* described in part 2:

> The first [float] was preceded by drums, trumpets, pages, heralds, and eight couples of both sexes, six of artisans, one of farmers, and one of field hands, each holding the tools of their profession. They were followed by the orchestra and immediately thereafter by another float, pulled like the rest by six horses, on which the Statue of Atlantis, with several mottos, held the sky. Our August Monarch Charles III, with his heroic virtues and happy government, held the Spanish Monarchy. Spaniards love and venerate their glorious Monarch, the Princes, and the Royal Family, so worthy of the love bestowed on them by the Nation. . . . The last float . . . was preceded by eight couples on horseback armed with lance and shield. Then two pages, and nine couples symbolizing the Provinces of Spain, whose costumes they wore.[92]

This vision of the Spanish nation, assuredly a reproduction of those that appeared in performances throughout the monarchy, was led off by inhabitants of Mexico dressed up as Spanish workers and peasants who somehow symbolized the unitary nature of the monarchy and at the same time the regional diversity of the Iberian Peninsula. Perhaps work in the interest of progress and a better future (embodied in the newborn twins) could transcend distance and boundaries and race and geography. Perhaps the new economic language could supplant the old racial and meteorological language. Perhaps the Bourbon monarchy could continue to extract the American wealth it so badly needed, but now from a willing, multicultural workforce.

Disaster

The last Cuban revolt for independence began in 1895. The following year, news that a second colonial war had erupted in the Philippines prompted protests in Spain by urban workers, peasants, and hungry, unemployed men and women. "As they witness the departure of the troops, they weep and groan and pray," the *New York Times* reported.[93] Though Spanish newspapers at first ran patriotic images of bullfighters plunging their swords into the bellies of pigs draped in American flags, money

[92] Claudio Lomnitz, "Nationalism as a Practical System: Benedict Anderson's Theory of Nationalism from the Vantage Point of Spanish America," in *The Other Mirror: Grand Theory through the Lens of Latin America*, ed. Miguel Angel Centeno and Fernando López-Alves (Princeton University Press, 2001), 345–346. Lomnitz cites *La Gazeta de Mexico*.

[93] Louis A. Pérez Jr., *Cuba between Empires, 1878–1902* (University of Pittsburgh Press, 1983), 83.

spilling out of their rent guts, the real battle did not prove so easy.[94] Soldiers mutinied or deserted, thousands more fled to France, and officers refused to carry out orders. The government of Sagasta (his predecessor, Cánovas, had been assassinated by an anarchist) coexisted unhappily with a regency awaiting Alfonso XIII's majority. Republican sentiment and rejection of the Restoration monarchy grew as the Cuban and Filipino insurgents advanced.

On 4 April 1898, two weeks before the United States declared war on Spain, the *New York Times* published an article on "The Spanish Character." The imminent enemy was "situated between two continents, the most advanced and most backward, the most illumed and the darkest—Europe and Africa. The institutions of Spain naturally enough respond to the influences of each. . . . There are, then, in the Spanish national character, dwelling side by side, and most of the time blended into one, these two forces—civilization and barbarism."[95] Exactly one month later, the British prime minister, Lord Salisbury, instructed a gathering of Tories on the Darwinian nature of the new imperialism: "You may roughly divide the nations of the world as the living and the dying . . . the weak states are becoming weaker and the strong states are becoming stronger. . . . [The] living nations will gradually encroach on the territory of the dying, and the seeds and causes of conflict among civilized nations will speedily appear."[96] After the last shots had been fired, *El Liberal,* which billed itself as the largest-circulation daily newspaper in Spain, made it clear that it counted Spain among the dying: "After four hundred years we return from the West Indies, which we discovered, and from the Far East, which we civilized, as evicted tenants, expelled intruders, incapacitated prodigals, disorderly elements who must be confined."[97]

We discovered; we were evicted. This was most decidedly the reaction of self-appointed spokesmen for a nation who explicitly linked what they described as a national catastrophe to a much older (even eternal) phenomenon, a national character. In this character, many found the explanations for Spain's defeat; in that same character, they sought hope for regeneration. Just as Spanish Americans at the start of the nineteenth

[94] José Alvarez Junco, "La nación en duda," in *Más se perdió en Cuba: España, 1898 y la crisis de fin de siglo,* ed. Juan Pan-Montojo et al. (Madrid: Alianza Editorial, 1998), 405. The pigs sometimes bore stereotypically Jewish features.

[95] Cited in Richard Kagan, "U.S. Historical Scholarship on Spain," in his *Spain in America,* 25. Kagan credits a graduate student with having found this quote.

[96] Lord Salisbury, speech of 4 May 1898 to the Tory Primrose League. In an interesting inversion of this logic, the U.S. political scientist and social Darwinist William Graham Sumner argued at the time that U.S. expansion in Cuba was simply a wrongheaded adoption of Spain's corrupt imperial ways. The United States' future lay in industrialism, he argued, not militarism (*War and Other Essays* [New Haven: Yale University Press, 1911], 297–334). I am grateful to Jeff Sklansky for this reference.

[97] 28 November 1898, cited in Ramsden, *The 1898 Movement in Spain,* 106.

century attempted to create a national identity (or identities), a project akin to those they had observed in the United States and revolutionary France and which was deeply influenced by the example and counter-example of Spain, Spaniards themselves by the end of the century were trying to uncover the identity they had lost and determine where they had gone wrong. The authentic Spain had disappeared amid vices either imported from abroad or self-imposed, the result of delusions of imperial grandeur and mistaken notions of honor. There was little disagreement, after centuries of self-examination, on what their traits were: bravery, austerity, stoicism, pride, sobriety, honor, spirit, individualism. The problem was deciding the extent to which these were virtues or defects and the degree to which they hindered or encouraged collective action in favor of the common good. The loss of all Spain's colonies (except minor outposts in Africa, more trouble than they were worth) lent a new, explicitly national tinge to the old introspective anguish. As before, the three-way correspondence of Europe's vision of Spain, Spain's vision of its colonies, and the colonies' vision of the mother country worked together to mold and fix the image of Spain that not only would survive but would be presented as always having been there.

In the dark and depressed minds of many of its intellectuals, nothing could redeem Spain. "Spain is an absurd and metaphysically impossible nation, and absurdity is her sinew and her principal sustenance," the diplomat and essayist Angel Ganivet (1865–1898) wrote to the philosopher Unamuno (1864–1936) at the turn of the century.[98] There were precedents for such thoughts, of course; and when the anniversary of 1898 was commemorated in 1998, few commentators missed the opportunity to point to the echoes from the early seventeenth century. Even some of the tropes were the same. In one of the most celebrated *arbitrios,* or tracts lamenting Spain's lost fortunes, Martín González de Cellorigo complained that "it would appear that they want to reduce these kingdoms to a republic of enchanted men living outside the natural order."[99] In 1621, a *memorial* to Philip IV outlined the causes of depopulation thus:

What has most estranged our people from the legitimate occupations so important to a Republic is the honor and authority placed on avoiding work and the little esteem paid to those who attend to agriculture, cattle, shopkeeping, business, and any sort of manufacturing, defying all good sense, even ex-

---

[98] Angel Ganivet, *Idearium español. El porvenir de España* (Madrid: Espasa-Calpe, 1999), 204–205.

[99] Martín González de Cellorigo, "Memorial de la política necesaria y útil restauración a la república de España," (Valladolid, 1600), cited in Pierre Vilar, *Crecimiento y desarrollo* (Barcelona: Ariel, 1980), 341. Vilar's famous 1956 essay appeared in English as "The Age of Don Quixote"; it was republished in Peter Earle, ed., *Essays in European Economic History 1500–1800* (Oxford: Clarendon Press, 1974), 100–112.

cluding vendors, merchants, and journeymen from honors and offices, such that it would appear they want to reduce these kingdoms to a Republic of enchanted men, lost souls, and idlers.[100]

In the mid-nineteenth century, the poet and social critic Mariano José de Larra wrote optimistically that Spain "was beginning to awake from a dream."[101] In 1890 (eight years before the Cuban disaster), the Spanish engineer Lucas Mallada outlined Spaniards' four principal defects: laziness, ignorance, a lack of patriotism, and fantasy. Regarding the fourth, he wrote: "The land of Don Quixote is a land of dreamers. With all that dreaming, we sleep a great deal; and though we do not drug ourselves with opium as the Chinese do, we see visions and perpetual illusions without stirring from our slumber." Later he referred to "this cursed fantasy" (*maldita fantasía*).[102] In 1900, Joaquín Costa, reflecting his generation's deep cultural ambivalence, turned the Quixote legacy to his own purpose by declaring (in a new commonplace) that a new Spanish *raza* was needed

> as a counterweight to the Saxon race, to maintain the moral equilibrium in the infinite game of history. . . . To confront the Saxon Sancho there must always be the pure, luminous Spanish Quixote, filling the world with his madness, affirming through the centuries the Utopia of the Golden Age and maintaining perennially here below this spiritual chivalry committed to belief in something and prepared to sacrifice for something; a Quixote who through passion and faith and sacrifice makes the earth become something more than a factory and a market where things are bought and sold.[103]

In a similarly ambivalent vein, Unamuno wrote that if Spaniards were to relinquish their sobriety and become more like the rest of Europe, "we would [renounce] the possibility of a new Quixote."[104] For Unamuno, Quixote was the essence of Spain, the triumph of will and goodness, the

[100] Anonymous *memorial* to Felipe IV, 1621 (?), AHN Consejos Libro 1427, ff. 12–35, published in Angel González Palencia, ed., *La Junta de Reformación, 1618–1625*, vol. 5 of *Colección de documentos inéditos para la historia de España y de sus Indias* (Valladolid: Archivo Histórico Español, 1932), 235. The writer may have been Cellorigo again, though he died in 1620, or someone else who used his language.

[101] Mariano José de Larra, "Revista del año 1834," cited in Gies, "Dos preguntas regeneracionistas," 320.

[102] Lucas Mallada, *Los males de la patria* (1900) (Madrid: Alianza Editorial, 1969), 40, 129.

[103] Cited in Fredrick B. Pike, *Hispanismo 1989–1936: Spanish Conservatives and Liberals and Their Relations with Spanish America* (South Bend, Ind.: University of Notre Dame Press, 1971), 57–58. Costa (1846–1911) was a progressive journalist, an educator, and an important advocate of agrarian reform. He was also, according to one of his later editors, "the new Moses of a Spain in exodus." See Joaquín Costa, *Historia, política social, patria,* ed. José García Mercadal (Madrid: Aguilar, 1961), 27.

[104] Miguel de Unamuno, "Sobre la europeización," cited in Pike, *Hispanismo 1989–1936*, 129–130.

refusal to accept the inevitability of death; Quixote's niece Antonia, who persuaded him to lay down his arms and come home, signified the utter vanquishment of glory at the hands of common sense.[105] Spain's greatest nineteenth-century novelist, Benito Pérez Galdós, wrote that after the loss of the colonies, Quixote was all Spain had left to be proud of.[106]

Like their arbitrista, Enlightenment, and liberal predecessors, members of the so-called Generation of '98 saw empire as the problem. It had brought wealth that led to poverty, dreams that spawned disaster, opportunities that foundered in perversion. In the aftermath of Cuba, the journalist and lawyer Luis Morote, in *La moral de la derrota*, observed that there was a patriotism of empire and a patriotism of labor, two very different things. "We were the masters of Italians, of the Dutch, of the English, and of the French in commerce, in industry, and in naval science. Today," he wrote, with a passing nod at the Boer War, "we look like disciples of an African Empire."[107] The Hapsburg monarchy—said to have ruled during a time of vice, fanaticism, and decadence—was faulted for steering Spain away from its true self. "There is nothing more frightful, more abominable than that great Spanish empire, a shroud that extended over the planet," proclaimed the Republican orator Emilio Castelar in 1868, the year of the Republican revolution, a point of reference for subsequent liberal thinkers.[108] "With locks, keys, and padlocks, we must close all the passages through which the Spanish spirit has escaped and extended itself out over the four points of the globe," Ganivet insisted.[109] If imperialist Spain had erred by going astray, then the solution was to look inward. In the seventeenth century, the bywords were *restauración, declinación,* and *conservación.* At the turn of the twentieth century, it was *regeneración.* The aim was similar: to go back to the beginning and regain one's bearings to find the essence of Spain. Rebirth, resuscitation, even resurrection was required. The moral qualities that had made Spain so admirable had softened and become a parody of themselves. Instead of laboring and competing, Quixote's children just dreamed.

Though 1898 was the impetus for much of the pessimistic and soul-searching literature of the turn of the century, many critics believed poli-

[105] See Unamuno's *Vida de Don Quixote y Sancho* (1905); also Eric Storm, *La perspectiva del progreso: Pensamiento político en la España del cambio de siglo (1890–1914)* (Madrid: Biblioteca Nueva, 2001), 291–306.

[106] For a very interesting study of the discourse of national character, patriotism, effeminacy, and indolence in nineteenth-century Italy, see Silvana Patriarca, "Indolence and Regeneration: Tropes and Tensions of Risorgimiento Patriotism," *American Historical Review* 110 (April 2005): 380–408.

[107] Luis Morote, *La moral de la derrota* (1900) (Madrid: Biblioteca Nueva, 1997), 153. Morote (1862–1913), a Republican, had reported on the Cuban war.

[108] Cited in Boyd, *Historia Patria*, 123.

[109] Cited in Inman Fox's introduction to Ganivet, *Idearium español*, 20.

tics had been rotten for a long time, certainly since the monarchy returned after the failed Republican experiment in the 1860s. In 1895, Unamuno wrote:

> Spanish society is going through a deep crisis. . . . There are no live internal currents in our intellectual and moral life. This is a reservoir of stagnant water, not a rushing stream. Ever so often a pebble disturbs the water's surface, and at most the slime at the bottom gets stirred up and muddies the depths. Beneath a soporific atmosphere there extends a spiritual plain so arid it is frightening. There is no fresh air, no spontaneity, no youth.

"The same dogs, with the same collars," he added memorably.[110] It was not just the military defeat, in short, that brought about the despair. Incipient industrialization, enormous economic disparities, working-class radicalism, and years of political instability and frustration all impelled a new class of intellectuals to ask themselves what would happen with their country and, more important, what should have happened. Their vision of the future was, as always in Spain, strictly conditioned by their vision of the past.

The dates of the movement of 1898 and its membership are matters for debate among historians of the era. In addition to academics and political reformers, the very diffuse group more famously included a group of brilliant writers including the modernist novelist and playwright Ramón Valle-Inclán, the dramatist Jacinto Benavente, the novelist Pío Baroja, the journalist José Martínez Ruiz (known as Azorín), and the poet Antonio Machado. Two of the outstanding members of the first wave of late-nineteenth-century reformers were Costa, best known for his ideas on agrarian reform, and the pedagogue Francisco Giner de los Ríos, founder of the famed Institución Libre de Enseñanza. Many of the regenerationists were influenced by the work of the German philosopher Karl Krause, who appealed equally to Spaniards steeped in mysticism and to those who were enthusiastic positivists. In general, Krause's followers shared a conviction that Spain must modernize and that new rational and moral citizens needed to be formed. The project was not to impose an ideal or to mold Spaniards; rather, it was to transform the nation by enabling individuals to transform (or regenerate) themselves. Ultimately, therefore, because it was predicated on individual choices, "regeneration" could mean just about anything. In the twentieth century, some adherents ended up as socialists; others became fascists or retreated to the comfort of their books. Though they all agreed there was something special about Spain that

---

[110] Miguel de Unamuno, *En torno al casticismo* (Madrid: Espasa-Calpe, 1972), 127, 132, 133. The words of the sixteenth-century preacher Diego de Estella, cited in chapter 1, are worth recalling: "Running water breeds delicious fish, but stagnant and idle water breeds only toads and snakes."

needed to survive yet had to be changed, they differed on the solution. But the two options were familiar: either what Costa called Europeanization, or the path taken a century earlier by Forner, for whom there was little to be gained by crossing the Pyrenees.

In some ways, of course, the 1898 project of reform and self-analysis recalls the Enlightenment-era Economic Societies. But there were sharp differences. The pessimism, essentialism, and obsessive concern for the meaning and identity of Spain in the late nineteenth century bore little resemblance to the Enlightened near-cult of rationalism and empiricism. Bad government and bad science, not bad character, bore the blame for Spain's problems in the earlier era. In another contrast, the regenerationists were outsiders and had little or no power to put ideas into practice. Unlike Campomanes and his cohort, who mostly were employed by the Bourbon courts, they had only scorn for those in power. The Restoration governments, in their opinion, had destroyed Spain. In that respect, they were more like the arbitristas, who from afar insisted that the monarchy's councilors were betraying the true interests of the king and his vassals. In any case, the regenerationists were isolated not only from the highest circles of power but also from society at large, and the movement can safely said to have expired a decade after it appeared.

The most brilliant intellectual figure of the period was Unamuno, a professor of Greek at the University of Salamanca. Unusually for the era, he read both English and German (in addition to the usual French) and thus was able to introduce new works to Spanish readers. Though he went through various philosophical and political phases (he abandoned positivism early on, had sympathies for the new Spanish Socialist Party, became increasingly mystical, and very briefly in 1936 expressed support for Franco before dying, profoundly disappointed), his vision of Spain remained fairly constant: Castilian, tragic, idealistic, and Catholic. In 1895, he wrote five essays (published in 1902 as *En torno al casticismo*) in which he set out his notion of national character.[111] Delving deep into the eternal Castilian popular soul, he advocated what he called intrahistory, sort of the *longue durée* or thick description of national character. Landscape and climate were a crucial influence; the intense heat and cold of Castile, rather than canceling each other out in an Aristotelian balance, made inhabitants both enormously energetic and enormously passive, and the arid, austere expanse of the meseta forged individualists. Castilians could do nothing to change this. This was their history, their destiny, their historical consciousness, their *volksgeist*.

In 1897, Unamuno underwent an intense personal crisis of faith and

[111] The word *castizo* can mean pure, traditional, or authentic; however, in America it was used to denote the offspring of one Spanish parent and one mestizo parent.

thereafter increasingly doubted the possibility of utopia or even of progress. He became more introspective, believing that everything, certainly politics, was subjective: "Say inward! instead of onward!" he counseled.[112] The following year he engaged in a public correspondence with Ganivet, also a classics scholar by training but a diplomat by profession, that was published as *El porvenir de España*. Ganivet in 1896 had published *Idearium español*, originally written for a restricted audience of his friends. In the words of a contemporary, *Idearium* was about "national psychology."[113] It was a collection of observations, many based on false nostalgia, faulty history, and bad theology, about what was right and wrong with Spain, and it struck a chord with Unamuno. Ganivet, who was clinically depressed (he ended up commiting suicide), was certainly Unamuno's intellectual inferior, but the two former university friends both believed Spain's history could be explained through its character, most firmly lodged in the common people of Castile. For both, Spain as nation was an end in itself. People must live as who they are. The two men parted ways, however, in their solution: Unamuno looked abroad (though he later changed his mind on this); Ganivet wanted to lock the gate.[114]

Neither was enthusiastic about material progress when placed alongside spiritual progress, and though both admitted that Spaniards' work ethic was not that of other nations—"our scorn for manual labor grows day by day," Ganivet wrote—they were not overly concerned.[115] After visiting the World's Fair in Antwerp in 1894, Ganivet described the English Pavilion, where a weaver was so utterly absorbed by his labor that he appeared to be part of his own loom. That was how England grew to rule the world, Ganivet admitted, but the prospect held out little appeal.[116] Unamuno in *En torno al casticismo* recited all the common wisdom: nothing ruins a man as quickly as a mechanical occupation, the Golden Age was populated by beggars who enjoyed the sun's rays and then a free lunch at the local convent, and hidalgos would rather die than work (for which he cited Huarte de San Juan's 1575 *Examen de ingenios*). Even the puzzled Indians in Peru asked Spaniards why they didn't reap and sow, Unamuno reported. The traditional soul, the *alma castiza*, was "warlike and indolent."[117] In his diary, Unamuno asked:

[112] Cited in Storm, *La perspectiva del progreso*, 201.

[113] Rafael Altamira, *Psicología del pueblo español* (Madrid: Biblioteca Moderna de Ciencias Sociales, 1902), 75.

[114] Not coincidentally, *Idearium* was a favorite of the extreme right wing during the twentieth century.

[115] Ganivet, *Idearium español*, 82.

[116] See Storm, *La perspectiva del progreso*, 159.

[117] Unamuno, *En torno al casticismo*, 78–82.

Work? What for? Work in order to work more? Produce in order to consume and consume in order to produce, like a donkey in a vicious circle? That is the essence of the social question. If the human race is merely a series of men with no permanent common substance, if there is no communion between the living and the dead, and the dead live only in the memory of the living, then what is progress for?[118]

Mallada was a lesser member of the group, but his 1890 book beautifully distilled the contemporary issues. Its title—*Los males de la patria*—left no room for doubt. Itemizing Spain's four principal defects, which were all related (indolence led to immorality, fantasy led to ignorance, etc.), he remarked that his compatriots' laziness (*pereza*) was "as deep as the sea."[119] However, though they apathetically would nod their heads when told how lazy they were, he wrote, they indignantly would jump to attention if their patriotism were placed in doubt. Mallada found this especially reprehensible, as would Morote a decade later when he distinguished patriotism of empire from patriotism of labor. An apathetic patriot is not a "true" patriot, Mallada wrote.[120] Fantasy, though, was the worst of the four defects, the principal cause of Spain's industrial backwardness. "It is a general rule of every era that among peoples where imagination exceeds intelligence, arts, industry and commerce will flourish to a lesser degree than among peoples with a more reflective spirit and calmer attitude," he wrote.[121] The Anglo-Saxon and Latin races were the prime examples of this general rule, he added, using the opposition so favored by his contemporaries even though the trope of the fantastic Spaniard corresponded poorly with the age-old one of Castilian sobriety.

The importance of the Generation of 1898 for me lies less in what its participants said than in the role they played in subsequent historiography and in the creation of a peculiarly Spanish metanarrative. Though the words "grief," "tragedy," and "disaster" abound in twentieth-century accounts, it is inexplicable that the trauma of losing Cuba and the Philippines has loomed larger for historians than the previous loss of practically all of America. The very existence of an 1898 "movement" has come to be assumed, though there was little that bound them together and most of their works quickly vanished from bookshelves. Their essays are taken as a meaningful reflection of how Spaniards thought about themselves, their countrymen, and their history at a moment of national and imperial cri-

---

[118] Cited in Storm, *La perspectiva del progreso,* 197.

[119] Mallada, *Los males de la patria,* 42. The practice of listing a nation's virtues and defects, as we saw earlier, was frequent in the late Middle Ages and early modern period.

[120] Ibid., 45–46. Giner de los Ríos also spoke of "false patriotism."

[121] Ibid., 126.

sis. In fact, they may not have been particularly representative. Their diagnoses often contained implicit or explicit judgments about Spain's past in general (there were frequent comparisons between 1898 and that other great disaster, the French invasion of 1808) and about Spaniards' industriousness in particular as a partial explanation for their nation's eternal predicament. As far as I can tell, however, none was particularly interested in the actual mechanics of labor and society. So in this study, they are significant only insofar as they participate in our representation of the character forces and prejudices allegedly imprinted on social organization and failure in early modern Castile. They assumed work was of little interest to their ancestors; for some that was good, for others that was bad, but in any case it was regarded as an intrinsic component of national character, one that arose as a result of Spain's peculiar conquest (and Reconquest) history.

CHAPTER SIX

The Narrative

Spaniards, it seems, have always borne an especially heavy burden of explaining their past. They point accusing fingers at their ancestors and blame them for the invasion by the Moors, the expulsion of the Jews, the disasters on the battlefields, the loss of so much treasure, the folly of ignoring their true destiny, the reluctance to get their hands dirty. "The compulsion to redress the deficiencies of history's actors is . . . a feature of Spain's emergence as a nation-state," according to one writer. Chroniclers during the reign of the Catholic Monarchs provided "an artistic, judicial, and philosophical framework that was not only propitious to the interests of the crown but mindful of more transcendent and exacting criteria of the sort that might guide the nation in the future."[1] History was an instructional tool. It would help remedy errors and ensure a more noble, more prosperous, more rational future. It would enable Spaniards to seize that downward curve of decline and push it back up.

This is Spanish exceptionalism. Sometimes it was good that Spain was different. In the hands of that great apologist of laziness, Paul Lafargue, Spain's oddity became its triumph. Marx's son-in-law, who visited Spain after the defeat of the Paris Commune, largely to keep an eye on the anar-

---

[1] David A. Boruchoff, "Historiography with License: Isabel, the Catholic Monarch and the Kingdom of God," in his *Isabel la Católica, Queen of Castile: Critical Essays* (New York: Palgrave MacMillan, 2003), 229. A historian of medieval France has pointed out that historical writing in the Middle Ages could "address contemporary political life via a displacement to the past." Writers wrote the past according to present necessities, and present leaders staged political acts according to past events. See Gabrielle M. Spiegel, *The Past as Text: The Theory and Practice of Medieval Historiography* (Baltimore: Johns Hopkins University Press, 1997), xiii, 86.

chists, was delighted with what he found: "The heart leaps at hearing the beggar, superbly draped in his ragged *capa*, parlaying on terms of equality with the duke of Ossuna [*sic*]. For the Spaniards, in whom the primitive animal has not been atrophied, work is the worst sort of slavery."[2] Or, it was bad that Spain was different: A twentieth-century American historian wrote:

> Spain [in the nineteenth century] held tenaciously onto her medieval dream. Gutted and prostrate, she still spouted about her sacred faith, her glorious past, her splendid character, her matchless courage and unique zeal. It was like standing in a graveyard and boasting about the exploits of the deceased, as if such boasts would cause the dead to arise again and take a new lease on life.[3]

On both counts there were plenty of Spaniards who agreed with the foreign commentators. "Men naturally love honor, and Spaniards more than others. Everyone wants to be or to resemble a nobleman," the historian Manuel Dánvila wrote in the late nineteenth century.[4] There was a gulf between Spain and the rest of civilized Europe. That gulf had to be justified.

In this final chapter I first explore this historiographic responsibility as it was acquitted by nineteenth- and twentieth-century historians from Spain, who pondered what they were sure was a unique legacy, a crucial part of which included disdain for manual labor. Next, I return to the eighteenth century, which itself, in the eyes of its protagonists and its historians, has been regarded as an exception to the exception. I consider how its thinkers understood their place in time and how we inherited their vision, not only of labor in particular but of Spanish history in general and of the Enlightenment as a turning point. Finally, I consider some of the larger issues that this study of early modern Castile has forced me (and, I hope, readers) to confront. Among them are historians' avid interest in "marginality" or "margination" as an explanation and description of early modern Spanish social organization. Such a scheme inevitably considers an implausibly vast array of qualities as "marginal" and misrepresents power relationships. Drawing a stark demarcation between insiders and outsiders sorely distorts the fluid and often ambiguous nature of politics

---

[2] Paul Lafargue, *The Right to be Lazy* (1883) (Chicago: Charles H. Kerr, 1975), 37.

[3] John Armstrong Crow, *Spain: The Root and the Flower: An Interpretation of Spain and the Spanish People* (1963), 3d ed. (Berkeley: University of California Press, 1985), 250. Crow, a professor of Spanish political and literary history, first traveled to Spain in 1928. His dim view of Spain may well have been influenced by the pessimism of Spanish intellectual circles at the time. See William D. Phillips Jr., "Images of Spanish History in the United States," *Bulletin of the Society for Spanish and Portuguese Historical Studies* 27 (Summer–Winter 2002): 40–49.

[4] Manuel Dánvila y Collado, *El Reinado de Carlos III*, 6 vols. (Madrid: Real Academia de la Historia, 1894), vol. 5, 513.

and participation in early modern Castile (and elsewhere) and belittles those on both sides of the lines. Returning to themes introduced in previous chapters, I argue that narrow definitions of citizenship fail to account for even passive political participation on the part of Castilian workers or for the favorable regard in which workers were held, narrow definitions of the economic fail to detect the political nature of market transactions or the cultural trusses of guild organization, and narrow definitions of legality overlook the imprecision and contingency that defined early modern society. Paying excessive heed to stereotypes and dramatic works, taking normative treatises as descriptive, and ignoring the words actually spoken by the people allegedly living on the margins can lead us to believe that labor and its practitioners were despised. But there is no shortage of evidence that that was not the case.

Exceptionalism and the Exceptional Century

It is no coincidence that some of the most influential modern authorities on Spain's past and its national character were not historians. Unamuno was a classicist and a philosopher, Marcelino Menéndez y Pelayo an extraordinarily erudite man devoted primarily to literature, Ramón Menéndez Pidal a scholar of medieval literature, and José Ortega y Gasset a philosopher. Américo Castro taught literature and philology. For Hayden White, the difference between history and the philosophy of history is that the latter "brings the conceptual apparatus by which the facts are ordered in the discourse to the surface of the text, while history proper (as it is called) buries it in the interior of the narrative, where it serves as a hidden or implicit shaping device."[5] But at least in the case of Spain, the difference is not simply that one conceptual apparatus is explicit and another implicit. The apparatus wielded by writers such as Menéndez y Pelayo and Unamuno, who I think would safely fall into White's category of philosophers of history, cannot be compared to that of "proper" historians because their normative weights are so radically distinct. They are not merely located at different depths of their respective narratives; they are entirely different animals. For these writers around the turn of the twentieth century, history was identity; it was the nation. They found it, alive but wounded, in the romances and dramas of the Siglo de Oro and before. They sought it in few other places.

In their immediate past, the nineteenth century, Spanish historiography was, in Carolyn Boyd's words, "an eclectic methodology derived from

[5] Hayden White, *Tropics of Discourse: Essays in Cultural Criticism* (Baltimore: Johns Hopkins University Press, 1978), 127.

Enlightenment philosophy, Romantic idealism, and empiricism."[6] Liberal historians' goal was to legitimate the liberal state, which they believed had inherited the mantle of the *ilustrados* and the *comuneros,* whose 1520 revolt they celebrated just as they mourned the seeds of democracy in Old Castile that had been trampled by the imperial Hapsburgs in the person of Charles V. Francisco Martínez de la Rosa (1787–1862), for example, a politician, poet, and dramatist who served several times as a government minister and also as ambassador to France, wrote a play, *La Viuda de Padilla,* about the *comuneros.* In it, he told the story of María de Padilla, who led the city of Toledo in the months after the revolt's defeat, heroically refusing to surrender to royal authorities. He wrote the tragedy (he described it as such) while living in Cádiz when it was the site of the liberal Cortes; its 1814 premiere took place as the French invaders' bombs fell around the makeshift theater.[7]

The overtly political agenda of Martínez de la Rosa and his contemporaries was gradually overtaken by a more philosophical, introspective one. Among the giants of late nineteenth-century Spanish history and intellectual thought and an inevitable point of reference for subsequent generations was Menéndez y Pelayo (1856–1912). His entry onto the public stage came in 1876 in a debate with Manuel de la Revilla, an anticlerical Krausian. The terms of the argument could easily lead one to believe that time had stood still: Spain was backward, Revilla said, on account of the church, with which science was incompatible. The Spanish nation, Menéndez y Pelayo replied, was inseparable from Catholicism. Reject one and you reject the other, and neither is incompatible with science.[8] Four years later, he published *Historia de los heterodoxos españoles,* an impassioned defense of Spanish orthodoxy that insisted that phenomena such as the French Revolution and the Enlightenment were for others, but not for Spain. Today, despite the obviously enormous breadth of his knowledge, his book is practically unreadable, his erudition disappearing beneath the rant. Menéndez y Pelayo's most notable student and successor was Ramón Menéndez Pidal (1869–1968), a scholar of medieval literature. In his long, well-known historical essay, "Los españoles en la historia," which in 1947 opened the multivolume *Historia de España* that he directed (and which continued appearing after his death), one reads of Spaniards' "per-

[6] Carolyn Boyd, *Historia Patria: Politics, History, and National Identity in Spain, 1875–1975* (Princeton University Press, 1997), 70 and chap. 3.

[7] Francisco Martínez de la Rosa, *Obras dramáticas* (Madrid: Espasa-Calpe, 1947). Martínez de la Rosa was a member of both the Real Academia de Historia and the Real Academia Española. He was best known as a dramatist but also wrote works of history.

[8] Marcelino Menéndez y Pelayo, *La ciencia española (Polémicas, proyectos y bibliografía)*, 3 vols., Colección de Escritores Castellanos Críticos, vols. 52, 57, 64 (Madrid: Pérez Dubrull, 1887–1888). One of his replies to Revilla was significantly entitled "Mr. Masson redivivo," or "Mr. Masson [he who asked 'What is owed to Spain?'] resuscitated."

manent identity," largely inherited from the Stoics, so like the Castilian landscape in their sobriety, austerity, and extremity. Referring to Guicciardini's observations on Spaniards' lethargy and supporting himself with lines of poetry and foreign travelers' disparaging remarks, he wrote: "This indifference toward work, so marked through the centuries, finds rectifications of a general sort both easily and not infrequently."[9] Such rectifications, it was understood, were the exceptions that confirmed the rule of indifference. The fifth section of the essay was called "Las dos Españas." Like his teacher, he saw Spanish history as a series of markers setting some Spaniards apart from others, and all Spaniards apart from everyone else, but for him the chasm was a source of sorrow. Writing in the darkest years of postwar Francoist Spain, he believed that foreign influences in the eighteenth century had driven a wedge into what had been a spiritually united nation. The divide continued into the nineteenth century, when political polarization was epitomized by the ideologies of the Cortes of Cádiz and the reactionary reign of Ferdinand VII. His vision, which Américo Castro called "radical melancholy" and which in fact was quite optimistic, given the circumstances, was this:

> The hard reality of facts will reinforce tolerance, that priceless historical quality granted to the noblest of peoples through experience, which cannot be extinguished by collective extremism, so prevelant today throughout the world. It will not be one of the warring semi-Spains that will prevail alone, one writing an epitaph for the other. It will not be a Spain of the left or a Spain of the right; it will be all of Spain, yearned for by so many, which does not amputate one of its arms, which puts all its efforts toward occupying a place among those peoples who strive for modernity.[10]

History is a cross we bear. But, according to a remarkable suggestion by Luis Morote, writing earlier in the twentieth century, we have a choice. We (or, more correctly, Spaniards) can use crosses selectively:

> The first step on the road to this sought-after national resurrection is knowing *which historical era truly corresponds to our ideal* and satisfaction and which Spaniards we wish to resemble, those who were everywhere ruined as they fought and triumphed, or those who worked in their workshops in Seville, in Barcelona factories, in the fields of Valencia and Aragón and the fertile Andalucía and even the forbidding Alpujarra, who attracted visitors to the famed

---

[9] Ramón Menéndez Pidal, "Los españoles en la historia," in *Historia de España,* ed. Ramón Menéndez Pidal, vol. 1: *España prehistórica* (Madrid: Espasa-Calpe, 1947), xiii. See also Ramón Menéndez Pidal and Walter Starkie, *The Spaniards in Their History* (London: Hollis and Carter, 1950), for the text in English and an interpretive essay by Starkie.

[10] Menéndez Pidal, "Los españoles en la historia," c; Américo Castro, *De la edad conflictiva,* 2d ed. (Madrid: Taurus, 1963), 136.

fairs of Castile, who navigated the seas so well they appeared to be made for them.[11]

However, in the opinion of Ramiro de Maeztu, who also formed part of the Generation of '98, though he later became chief apologist for dictator Miguel Primo de Rivera and eventually was shot by the Republicans in the civil war, "We ought to forget all our history and place our eyes only on the supreme ideal, there in the future."[12] The past had not done right by the Spanish people. Yet rather than cede it to the right, progressives had to search around in the past to claim that part that corresponded to true Spaniards. Morote found it in the workshops. Joaquín Costa found it in the seventeenth and eighteenth centuries, devoting essays to Alvarez Osorio (who wrote during the reign of Charles II), Campomanes, and the count of Aranda.[13] For Ortega y Gasset (1883–1955), the outstanding intellectual of the generation that followed 1898, too, history was a matter of looking back to find the point at which things starting going wrong. According to his reading of the past in *Invertebrate Spain,* "the secret of Spanish misfortune" lay in the Middle Ages because there had been no proper feudal era, thanks to the Christian Visigoths having allowed themselves to be conquered by North African Muslims.[14] In the 1920s, the diplomat Salvador de Madariaga in *Englishmen Frenchmen Spaniards* meditated on the differences among those three peoples using what he called international psychology. Spaniards were not lazy, just choosy about what they did and did not do, he said. "A nation is a character," he said in the introduction, and he went on to describe that of Spain:

> The Spanish character abounds in conflicting tendencies. It is hard and human, it is resigned and rebellious, it is energetic and indolent. For in reality it is both spontaneous and complete, and therefore it allows the manifestation of all the tendencies which are to be found in the human microcosm. The combination of this wholeness with the reserve, which we have also observed in the Spanish character, contributes to the richness and complexity

[11] Luis Morote, *La moral de la derrota* (1900) (Madrid: Biblioteca Nueva, 1997), 150. My emphasis.

[12] Cited in Fredrick B. Pike, *Hispanismo 1989–1936: Spanish Conservatives and Liberals and Their Relations with Spanish America* (South Bend, Ind.: University of Notre Dame Press, 1971), 50.

[13] Joaquín Costa, *Historia política social patria,* ed. José García Mercadal (Madrid: Aguilar, 1961). The book also contains essays on the Catholic Monarchs and El Cid.

[14] José Ortega y Gasset, *Invertebrate Spain,* ed. and trans. Mildred Adams (New York: W. W. Norton, 1937). The chapter on Andalucía bears the subhead "The Vegetative Ideal." "The Andaluz has worn his indolence for four thousand years and it seems to do him no harm. . . . That famous Andalusian indolence is the formula for its culture," a culture that he rather admired, perhaps along the lines of Lafargue (95–97). Ortega was a professor of philosophy, a Republican politician, and the founder (in 1921) of the journal *Revista de Occidente,* which continues to be published.

of the famous Spanish indifference. Indifference, laziness, passivity, are but various apprearances of passionate life quietly flowing.[15]

Similarly, for Unamuno, "disinterested knowledge of its history gives people strength and knowledge of themselves, enabling them to remove the disassimilationist debris that clutters their lives. . . . To reach the enduring nature of our *casticismo,* its living mass [*roca viva*], we must study how our *casa histórica* was formed and revealed in History."[16] Yet in similar terms he also told Ganivet, "History, damned history, in large part an imposition of the environment, has hidden from us the living mass of the *constitución patria;* history, while it has revealed to us in our acts much of our spirit, also has prevented us from seeing the most intimate parts of that spirit."[17] There is a disjuncture between us and our history; this theme runs through the work of most of the leading historical writers of the early twentieth century.

The most influential Spanish historian of the early twentieth century was Castro (1885–1972). Influenced, like so many of his predecessors, by German philosophy (he served as the Second Republic's ambassador to Germany in 1931), Castro's explanation for why Spain was different was the cohabitation (*convivencia*) on the Iberian peninsula of Jews, Muslims, and Christians, each of which he said constituted a caste. As a result of pogroms and the Christians' eventual expulsion of Jews and Muslims, fear of tainted blood and the subsequent anxiety to attain limpieza defined Spain's peculiarity. "The Iberian past consists in a series of political and economic errors, the results of which were failure and decadence," he asserted at the start of his mammoth *The Structure of Spanish History,* primarily devoted to the medieval period, in which Castro sought not psychology but the structures that he said determined the shape of peoples' lives: "The primary task of the historian's history should be to show the basic position of a people inside its own inescapable life." One of the inescapable structures for Spaniards was the inability, because of the enormous risks to one's honor, to perform manual labor. Basing himself on literary sources, mostly from the fifteenth and sixteenth centuries (for him, the Spanish structure did not change after that), he asserted that Christian Spaniards became attuned only to their inner essence, not to the exterior world. Honor, not work, was what interested them. The true value of things, not material reality, inspired them. Christian Spaniards were entirely devoted to simply

[15] Salvador de Madariaga, *Englishmen Frenchmen Spaniards* (Oxford University Press, 1928), 43. Madariaga was a professor at Oxford and director of disarmament at the League of Nations.

[16] Miguel de Unamuno, *En torno al casticismo* (Madrid: Espasa-Calpe, 1972), 40.

[17] Unamuno, in Angel Ganivet, *Idearium español. El porvenir de España* (Madrid: Espasa-Calpe, 1999), 212.

existing, to being men, to believing instead of thinking: "As early as the Middle Ages, the Spanish Christian scorned mechanical, rational labor that was without mystery, without a background of eternity to transcend it," he wrote. "No other European country so stigmatized manual labor, which was not accorded legal dignity until the reign of Charles III." No practical affairs of life were in the hands of Christians, he said. Moors were tailors, barbers, muleteers, masons, architects, and shoemakers; Jews collected taxes and were physicians, pharmacists, astrologers, and assorted tradesmen.[18] Life in post-expulsion Spain for Castro was a daily drama that combined the horror of heresy, the obsession with purity, and the dangers of losing one's honor. Many people, he said perfectly seriously in another major work, would die of hunger rather than lose the esteem of their neighbors by working.[19] This, indeed, was a world that had nothing to do with the rest of Europe.

Though Castro's work was bereft of documentation other than literary sources and today is not taken seriously as a work of history except insofar as it pointed out (finally) that Spain had three religious heritages, not just one, his portrait of a Christian Spaniard who did practically nothing (except dream, perhaps) has had an extraordinary shelf life. A tedious and nasty debate between him and Claudio Sánchez Albornoz in the 1950s contributed to its longevity. The issue, again, was to what to attribute Spain's unique status among nations. Sánchez Albornoz, an expert on the Visigoths and institutional history, rejected, point by point, Castro's vision of a happy religious threesome and insisted that more attention be paid to the Christian Visigoths and the Romans before them. While Castro stressed diversity and rupture, Sánchez-Albornoz stressed unity and continuity.[20] Both, however, though breaking with Menéndez y Pelayo's Christocentricism, understood Spanish history as a religous narrative of one sort or another. Both, too, went into exile after Franco triumphed, and both spent the rest of their careers trying to figure out how things had come to this.

If there is something unbearable about reading historical pronouncements and generalizations based on equal parts of psychology, poetry, re-

---

[18] Américo Castro, *The Structure of Spanish History*, trans. Edmund L. King (Princeton University Press, 1954), 5, 643, 23, 630, 609. This is an expanded version of the 1948 Spanish original.

[19] Américo Castro, *La realidad histórica de España* (1954) (Mexico: Editorial Porrúa, 1982), 235.

[20] Claudio Sánchez-Albornoz, *Spain: A Historical Enigma*, 2 vols. (Madrid: Fundación Universitaria Española, 1975). First published in Spanish in 1956 as *España, un enigma histórico*. Eugenio Asensio in his famous critique of Castro's *Realidad Histórica* referred to Sánchez-Albornoz's 1,600-page refutation as the "anti-Castro" (Eugenio Asensio, "Américo Castro historiador: Reflexiones sobre 'La realidad histórica de España,'" *MLN* 81 [December 1966]: 596). Asensio argued persuasively that Castro, in "orientalizing" Hispanic culture, vastly overestimated the impact of the Jews. He also accused him of bad scholarship, overlooking contrary evidence, and leaping to conclusions that confirmed his racial thesis.

ligiosity, and anguish, the antidote arrived in the second half of the twentieth century with the influence of Marxism and French and English social historical methods. While Franco's sycophants continued exploring themselves and paying repetitive and ardent homage to *don* Marcelino, a new generation of Spanish scholars with yet another burden to explain—the genesis of the Civil War and the resulting dictatorship—found an explanation for its country's tortured past and faulty development in the absence of a proper bourgeoisie.[21] José Antonio Maravall wrote his famed study of the Revolt of the Comuneros in 1963, claiming that the revolt had indeed been a modern revolution, one that occurred long before the English or French versions. So Spain could have had a middle class, in fact was on its way to having one, but the Hapsburgs interrupted it and the incipient bourgeoisie was only too willing to betray its historical mission. Castile, the great Catalan historian Jaime Vicens Vives wrote in 1952, simply had an "incomprehension of the capitalist world."[22] Faced with the occasional sign of modern behavior or language in the early modern era (such as praise for noblemen who labored), these and other social historians detected merely unsuccessful attempts to shift the dominant ideology away from the unproductive past and toward the dawn of capitalism. Michel Cavillac called it the "grafting of certain capitalist values onto the aristocratic axiology," an operation that sadly had to wait for its success until the Enlightenment.[23]

The historians of the 1960s and 1970s, especially those working in Spain, were a brave and extraordinary group, and citations to their work can be found throughout this book. Where I take issue with them, it should be obvious, is in their assurance that early modern Spaniards had an antipathy to labor that was the outcome of the hegemony of a medieval, or aristocratic, or at any rate antimodern ideology. There was no other possi-

---

[21] They also, similarly to twentieth-century German historians, sought clues that proved fascism inevitable and saw the nineteenth century as a trail of crumbs leading to the Primo de Rivera dictatorship, left-wing radicalism, and the Civil War. Thus, for example, Tierno Galván called Joaquin Costa a "pre-fascist" (Enrique Tierno Galván, *Costa y el regeneracionismo* [Barcelona: Editorial Barna, 1961], 10).

[22] Jaime Vicens Vives, *Aproximación a la historia de España*, 2d ed. (Universidad de Barcelona, 1960), 150.

[23] Michel Cavillac, "Le marchand, l'honneur et la noblesse en Castille au siècle d'or," in *Les sociétés fermés dans le monde Iberique (XVI–XVIIe siècles). Actes de la table ronde des 8 et 9 février 1985* (Paris: CNRS, 1986), 55, 59. A more plausible case of grafting is found in the very interesting study by Laura Caroline Stevenson of literary images of late-sixteenth-century English craftsmen and merchants. They often were depicted in positive ways but in settings that were feudal, royal, or aristocratic. Hard work could earn an apprentice glory, but divine intervention by a benevolent monarch also was frequent. Stevenson suggests that writers did not have the literary tools with which to depict workers: "There was no place in the pastoral ideal for the celebration of diligent work that got a man *out* of a low social position" (Laura Caroline Stevenson, *Praise and Paradox: Merchants and Craftsmen in Elizabethan Popular Literature* [Cambridge University Press, 1984], 210).

ble explanation for their country's development, which they were convinced was peculiar. They sought their explanations in class analysis, not in national essence, which I, at least, take as an improvement. But the assumption was as rooted in literature, stereotypes, and passive repetition of previous sources as it had been before. Even the greatest of the archival historians of the era, Antonio Domínguez Ortiz, seemed unwilling to question the paradigm of the Spaniard imprisoned by a code of honor.

For Domínguez Ortiz and his cohort, the code was broken only in the eighteenth century, the turning point that confirmed the oddness and badness of the previous era. When Campomanes wrote that not all centuries are enlightened, he might have added that he had absolutely no doubt that his was.[24] His confidence was infectious, and it has become a problem for historians. It is easy to take for granted that the *ilustrados'* self-praise was entirely deserved, and easy to forget that their critical and programmatic writings and acts were themselves interpretive. How they saw their past and themselves—Sempere referred to "the centuries of ignorance" behind him—and how we see them constitute two of the most fundamental stumbling blocks for understanding how work, not-work, and antiwork were experienced and theorized in the early modern era.[25] Historical presuppositions regarding symmetry between the Enlightenment and economic progress, broken social barriers, and enhanced dignity are not unambiguously true. The symmetry can be attenuated, contingent, or filtered through discourses either imposed by us or anachronistically understood. "Everything is now different in Europe," proclaimed Jovellanos, an unreliable albeit brilliant witness to his own revolution.[26] But everything was not.

What allowed them to be so original and audacious, the *ilustrados* said, was the Bourbon dynasty. "As soon as Philip V reached the throne, the human spirit in Spain began struggling to free itself from the slavery and dejection [*abatimiento*] that public opinion [*el imperio de la opinión*] had imposed on it," Sempere wrote in the first volume of his collection of the most important works of his era. Later, explaining the purpose of such a work, he credited "the vigorous efforts by our monarchs, particularly the august house of Bourbon, to banish barbarism and spread enlightenment."[27] It is no surprise that writers laced their works with praise for their

[24] Concepción de Castro, *Campomanes: Estado y reformismo ilustrado* (Madrid: Alianza Editorial, 1996), 303. The citation, also used in part 2, is from "Respuesta fiscal sobre abolir la tasa . . . " (1764).

[25] Juan Sempere y Guarinos, *Historia del luxo y de las leyes suntuarias de España* (Madrid, 1788), 126.

[26] Gaspar Melchor de Jovellanos, "Informe dado a la Junta General de Comercio y Moneda sobre el libre ejercicio de las artes," in *Obras*, vol. 2, ed. Cándido Nocedal, Biblioteca de Autores Españoles, vol. 50 (Madrid, 1859), 38.

[27] Juan Sempere y Guarinos, *Ensayo de una biblioteca española de los mejores escritores del reynado de Carlos III*, vol. 1 (Madrid: Impr. Real, 1785), 53; vol. 5 (Madrid: Impr. Real, 1789), 1.

monarch. They did so in Spain and elsewhere, regardless of the dynasty. But the fact that the Bourbons in eighteenth-century Spain were a new dynasty and that the previous century was perceived to have been catastrophic gave their praise additional purpose. It converted them into the protagonists of something entirely new.[28]

One of the most eloquent examples of this self-assurance combined with extravagant adulation was Jovellanos's speech to the Madrid Economic Society after the death of Charles III, one of the first of a very long list of hagiographic tributes.[29] The genre illuminates not only how its practitioners venerated the king (and Campomanes, who received his own considerable share of exaltation) but how they venerated themselves, or at least their historical role. The speech began, as many subsequent biographies did, by recounting the story of Charles's arrival from afar. He was ruler of Naples from 1734 to 1759, learning his kingly trade while his brother, Ferdinand VI, ruled Spain, and Charles had no reason to expect the larger kingdom. But on his brother's death, he was summoned, "brought by providence to occupy the throne of his forefathers." When the new monarch arrived in Spain, Jovellanos told his listeners, it was a time of darkness and ignorance. Knowledge was speculative, religion oppressive, science nonexistent, misery widespread, and fields fallow: "Everywhere there was horror and sadness." Faced with this alarming scenario, Charles immediately understood that he could do nothing for his people without first preparing them for the inevitable reforms, instilling them with a spirit that would enable them to receive the good news. Jovellanos, like others of his generation, knew the work of the arbitristas, and he contrasted their fate with that of their followers. Their intellectual efforts, he said, had fallen on sterile ground and there was no order to their inquiries because they had lacked the necessary spiritual guidance of a wise monarch. Their work was for naught. Finally, finally, the seventeenth century came to an end, and slowly philosophy and science were freed from their fetters. Like a gardener nursing along fragile plants in barren soil, Charles rescued the wisdom left behind by such men as Bernardo Ward and Jerónimo Ustariz, advisers to the deceased king's father. In short, "heaven had reserved for the Bourbons the restoration of [Spain's] splendor and its force."

The men of the Spanish Enlightenment saw themselves as historical actors, which meant they had to differentiate themselves (and their monarchs) from their predecessors. Like Morote two hundred years later, the *ilustrados* sought in history that which corresponded to what they thought

[28] It is not out of place to point out that the present-day, highly praised Bourbon monarchy in Spain is a restoration monarchy that came to power after decades of dictatorship.

[29] Gaspar Melchor de Jovellanos, "Elogio de Carlos III, leído en la Real Sociedad Económica de Madrid, 8 November 1788," in *Obras*, vol. 1, ed. Cándido Nocedal, Biblioteca de Autores Españoles, vol. 46 (Madrid, 1858), 311–317.

was their authentic self. (Not coincidentally, Morote devoted a chapter of his book to the many accomplishments of Charles III: "A glorious reign in which there was no sort of human activity that did not bear the mark, the deep imprint, of civilization.")[30] The Visigoths were of exceptional interest, being, as they were, Christians, united, and sovereign; thousands of their documents were transcribed during the late eighteenth century. Jovellanos told the Royal Academy in 1780 that all patriots should study legal history, especially from the Visigothic era, and he deplored Spain's failure "to conserve the [Visigoths'] constitution [i.e., laws] in its primitive purity."[31] Campomanes also liked the Visigoths, primarily because they had resisted Rome's efforts to run their church, which is exactly what he was trying to do. The Valencian Gregorio Mayans, one of Spain's leading men of letters in the years just preceding the Enlightenment, wrote a defense of King Witiza, the penultimate Visigothic king before the Muslim invasion. After the Reconquest and the restoration of peninsular unity, Sempere wrote, the Catholic Monarchs had had the opportunity to restore the old ways but their "horrifying failure" indicated the "limitations of our enlightenment" (la cortedad de nuestras luces).[32]

It was not enough to criticize the past; the ilustrados had to write history anew.[33] The Royal Academy of History was established in 1738 during the reign of Philip V, and historical publications, both new and republished, flourished in the later part of the century. What is usually considered the first general history of Spain, Juan de Mariana's 1601 Historia general de España, was reedited several times. Periodicals reprinted primary documents, and dramatic works incorporated historical themes. Economic Societies offered classes on historical research. They rejected the old chronicles and heroic epics, often based on fanciful stories, and wanted them supplanted with a truthful civic history. Juan Francisco de Masdeu's massive opus in the 1780s was the most serious work of general history since Mariana's. Pedro and Rafael Rodríguez Mohedano, brothers and Franciscans, published a ten-volume history of Spain that began with the Phoenicians and ended with the first

---

[30] Morote, La moral de la derrota, 159.

[31] Gaspar Melchor de Jovellanos, "Discurso leido por el autor en su recepción a la Real Academia de la Historia," in Obras, vol. 1.

[32] Sempere y Guarinos, Historia del luxo, 14–15.

[33] On the writing of history in the Enlightenment era, see José Alvarez Junco, Mater dolorosa: La idea de España en el siglo XIX (Madrid: Taurus, 2001), 195–226; Richard Herr, The Eighteenth Century Revolution in Spain (Princeton University Press, 1958), chap. 12; Antonio Mestre Sanchis, "Conciencia histórica e historiografía," in Historia de España, ed. Menéndez Pidal, vol. 31, pt. 1: La época de la ilustración. El estado y la cultura (1759–1808) (Madrid: Espasa-Calpe, 1987), 301–345. In a different vein, see Jorge Cañizares-Esguerra, "Eighteenth-Century Spanish Political Economy: Epistemology and Decline." Eighteenth-Century Thought, no. 1 (2003): 295–314.

century A.D.[34] All these writers celebrated their newness and denigrated their past, the latter meaning both the events themselves and how they had been written, exhibiting a new patriotism (and national myth) and redefining the standard by which societies should be judged.

In the center of both the Enlightenment's and our re-creations of Spanish history stands Campomanes, for whom history was a constant struggle between reason and nonreason. The hagiography of the king's *fiscal* is every bit as impressive as that of Charles III and leaves no doubt that reason—that is, his version—won out. His contemporaries regarded him as the great helmsman of the Enlightenment, a reputation that survived unscathed. He was as brave as he was learned. From one of his twentieth-century editors we read:

> To ennoble occupations vilified by custom and the prejudices of caste and blood was not a matter of theoretical digressions or legal writs. Generations would be necessary. But the first step had been taken. And Campomanes had the courage to take it in a hostile environment. . . . [T]he *Discurso* is a milestone of labor theory, essential reading for a correct understanding of the historical evolution of Spain.[35]

A Madrid exhibition in 2003 on "Campomanes and His Times" proclaimed that the count "embodied like no one else the distinguished men of an Administration that was humanistically trained, fighting for change."[36] He fought for change armed with *luces;* yet as we have seen, the famous appendices to the *Discurso sobre la educación popular* relied almost entirely on writers from the sixteenth and seventeenth centuries. He used their language and their logic. His explanations for the origin of the arts and crafts was no different from theirs, and his opinion of their status was no closer to the truth. His obsession with distinguishing the true from the false poor was the same, as were his remedies. Even the patriotic schools were reminiscent of the solutions of Miguel de Giginta and Juan Luis Vives.

Echoes of Campomanes's enlightened self-consciousness also reached the nineteenth century, when liberal historians reiterated Sempere's sentiments that the world had changed once Philip V sat on the throne: "It is of greater interest to examine the politics of Spain since the august house of Bourbon occupied the throne than to examine the same matter under the Austrian dynasty. The latter was, so to speak, *ancient history.* The former

---

[34] Pedro and Rafael Rodríguez Mohedano, *Historia literaria de España: origen, progresos, decadencia y restauración de la literature española* (Madrid 1766–1791).

[35] Pedro Rodríguez de Campomanes, *Discurso sobre la educación popular* (1775), ed. F. Aguilar Piñal (Madrid: Editora Nacional, 1978), 36.

[36] *Campomanes y su tiempo* (Madrid: Fundación Santander Central Hispano), 21. The catalogue also informs us that Campomanes was a pioneer in the fight for women's rights.

is *modern*," Martínez de la Rosa wrote in 1857.[37] Massive biographies of Charles III appeared in the nineteenth century depicting a kindly, chaste, wise, and generous monarch. One such work was a four-volume opus by Antonio Ferrer del Río which began with a catastrophic portrait of the times preceding Charles's reign. All that was left of the merchants and artisans who bravely fought under Juan de Padilla's orders in the *comuneros* revolt, he wrote, were ragtag bands of beggars and bums, the same who threw furniture and tapestries off the balconies of the count of Oropesa's palace in 1699.[38] In a chapter titled "Improvements in All Fields," Ferrer del Río reported that "no one excelled in industry without receiving immediate reward, according to his class and circumstances," following which he provided a list of industrial innovators and factory owners: "Such direct, painstaking, continuous protection for Spanish industry had never before been expended," a triumph he laid at the feet of Campomanes as well as at those of the king.[39] *Discurso sobre la educación popular* is described as "one of the most precious books ever published in Spain and the true cradle of those beneficent and popular corporations," a reference to the Economic Societies, whose work on behalf of the poor is described amid citations from Vives, Soto, and Pérez de Herrera, whose works by then had existed for some three hundred years.[40] Simply put, there was nothing that was not wonderful during the reign: foreign policy, social policy, finance, military adventures, the royal cabinets—and, of course, the recovery of dignity for working people: "When posterity judges kings, it heeds nothing but the people's love. Spaniards gave unmistakable proof of theirs toward Charles III, bathing his tomb with tears. Fathers transmitted to sons reverence for his memory, and they called his times happy ones."[41] The monarch also

[37] Francisco Martínez de la Rosa, *Bosquejo histórico de la política de España desde los tiempos de los Reyes Católicos hasta nuestros días*, 2 vols. (Madrid: M. Rivadeneyra, 1857), vol. 1, vi. Emphasis is in the original and is curious given the same author's enthusiasm for the *comuneros,* by definition more ancient than the Hapsburgs who defeated them.

[38] Antonio Ferrer del Río, *Historia del reinado de Carlos III en España*, 4 vols. (Madrid: Impr. de Matute y Compagni, 1856), vol. 1, 69–70. Ferrer del Río in 1850 wrote a history of the *comuneros* whose title began with the words *Decadencia de España.* For a similar work see Carlos Gutiérrez de los Ríos, count of Fernán Núñez, *Vida de Carlos III*, 2 vols. (Madrid: F. Fé, 1898). The author, Spain's ambassador to France during the French Revolution, wrote the biography early in the nineteenth century. It was republished in Madrid in 1988 by Fundación Universitaria Española. Mauro Hernández, "Carlos III: Un mito progresista," in Equipo Madrid, *Carlos III, Madrid y la Ilustración* (Madrid: Siglo Veintiuno, 1988), 20, calls the Fernán Núñez biography a "key work in the construction of Charles III's personal myth." See also Manuel Dánvila y Collado, *El Reinado de Carlos III*, 6 vols. (Madrid: Real Academia de la Historia, 1894), for whom "industry [in the era of Charles III] grew as the destructive echo of war was replaced with the calm artistry of peace and manual labor freed itself with the first signs of freedom and science" (vol. 6, 233).

[39] Ferrer del Río, *Historia del reinado de Carlos III en España*, vol. 3, 228–231.

[40] Ibid., vol. 4, 64.

[41] Ibid., vol. 4, 294.

"broadened the horizons of thought" by granting "freedom of the press" in a way that met the liberal Ferrer del Río's approval: "Not unbridled and licentious freedom, which is like a fury and threatens to unhinge everything, but *just and moderate freedom that respects religion and its practices, that recognizes sovereign authority and legitimate power, that abstains from besmirching the honor of one's neighbors with distractions and calumny.*" The king, finally, had neither "innovated nor copied foreigners but reestablished ancient practices."[42]

If we assume that present-day historians make choices in their narrative strategies such that self-evident explanations emerge for the way things turned out, the same is true for past historians. Unfortunately, however, our predecessors often escape the critical eye we cast on our peers. Their works are for some reason regarded as transparent because they are closer to the events and processes in question. But in the words of a contemporary historian of the Ottoman Empire, "the formless reality of the past has already been ordered by people from the past."[43] The idea that "the Enlightenment," in Spain or anywhere else, was a unitary project with a logical, coherent, and predictable set of precepts, among which were secularism and progress, is one of many problems confronting us as we peer through the thicket of words of *nuestros ilustrados,* as Spanish historians often tellingly refer to them, to see what it was they saw in their past. The eighteenth century becomes a turning point or an exception only if we regard it as a discrete object of analysis and only if we abandon our critical vantage point and forget that historical eras do not line up like dominos, one following the next, each with its own set of ideas, ours being the culmination. As Giovanni Levi once pointed out, the decline of magic did not automatically result in the ascent of science.[44] The decline of artisanal practices and institutions was not necessarily the occasion for the triumph of political economy. The view from here is not always the best one, though the close-up has its own problems.

If our vision is skewed by artificial temporal divisions, it is equally skewed by social divisions that too often correspond to anachronistic schematics instead of to the lives of the men and women whose petitions were read in city council chambers. To complete this study of the discourse of labor in early modern Castile, I now return to them.

---

[42] Ibid., vol. 4, 553–554, emphasis in original.

[43] Gabriel Piterberg, *An Ottoman Tragedy: History and Historiography at Play* (Berkeley: University of California Press, 2003), 59.

[44] Giovanni Levi, *Inheriting Power: The Story of an Exorcist,* trans. Lydia G. Cochrane (University of Chicago Press, 1988), 23.

CHAPTER 6

Conclusion

Workers, it will be recalled, are said to have lived on the margins, a place one would think undesirable but which in recent years has positively teemed with inhabitants. Women, of course, were there: "Deviant from the male norm, all women floated along the margins of respectability, bobbing between ostracism and integration, in an ambiguous area where social rules can be played with, questioned, or waived."[45] Craftsmen and the poor (often interchangeable) were there: guild confraternities "contributed to swell the ranks of the *marginados*—and potentially dangerous subjects—of Old Regime society."[46] Conversos and moriscos were there. Gypsies were there.

Spain lends itself to such a construct. Spaniards' own history of themselves has placed Spain on the margins, as we have seen, and the dueling versions of Spanish history as a nation at war with itself or as a nation that arose from accommodation among competing religious and ethnic strains both contain enormous possibilities for exclusionary paradigms. The racial and religious complexity of Spanish society provides a particularly apt setting for representations of otherness, which have prospered in recent years.[47] The influence of anthropology, feminist theory, and Foucault's conception of fragmented power have made it almost imperative over the past few decades that certain people on the peninsula be designated *marginados*, dangerous, or disorderly.[48] These are culturally laden categories that supplant explanations of hierarchy, injustice, and conflict that rely on class or politics. I do not mean to minimize the importance of any of these theories or disciplines or to suggest that class and politics themselves are not culturally laden. Nor do I want to enter into a debate over definitions of culture and economics, which I do not find useful. I do, however, object to a stripping-away of political and production relations and to an in-or-out approach that appears determined to locate otherness where it does not exist. Pointing to a series of subjects on the margins too often begs the questions—which could be better answered with a broader theoretical argument about society at large—of how they got there and how "there" sits relative to the rest, if indeed it is a margin.

[45] Mary Elizabeth Perry, *Gender and Disorder in Early Modern Seville* (Princeton University Press, 1990), 9.

[46] José María Vallejo García-Hevia, "Campomanes, jurista y ministro de la monarquía," in *Campomanes y su tiempo*, 40.

[47] Josiah Blackmore and Gregory S. Hutcheson, eds., *Queer Iberia: Sexualities, Cultures, and Crossings from the Middle Ages to the Renaissance* (Durham, N.C.: Duke University Press, 1999), starts off by announcing that Iberia "has lain on the margins of Europe's consciousness, always the site of difference, always 'queer' Iberia." See my review of the anthology in *Sixteenth Century Journal* 31, no. 2 (2000): 520–521.

[48] See Scott Taylor, "Credit, Debt, and Honor in Castile, 1600–1650," *Journal of Early Modern History* 7, no. 1–2 (2003): 23–27, for a particularly articulate criticism of anthropology's impact on Spanish historiography.

The vile and mechanical craftsmen of early modern Spain, be they real, legal constructs, or literary figures, are the quintessential *marginados* of the era. They suit the decline narrative, the enlightened narrative, the disaster narrative, and the marginal narrative. The world of not-work and anti-work took the place of a Castilian republic inhabited by common citizens, some of whom worked, some of whom did not, and whose actions and language cannot be accounted for by "margination." If political economy was in many ways inadequate for grasping the meaning of guild ordinances or appreciating contemporary attitudes toward labor, a stark exclusionary schema that substitutes culturally driven lateral barriers for class-driven vertical barriers is equally inadequate. Both not only miss documentary evidence of oral and physical (passive and active) participation in the republic, because they do not seek it, but they misread the sources.

My objections to strict chronological and social dividing lines come together when we consider the language used by and about artisans and their work. Vice and virtue were never clear-cut, and one behavior or action could summon up two judgments: respecting a religious holiday, for instance, could be construed as piety or laziness. Constructing an elaborate piece of furniture or embroidering an item of fancy clothing could be a display of excellence or excess. The judgments easily could coexist; one was not swapped for another at a certain chronological point, though, of course, ideas eventually come and go. But modes of thought are neither easily extinguished nor suddenly ignited, and both scenarios were implicit in the tale of Castile's vile and mechanical workers. Similarly, there were few signposts between the political and economic realms, showing us when we were leaving one and entering the next. The passions could become interests, Albert O. Hirschman wrote in a little book a quarter of a century ago; avarice, properly channeled, could be of benefit to all. Thus something formerly in the realm of statecraft—the temptation of extravagance—acquired economic meaning and virtue. He beautifully described the passions' metamorphosis into interests as an illustration of how "unintended consequences flow from human thought (and from the shape it is given through language), no less than from human actions."[49] For my purposes, Hirschman's argument helps elucidate how things such as guild ordinances and occupational status were subsequently interpreted. Something once in one realm and then in another possibly is not recognized. Or, the realm itself can be refigured to account for its new inhabitant. In referring to realms, I do not mean to identify certain spheres of human activity as political or economic, as that would undermine my point. I mean to say simply that certain activities were later considered as one or another

[49] Albert O. Hirschman, *The Passions and the Interests: Political Arguments for Capitalism Before Its Triumph* (Princeton University Press, 1997, 20th anniversary edition), 41.

in a manner that distorted their original context. As least as far as common artisans were concerned, both the eighteenth-century reformers and later historians overlooked the porous nature of the old world and the instability of its language. The common good, to return to an early theme of this book, was a political virtue easily translated by artisans into economic terms. In the same manner, rules of production for them were rules of harmonious living. Though artisans and the *ilustrados* understood fraud in different fashions, both usages rested on a belief that exchange and production relations could be free of perversion. Churchmen attacked business practices both in the fifteenth century and in the eighteenth, and their terms were defined by their very different opponents. To focus only on the recurrence of words, ignoring their varied contexts, could presume unwarranted cohesion; but to focus only on colliding realms could overlook deep discursive resonance. The boundless, timeless nature of vices and virtues in the minds of early modern artisans and writers can be a challenge to ours; likewise, the contingent nature of the category of vile and mechanical should not be exaggerated by us into something larger than it was. As political economy gradually gave rise to a new language of labor in the late eighteenth century, the practices that had accompanied the old language became scorned, overlooked, or misunderstood. There literally was no longer a way to read the past.

Labor as an autonomous, economic concept would not have been a familiar notion to anybody in the seventeenth century. Indeed, the apparent inevitability and permanence of certain "economic" concepts is altogether problematic. Karl Polanyi wrote many years ago that economic language was "embedded" in earlier eras.[50] Extrapolating a bit from his words, labor practices and commentary on those practices, either descriptive or normative, may offer us a better perspective on other problems—empire or nationalism, for example—than on what we today call labor. Yet at the same time, the commentary was not written in isolation from labor. Economic facts and relations obviously existed in the early modern era but were not necessarily understood as such. Linkages between linguistic practices and political-economic activity, then, become crucial to us as we look back, step by step, through centuries of observation and judgment. The eighteenth-century Spanish thinkers embraced Adam Smith's assumptions about the economic motivations of mankind, the value of labor, and the power of reason, and they understood "freedom" to be liberation from unhappy obligations. They were wrong, and we also are wrong if we consider their remedies to be the first stirrings of a long, economic process.

[50] Karl Polanyi, "Aristotle Discovers the Economy," in *Trade and Market in the Early Empires. Economies in History and Theory*, ed. Karl Polanyi, Conrad M. Arensberg and Harry W. Pearson (Chicago: Henry Regency, 1971), 67–71; Karl Polanyi, *The Great Transformation: The Political and Economic Origins of Our Time* (Boston: Beacon Press, 1957).

In a similar fashion, if we choose to see "vile and mechanical" as a legal category we inevitably run into trouble. Partly, as I have shown, this is because there was no such legal category in the strict sense that we understand the term. Neither the list of proscribed occupations nor the occasions on which they were proscribed was fixed or consistent, and, therefore, nor were transgressions. Beyond that consideration, however, lies a larger one: law itself was an ill-defined category. Practice rarely coincided with legality, not so much because disobedience was widespread but because the fetters were so loosely bound. Several times in this book, we saw how guilds and confraternities were abolished, but they continued to exist. Guilds spent decades arguing over what was law and what was custom. One could become the other, which is not the same as saying that customs were all either discarded or codified as time went on. Laws, too, were ignored if they made no sense. Their very existence as "laws" was disputed; a rule could not constitute a law if no one took it seriously, even if it was written down and even if it was signed by the king. In the words of Michael Sonenscher, law "was always exceptional. It marked a point at which the universal claims of nature were obliged to defer to the rights embodied in a particular form of words."[51] But the point at which that was necessary was not the same in all circumstances. Your law was not necessarily the same as mine. A tanner was not always, perhaps not ever, a vile neighbor. The acceptability of a certain person, religion, or occupation for a given position or status was almost always a function of a particular community's sense of pragmatism and rights. The value attached to crafts guilds and their members in a community grew out of their daily contributions to the common good and to their discursive articulation of those practices, not to any prior occupational hierarchy.

This book is about a multiplicity of discourses, some of them simultaneous, some contradictory, that have as their common point the place of labor in early modern Castile. These discourses address, describe, and enact history, failure, decline, crisis, patriotism, community, sin, and family. Each has specific content and context, but they also overlap. Each portrays a successive vision of Spain, and each includes its own subdiscourse of labor. Only gradually, "work" itself became a discourse, a collection of discrete practices and attitudes. Going back to unintended consequences, one discourse can set in motion a process of an entirely different nature, growing out of one other but to a different end. One way to settle secular concerns was by using religious language. A way to settle personal disputes was by using political language. A way to settle wage disputes was by using the language of deference. And the way to evaluate Spain's health, its past, its future, its essence, was, in part, by looking at Spaniards' capacity and aversion for labor.

[51] Michael Sonenscher, *Work and Wages: Natural Law, Politics, and the Eighteenth-Century French Trades* (Cambridge University Press, 1989), 54.

Bibliography

Abreu-Ferreira, Darlene. "Work and Identity in Early Modern Portugal: What Did Gender Have to Do with It?" *Journal of Social History* 35, no. 4 (2002): 859–887.

Adler, Hans, and Ernest A. Menze, eds. *On World History: Johann Gottfried Herder, An Anthology*. New York: M. E. Sharpe, 1997.

Alatas, Syed Hussein. *The Myth of the Lazy Native: A Study of the Image of the Malays, Filipinos and Javanese from the 16th to the 20th Century and Its Function in the Ideology of Colonial Capitalism*. London: Frank Cass, 1977.

Altamira, Rafael. *Psicología del pueblo español*. Madrid, 1902.

Altman, Ida. *Emigrants and Society: Extremadura and America in the Sixteenth Century*. Berkeley: University of California Press, 1989.

———. *Transatlantic Ties in the Spanish Empire*. Stanford University Press, 2000.

Alvarez Junco, José. *Mater dolorosa: La idea de España en el siglo XIX*. Madrid: Taurus, 2001.

———. "La nación en duda." In *Más se perdió en Cuba: España, 1898 y la crisis de fin de siglo*, ed. Juan Pan-Montojo et al., 405–475. Madrid: Alianza Editorial, 1998.

———. "La Sociedad Aragonesa de Amigos del País en el siglo XVIII." *Revista de Occidente*, no. 69 (December 1968).

Alvarez Osorio y Redín, Miguel. *Tres memoriales a Carlos II*. 1680s. BN ms. 6659.

Amelang, James. *The Flight of Icarus: Artisan Autobiography in Early Modern Europe*. Stanford University Press, 1999.

———, ed. *A Journal of the Plague Year: The Diary of the Barcelona Tanner Miquel Parets, 1651*. New York: Oxford University Press, 1991.

Amezúa, Agustín G. de. "El bando de policía de 1591 y el pregón general de 1613 para la villa de Madrid." *Revista de la Biblioteca, Archivo y Museo*, no. 38 (April 1933).

———. *La vida privada española en el protocolo notarial. Selección de los siglos XVI, XVII y XVIII del Archivo Notarial de Madrid*. Colegio Notarial de Madrid, 1950.

Anderson, Benedict. *Imagined Communities*. London: Verso, 1991.

Anes de Castrillón, Gonzalo. "Pedro Antonio Sánchez y la honradez de los oficios." *Torre de los Lujanes*, no. 25 (1993).

Archivo General de Indias. *Catálogo de pasajeros a Indias durante los siglos XVI, XVII y XVIII.* 7 vols. Seville: Archivo General de Indias, 1940–1986.

Ardemans, Theodoro. *Ordenanzas de Madrid, y otras diferentes, que se practican en las ciudades de Toledo, y Sevilla con algunas advertencias a los Alarifes, y particulares, y otros capítulos añadidos a la perfecta inteligencia de la materia, que todo se cifra en el govierno político de las fábrica.* 1719. Reprint, Madrid, 1760.

Ariño, Francisco de. *Sucesos de Sevilla de 1592–1604.* Seville: Ayuntamiento de Sevilla, 1993.

Aristotle. *Aristotle's Metaphysics.* Trans. Hippocrates G. Apostle. Bloomington: Indiana University Press, 1966.

——. *The Ethics of Aristotle.* Ed. J. A. K. Thomson. Baltimore: Penguin, 1953.

——. *The Politics of Aristotle.* Ed. and trans. Ernest Barker. Oxford University Press, 1962.

Arphe, Joan. *Quilatador de la plata, oro, y piedras.* Valladolid, 1572.

Arteta de Monteseguro, Antonio. *Disertación sobre el aprecio y estimación que se debe hacer de las artes prácticas y de los que las exercen con honradez, inteligencia y aplicación.* Zaragoza, 1781.

Asenjo González, María. "El obraje de paños en Segovia tras las ordenanzas de los RRCC." In *La manufactura urbana i els menestrales (ss. XIII–XVI) (Actas, IX jornades d'estudis historics locals).* Palma de Mallorca: Govern Balear, 1991.

Asensio, Eugenio. "Américo Castro historiador: Reflexiones sobre 'La realidad histórica de España.'" *MLN* 81 (December 1966): 595–637.

——. *La España imaginada de Américo Castro.* Barcelona: Editorial Crítica, 1992.

Asso y del Río, Ignacio. *Historia de la economía política de Aragón.* 1798. Reprint, Zaragoza: CSIC, 1947.

Aston, T. H., and C. H. E. Philpin, eds. *The Brenner Debate: Agrarian Class Structure and Economic Development in Pre-Industrial Europe.* Cambridge University Press, 1985.

Avila, Juan de. *Obras del Padre Maestro Juan de Avila, Predicador en el Andaluzia.* Madrid, 1588.

Bacigalupo, Mario Ford. "An Ambiguous Image: English Travel Accounts of Spain (1750–1787)." *Dieciocho* 1 (Fall 1978).

Baldwin, John W. *The Medieval Theories of the Just Price: Romanists, Canonists, and Theologians in the Twelfth and Thirteenth Centuries.* Transactions of the American Philosophical Society, vol. 49, pt. 4. Philadelphia: American Philosophical Society, 1959.

Barahona, Renato. *Sex Crimes, Honour, and the Law in Early Modern Spain: Vizcaya, 1528–1735.* University of Toronto Press, 2003.

Barrenechea, José Manuel. *Valentín de Foronda, reformador y economista ilustrado.* Vitoria: Diputación Foral de Alava, 1984.

Barrientos García, José, "El pensamiento económico en la perspectiva filosófico-teológica." In *El pensamiento económico en la Escuela de Salamanca,* ed. Francisco Gómez Camacho and Ricardo Robledo. Universidad de Salamanca, 1998.

Barrientos García, José. *Un siglo de moral económica en Salamanca (1526–1629).* Vol. 1: *Francisco de Vitoria y Domingo de Soto.* Universidad de Salamanca, 1985.

Bazan Diaz, Iñaki. *Delincuencia y criminalidad en el Pais Vasco en la transición de la Edad Media a la moderna.* Vitoria: Gobierno Vasco, 1995.

Bell, David. *The Cult of the Nation in France: Inventing Nationalism, 1680–1800.* Cambridge, Mass.: Harvard University Press, 2001.

——. "Recent Works on Early Modern French National Identity." *Journal of Modern History* 68 (March 1996): 84–113.

Berkhofer, Robert Jr. *Beyond the Great Story: History as Text and Discourse.* Cambridge, Mass.: Belknap Press, 1997.

Berman, Harold. *Law and Revolution.* Cambridge, Mass.: Harvard University Press, 1983.

Bernal, Antonio Miguel, Antonio Collantes de Terán, and Antonio García-Baquero. "Sevilla: De los gremios a la industrialización." *Estudios de Historia Social,* no. 5–6 (1978).

Berry, Christopher J. *The Idea of Luxury: A Conceptual and Historical Investigation.* Cambridge University Press, 1994.

Black, Antony. *Guilds and Civil Society in European Political Thought from the Twelfth Century to the Present.* Ithaca, N.Y.: Cornell University Press, 1984.

Black, Charlene Villaseñor. "Love and Marriage in the Spanish Empire: Depictions of Holy Matrimony and Gender Discourses in the Seventeenth Century." *Sixteenth Century Journal* 32, no. 3 (2001): 637–665.

——. "Trabajo y redención en la España del Siglo de Oro: Imágenes de San José en el taller de carpintero." *Estudios Josefinos* (Valladolid), no. 101 (January–June 1997): 3–23.

Bodin, Jean. *The Six Bookes of a Commonweale* (facs.). Ed. Kenneth Douglass McRae. Cambridge, Mass.: Harvard University Press, 1962.

Boruchoff, David A. "Historiography with License: Isabel, the Catholic Monarch and the Kingdom of God." In *Isabel la Católica, Queen of Castile: Critical Essays,* ed. David A. Boruchoff, 225–294. New York: Palgrave MacMillan, 2003.

Bosch, Alberto. *El Centenario: Apuntes para la historia de la Sociedad Económica Matritense.* Madrid: Impr. y fundición de M. Tello, 1875.

Bossenga, Gail. *The Politics of Privilege: Old Regime and Revolution in Lille.* Cambridge University Press, 1991.

Bossy, John. *Christianity in the West, 1400–1700.* Oxford University Press, 1985.

Boyd, Carolyn. *Historia Patria: Politics, History, and National Identity in Spain, 1875–1975.* Princeton University Press, 1997.

Boyer, Richard. "Honor among Plebeians: 'Mala Sangre' and Social Reputation." In *The Faces of Honor: Sex, Shame, and Violence in Colonial Latin America,* ed. Lyman L. Johnson and Sonya Lipsett-Rivera, 152–178. Albuquerque: University of New Mexico Press, 1998.

Brading, D. A. *The First America: The Spanish Monarchy, Creole Patriots and the Liberal State, 1492–1867.* Cambridge University Press, 1991.

Bravo, Paloma, "El Pasquín: Condiciones de escritura, difusión y recepción en la revuelta aragonesa de 1591." In *L'écrit dans l'Espagne du siècle d'or: Practiques et représentations,* ed. Pedro M. Cátedra. Universidad de Salamanca and Publications de la Sorbonne, 1998.

Breen, Timothy Hall. "The Non-Existent Controversy: Puritan and Anglican Attitudes on Work and Wealth, 1600–1640." *Church History* 35 (1966): 273–287.

Brigden, Susan. "Religion and Social Obligation in Early Sixteenth-Century London." *Past and Present,* no. 103 (May 1984): 67–112.

Broadhead, P. J. "Guildsmen, Religious Reform and the Search for the Common

Good: The Role of the Guilds in the Early Reformation in Augsburg." *Historical Journal* 39, no. 3 (1996): 577–597.

Brown, Jonathan. *Images and Ideas in Seventeenth-Century Spanish Painting.* Princeton University Press, 1978.

Browning, John D. "Cornelius de Pauw and Exiled Jesuits: The Development of Nationalism in Spanish America." *Eighteenth-Century Studies* 11 (Spring 1978): 289–307.

——. "The Periodical Press: Voice of the Enlightenment in Spanish America." *Dieciocho* 3, no. 1 (1980).

Brumont, Francis. *Campo y campesinos de Castila la Vieja en tiempos de Felipe II.* Madrid: Siglo Veintiuno, 1984.

——. *Paysans de Vieille-Castille aux XVI et XVII siècles.* Madrid: Casa de Velázquez, 1993.

Burstin, Haim. "Unskilled Labor in Paris at the End of the Eighteenth Century." In *The Workplace before the Factory: Artisans and Proletarians, 1500–1800,* ed. Thomas Max Safley and Leonard N. Rosenband, 63–72. Ithaca, N.Y.: Cornell University Press, 1993.

Cabrera, Fr. Alonso de. *Sermones.* Ed. Miguel Mir. Nueva Biblioteca de Autores Españoles. Madrid: Casa Editorial Bailly, 1930.

Cabrera, Padre Juan de. *Crisis política determina el mas florido imperio y la mejor institución de príncipes y ministros.* Madrid, 1715.

Cabrera Nuñez de Guzmán, Melchor de. *Discurso legal histórico y político en prueba del origen, progresos, utilidad, nobleza, y excelencias del arte de la Imprenta.* Madrid, 1675.

Cadalso, José. *Cartas marruecas.* 1793. Reprint ed. Joaquin Marco. Madrid: Planeta, 1985.

Calatayud, Padre Pedro de. *Cathecismo práctico y muy útil para la instrucción y enseñanza fácil de los fieles, y para el uso y alivio de los señores parrochos y sacerdotes.* Valladolid, 1747.

——. *Doctrinas prácticas que suele explicar en sus misiones el padre Pedro de Calatayud,* 2 vols. Valencia 1739.

Callahan, William J. *Church, Politics, and Society in Spain, 1750–1874.* Cambridge, Mass.: Harvard University Press, 1984.

——. *Honor, Commerce and Industry in Eighteenth-Century Spain.* Boston: Baker Library, Harvard University, 1972.

——. "Moralidad católica y cambio económico." *Manuscrits,* no. 20 (2002).

——. "A Note on the Real y General Junta de Comercio, 1679–1814." *Economic History Review* 21 (December 1968): 519–528.

——. *La Santa y Real Hermandad del Refugio y Piedad de Madrid, 1618–1832.* Madrid: CSIC, 1980.

——. "Utility, Material Progress, and Morality in 18th Century Spain." In *The Triumph of Culture: 18th Century Perspectives,* ed. Paul Fritz and David Williams, 353–368. Toronto: A. M. Hakkert, 1972.

Cámara Muñoz, Alicia. *Arquitectura y sociedad en el Siglo de Oro.* Madrid: Ediciones El Arquero, 1990.

Camós de Requesens, Marco Antonio. *Microcosmia y govierno universal del hombre christiano para todos los estados y qualquiera de ellos.* Barcelona, 1592.

Campillo y Cosío, José. *Lo que hay de mas y de menos en España para que sea lo que debe ser y no lo que es.* Ed. Antonio Elorza. Universidad de Madrid, 1969.

——. *Nuevo sistema económico para America.* 1789. Reprint ed. Manuel Ballesteros Gaibois. Oviedo: Grupo Editorial Asturiano, 1993.

Campomanes, Pedro Rodríguez de. *Apéndice a la Educación Popular.* 4 vols. Madrid, 1775.

——. *Discurso sobre la educación popular.* 1775. Reprint ed. F. Aguilar Piñal. Madrid: Editora Nacional, 1978.

——. *Discurso sobre el fomento de la industria popular.* Madrid, 1774.

Campomanes y su tiempo (exhibit catalogue). Madrid: Fundación Santander Central Hispano, 2003.

Cañabata Navarro, Eduardo. *Ordenanza [sic] de los gremios de Cartagena en el siglo XVIII.* Murcia, 1962.

Cañizares-Esguerra, Jorge. "Eighteenth-Century Spanish Political Economy: Epistemology and Decline." *Eighteenth-Century Thought,* no. 1 (2003): 295–314.

——. *How to Write the History of the New World. Histories, Epistemologies, and Identities in the Eighteenth-Century Atlantic World.* Stanford University Press, 2001.

——. "New World, New Stars: Patriotic Astrology and the Invention of Indian and Creole Bodies in Colonial Spanish America, 1600–1650." *American Historical Review* 104 (February 1999): 33–68.

Capella, Miguel, and Antonio Matilla Tascón. *Los Cinco Gremios Mayores de Madrid.* Madrid, 1957.

Capmany, Antonio de [Ramón Miguel Palacio, pseud.]. *Discurso político económico en defensa del trabajo mecánico de los menestrales y de la influencia de sus gremios en las costumbres populares, conservacion de las artes y honor de los artesanos.* 1778. Reprint, Madrid: Almarabu, 1986.

Capmany, Aureli, and Agustí Durán. *El gremio de los maestros zapateros.* Barcelona: Ediciones Aymá, 1944.

Carbajo Isla, María F. *La población de la villa de Madrid desde finales del siglo XVI hasta mediados del siglo XIX.* Madrid: Siglo Veintiuno, 1987.

Caro Baroja, Julio. *El mito del caracter nacional. Meditaciones a contrapelo.* Madrid: Seminarios y Ediciones, 1970.

Carr, Raymond. *Spain, 1808–1975.* 2d ed. Oxford University Press, 1989.

Carrera Stampa, Manuel. *Los gremios mexicanos: La organización gremial en Nueva España, 1521–1861.* Mexico City: EDIAPSA, 1954.

Carreras Panchon, Antonio. "Las actividades de los barberos durante los siglos XVI al XVIII." *Cuadernos de historia de la medicina española,* no. 13 (1974).

Casanova, Giacomo. *The Memoirs of Jacques Casanova: An Autobiography.* London: Venetian Society, 1928.

Casey, James. *Early Modern Spain: A Social History.* London: Routledge, 1999.

——. "Household Disputes and the Law in Early Modern Andalusia." In *Disputes and Settlements: Law and Human Relations in the West,* ed. John Bossy, 189–217. Cambridge University Press, 1983.

Casey, James, and Bernard Vincent. "Casa y familia en la Granada del Antiguo Régimen." In *La familia en la España mediterránea,* ed. James Casey et al., 172–211. Barcelona: Crítica, 1987.

Castilla, Francisco. *Theórica de virtudes en coplas de arte humilde con comento.* Murcia, 1518.

Castillo de Bobadilla, Jerónimo. *Política para corregidores y señores de vasallos.* 2 vols. Madrid, 1597.

Castro, Américo. *De la edad conflictiva*. 2d ed. Madrid: Taurus, 1963.
——. *La realidad histórica de España*. 1954. Reprint, México: Ed. Porrúa, 1982.
——. *The Structure of Spanish History*. Trans. Edmund L. King. Princeton University Press, 1954.
Castro, Concepción. *Campomanes: Estado y reformismo ilustrado*. Madrid: Alianza Editorial, 1996.
Castro y Bravo, Federico de. *Las naos españolas en la carrera de las Indias. Armadas y flotas en la segunda mitad del siglo XVI*. Madrid: Editorial Voluntad, 1927.
Cavillac, Michel. *Gueux et marchands dans le "Guzmán de Alfarache" (1599–1604): Roman picaresque et mentalité bourgeoise dans l'Espagne du Siècle d'Or*. Université de Bordeaux, 1983.
——. "Le marchand, l'honneur et la noblesse en Castille au siècle d'or." In *Les sociétés fermées dans le monde iberique (xvi–xviii siècles)*. Paris: CNRS, 1986.
El Censor: Obra periódica, comenzada a publicar en 1781 y terminada en 1787. Ed. José María Caso González et al. Oviedo: Instituto Feijóo de Estudios del Siglo XVIII, 1989.
Cerutti, Simona. "Group Strategies and Trade Strategies: The Turin Tailors' Guild in the Late Seventeenth and Early Eighteenth Centuries." In *Domestic Strategies: Work and Family in France and Italy 1600{endash}1800*, ed. S. Woolf, 102–147. Cambridge University Press, 1991.
——. *La ville et les métiers: Naissance d'un langage corporatif (Turin, 17–18 siècles)*. Paris: Editions de l'École des Hautes Études en Sciences Sociales, 1990.
Cervantes, Miguel de. *El ingenioso hidalgo Don Quijote de la Mancha*. Madrid: Clásicos Castalia, 1978.
Chartier, Roger. *The Cultural Origins of the French Revolution*. Trans. Lydia G. Cochrane. Durham, N.C.: Duke University Press, 1991.
Chauchadis, Claude. "Les modalités de la fermeture dans les confréries religieuses espagnoles (XVI–XVIII siècles)." In *Les sociétés fermées dans le monde iberique (xvi–xviii siècles)*. Paris: CNRS, 1986.
Chevalier, Maxime. *Lectura y lectores en la España de los siglos XVI y XVII*. Madrid: Ediciones Turner, 1976.
Christian, William A., Jr. *Local Religion in Sixteenth-Century Spain*. Princeton University Press, 1981.
Cicero. *On Duties*. Trans. and ed. M. T. Griffin and E. M. Atkins. Cambridge University Press, 1991.
Clavijo y Faxardo, José. *El Pensador*. 1763. Reprint, Universidad de Las Palmas de Gran Canaria, 1999.
Cohn, Samuel Kline, Jr. *The Laboring Classes in Renaissance Florence*. New York: Academic Press, 1980.
Colish, Marcia L. *Medieval Foundations of the Western Intellectual Tradition 400–1400*. New Haven: Yale University Press, 1997.
——. *The Stoic Tradition from Antiquity to the Early Middle Ages*. Leiden: E. J. Brill, 1985.
Collantes de Terán Sánchez, Antonio. "Los poderes públicos y las ordenanzas de oficios." In *La manufactura urbana i els menestrales (ss. XIII–XVI) (Actas, IX jornades d'estudis historics locals.)* Palma de Mallorca: Govern Balear, 1991
Cope, R. Douglas. *The Limits of Racial Domination: Plebeian Society in Colonial Mexico City, 1660–1720*. Madison: University of Wisconsin Press, 1994.
"Copia paleográfica de los antiguos Libros de Cabildo del Exmo. Ayuntamiento de Esta Capital," 6 vols. Mexico, 1849. Newberry Library. Ayer ms. 1143.

Córdoba, Fr. Antonio de. *Tratado de casos de consciencia.* Zaragoza, 1581.

Corteguera, Luis. "The Painter Who Lost His Hat: Artisans and Justice in Early Modern Barcelona." *Sixteenth Century Journal* 29, no. 4 (1998): 1023–1042.

Costa, Joaquín. *Historia política social patria.* Ed. José García Mercadal. Madrid: Aguilar, 1961.

Coxe, William. *Memoirs of the Kings of Spain of the House of Bourbon,* 3 vols. London, 1813.

Crossick, Geoffrey. "Past Masters: In Search of the Artisan in European History." In *The Artisan and the European Town, 1500–1900,* ed. G. Crossick, 1–40. Aldershot, U.K.: Ashgate, 1997.

Crowston, Clare Haru. *Fabricating Women: The Seamstresses of Old Regime France, 1675–1791.* Durham, N.C.: Duke University Press, 2001.

Cruz, Anne J. *Discourses of Poverty: Social Reform and the Picaresque Novel in Early Modern Spain.* University of Toronto Press, 1999.

Curcio-Nagy, Linda A. *The Great Festivals of Colonial Mexico City. Performing Power and Identity.* Albuquerque: University of New Mexico Press, 2004.

Dánvila y Collado, Manuel. *Reinado de Carlos III,* 6 vols. Madrid: Real Academia de la Historia, 1894.

Davis, Natalie Zemon. *Women on the Margins: Three Seventeenth-Century Lives.* Cambridge, Mass.: Harvard University Press, 1995.

Davis, Robert C. *Shipbuilders of the Venetian Arsenal: Workers and Workplace in the Preindustrial City.* Baltimore: Johns Hopkins University Press, 1991.

Deceulaer, Harald. "Guilds and Litigation: Conflict Settlement in Antwerp (1585–1796)." In *Statuts individuels, statuts corporatifs et statuts justiciaires dans les villes européennes (Moyen âge et temps modernes). Actes du colloque tenu à Gand les 12–14 Oct. 1996,* ed. Marc Boone and Maarten Prak. Leuven: Garant, 1996.

Dedieu, Jean-Pierre. "*Limpieza,* pouvoir et richesse: Conditions d'entrée dans le corps des ministres de l'inquisition Tribunal de Tolède—XVIe–XVIIe siècles." In *Les sociétés fermées dans le monde iberique (xvi–xviii siècles).* Paris: CNRS, 1986.

Demerson, Jorge. *La Real Sociedad Económica de Valladolid (1784–1808).* Universidad de Valladolid, 1969.

Desportes Bielsa, Pablo. "Entre mecánicos y honorables. La 'élite popular' en la Zaragoza del siglo XVII." *Revista de Historia Jerónimo Zurita,* no. 75 (2000): 55–74.

Deza, Lope de. *Gobierno político de agricultura.* 1618. Reprint, ed. Angel García Sanz. Madrid: Instituto de Estudios Fiscales, 1991.

Díez, Fernando. "El gremialismo de Antonio de Capmany (1742–1813). La idea del trabajo de un conservador ingénuo." *Historia y política: Ideas, procesos y movimientos sociales,* no. 5 (2001).

——. *Viles y mecánicos: Trabajo y sociedad en la Valencia preindustrial.* Valencia: Institució valenciana d'estudis i investigació, 1990.

Domínguez Ortiz, Antonio. *Alteraciones andaluzas.* Madrid: Narcea, S.A., 1973.

——. *Las clases privilegiadas en el Antiguo Régimen.* 3d ed. Madrid: Istmo, 1985.

——. "Notas sobre la consideración social del trabajo manual y el comercio en el antiguo régimen." *Revista del trabajo,* no. 7–8 (July–August 1945).

——. *Política y hacienda de Felipe IV.* Madrid: Ediciones Pegaso, 1983.

——. *Sociedad y estado en el siglo XVIII español.* Barcelona: Ariel, 1990.

Dyer, Abigail. "Seduction by Promise of Marriage: Law, Sex, and Culture in Seventeenth-Century Spain." *Sixteenth Century Journal* 34, no. 2 (2003): 439–455.

Eamon, William. *Science and the Secrets of Nature: Books of Secrets in Medieval and Early Modern Culture*. Princeton University Press, 1994.

Earle, Rebecca. "Consumption and Excess in Spanish America (1700–1830)," working paper, Centre for Latin American Cultural Studies, University of Manchester, April 2003.

———. "Creole Patriotism and the Myth of the 'Loyal Indian.'" *Past and Present*, no. 172 (August 2001): 125–45.

Edwards, John. "The Beginnings of a Scientific Theory of Race? Spain, 1450–1600." In *From Iberia to Diaspora: Studies in Sephardic History and Culture*, ed. Yedida K. Stillman and Norman A. Stillman, 179–196. Leiden: E. J. Brill, 1999.

Elliott, J. H. "A Europe of Composite Monarchies." *Past and Present*, no. 137 (November 1992): 48–71.

———. "Nueva luz sobre la prisión de Quevedo y Adam de la Parra." *Boletín de la Real Academia de la Historia* 169 (January–April 1972).

———. *Spain and Its World 1500–1700*. New Haven: Yale University Press, 1989.

Elorza, Antonio. *La ideología liberal en la ilustración española*. Madrid: Editorial Tecnos, 1970.

———. "Introducción: La formación de los artesanos y la ideología ilustrada." *Revista de trabajo*, no. 24 (1968).

———. "La polémica sobre los oficios viles en la España del siglo XVIII." *Revista de trabajo*, no. 22 (1968).

Epstein, S. R. "Craft Guilds, Apprenticeship, and Technological Change in Preindustrial Europe." *Journal of Economic History* 58 (September 1998): 684–713.

Epstein, Steven. *Wage Labor and Guilds in Medieval Europe*. Chapel Hill: University of North Carolina Press, 1991.

Estella, Diego de. *Libro de la vanidad del mundo*, 3 vols. Barcelona, 1582.

Fabié, Antonio María, ed. *Viajes por España*. Madrid: Librería de los Bibliófilos, 1879.

Fairman, Patricia Shaw. *España vista por los ingleses del siglo XVII*. Madrid: Sociedad General Española de Librería, 1981.

Fanshawe, Richard. *Original Letters of His Excellency Sir Richard Fanshawe during his Embassies in Spain and Portugal*. London, 1702.

Farr, James R. *Artisans in Europe, 1300–1914*. Cambridge University Press, 2000.

———. "Cultural Analysis and Early Modern Artisans." In *The Artisan and the European Town, 1500–1900*, ed. Geoffrey Crossick, 56–74. Aldershot, U.K.: Ashgate, 1997.

———. *Hands of Honor: Artisans and Their World in Dijon 1550–1650*. Ithaca, N.Y.: Cornell University Press, 1988.

———. "On the Shop Floor: Guilds, Artisans, and the European Market Economy, 1350–1750." *Journal of Early Modern History* 1 (February 1997): 24–54.

Fayard, Janine. *Les membres du Conseil de Castille a l'époque moderne 1621–1746*. Geneva: Droz, 1979.

Feijóo, Benito Jerónimo, "Glorias de España" (1730). Biblioteca de Autores Españoles, vol. 56. Madrid, 1952.

———. *Teatro crítico universal*. Ed. Giovanni Stiffoni. Madrid: Clásicos Castalia, 1986.

Fernández Albaladejo, Pablo. *Fragmentos de monarquía*. Madrid: Alianza Universidad, 1992.

Fernández de Lizardi, José Joaquín. *El Periquillo Sarniento*. Mexico: Editorial Stylo, 1942.

Fernández Navarrete, Pedro. *Conservación de monarquías.* Madrid, 1626.

Fernández-Santamaría, J. A. *The State, War, and Peace: Spanish Political Thought in the Renaissance 1516–1559.* Cambridge University Press, 1977.

Ferrer del Río, Antonio. *Historia del reinado de Carlos III en España.* 4 vols. Madrid: Impr. de Matute y Compagni, 1856.

Flynn, Maureen. "Baroque Piety and Spanish Confraternities." In *Confraternities and Catholic Reform in Italy, France, and Spain,* ed. John Patrick Donnelly, S.J., and Michael Maher. Kirksville, Mo.: Thomas Jefferson University Press, 1999.

———. *Sacred Charity: Confraternities and Social Welfare in Spain, 1400–1700.* Ithaca, N.Y.: Cornell University Press, 1989.

Foronda, Valentín de. *Miscelánea o colección de varios discursos en que se tratan los asuntos siguientes . . .* Madrid, 1787.

Fortea Pérez, José Ignacio. "Los abusos del poder: El común y el gobierno de las ciudades de Castilla tras la rebelión de las Comunidades." In *Furor et rabies: Violencia, conflicto y marginación en la Edad Moderna,* ed. José Ignacio Fortea Pérez et al. Santander: Universidad de Cantabria, 2003.

———. *Córdoba en el siglo XVI: Las bases demográficas y económicas de una expansión urbana.* Córdoba: Monte Piedad y Caja de Ahorros de Córdoba, 1981.

———. "The Textile Industry in the Economy of Córdoba at the End of the Seventeenth and the Start of the Eighteenth Centuries: A Frustrated Recovery." In *The Castilian Crisis of the Seventeenth Century: New Perspectives on the Economic and Social History of Seventeenth-Century Spain,* ed. I. A. A. Thompson and Bartolomé Yun Casalilla, 136–168. Cambridge University Press, 1994.

Fox, Inman. *La invención de España.* Madrid: Cátedra, 1997.

Fradera, Josep M. "Spanish Colonial Historiography: Everyone in Their Place." *Social History* 29 (August 2004): 368–372.

Fraser, Angus. *The Gypsies.* Oxford: Blackwell, 1992.

Freedman, Paul. *Images of the Medieval Peasant.* Stanford University Press, 1999.

Fusi, Juan Pablo. *España: La evolución de la identidad nacional.* Madrid: Temas de Hoy, 2000.

Galinsky, G. Karl. *The Herakles Theme: The Adaptations of the Hero in Literature from Homer to the Twentieth Century.* Oxford: Blackwell, 1972.

Ganivet, Angel. *Idearium español. El porvenir de España.* Madrid: Espasa-Calpe, 1999.

García Calonga, Milagros. *El poder municipal de Calahorra en el siglo XVII.* Amigos de la Historia de Calahorra, 1998.

García de la Torre, Fuensanta. *Estudio histórico-artístico de la Hermandad del Gremio de Toneleros de Sevilla.* Seville: Consejo General de Hermandades y Cofradías, 1979.

García Fernández, Máximo. *Los viejos oficios vallisoletanos.* Valladolid: Neumáticos Michelin, 1996.

García Mercadal, José, ed. *Viajes por España.* 2d ed. Madrid: Alianza, 1972.

García-Oliva Pérez, Mario. "'Oficios mecánicos' en la nobleza montañesa." *Hidalguia,* no. 46 (May–June 1961).

García Sáiz, María Concepción. *Las castas mexicanas: Un género pictórico americano.* Milan: Olivetti, 1989.

García Sanz, Angel. "El contexto económico del pensamiento escolástico: El florecimiento del capital mercantil en la España del siglo XVI." In *El pensamiento económico en la Escuela de Salamanca,* ed. Francisco Gómez Camacho and Ricardo Robledo. Universidad de Salamanca, 1998.

———. "Organización productiva y relaciones contractuales en la pañería segoviana en el siglo XVI." In *La manufactura urbana i els menestrales (ss. XIII–XVI) (Actas, IX jornades d'estudis historics locals.)* Palma de Mallorca: Govern Balear, 1991.

Garmendia Larrañaga, Juan. *Gremios, oficios y cofradias en el Pais Vasco.* San Sebastian: Caja de Ahorros de Guipuzcoa, 1979.

Garrioch, David. *Neighborhood and Community in Paris 1740–1790.* Cambridge University Press, 1986.

Garzoni, Tommaso. *La piazza universale di tutte le professioni del mondo.* 1585. Ed. Giovanni Battista Bronzini. 2 vols. Reprint, Florence: Leo S. Olschki Editore, 1996.

Garzoni, Tomaso. *Plaza universal de todas ciencias y artes.* Spanish ed. and trans. by Christobal Suárez de Figueroa. Madrid, 1615.

Generés, Miguel Dámaso. *Reflexiones políticas y económicas sobre la población, agricultura, artes, fábricas y comercio del Reino de Aragón.* 1793. Reprint ed. Ernest Lluch and Alfonso Sánchez Hormigo. Zaragoza: Institución Fernando el Católico, 1996.

Gerbi, Antonello. *The Dispute of the New World: The History of a Polemic, 1750–1900.* 1955. Trans. Jeremy Moyle. Reprint, University of Pittsburgh Press, 1973.

Gies, David T. "Dos preguntas regeneracionistas: '¿Qué se debe a España?' y '¿Qué es España?' Identidad nacional en Forner, Moratín, Jovellanos y la Generación de 1898." *Dieciocho* 22 (Fall 1999).

Giginta, Miguel. *Tratado de remedio de pobres* (Coimbra, 1579). Barcelona: Editorial Ariel, 2000.

Gil Pujol, Xavier. "Ciudadanía, patria y humanismo cívico en el Aragón foral: Juan Costa." *Manuscrits* 19 (2001).

Gilabert, Francisco de. *Discurso sobre la verdadera nobleza, efectos de la justa, y injusta guerra: dirigido al branco militar del Principado de Cataluña . . .* Lérida, 1616.

Gilchrist, J. *The Church and Economic Activity in the Middle Ages.* London: Macmillan, 1969.

Glendinning, Nigel. *A Literary History of Spain: The Eighteenth Century.* New York: Barnes and Noble, 1972.

Gómez Camacho, Francisco, ed. *Luis de Molina: La teoría del justo precio.* Madrid: Editora Nacional, 1981.

Gómez Zorraquino, José Ignacio. "Ni señores, ni campesinos/artesanos. El gobierno de los ciudadanos en Aragón." In *Burgueses o ciudadanos en la España moderna*, ed. Francisco José Aranda Pérez. Cuenca: Universidad de Castilla-La Mancha, 2003.

González Alonso, Benjamín. *Sobre el estado y la administración de la corona de Castilla en el antiguo régimen.* Madrid: Siglo Veintiuno, 1981.

González Arce, José Damián. *Gremios, producción artesanal y mercado: Murcia, siglos XIV y XV.* Universidad de Murcia, 2000.

González Castillejo, María José. "Los héroes del deber, o el trabajo como virtud en España durante la dictadura de Primo de Rivera." *Baética,* no. 24 (2002).

González de Cellorigo, Martín. *Memorial de la política necesaria y util restauración a la Repúblicade España y estados de ella y del desempeño universal de estos reinos.* 1600. Reprint ed. José L. Pérez de Ayala. Madrid: Instituto de Estudios Fiscales, 1991.

González Mínguez, César. "Los tejedores de Palencia durante la Edad Media." *Publicaciones de la Institución Tello Tellez de Meneses,* no. 63 (1992).

González Múñoz, María del Carmen. "Datos para un estudio de Madrid en la primera mitad del siglo XVII." *Anales del Instituto de Estudios Madrileños* 18 (1981): 149–185.

González Palencia, Angel, ed. *La Junta de Reformación, 1618–1625.* Vol. 5 of *Colección de documentos inéditos para la historia de España y de sus Indias.* Valladolid: Archivo Histórico Español, 1932.

Goodman, David. *Spanish Naval Power, 1589–1665: Reconstruction and Defeat.* Cambridge University Press, 1997.

Granada, Luis de. *Guía de Pecadores.* Barcelona, 1625.

Green, Otis H. "On the Attitude toward the Vulgo in the Spanish Siglo de Oro." *Studies in the Renaissance* 4 (1957): 190–200.

Gremios y cofradías en la Nueva España (exhibit catalogue). Mexico: Museo Nacional del Virreinato, 1996.

Grice-Hutchinson, Marjorie. *Early Economic Thought in Spain 1177–1740.* London: Allen and Unwin, 1978.

Groppi, Angela. "Jews, Women, Soldiers, and Neophytes: The Practice of Trades under Exclusions and Privileges (Rome from the Seventeenth to the Early Nineteenth Centuries)." In *Guilds, Markets and Work Regulations in Italy, 16th–19th Centuries,* ed. Alberto Guenzi et al., 372–392. Aldershot, U.K.: Ashgate, 1998.

Guenzi, Alberto, Paola Massa, Fausto Piola Caselli, eds. *Guilds, Markets and Work Regulations in Italy, 16th–19th Centuries.* Aldershot, U.K.: Ashgate, 1998.

Guerrero Mayllo, Ana. *Familia y vida cotidiana de una élite de poder: Los regidores madrileños en tiempos de Felipe II.* Madrid: Siglo Veintiuno, 1993.

Guevara, Antonio de. *Menosprecio de Corte y Alabanza de Aldea.* 1539. Reprint ed. Asunción Rallo. Madrid: Cátedra, 1984.

Guichot y Parody, Joaquín. *Historia de la ciudad de Sevilla.* Seville, 1889.

———. *Historia del Excmo. Ayuntamiento de la muy noble, muy leal, muy heróica é invicta Ciudad de Sevilla.* Seville, 1897.

Guillamon Alvarez, Javier. *Honor y honra en la España del siglo XVIII.* Madrid: Universidad Complutense, 1981.

Guthrie, William. *A New Geographical, Historical, and Commercial Grammar and Present State of the Several Kingdoms of the World.* 12th ed. London, 1790.

Gutiérrez Alonso, Adriano. *Estudio sobre la decadencia de Castilla: La ciudad de Valladolid en el siglo XVII.* Universidad de Valladolid, 1989.

Gutiérrez de los Ríos, Carlos, count of Fernán Núñez. *Vida de Carlos III.* 2 vols. Madrid: F. Fé, 1898.

Gutiérrez de los Ríos, Gaspar. *Noticia general para la estimación de las artes y de la manera en que se conocen las liberales de las que son mecánicas y serviles, con una exortación a la honra de la virtud y el trabajo contra los ociosos y otras particulares para las personas de todos los estados.* Madrid, 1600.

Gutiérrez Nieto, Juan Ignacio. "El pensamiento económico político y social de los arbitristas." In *Historia de España,* ed. Ramón Menéndez Pidal. Vol. 26, pt. 1: *El Siglo de Quixote: Religión, filosofía, ciencia,* 235–351. Madrid: Espasa Calpe, 1986.

———. "Semántica del término 'comunidad' antes de 1520: Las asociaciones juramentadas de defensa." *Hispania,* no. 136 (1977).

Guzmán, Pedro de. *Bienes del honesto trabajo y daños de la ociosidad, en ocho discursos.* Madrid, 1614.

Hamilton, Bernice. *Political Thought in Sixteenth-Century Spain.* Oxford University Press, 1963.

Hanke, Lewis. *The Spanish Struggle for Justice in the Conquest of America.* University Park, Penn.: University of Pennsylvania Press, 1949.

Herder, Johann Gottfried von. *Reflections on the Philosophy of the History of Mankind.* Ed. and abridged Frank E. Manuel. University of Chicago Press, 1968.

Heredia Moreno, María Carmen. *Estudio de los contratos de aprendizaje artístico en Sevilla a comienzos del S. XVIII.* Seville, 1975.

Hernández Benítez, Mauro. "Carlos III: Un mito progresista." In *Carlos III, Madrid y la Ilustración,* ed. Equipo Madrid, 1–23. Madrid: Siglo Veintiuno, 1988.

Herr, Richard. *The Eighteenth-Century Revolution in Spain.* Princeton University Press, 1958.

——. *Rural Change and Royal Finances in Spain at the End of the Old Regime.* Berkeley: University of California Press, 1989.

Herrera, Gabriel Alonso de. *Libro de agricultura copilado de diversos autores por Gabriel Alonso de Herrera.* Zaragoza, 1524.

Herrero García, Miguel. *Ideas de los españoles del siglo XVII.* 1927. Reprint, Madrid: Editorial Gredos, 1966.

——. *Oficios populares en la sociedad de Lope de Vega.* Madrid: Editorial Castalia, 1977.

Herrero Salgado, Félix. *La oratoria sagrada en los siglos XVI y XVII.* Madrid: Fundación Universitaria Española, 1996.

Herzog, Tamar. *Defining Nations: Immigrants and Citizens in Early Modern Spain and Spanish America.* New Haven: Yale University Press, 2003.

——. "Vecindad y oficio en Castilla: La actividad económica y la exclusión política en el siglo XVIII." In *Furor et Rabies: Violencia, conflicto y marginación en la Edad Moderna,* ed. José I. Fortea et al., 239–252. Santander: Universidad de Cantabria, 2002.

Hill, Christopher. "Pottage for Freeborn Englishmen: Attitudes to Wage Labour in the Sixteenth and Seventeenth Centuries." In *Socialism, Capitalism and Economic Growth: Essays Presented to Maurice Dobb,* ed. C. H. Feinstein, 338–350. Cambridge University Press, 1967.

——. *Society and Puritanism in Pre-Revolutionary England.* 2d ed. New York: Schocken Books, 1967.

Hillgarth, J. N. *The Mirror of Spain, 1500–1700: The Formation of a Myth. History, Languages and Cultures of the Spanish and Portuguese Worlds.* Ann Arbor: University of Michigan Press, 2000.

——. "Spanish Historiography and Iberian Reality." *History and Theory* 24, no. 1 (1985): 23–43.

——. *The Spanish Kingdoms, 1250–1516,* 2 vols. Oxford: Clarendon Press, 1976.

Hirschman, Albert O. *The Passions and the Interests: Political Arguments for Capitalism before Its Triumph.* 20th anniversary edition. Princeton University Press, 1997.

Homza, Lu Ann. *Religious Authority in the Spanish Renaissance.* Baltimore: John Hopkins University Press, 2000.

Hoyland, John. *A Historical Survey of the Customs, Habits, and Present State of The Gypsies; Designed to Develope the Origin of this Singular People and to Promote the Amelioration of their Condition.* London, 1816.

Hume, David. "Of National Characters." In his *Essays, Moral, Political, and Literary.* 1742. Available at www.econlib.org/library/LFBooks/Hume/hmMPL21.html

Hunt, Lynn, and George Sheridan. "Corporativism, Association, and the Language of Labor in France, 1750–1850." *Journal of Modern History* 58 (December 1986): 813–844.

Iglesias, María Carmen. "Montesquieu and Spain: Iberian Identity as Seen through the Eyes of a Non-Spaniard of the Eighteenth Century." In *Iberian Identity: Essays on the Nature of Identity in Portugal and Spain,* ed. Richard Herr and John H. R. Polt. Berkeley: University of California Press, 1989.

Ilie, Paul. "Exomorphism: Cultural Bias and the French Image of Spain from the War of Succession to the Age of Voltaire." *Eighteenth-Century Studies* 9 (Spring 1976): 375–389.

Iradiel Murugarren, Paulino. *Evolucion de la industria textil castellana en los siglos XIII–XVI: Factores de desarrollo, organización y costes de la producción manufactura en Cuenca.* Universidad de Salamanca, 1974.

Israel, Jonathan I. *Race, Class and Politics in Colonial Mexico 1610–1670.* Oxford University Press, 1975.

———. *Radical Enlightenment: Philosophy and the Making of Modernity, 1650–1750.* Oxford University Press, 2001.

Jago, Charles. "The 18th-Century Economic Analysis of the Decline of Spain." In *The Triumph of Culture: 18th-Century Perspectives,* ed. Paul Fritz and David Williams, 335–352. Toronto: A. M. Hakkert, 1972.

Johnson, Lyman. "Artisans." In *Cities and Society in Colonial Latin America,* ed. Louisa Schell Hoberman and Susan Migden Socolow. Albuquerque: University of New Mexico Press, 1986.

Jovellanos, Gaspar Melchor de. *Obras,* 5 vols. Ed. Cándido Nocedal (1–2) and Miguel Artola (3–5). Biblioteca de Autores Españoles, vols. 46, 50, 85, 86, 87. Madrid, 1858–1956.

Joyce, Patrick, ed. *The Historical Meanings of Work.* Cambridge University Press, 1987.

Juan, Jorge, and Antonio de Ulloa. *Noticias secretas de América.* Ed. David Barry. London, 1826.

Juderías, Julián. *La leyenda negra: Estudios acerca del concepto de España en el extranjero.* 1914. Reprint, Salamanca: Junta de Castilla y León, 1997.

Jütte, Robert. *Poverty and Deviance in Early Modern Europe.* Cambridge University Press, 1994.

Kagan, Richard. "Clio and the Crown: Writing History in Habsburg Spain." In *Spain, Europe and the Atlantic World: Essays in Honour of John H. Elliott,* ed. Richard L. Kagan and Geoffrey Parker, 73–99. Cambridge University Press, 1995.

———, ed. *Spain in America: The Origins of Hispanism in the United States.* Urbana: University of Illinois Press, 2002.

Kamen, Henry. "Una crisis de conciencia en la Edad de Oro en España: Inquisición contra 'limpieza de sangre.'" *Bulletin Hispanique* 88 (July–December 1986): 321–356.

———. "Limpieza and the Ghost of Américo Castro: Racism as a Tool of Literary Analysis." *Hispanic Review* 64 (Winter 1996): 19–29.

———. *Spain in the Later Seventeenth Century (1665–1700).* London: Longman, 1980.

Katzew, Ilona. "Casta Painting: Identity and Social Stratification in Colonial Mexico." In *New World Orders: Casta Painting and Colonial Latin America,* ed. Ilona Katzew et al. New York: Americas Society Art Gallery, 1996.

Kollmann, Nancy Shields. *By Honor Bound: State and Society in Early Modern Russia.* Ithaca, N.Y.: Cornell University Press, 1999.

Konetzke, Richard. "Las ordenanzas de gremios como documentos para la historia social de Hispano-américa durante la época colonial." *Estudios de historia social de España* 1 (1949).

———, ed. *Colección de documentos para la historia de la formación social de Hispanoamérica, 1493–1810.* 5 vols. Madrid: CSIC, 1953–1962.

Krebs Wilckens, Ricardo. *El pensamiento histórico, político y económico del conde de Campomanes.* Santiago de Chile: Universidad de Chile, 1960.

Kupperman, Karen Ordahl. *Indians and English: Facing Off in Early America.* Ithaca, N.Y.: Cornell University Press, 2000.

——. *Settling With the Indians: The Meeting of English and Indian Cultures in America, 1580–1640.* Totowa, N.J.: Rowman and Littlefield, 1980.

Lafargue, Paul. *The Right to Be Lazy.* 1883. Reprint, Chicago: Charles H. Kerr, 1975.

La Force, James Clayburn. *The Development of the Spanish Textile Industry, 1750–1800.* Berkeley: University of California Press, 1965.

Lario, Dámaso de. "El requisito de pobreza en los colegios mayores españoles." *Pedralbes,* no. 15 (1995).

Larquié, Claude. "La alfabetizacion de los madrileños en 1650." *Anales del Instituto de Estudios Madrileños* 17 (1980).

——. "Barrios y parroquias urbanas: El ejemplo de Madrid en el siglo XVII." *Anales del Instituto de Estudios Madrileños* 12 (1976).

Larruga y Boneta, Eugenio. *Historia de la Real y General Junta de Comercio, Moneda y Minas y Dependiencias Estrangeros y colección integra de los reales decretos, pragmáticas, resoluciones, órdenes y reglamentos.* 12 vols. Madrid, 1779–1789.

——. *Memorias políticas y económicas sobre los frutos, comercio, fábricas y minas de España, con inclusión de los reales decretos, ordenes, cédulas, aranceles y ordenanzas expedidas para su gobierno y fomento.* 45 vols. Madrid, 1787.

Lavallé, Bernard. *Concepción, representación y papel del espacio en la reivindicación criolla en el Perú colonial.* Lima: Universidad Nacional Federico Villarreal, 1982.

——. *Las promesas ambiguas. Criollismo colonial en los Andes.* Lima: Pontificia Universidad Católica del Perú, 1993.

Le Goff, Jacques. *Time, Work, and Culture in the Middle Ages.* University of Chicago Press, 1980.

——. *Your Money or Your Life: Economy and Religion in the Middle Ages.* New York: Zone Books, 1988.

León, Fr. Luís de. *La Perfecta Casada.* 1583. Reprint, Madrid: Taurus, 1987.

Levi, Giovanni. *Inheriting Power: The Story of an Exorcist.* University of Chicago Press, 1988.

——. "Reciprocidad mediterránea." *Hispania* 60/1, no. 204 (2000).

Lewis, A. H. *A Critical History of the Sabbath and the Sunday in the Christian Church.* Plainfield, N.J.: American Sabbath Tract Society, 1903.

Lida, Raimundo. "Quevedo y su España antigua." *Romance Philology* 17 (November 1963): 253–271.

Lisón Tolosana, Carmelo. "Las Españas de los españoles." *Revista española de investigaciones sociológicas,* no. 40 (1987).

Liss, Peggy J. *Atlantic Empires: The Network of Trade and Revolution, 1713–1826.* Baltimore: Johns Hopkins University Press, 1983.

——. *Mexico under Spain, 1521–1556.* University of Chicago Press, 1975.

Llombart, Vicent. *Campomanes, economista y político de Carlos III.* Madrid: Alianza Universidad, 1992.

Llordén, Andrés. *Ensayo histórico-documental de los maestros plateros malagueños en los siglos XVI y XVII.* Málaga: Ricardo Sánchez, 1947.

——. *Arquitectos y canteros malagueños: Ensayo histórico documental (siglos XVI–XVII).* Avila, 1962.

Locke, John. *The Second Treatise of Government.* New York: Bobbs-Merrill, 1952.

Lomnitz, Claudio. "Nationalism as a Practical System: Benedict Anderson's Theory of Nationalism from the Vantage Point of Spanish America." In *The Other Mirror: Grand Theory through the Lens of Latin America*, ed. Miguel Angel Centeno and Fernando López-Alves, 329–359. Princeton University Press, 2001.

Long, Pamela O. *Openness, Secrecy, Authorship: Technical Arts and the Culture of Knowledge from Antiquity to the Renaissance*. Baltimore: Johns Hopkins University Press, 2001.

López, François. *Juan Pablo Forner et la crise de la conscience espagnole au XVIII siècle*. Université de Bordeaux, 1976.

Luján, Pedro de. *Coloquios matrimoniales*. 1550. Reprint ed. Asunción Rallo Gruss. Madrid: Real Academia Española, 1990.

Luque Faxardo, Francisco de. *Fiel desengaño contra la ociosidad y los juegos*. 1603. Reprint ed. Martín de Riquer. Madrid: Real Academia Española, 1955.

Lynch, John. *Bourbon Spain, 1700–1808*. Oxford: Blackwell, 1989.

———. *The Hispanic World in Crisis and Change, 1598–1700*. Oxford: Blackwell, 1992.

———. *Spain 1516–1598: From Nation State to World Empire*. Oxford: Blackwell, 1991.

———. *The Spanish American Revolutions 1808–1826*. 2d ed. New York: W. W. Norton, 1986.

Macías Delgado, Jacinta, ed. *El motin de Esquilache a la luz de los documentos*. Madrid: Centro de Estudios Constitucionales, 1988.

Macías Picavea, Ricardo. *El problema nacional*. 1899. Reprint, Madrid: Fundación Banco Exterior, 1992.

MacKay, Ruth. *The Limits of Royal Authority: Resistance and Obedience in Seventeenth-Century Castile*. Cambridge University Press, 1999.

MacKenney, Richard. *Tradesmen and Traders: The World of the Guilds in Venice and Europe, c. 1250–c. 1650*. Totowa, N.J.: Barnes and Noble Books, 1987.

Madariaga, Salvador de. *Englishmen Frenchmen Spaniards*. Oxford University Press, 1928.

Mallada, Lucas. *Los males de la patria*. 1900. Reprint, Madrid: Alianza Editorial, 1969.

Maltby, William S. *The Black Legend in England: The Development of Anti-Spanish Sentiment, 1558–1660*. Durham, N.C.: Duke University Press, 1971.

Mandeville, Bernard de. *The Fable of the Bees, or Private Vices, Public Benefits*. London, 1714.

Maravall, José Antonio. *Las Comunidades de Castilla: Una primera revolución moderna*. Madrid: Alianza Universidad, 1963.

———. "De la misericordia a la justicia social en la economía del trabajo: la obra de fray Juan de Robles." *Moneda y Crédito*, no. 148 (March 1979).

———. *Estado moderno y mentalidad social*. 2 vols. Madrid: Alianza Editorial, 1972.

———. *La literatura picaresca desde la historia social*. Madrid: Taurus, 1986.

———. *Poder, honor y élites en el siglo XVII*. Madrid: Siglo Veintiuno, 1979.

———. "Reformismo social-agrario en la crisis del siglo XVII: Tierra, trabajo y salario según Pedro de Valencia." *Bulletin Hispanique* 72 (January–June 1970).

———. "Trabajo y exclusión: El trabajador manual en el sistema social español de la primera modernidad." In *Les Problemes de l'exclusión en Espagne (XVI–XVII siècles)*, ed. Augustin Redondo. Paris: Publications de la Sorbonne, 1983.

Marín López, Rafael. "El cabildo eclesiástico granadino y las obras de la catedral en el siglo XVI." *Chronica Nova* 22 (1995).

Márquez Villanueva, Francisco. *"Menosprecio de Corte y Alabanza de Aldea" (Valladolid,*

1539) y el tema áulico en la obra de Fray Antonio de Guevara. Santander: Universidad de Cantabria, 1999.

Martín González, Juan José. *El artista en la sociedad española del siglo XVII.* Madrid: Cátedra, 1993.

Martínez Alcubilla, Marcelo, ed. *Códigos antiguos de España.* 2 vols. Madrid: J. López Comancho, 1885.

Martínez de la Mata, Francisco. *Memoriales y discursos de Francisco Martínez de Mata* [*sic*]. Ed. Gonzalo Anes. Madrid: Editorial Moneda y Crédito, 1971.

Martínez de la Rosa, Francisco. *Bosquejo histórico de la política de España desde los tiempos de los Reyes Católicos hasta nuestros dias.* 2 vols. Madrid: M. Rivadeneyra, 1857.

——. *Obras dramáticas.* Madrid: Espasa-Calpe, 1947.

Martínez López, María Elena. "The Spanish Concept of 'Limpieza de Sangre' and the Emergence of the 'Race/Caste' System in the Viceroyalty of New Spain." Ph.D. diss., University of Chicago, 2002.

Martz, Linda. *Poverty and Welfare in Habsburg Spain.* Cambridge University Press, 1983.

Masdeu, Juan Francisco de. *Historia crítica de España y de la cultura española.* 20 vols. Madrid, 1783–1805.

Maza Zorrilla, Elena. *Pobreza y asistencia social en España.* Universidad de Valladolid, 1987.

Mechoulan, Henry, ed. *Mateo López Bravo: Un socialista español del siglo XVII.* Madrid: Editora Nacional, 1977.

Medina, Pedro de. *Obras de Pedro de Medina.* Ed. Angel González Palencia. Madrid: CSIC, 1944.

Meek, Ronald L. *Studies in the Labor Theory of Value.* New York: Monthly Review Press, 1956.

Mejía Ponce de León, Luis de. *Apólogo de la ociosidad i el trabajo.* 1546. In *Obras que Francisco Cervantes de Salazar ha hecho glosado i traducido,* ed. Francisco de Salazar. Madrid, 1772.

Meléndez Valdés, Juan. *Discursos forenses.* Madrid: Imprenta Real, 1821.

Menéndez Pidal, Ramón. "Los españoles en la historia." In *Historia de España,* ed. Ramón Menéndez Pidal. Vol. 1: *España prehistórica,* ix–ciii. Madrid: Espasa-Calpe, 1947.

Menéndez y Pelayo, Marcelino. *La ciencia española (Polémicas, proyectos y bibliografía).* 3 vols. Colección de Escritores Castellanos Críticos, vols. 52, 57, 64. Madrid: Pérez Dubrull, 1887–1888.

Menjot, Denis. "Les métiers en Castille au bas moyen âge: Approche des 'vécus socio-économiques.'" In *Les métiers au moyen âge: Aspects économiques et sociaux.* Université Catholique de Louvain, 1994.

Mercado, Tomas de. *Suma de Tratos y Contratos.* 1571. 2 vols. Reprint ed. Nicolás Sánchez Albornoz. Madrid: Instituto de Estudios Fiscales, 1977.

Merlo, Elisabetta. "El trabajo de las pieles en Milán en los siglos XVII y XVIII: entre el divorcio y la unión corporativa." In *El trabajo en la encrucijada. Artesanos urbanos en la Europa de la Edad Moderna,* ed. Victoria López and José A. Nieto, 179–202. Madrid: Los Libros de la Catarata, 1996.

Mestre Sanchis, Antonio. "Conciencia histórica e historiografía." In *Historia de España,* ed. Ramón Menéndez Pidal. Vol. 31, pt. 1: *La época de la ilustración. El estado y la cultura (1759–1808),* 301–345. Madrid: Espasa-Calpe, 1987.

Mettam, Roger. "Definitions of Nobility in Seventeenth-Century France." In *Lan-*

guage, History, and Class, ed. Penelope J. Corfield, 79–100. Oxford: Blackwell, 1991.

Milhou, Alain. "El labrador casado." *Estudios de Historia Social,* no. 36–37 (1986).

Milhou, Alain, and Anne Milhou-Roudié. "Le concept de travail dans les courants utopiques en Espagne et en Amérique (1516–1558)." In *Les utopies dans le monde hispanique,* ed. Jean-Pierre Etienvre, 171–190. Madrid: Casa de Velázquez, 1990.

——. "El pecado de pereza en el Criticón: 'dejamiento' sin obras." In *Estado actual de los estudios sobre el Siglo de Oro,* vol. 2, ed. M. G. Martín. Universidad de Salamanca, 1993.

Milhou-Roudie, Anne. "L'évolution du concept de paresse jusqu'aux moralistes espagnols du XVI siècle." *Voces* 2. Salamanca 1991.

Millán, Jesús, and María Cruz Romeo. "Was the Liberal Revolution Important to Modern Spain? Political Cultures and Citizenship in Spanish History." *Social History* 29 (August 2004): 284–300.

Millares Carlos, Agustín, and T. Díaz Galdós. "Incendio de la Plaza Mayor en 1631." *Revista de la Biblioteca, Archivo y Museo,* no. 13 (January 1927).

Milton, Cynthia. "The Many Meanings of Poverty: Colonial Compacts and Social Assistance in Eighteenth-Century Quito." Ph.D. diss., University of Wisconsin, 2002.

Mindek, Dubravka. *Fiestas de gremios ayer y hoy.* Mexico City: Consejo Nacional para la Cultura y las Artes, 2001.

Molas Ribalta, Pere. *La burguesía mercantil en la España del Antiguo Régimen.* Madrid: Cátedra, 1985.

——. "El exclusivismo en los gremios de la Corona de Aragon: Limpieza de sangre y limpieza de oficios." In *Les sociétés fermées dans le monde iberique (xvi–xviii siècles).* Paris: CNRS, 1986.

——. *Los gremios barceloneses del siglo XVIII.* Madrid: Confederación Española de Cajas de Ahorro, 1970.

Monahan, Arthur P. *From Personal Duties towards Personal Rights: Late Medieval and Early Modern Political Thought, 1300–1600.* Montreal: McGill-Queen's University Press, 1994.

Moncada, Sancho de. *Restauración política de España.* 1619. Reprint ed. Jean Vilar. Madrid: Instituto de Estudios Fiscales, 1974.

Montesquieu, Charles Louis de Secondat, baron de. *The Persian Letters of Montesquieu.* Ed. Manuel Komroff. New York: Library of Living Classics, 1929.

Montoro Ballesteros, Alberto. "El 'Tratado de República' de Alonso de Castrillo." *Revista de Estudios Políticos* 188 (March–April 1973).

Moral Roncal, Antonio Manuel. *Gremios e Ilustración en Madrid (1775–1836).* Madrid: Actas Editorial, 1998.

Morán, Miguel, and Bernardo J. García, eds. *El Madrid de Velázquez y Calderón. Villa y Corte en el siglo XVII.* 2 vols. Madrid: Ayuntamiento de Madrid, 2000.

Moreno de Vargas, Bernabé. *Discursos de la nobleza de España.* Madrid, 1659.

Morgado, Alonso. *Historia de Sevilla.* Seville, 1587.

Morgan, Edmund S. *American Slavery, American Freedom: The Ordeal of Colonial Virginia.* New York: W. W. Norton, 1975.

Morote, Luis. *La moral de la derrota.* 1900. Reprint, Madrid: Biblioteca Nueva, 1997.

Munro, John. "The Symbiosis of Towns and Textiles: Urban Institutions and the Changing Fortunes of Cloth Manufacturing in the Low Countries and England, 1270–1570." *Journal of Early Modern History* 3 (February 1999): 1–74.

Muñoz Barberán, Manuel, and Juan Guirao García. *De la vida murciana de Ginés Pérez de Hita*. Murcia, 1987.

Negrín, Olegario. *Ilustración y educación: La sociedad económica matritense*. Madrid: Editora Nacional, 1984.

Nieto Sánchez, José A. "Asociación y conflicto laboral en el Madrid del siglo XVIII." In *El trabajo en la encrucijada. Artesanos urbanos en la Europa de la Edad Moderna*, ed. Victoria López and José A. Nieto, 248–287. Madrid: Los Libros de la Catarata, 1996.

———. "La conflictividad laboral en Madrid durante el siglo XVII: El gremio de sastres." Paper read at I Congreso de Jóvenes Geógrafos e Historiadores, Seville, November 1990.

———. "Labour, Capital and the Structure of the Textile Industry in Seventeenth-century Madrid." In *Occupational Titles and Their Classification: The Case of the Textile Trade in Past Times*, ed. Herman Diederiks and Marjan Balkestein, 217–229. St. Katharinen: Max-Planck-Institut für Geschichte, 1995.

———. "'Nebulosas industriales' y capital mercantil urbano: Castilla la Nueva y Madrid, 1750–1850." *Sociología del Trabajo*, nueva época, no. 39 (Spring 2000): 85–109.

———. "La organización social del trabajo en una ciudad preindustrial europea. Las corporaciones de oficio madrileñas durante el feudalismo tardío." Lic. diss., Universidad Autónoma de Madrid, 1993.

Noel, Charles C. "Missionary Preachers in Spain: Teaching Social Virtue in the Eighteenth Century." *American Historical Review* 90 (October 1985): 866–892.

Normante y Carcavilla, Lorenzo. *Discurso sobre la utilidad de los conocimientos Económico-Políticos y la necesidad de su estudio metódico. Proposiciones de Economía Civil y Comercio. Espíritu del Señor Melón en su Ensayo político sobre el Comercio*, ed. Antonio Peiró Arroyo. Zaragoza: Diputación General de Aragón, 1984.

Nuñez de Castro, Alonso. *Libro histórico político. Sólo Madrid es Corte, y el cortesano en Madrid*. Madrid, 1658.

Nussdorfer, Laurie. *Civic Politics in the Rome of Urban VIII*. Princeton University Press, 1992.

———. "Writing and the Power of Speech: Notaries and Artisans in Baroque Rome." In *Culture and Identity in Early Modern Europe (1500–1800): Essays in Honor of Natalie Zemon Davis*, ed. Barbara B. Diefendorf and Carla Hesse, 103–118. Ann Arbor: University of Michigan Press, 1993.

Ogilvie, Sheilagh. *State Corporatism and Proto-Industry: The Württemberg Black Forest, 1580–1797*. Cambridge University Press, 1997.

Ordenanzas para el buen régimen y gobierno de la muy noble, muy leal e imperial Ciudad de Toledo. Toledo: José de Cea, 1858.

Ortega y Gasset, José. *Invertebrate Spain*. Ed. and trans. Mildred Adams. New York: W. W. Norton, 1937.

Ortiz, Luis. *Memorial del contador Luis Ortiz a Felipe II* (1558). Madrid: Instituto de España, 1970.

Osuna, Francisco de. *Quinta Parte del Abecedario Espiritual que es Consuelo de Pobres y Aviso de Ricos*. Medina del Campo, 1554.

Otte, Enrique, ed. *Cartas privadas de emigrantes a Indias, 1540–1616*. Seville: Junta de Andalucía, 1988.

Ovitt, George, Jr. *The Restoration of Perfection: Labor and Technology in Medieval Culture*. New Brunswick, N.J.: Rutgers University Press. 1987.

Pagden, Anthony. *European Encounters with the New World: From Renaissance to Romanticism.* New Haven: Yale University Press, 1993.

Palacio Atard, Vicente. *Los Españoles de la Ilustración.* Madrid: Ediciones Guadarrama, 1964.

Palomero Páramo, Jesus M. *El retablo sevillano del Renacimiento.* Seville, 1983.

Panciera, Walter. "Padova, 1704: 'L'antica unione de' poveri laneri' contro 'la ricca università dell'arte della lana.'" *Quaderni Storici* 87 (December 1994).

Patriarca, Silvana. "Indolence and Regeneration: Tropes and Tensions of Resorgimiento Patriotism." *American Historical Review* 110 (April 2005): 380–408.

Patterson, Annabel. *Reading between the Lines.* Madison: University of Wisconsin Press, 1993.

Payne, Stanley G. *A History of Spain and Portugal in Two Volumes.* Madison: University of Wisconsin Press, 1973.

Pelorson, Jean-Marc. "'Hommes moyens,' 'pouvoir moyen' au siècle d'or." In *Hommage des hispanistes francais a Noël Salomon.* Barcelona: Editorial Laia, 1979.

Peñalosa y Mondragon, Fr. Benito de. *Libro de las cinco excelencias del español que despueblan a España para su mayor potencia y dilatación . . .* Pamplona, 1629.

Pérez, Joseph. "A propos de l'exclusion des mendiants: Bienfaisance et esprit bourgeois au XVI siècle." In Augustin Redondo, ed. *Les problèmes de l'exclusion en Espagne (XVI–XVII siècles).* Paris: Publications de la Sorbonne, 1983.

Pérez, Louis A., Jr. *Cuba between Empires, 1878–1902.* University of Pittsburgh Press, 1983.

Pérez, Ventura. *Diario de Valladolid* (1885). Valladolid, 1983.

Pérez de Herrera, Cristóbal. *Amparo de pobres.* 1598. Reprint ed. Michel Cavillac. Madrid: Espasa-Calpe, 1975.

———. *Remedios para el bien de la salud del cuerpo de la Republica.* Madrid, 1610.

Pérez Escolano, Víctor, and Fernando Villanueva Sandino, eds. *Ordenanzas de Sevilla.* 1632. Reprint, Seville: Oficina Técnica de Arquitectura e Ingeniería, 1975.

Pérez Estévez, Rosa María. *El problema de los vagos en la España del siglo XVIII.* Madrid: Confederación Española de Cajas de Ahorros, 1976.

Pérez y López, Antonio Javier. *Discurso sobre la honra y la deshonra legal.* Madrid, 1781.

Pérez-Mallaína, Pablo E. *Spain's Men of the Sea: Daily Life on the Indies Fleets in the Sixteenth Century.* Trans. Carla Rahn Phillips. Baltimore: Johns Hopkins University Press, 1998.

Perry, Mary Elizabeth. *Gender and Disorder in Early Modern Seville.* Princeton University Press, 1990.

Pescador del Hoyo, María del Carmen. "Los gremios de artesanos en Zamora." *Revista de Archivos, Bibliotecas y Museos* 75 (January 1968–December 1972): 183–200; 76 (January–June 1973): 13–60; 77 (January–June 1974): 67–101; 77 (July–December 1974): 449–520; 78 (January–June 1975): 111–188; 78 (July–December 1975): 605–691.

Phelan, John Leddy. *The Kingdom of Quito in the Seventeenth Century.* Madison: University of Wisconsin Press, 1967.

Phillips, Carla Rahn. *Six Galleons for the King of Spain: Imperial Defense in the Early Seventeenth Century.* Baltimore: Johns Hopkins University Press, 1986.

Phillips, William, Jr., "Images of Spanish History in the United States." *Bulletin of the Society for Spanish and Portuguese Historical Studies* 27 (Summer–Winter 2002): 40–49.

Pike, Fredrick B. *Hispanismo 1989–1936: Spanish Conservatives and Liberals and Their Relations with Spanish America*. South Bend, Ind.: University of Notre Dame Press, 1971.

Pike, Ruth. *Aristocrats and Traders: Sevillian Society in the Sixteenth Century*. Ithaca, N.Y.: Cornell University Press, 1972.

Pineda, Juan de. *Diálogos familiares de la agricultura cristiana*. 5 vols. Biblioteca de Autores Españoles, vols. 161–163, 169–170. Madrid: Atlas, 1963–1964.

Pinkerson, John, ed. *A General Collection of the Best and Most Interesting Voyages and Travels In All Parts of the World*. Vol. 14. London, 1813.

Pinto Crespo, Virgilio, and Santos Madrazo Madrazo, eds. *Madrid: Atlas histórico de la ciudad. Siglos IX–XIX*. Madrid: Lunwerg Editores, 1995.

Piterberg, Gabriel. *An Ottoman Tragedy: History and Historiography at Play*. Berkeley: University of California Press, 2003.

Pitt-Rivers, Julian. "Honour and Social Status." In *Honour and Shame: The Values of Mediterranean Society*, ed. J. G. Peristiany, 19–77. University of Chicago Press, 1966.

Pocock, J. G. A. *The Machiavellian Moment: Florentine Political Thought and the Atlantic Republican Tradition*. Princeton University Press, 1975.

Polanyi, Karl. "Aristotle Discovers the Economy." In *Trade and Market in the Early Empires. Economies in History and Theory*, ed. Karl Polanyi, Conrad M. Arensberg, and Harry W. Pearson, 64–94. Chicago: Henry Regency, 1971.

———. *The Great Transformation: The Political and Economic Origins of Our Time*. Boston: Beacon Press, 1957.

Polt, John H. R. *Jovellanos and His English Sources: Economic, Philosophical and Political Writings*. Transactions of the American Philosophical Society, vol. 54, pt. 7. Philadelphia: American Philosophical Society, 1964.

Pond, Kathleen. *The Spirit of the Spanish Mystics: An Anthology of Spanish Religious Prose from the Fifteenth to the Seventeenth Century*. New York: P. J. Kennedy and Sons, 1958.

Poni, Carlo. "Per la storia del distretto industriale serico di Bologna (secoli XVI–XIX)." *Quaderni Storici* 25 (April 1990): 93–168.

———. "Local Market Rules and Practices: Three Guilds in the Same Line of Production in Early Modern Bologna." In *Domestic Strategies: Work and family in France and Italy 1600–1800*, ed. S. Woolf, 69–101. Cambridge University Press, 1991.

Poole, Stafford, C. M. "The Politics of 'Limpieza de Sangre': Juan de Ovando and his Circle in the Reign of Philip II." *The Americas* 55 (January 1999).

Poska, Allyson M. "From Parties to Pieties: Redefining Confraternal Activity in Seventeenth-Century Ourense." In *Confraternities and Catholic Reform in Italy, France, and Spain*, ed. John Patrick Donnelly, S. J. Kirksville, Mo.: Thomas Jefferson University Press, 1999.

Postigo Castellanos, Elena. *Honor y privilegio en la Corona de Castilla: El Consejo de las Ordenes y los Caballeros de Hábito en el s. XVII*. Soria: Junta de Castilla y León, 1988.

Prescott, William. *History of the Conquest of Mexico*. 1843. Reprint, University of Chicago Press, 1966.

———. *History of the Reign of Ferdinand and Isabella the Catholic*. 2 vols. Philadelphia: J. B. Lippincott Co, 1892.

Quevedo, Francisco de. *El Buscón*. 1626. Reprint, Madrid: Clásicos Castalia, 1990.

———. "España defendida y los tiempos de ahora de las calumnias de los noveleros y sediciosos." In *Obras completas*, 2 vols. Ed. Felicidad Buendía. Madrid: Aguilar, 1969.

Quiroz Chueca, Francisco, and Gerardo Quiroz Chueca, eds. *Las ordenanzas de gremios de Lima (s. XVI–XVIII)*. Lima, 1986.

Ramsden, H. *The 1898 Movement in Spain: Towards a Reinterpretation, With Special Reference to 'En Torno al Casticismo' and 'Idearium Español'*. Manchester University Press, 1974.

Rancière, Jacques. "The Myth of the Artisan: Critical Reflections on a Category of Social History." In *Work in France: Representations, Meaning, Organization and Practice*, ed. Steven Laurence Kaplan and Cynthia J. Koepp, 317–334. Ithaca, N.Y.: Cornell University Press, 1986.

———. *The Nights of Labor: The Workers' Dream in Nineteenth-Century France*. Trans. John Drury. Philadelphia: Temple University Press, 1989.

Rappaport, Steve. *Worlds within Worlds: Structures of Life in Sixteenth-Century London*. Cambridge University Press, 1989.

Real Sociedad Económica de Amigos del País. *Colección de las memorias premiadas y de las que se acordó se imprimiesen sobre . . . el ejercicio de la caridad y socorro de los verdaderos pobres . . .* Madrid, 1784.

Redondo, Augustin. "Pauperismo y mendicidad en Toledo en época del 'Lazarillo.'" In *Hommage des hispanistes français a Noël Salomon*, 703–717. Barcelona: Editorial Laia, 1979.

Redondo Veintemillas, Guillermo. *Las corporaciones de artesanos de Zaragoza en el siglo XVII*. Zaragoza: Institución "Fernando El Católico," 1982.

———. *El gremio de libreros de Zaragoza y sus antiguas ordinaciones (1573, 1600, 1679)*. Zaragoza, 1979.

Reid, Douglas A. "The Decline of Saint Monday 1766–1876." *Past and Present*, no. 71 (May 1976): 76–101.

Relaciones topográficas de Guadalajara. Memorial Histórico Español, vols. 41–43 and 45–47. Madrid: Real Academia de la Historia, 1903.

Ringrose, David. *Spain, Europe, and the "Spanish Miracle," 1700–1900*. Cambridge University Press, 1996.

Río, María José del. "Representaciones dramáticas en casa de un artesano del Madrid de principios del siglo XVII." In *Teatros y vida teatral en el Siglo de Oro através de las fuentes documentales*, ed. Luciano García Lorenzo and J. E. Varey, 245–258. London: Tamesis Books, 1991.

———. "El simbolismo social de las procesiones de corte en el Madrid de la Edad Moderna." *Actas del III Congreso Nacional de Cofradías de Semana Santa*. Córdoba: Cajasur, 1997.

Rizal, José. *Selected Essays and Letters of José Rizal* Ed. and trans. Encarnación Alzona. Manila: G. Rangel, 1964.

Roberts, Andrew. "Salisbury: The Empire Builder Who Never Was." *History Today* 49 (October 1999).

Rodríguez Díaz, Laura. *Reforma e ilustración en la España del siglo XVIII: Pedro Rodríguez de Campomanes*. Madrid: Fundación Universitaria Española, 1975.

Romá i Rosell, Francisco. *Las señales de la felicidad de España y medios de hacerlas eficaces*. Madrid, 1768.

Román, Fr. Hierónimo. *Las republicas del mundo*. 2 vols. Salamanca, 1595.

Romero Múñoz, Vicente. "La recopilación de ordenanzas gremiales de Sevilla en 1527." *Revista de Trabajo* (February 1950): 225–231.

Roper, Lyndal. *The Holy Household: Women and Morals in Reformation Augsburg*. Oxford: Clarendon Press, 1989.

Rose, Hugh James. *Among the Spanish People.* 2 vols. London: Richard Bentley and Son, 1877.

Rubio García, Luis. *La procesión de Corpus en el siglo XV en Murcia.* Murcia: Academia Alfonso X el Sabio, 1987.

Rubio Sánchez, Manuel. *Historia de la Sociedad Económica de Amigos del País.* Guatemala City: Editorial Académica Centroamericana, 1981.

Ruiz Lagos, Manuel, ed. *Historia de la Sociedad Económica de Amigos del País de Xerez de la Frontera.* Jeréz de la Frontera: Centro de Estudios Históricos Jerezanos, 1972.

Ruiz de Vergara, Francisco. *Regla y establecimientos de la Orden y Cavallería del glorioso Apostol Santiago.* Madrid, 1655.

Safley, Thomas Max. *Charity and Economy in the Orphanages of Early Modern Augsburg.* Atlantic Highlands, N.J.: Humanities Press, 1997.

Salomon, Noël. *Recherches sur le theme paysan dans la "comedia" au temps de Lope de Vega.* Bourdeaux: Feret et Fils, 1965.

———. *Lo villano en el teatro del Siglo de Oro.* Madrid: Editorial Castalia, 1985.

Samayoa Guevara, Hector Humberto. *Los gremios de artesanos en la Ciudad de Guatemala (1524–1821).* Guatemala City: Editorial Universitaria, 1962.

Sánchez, Pedro Antonio. "Memoria anónima bajo el nombre de Don Antonio Filántropo, sobre el modo de fomentar entre los labradores de Galicia las fábricas de curtidos." 1782. Reprinted in *Colección de los escritos del Dr. D. Pedro Antonio Sánchez.* Madrid: Imprenta de M. Minuesa, 1858.

Sánchez, Santos, ed. *Colección de pragmáticas, cédulas, provisiones, autos acordados, y otras providencias generales expedidas por el Consejo Real en el Reynado del Señor Don Carlos III.* 3d ed. Madrid, 1803.

———, ed. *Colección de todas las pragmáticas, cédulas, provisiones, circulares, autos acordados, vandos y otras providencias publicadas en el actual reynado del Señor Don Carlos IV.* 3 vols. Madrid, 1794–1801.

Sánchez-Blanco, Francisco. *El Absolutismo y las Luces en el reinado de Carlos III.* Madrid: Marcial Pons, 2002.

———. "La situación espiritual en España hacia mediados del siglo XVIII vista por Pedro Calatayud: Lo que un Jesuita predicaba antes de la expulsión." *Archivo Hispalense,* no. 217 (1988).

Sánchez de Arévalo, Rodrigo. *Spejo de la vida humana.* Zaragoza, 1491.

———. *Suma de la política.* 1454–1455. Reprint ed. Juan Beneyto Pérez. Madrid: CSIC, 1944.

Sánchez Ortega, María Helena, ed. *Documentación selecta sobre la situación de los gitanos españoles en el siglo XVIII.* Madrid: Editora Nacional, 1976.

San Juan, Huarte de. *Exámen de ingenios.* 1575. Reprint ed. Guillermo Serés. Madrid: Cátedra, 1989.

Sans Ferrán, José María. *Barcelona a través del gremio de zurradores.* Vich: Colomer Munmany, 1966.

Santa María, Juan de. *Tratado de república.* Valencia, 1615.

Sanz, María Jesus. *El gremio de plateros sevillano 1344–1867.* Universidad de Sevilla, 1991.

Sarat, Austin, and Thomas R. Kearns. "Writing History and Registering Memory in Legal Decisions and Legal Practices: An Introduction." In *History, Memory, and the Law,* ed. Austin Sarat and Thomas R. Kearns, 1–24. Ann Arbor: University of Michigan Press, 2002.

Sarrailh, Jean. *La España Ilustrada de la segunda mitad del siglo XVIII.* 1957. Reprint, Mexico City: Fondo de Cultura Económica, 1985.

Scott, H. M., ed. *The European Nobilities in the Seventeenth and Eighteenth Centuries.* 2 vols. London: Longman, 1995.

Scott, James C. *Weapons of the Weak: Everyday Forms of Peasant Resistance.* New Haven: Yale University Press, 1985.

Seaver, Paul. "The Puritan Work Ethic Revisited." *Journal of British Studies* 19, no. 2 (1980): 35–53.

Seluja Cecin, Antonio. *Los oficios en le época de Cervantes.* Montevideo: Universidad del Trabajo del Uruguay, 1972.

Sempere y Guarinos, Juan. *Ensayo de una biblioteca española de los mejores escritores del reynado de Carlos III.* 6 vols. Madrid: Impr. Real, 1785–1789.

———. *Historia del luxo y de las leyes suntuarias de España.* Madrid, 1788.

Sewell, William H., Jr., "Visions of Labor: Illustrations of the Mechanical Arts before, in, and after Diderot's Encyclopédie." In *Work in France: Representations, Meaning, Organization, and Practice,* ed. Steven Laurence Kaplan and Cynthia J. Koepp, 258–286. Ithaca, N.Y.: Cornell University Press, 1986.

———. *Work and Revolution in France: The Language of Labor from the Old Regime to 1848.* Cambridge University Press, 1980.

Shafer, Robert Jones. *The Economic Societies in the Spanish World (1763–1821).* Syracuse University Press, 1958.

Shaw Fairman, Patricia. *España vista por los ingleses del siglo XVII.* Madrid: Sociedad General Española de Librería, 1981.

Sierra Bravo, Restituto. *El pensamiento social y económica de la escolástica.* 2 vols. Madrid: CSIC, 1975.

Sigüenza, Fr. José de. *La fundación del monasterio de El Escorial.* 1605. Reprint, Madrid: Aguilar, 1963.

Silber, Nina. "Intemperate Men, Spiteful Women, and Jefferson Davis: Northern Views of the Defeated South." *American Quarterly* 41 (December 1989): 614–635.

Simpson, James. *Spanish Agriculture: The Long Siesta, 1765–1965.* Cambridge University Press, 1995.

Smith, Adam. *An Inquiry into the Nature and Causes of the Wealth of Nations.* Ed. R. H. Campbell and A. S. Skinner. 2 vols. Oxford: Clarendon Press, 1976.

Smith, Hilary Dansey. *Preaching in the Spanish Golden Age: A Study of Some Preachers of the Reign of Philip III.* Oxford University Press, 1978.

Smith, Pamela H. *The Body of the Artisan: Art and Experience in the Scientific Revolution.* University of Chicago Press, 2004.

———. *The Business of Alchemy: Science and Culture in the Holy Roman Empire.* Princeton University Press, 1994.

Smith, Robert Sydney. "The 'Wealth of Nations' in Spain and Hispanic America, 1780–1830." *Journal of Political Economy* 65 (April 1957): 104–125.

Sociedad Económica de Madrid. *Memorias de la Sociedad Económica.* 5 vols. Madrid: A. de Sancha, 1780–1795.

Solorzano, Juan de. *Política indiana.* 2 vols. Madrid, 1647.

Sonenscher, Michael. "Fashion's Empire: Trade and Power in Early 18th-Century France." In *Luxury Trades and Consumerism in Ancien Regime Paris: Studies in the History of the Skilled Workforce,* ed. R. F. A. Turner. Aldershot, U.K.: Ashgate, 1998.

———. *The Hatters of Eighteenth-Century France.* Berkeley: University of California Press, 1987.

———. "L'impero del gusto: Mestiere imprese e commerci nella Parigi del XVIII secolo." *Quaderni Storici* 87 (December 1994): 655–668.

———. "Mythical Work: Workshop Production and the Compagnonnages of Eighteenth-century France." In *The Historical Meanings of Work,* ed. Patrick Joyce, 31–63. Cambridge University Press, 1987.

———. *Work and Wages: Natural Law, Politics, and the Eighteenth-Century French Trades.* Cambridge University Press, 1989.

Soria, Melchor de. *Tratado de la justificación y conveniencia de la tassa de el pan.* 1627. Reprint ed. and intro. by Francisco Gómez Camacho. Madrid: Fundación Banco Exterior, 1992.

Soto, Fr. Domingo de. *De la justicia y del derecho.* 1556. Reprint, Madrid: Instituto de Estudios Políticos, 1967.

Soto, Fr. Domingo de, and Fr. Juan de Robles. *Deliberación en la causa de los pobres (y réplica de Robles).* 1545. Reprint, Madrid: Instituto de Estudios Políticos, 1967.

Spell, Jefferson Rea. *Rousseau in the Spanish World before 1833: A Study in Franco-Spanish Literary Relations.* 1938. Reprint, New York: Gordian Press, 1969.

Stanhope, Alexander. *Spain under Charles the Second; or Extracts from the Correspondence of the Hon. Alexander Stanhope.* London, 1840.

Stein, Stanley J., and Barbara H. Stein. *Apogee of Empire. Spain and New Spain in the Age of Charles III, 1759–1789.* Baltimore: Johns Hopkins University Press, 2003.

Stevenson, Laura Caroline. *Praise and Paradox: Merchants and Craftsmen in Elizabethan Popular Literature.* Cambridge University Press, 1984.

Stone, Lawrence. *The Crisis of the Aristocracy, 1558–1641.* Oxford: Clarendon Press, 1965.

Storm, Eric. *La perspectiva del progreso: Pensamiento político en la España del cambio de siglo (1890–1914).* Madrid: Biblioteca Nueva, 2001.

———. "El tercer centenario del Don Quijote en 1905 y el nationalismo español." *Hispania* 58/2, no. 199 (May–August 1998).

Stuart, Kathy. *Defiled Trades and Social Outcasts: Honor and Ritual Pollution in Early Modern Germany.* Cambridge University Press, 1999.

Sumner, William Graham. *War and Other Essays.* New Haven: Yale University Press, 1911.

Swanson, Heather. "The Illusion of Economic Structure: Craft Guilds in Late Medieval English Towns." *Past and Present,* no. 121 (1988): 29–48.

———. *Medieval Artisans: An Urban Class in Late Medieval England.* Oxford: Blackwell, 1989.

Taylor, Scott. "Credit, Debt, and Honor in Castile, 1600–1650." *Journal of Early Modern History* 7, no. 1–2 (2003): 8–27.

———. "Women, Honor, and Violence in a Castilian Town, 1600–1650." *Sixteenth Century Journal* 35, no. 4 (2004): 1079–1097.

Thirsk, Joan. "Luxury Trades and Consumerism." In *Luxury Trades and Consumerism in Ancien Regime Paris: Studies in the History of the Skilled Workforce,* ed. R. F. A. Turner. Aldershot, U.K.: Ashfield, 1998

Thomas, Keith. "Work and Leisure." *Past and Present,* no. 29 (1964): 50–66.

Thompson, I. A. A., "Hidalgo and Pechero: The Language of 'Estates' and 'Classes' in Early-modern Castile." In *Language, History and Class,* ed. Penelope J. Corfield, 53–78. Oxford: Blackwell, 1991.

———. "The Purchase of Nobility in Castile, 1552–1700." *Journal of European Economic History* 8 (Fall 1979): 313–360.

———. "The Rule of the Law in Early Modern Castile." *European History Quarterly* 14 (1984).

Thompson, I. A. A. and Bartolomé Yun Casalilla, eds. *The Castilian Crisis of the Seventeenth Century: New Perspectives on the Economic and Social History of Seventeenth-Century Spain.* Cambridge University Press, 1994.

Tikoff, Valentina K. "Assisted Transitions: Children and Adolescents in the Orphanages of Seville at the End of the Old Regime, 1681–1831." Ph.D. diss., Indiana University, 2000.

Toajas Roger, María Angeles. *Diego López de Arenas: Carpintero, alarife y tratadista en la Sevilla del siglo XVII.* Seville: Diputación Provincial de Sevilla, 1989.

Todorov, Tzvetan. *The Morals of History.* Trans. Alyson Waters. Minneapolis: University of Minnesota Press, 1995.

Topik, Steven. "Karl Polanyi and the Creation of the 'Market Society.'" In *The Other Mirror: Grand Theory through the Lens of Latin America,* ed. Miguel Angel Centeno and Fernando López-Alves, 81–104. Princeton University Press, 2001.

Torras, Jaume. "The Old and the New: Marketing Networks and Textile Growth in Eighteenth-Century Spain." In *Markets and Manufacture in Early Industrial Europe,* ed. Maxine Berg, 93–113. London: Routledge, 1991.

Townsend, Joseph. *A Journey through Spain in the Years 1786 and 1787, with Particular Attention to the Agriculture, Manufactures, Commerce, Population, Taxes, and Revenue of That Country; and Remarks in Passing Through a Part of France,* 3 vols. London, 1792.

Tramoyeres Blasco, Luis. *Instituciones gremiales: Su origen y organización en Valencia.* Valencia: Imprenta Domenech, 1889.

Trigueros, Cándido María. *Los Menestrales.* 1784. Ed. Francisco Aguilar Piñal. Universidad de Sevilla, 1997.

Truant, Cynthia Maria. "Independent and Insolent: Journeymen and Their Rites in the Old Regime Workplace." in *Work in France: Representations, Meaning, Organization, and Practice,* ed. Steven Laurence Kaplan and Cynthia J. Koepp, 131–175. Ithaca, N.Y.: Cornell University Press, 1986.

———. *The Rites of Labor: Brotherhoods of Compagnonnage in Old and New Regime France.* Ithaca, N.Y.: Cornell University Press, 1994.

Twinam, Ann. *Public Lives, Private Secrets: Gender, Honor, Sexuality, and Illegitimacy in Colonial Spanish America.* Stanford University Press, 1999.

Unamuno, Miguel de. *En torno al casticismo.* Madrid: Espasa-Calpe, 1972.

Underdown, David. *A Freeborn People: Politics and the Nation in Seventeenth-Century England.* Oxford: Clarendon Press, 1996.

Uña Sarthou, Juan. *Las asociaciones obreras en España.* Madrid: Estab. tip. de G. Juste, 1900.

Valencia, Pedro de. *Obras Completas.* Vol. 4, pt. 1: *Escritos económicos.* Ed. Rafael González Cañal. Universidad de León, 1994.

Valladares de Sotomayor, Antonio, ed. *Semanario erudito, que comprehende varias obras inéditas, críticas, morales, instructivas, políticas, históricas, satíricas y jocosas, de nuestros mejores autores antiguos y modernos.* 34 vols. Madrid, 1787.

Van den Hoven, Birgit. *Work in Ancient and Medieval Thought: Ancient Philosophers, Medieval Monks and Theologians, and Their Concept of Work, Occupations, and Technology.* Amsterdam: J. C. Gieben, 1996.

Vásquez, Genaro, ed. *Legislación del trabajo en los siglos XVI, XVII y XVIII. Relación entre la economía, las artes y los oficios en la Nueva España.* Mexico City: Departamento Autónomo del Trabajo, 1936.

Vassberg, David. *The Village and the Outside World in Golden Age Castile: Mobility and Migration in Everyday Rural Life*. Cambridge University Press, 1996.

Vega y de Luque, Carlos Luis de la. "Historia y evolución de los gremios de Teruel." *Teruel*, no. 77–78 (1987).

Venegas, Alejo. *Agonía del tránsito de la muerte*. 1537. Reprint, Nueva Biblioteca de Autores Españoles, vol. 16. Madrid: Bailly-Baillière, 1911.

Vicens Vives, Jaime. *Aproximación a la historia de España*. 2d ed. Universidad de Barcelona, 1960.

Vicente, Marta V. "Images and Realities of Work: Women and Guilds in Early Modern Barcelona." In *Spanish Women in the Golden Age. Images and Realities*, ed. Magdalena Sanchez and Alain Saint-Saëns, 127–139. Westport, Conn.: Greenwood Press, 1996.

Vila, Soledad. *La ciudad de Eiximenis: Un proyecto teórico de urbanismo en el siglo XIV*. Valencia: Diputación Provincial de Valencia, 1984.

Vilar, Pierre. *Crecimiento y desarrollo*. Barcelona: Ariel, 1980.

Vilar Berrogain, Jean. *Literatura y economia: La figura satírica del arbitrista en el Siglo de Oro*. Madrid: Revista de Occidente, 1973.

Villalón, Christobal de. *Provechoso tratado de cambios y contrataciones de mercaderes y reprobación de usura* (and enclosed pamphlet: *Instrucción de mercaderes*). Medina del Campo, 1547.

Villas Tinoco, Siro. *Los gremios malagueños (1700–1746)*. 2 vols. Universidad de Málaga, 1982.

Villena, Enrique de. *Los doze trabajos de Hércules*. 1483. Reprint ed. Margherita Morreale. Madrid: Real Academia Española, 1958.

Viñas y Mey, Carmelo, and Ramón Paz, eds. *Relaciones de los pueblos de España ordenadas por Felipe II*. 3 vols. Madrid: Instituto Balmes de Sociología, 1949.

Vives, Juan Luis. *Tratado del socorro de los pobres*. 1526. Reprint, Valencia: Prometeo, 1929.

Voltes, Pedro. *Carlos III y su tiempo*. Barcelona: Editorial Juventud, 1964.

Vyverberg, Henry. *Human Nature, Cultural Diversity, and the French Enlightenment*. Oxford University Press, 1989.

Walker, Mack. *German Home Towns*. Ithaca, N.Y.: Cornell University Press, 1971.

Ward, Bernardo. *Proyecto económico en que se proponen varias providencias, dirigidas a promover los intereses de España con los medios y fondos necesarios para su plantificación*. Madrid, 1779.

Webster, Susan Verdi. *Art and Ritual in Golden Age Spain: Sevillian Confraternities and the Processional Scupture of Holy Week*. Princeton University Press, 1998.

White, Hayden. *Tropics of Discourse: Essays in Cultural Criticism*. Baltimore: Johns Hopkins University Press, 1978.

Whitney, Elspeth. *Paradise Restored: The Mechanical Arts from Antiquity through the Thirteenth Century*. Transactions of the American Philosophical Society, vol. 80, pt. 1. Philadelphia: American Philosophical Society, 1990.

Wiesner, Merry E. *Working Women in Renaissance Germany*. New Brunswick, N.J.: Rutgers University Press, 1986.

Willughby, Francis. *A Relation of a Voyage Made through a Great Part of Spain*. London, 1673.

Wright, L. P. "The Military Orders in Sixteenth and Seventeenth Century Spanish Society. The Institutional Embodiment of a Historical Tradition." *Past and Present*, no. 43 (1969): 34–70.

Yun Casalilla, Bartolomé. *La gestión del poder: Corona y economías aristocráticas en Castilla (siglos XVI–XVIII)*. Madrid: Akal Ediciones, 2002.

Zarco-Bacas y Cuevas, Eusebio Julián, ed. *Relaciones de pueblos del Obispado de Cuenca hechas por orden de Felipe II*. 2 vols. Cuenca: Biblioteca diocesana conquense, 1927.

Zavala y Auñon, Miguel de. *Representación al Rey Nuestro Señor D. Phelipe V (que Dios guarde) dirigida al mas seguro aumento del real erario, y conseguir la felicidad, mayor alivio, riqueza, y abundancia de su monarquia*. 1732.

Zeller, Gaston. "Une notion de caractère historico-social: la dérogeance." In *Aspects de la politique française sous l'ancien régime*, ed. G. Zeller. Paris: Presses Universitaires de France, 1964.

Zofío Llorente, Juan Carlos. "Las culturas del trabajo en Madrid, 1500–1650. Familia, oficio y sociabilidad en el artesando preindustrial." Ph.D. diss, Universidad Complutense de Madrid, 2001.

Index

293